CONTRIBUTIONS
TO THE KNOWLEDGE
of
Mt. Carmel
BY DR. E GRAF VON MÜLINEN

Edited and prepared in Arabic and English
By
Mahmoud El Salman

Translated from German into English
By
Andrea Graves

 www.trafford.com

North America & international
toll-free: 1 888 232 4444 (USA & Canada)
fax: 812 355 4082

The book is didicated

To my beloved nephew, Dr. Wael Ammourah. Wael used to accompany me when I was conducting interviews for my studies on Tirat Haifa. He was a quiet person who motivated you and shared happiness through his small yet frequent smile. Wael's great spirit is still helping me and motivating me even though he has left us so early through the great effort of his wife, Andrea Graves, and the great help and motivation of my sister, Um Wael.

The Editor Mahmoud El Salman

CONTENTS

ACKNOWLEDGMENT

I would like to express my deepest gratitude to Palestine International Institute (Jordan-Amman) that supported the translation of the book from German into English. Thank you so much Prof As'ad Abdulrhaman, the director of the institute.

I would like also to express my deepest gratitude to Professor Aharon Kleinberger, who was the first to inform me about the book. Thank you, Prof Aharon Kleinberger.

The Editor Mahmoud El Salman

MULINEN, THE SCHOLAR
By Mahmoud El Salman

To begin, I would like to thank Mülinen for his outstanding work. It is very clear that he exerted great effort in order to carry out this very important study. He described details about the people and the place (the villages in Mt. Carmel) that would have been difficult to know in such detail without his exceptional work. However, it seems that sometimes a misunderstanding occurred when the informants conveyed their knowledge to Mülinen. The Arabic language may have been one of these difficulties while the second may have been that the informants themselves may have failed to properly convey their information. I believe this led the great scientist Mülinen to say one thing in one context and then something different in another. All in all, it seems as though when the information appeared inaccurate, it may have been the result of an unintentional misunderstanding. Therefore, this misunderstanding led to a vague or inaccurate description that could have been expressed differently had the information been more clearly and more precisely conveyed.

Because I have developed a great respect in my heart for this scholar since he wrote about a place I hold dear and about my people while they were living in our native villages, I tried my best to even visit Germany in order to know more about him and to be able to teach others about him. I found it possible to succeed in this through the Internet. As I am not familiar with the German language, Andrea Graves helped me in this regard. Little has been written about him in English and, unfortunately, in Arabic as well.

Mülinen was known as an Orientalist and German diplomat. He held offices as a diplomat in both Palestine and Turkey, then the Ottoman Empire. He was appointed the chamberlain of the Kaiser of Prussia. He began his public service in 1888 in Beirut and then went to work in the German Embassy in Constantinople in 1898.

Personally, I can now add that Mülinen is a great scholar who put tremendous effort into researching and authorizing one of the best books that I have ever read. Mülinen's name is linked to the name of my village, Et-Tire, and, on behalf of everybody who appreciates the value of knowledge, I heartily thank Dr. E. Graf von Mülinen

INTRODUCTION
By Prof. Mahmoud El Salman

When I first came across Mülinen's book *Contribution to the Knowledge of Mt. Carmel*, I was so happy to have found something about Mt. Carmel, and in particular, about my village "et-Tire," where my mother, father and some of my brothers and sisters were born, before their forced immigration to Jordan in 1948.

The first obstacle I faced once this book was in my hands was that it is written in German, a language of which I have little knowledge. So, I spent months merely looking at the pictures inside the book and trying to find anything that I might understand wherever the word et-Tire appeared. Nevertheless, the task became difficult; the language remained a frustrating obstacle. So, I began to search for someone whose knowledge of German I could trust and who could translate the text for me. It was not easy at all. After many attempts I found the best person to translate it. She was an American, Andrea Graves, who had obtained a bachelor's degree in the German language. Andrea is also my nephew's wife Dr. Wael Ammourah. She proved to be a great translator and, as expected, is a serious, motivated, enthusiastic person who clearly has a great deal of potential as a translator.

Thank you so much Andrea (Um Ibrahim). And a big thank also goes to my sister who continued to motivate Andrea to carry out her job. Thank you, Um Wael.

When I began to receive portions of the translation, the ambiguity and mysteriousness of the book eventually started to disappear.

The great effort exerted to write this book was adequately obvious. However, it also became adequately obvious that there are so many points considered contradictory and inaccurate to anyone who is familiar with the area and its society. Thus, the type of mistakes made could, from my viewpoint, clearly be divided into three types:

1) A mistake made as a result of Mülinen's unfamiliarity of the language (the Arabic language) and, as a result, of the linguistic context in the area. This sometimes led him to write whatever he heard from his informant as it is. To illustrate I shall give the following example. As a result of his unawareness of the linguistic

phenomenon known as the solar[1] lam and the lunar lam, he wrote the words as he heard them. Thus, words that have the (solar lam) without the phoneme (lam) are written with the lam as the lam is a phoneme but they are pronounced without the lam. Examples: *ez-alaqa* should be written *elzalaqa, though it is pronounced ez-alaqa*, *abu-eja* should be *abu alja*, *ess-yah* should be *alsyyah*, and many other examples of this type.

Mülinen decided to focus on et-Tire (my ntaive village) linguistically as he found it to be the village with the greatest population, and so, "In order to observe to the required consistency in the reproduction of the sounds, the example of the people from *et-tire*, whose fields lie on the larger portion of the mountain, is taken as a basis (p.5)."

Et-Tire has its very special dialect that differs from the dialects used in the rest of the adjacent areas. The uvular variant /q/ of the variable (Q) is its key feature unlike in the rest of the villages where the variant /k/ of the variable (Q) is its key feature. The /q/ is very specific to the Tirawi dialect. Thus, to choose et-Tire because it is the biggest village was, from the linguistic perspective, was perhaps not an ideal choice. Abdel-Jawad states that "because of the social and geographical importance of this variable [(Q)] as a carrier of local or regional loyalties, it has often been used by dialectologists as the main criterion for establishing the dialect boundaries or isoglosses in the Arabic dialects (Abdel-Jawad, 1981: 159)." According to El Salman, the social meanings of the linguistic features (i.e. the glottal stop of the people of Haifa and the /q/ of the Tirawis) came to be manipulated by both the people of et- Tire and those of Haifa to describe one another. The people of Haifa used to use the key feature of et-Tire, namely the [q] variant, humorously to describe the stubbornness and

---

1   The Arabic alphabet has 28 letters. Fourteen of them are classified as moon letters and 24 are classified as sun letters. This classification is based on the way these letters affect the pronunciation of the definite article (*al*) in Arabic which comes at the beginning of the word. The definite article is assimilated into the sun letters and loses its distinctive sound. As a result, the sound at the beginning of the word is doubled. Thus, a word like *elzalqa* becomes *ez-zalqa*, as "z" is a sun letter. And thus, the lam is assimilated into it. Whenever Mülinen found a word with the solar (lam), he omitted it and only wrote the pronunciation when, in fact, this misleads those who are unaware of Arabic into thinking that it is also written this way.

toughness of the Tirawis. For instance, if a man from Haifa wanted to know if somebody was from et-Tire he might humorously ask him: /inta min illi qawwasu ilbaħar/ 'Are you one of those who shot the sea/'. If the answer was yes, it was not uncommon for this question to be followed by a second typical question: /qarqaʕ babuur ittiirih willa baʕduh/ 'Has the grinding-machine of et-Tire started making a noise or not yet?' Notice the necessity of the appearance of the key feature [q] of this dialect in these phrases so as to convey this humorous and friendly social meaning. The [q] variant occurs twice in the word / qarqaʕ/ 'made a grinding noise' thus confirming the speaker's intention to signal the correlation between one's being a Tirawi and one's being a user of the [q].

My point in this discussion is to show that the key feature [q] became an enduring trait linked to the Tirawis. It is an identifying feature for a Tirawi whether he or she uses it or not (El Salman, 2003).

2) Errors made as a result of an imprecise viewpoint. In such inaccuracies, Mülinen wrote in general without any scientific evidence or convincing argument. Examples of this are clearly seen when he judged the people of my village, et-Tire, and of other villages and the Bedouin who lived among or around them, often without any further proof for what he said or the basis on which he formulated his argument. For example, on page 25, he claimed: "Universally, Bedouins are considered to be robbers and thieves, and an old ancestral rivalry prevails between them and the Druses." This is an inaccurate statement. In the Arab world, Bedouins are known to be very generous. They take pride in belonging to big tribes that have big names, and they strive to prove that they are good representatives of their tribal names. Thus, this very negative opinion was very general, and Mülinen did not give any evidence to support his opinion. He himself contradicted himself by stating: "Two hundred years ago, they [the Bedouins] were the lords of Carmel; it was so reported to me [Mülinen] that their Emirs (chiefs) from the Tarabīn tribe of that period have, however, long since moved to the region near Gaza" (p. 25). To be the lord or a prince (Emir) of an area requires the mastery of esteemed values and manners. Therefore, those who were once the lords of the Carmel could not also be described as thieves. Furthermore, the Bedouins have historically been known

to be very generous and were respected for their honerable values. "Needless to say, that Bedouin tribes also have some kind of social and historical prestige" (El Salman, 2016: 24). In addition, "Bedouins belong to tribes and normally they take the name of their tribes as their surnames" (El Salman, 2016:23). This is a socially known, obligatory practice to ensure the protection of the tribe's reputation through behaving according to the good values. Because Mülinen makes this statement in a vague and very general manner, the question arises if it is possible to consider his statement without any scientifically accepted evidence. Mahmoud Al Badawi (Badawi means Bedouin) was cited by Mülinen as his guide in the area and has the word Badawi (bedouni) as his surname. Did Mülinen recognize that? Mülinen himself said that Mahmoud Al Badawi was the best person to depend on during his journey. If he had been a thieving Bedouin as Mülinen described, how could Mülinen have accepted him as his guide throughout his journey and study in the area?

Moreover, Nimer ibn Asaf who belongs to the Bedouin group known as the Hariti, built the mosque in et-Tire. Building mosques is always linked to good behavior, values and strong faith. Thus, this also contradicts the very general statement that the Bedouins are robbers and thieves. Robbers and thieves do not build mosques, and they could not be princes among the Arabs. People who build mosques for a higher purpose do not exhibit poor morals. According to Mülinen, "Emīr 'Assāf, son of Nimr Bāy, ordered the construction of this blessed place [the mosque] in the year 987." He also continues, "According to tradition, Amīr 'Assāf was a member of the above-mentioned Bedouin family Hāriṯi" (p.102).

Mülinen said the same about the people of et-Tire. According to him, "The earlier reputation of the people [the people of et-Tire] was not a good one as conveyed in the already mentioned adage. ... They let their friends sell the livestock that they stole in East Jordan land; for this reason, the spoils of the latter are brought to market in *haifā*. Therefore, one frequently finds individuals among them who have spent a long time in the jail in *'akkā* for stealing or fighting."

Mülinen contradicted himself when he described the people of et-Tire in other contexts. He described them to be very honest and stated that stealing is considered dishonorable by them. He wrote, "Their [the people of et-Tire] conduct upon meeting is always appropriate, and every house is open to visitors. There is absolute security, namely for wayfarers and strangers, on the mountain during the day; women especially enjoy the protection of the custom which declares any injury committed against their decency strictly taboo. Stealing is also considered dishonorable (p.62)."

3) Erroneous claims as a result of his perceptions and observations being influenced by the general concept and discourse suggested by many orientalists of that period (see also Edward Said). Mülinen listed many characteristics as being inherent to the people he studied (especially, the people of et-Tire) while the actual situation and facts differed completely from what he stated. For example, he wrote (p.25):

All the same, can one really differ between two different types of Felläheen: one large, strong, relatively coarser, often blond and one smaller, well-proportioned, darker with more defined facial features and petite limbs and extremities. Of course, alone the color of skin and hair is not decisive since the mountain residents are on the average blonder than the peasants in the plain in all of Syria. Also, among the latter, a significant number of individuals are fair in their childhood but darken later. Nevertheless, one finds, for example, dark people in *et-tire*, whereas a reddish coloring prevails in *ikzim*, as confirmed by a proverb that will be cited later. In most cases, however, the two types have been mixed, so that striking varieties can be detected within the same family.

This is a rather limited description that is far from accurate. Many families in et-Tire were known to be fair-skinned and of a reddish hair. Some of these families were: Dar Alloh, Dar Elnajji, Dar Bakir, Dar Salman. For instance, my family, Hamolt al Hamolah, has so many people with fair-skin and a reddish coloring, while some families from Ijzim are known to be white and blond. Notice that Mülinen incorrectly wrote Ikzim, It is written and pronounced by the majority as it is written - Ijzim, and it could not be ikzim as the /k/ sound is not an allophone of the phoneme /j/.

It seems strange to divide the people of one area into two different types based on their appearance. It is as though the two groups were geologically and geographically so different that they would also be equally different in appearance. In other words, and based on my considerable knowledge of the people of this region, it is quite difficult to guess whether someone is from et-Tire, Balad alshikh or Ijzim when merely basing this on appearance or resemblance to others. In et-Tire alone, you can find people with large, strong frames and others with a significantly smaller stature.

In addition, a statement such as the following, "Also, among the latter, a significant number of individuals are fair in their childhood but darken later" (p.26) is not easily understood. This sounds as though he followed the people from their childhood through their youth in order to record the differences as they grew. Mülinen, however, only stayed there for a few years. Therefore, his judgment lacks facts and a scientific basis.

Mülinen also made statements regarding the religious faith of the people without citing the evidence for these statements. For example, he said:

"The Arab gypsies (*nawar*) characterize a special type of ethnic group. They occasionally roam through the Carmel region and are considered to be Muslims of doubtful orthodoxy. Aside from Arabic, they still speak their own language brought with them from their Indian homeland, the so-called *nawari*."

First of all, he contradicted himself when he said that the *nawar* are Arabs and then stated that they are from India, specifically an area called Nawari that exists in India.

Second, he did not provide any support or proof to claim that these people are of a doubtful faith. He even claimed that the people of el-Tire themselves are of a doubtful faith and that most of them are alcoholic. This also contradicts the facts and is a direct infringement against the principles of Islam as Islam completely forbids alcohol. He said: "Despite their fanaticism, they [the Tirawis] were considered to be given to consuming alcohol and, furthermore, marauding (p. 11)."

> This very general statement is refuted by a fact he himself mentioned. In et-Tire, there were two mosques. One was small, and the other was very big and called the Big Mosque. To have two mosques in a village at that time reflected the pious nature of the people. A new mosque is commonly established in an area once the number of the people who attending the prayers exceeds

the capacity of the already existing mosque. In addition to the two mosques, there were also two qur'anic houses about which Mülinen also wrote, "Other than the so-called small mosque (*jāmi' es-saghīr*), the great mosque (*jāmi' el-kebīr*) stands next to the palace in the southwest" (p. 102). In addition to these two mosques,"... *et-tīre* has two *zāwie* for accommodating travelers and two Quran schools [emphasis added] (p.3)." By the way, the small mosque mentioned by Mülinen was also called "*jami' alarb'iin*" (the forty-four mosque) (El Salman, 1991:14). It was called the forty-four mosque because incidentally 44 men died in that mosque as a result of an accident.

He also discussed the different Muslim sects in el-Tire. "The dominant faith is orthodox Sunni Islam; the prevailing school of thought (*medheb*) is Hanifi whereas there are a few followers of Imām Shāfi'i and scant followers of Imām Malik (p.26)." However, he did not cite any official records that documented the numbers of the followers of each sect. It is based merely on speculation, suggesting that he depended on general information from his informants which, in turn, was not based on any scientific method. At that time, et-Tire had the greatest population, as Mülinen also stated. All Tirawis are followers of Imam Shafi'i. Even now when we, the people of el-Tire, go to the cemetery, the *khatib* (who is normally also from et-Tire) who prays for the dead, reminds us that we follow the Shafi'i *medheb*. It is, however, worth noting that, presently, many Muslims know which *medheb* they follow but know little of the differences between his/her *medheb* and the other *medahebs*. Nonetheless, all *medhebs* are Sunni with few significant differences between them.

Another example of an error in Mülinen's work is in the instance of perceiving the name Nimr as 'Omar. According to him, "The inscription has been well preserved but is not executed very skillfully. I read the second name in the last line as Nimr but one could also just as easily think of 'Omar."

Indeed, the name is Nimr not 'Omar. I myself have heard it from many Tirawis whom I interviewed in 1991. One of those informants was the last *makhtar* of et-Tire and was born in 1885. He himself read to me what was written in the mosque.

Mülinen also claimed that the people did not even know the different types of fish and that they only ate the edible fish. This is not true at all, and they were not ignorant to eat fish that was inedible. The people of et-Tire were good fishers, and they were able to name at least 6 types of good fish found in the Mediterranean. Some of the people I met were old enough to have lived in a period of time close to the time of Mülinen. According to him, "[t]he Felläheen are not very knowledgeable concerning fish." He added that the best ocean fish was the large white *sulbi*, followed by *samak gharīb*, about the circumference of an arm, and the overall favored red *sultān ibrahīm*. The *bōri* is the same fish which is held in a pond by Saint Anthony of Padua in Tripoli. Otherwise, the Felläheen only knew the flat white shimmering *serghōs* and the inedible *burraqa*.

According to Abu Rashid, Al Manzol (a name of a place in et-Tire) was a central market for selling different types of fish, such as al *bouri, sultan ibrahim, koban safarini* and many other types. Women also were able to prepare very good fish meals (Abu Rasihd, 1993: 142).

Mülinen claimed that you could see goats on the mountain but not sheep; thus, he thought that "One does not see sheep[1] on Mount Carmel itself as the many thorny plants irritate their fleece greatly (p. 23)." This is also a false claim. The people of et-Tire did not keep sheep (*aghnam*) on the mountain because they are heavy animals and cannot climb the mountains and move as easily as goats can. Goats are lighter, and they can adapt to life on mountains as they can move easily (El Salman, 1991: 22)

In discussing the songs sung by the people of the area, Mülinen did not recognize the meaning of an important word, which is the key word in classical Arabic songs, namely the word "*mudschina* (p.59)." This word is basically "*ya ma jana.*" It means that our tragedies and problems are many. It also comes as a result of a man who had an incident that caused him to suffer a great deal. Thus, he uttered this important and historical phrase.

It is also worth mentioning that the older songs contain numerous lexical items relating to romantic love (wishes, besotted and waiting), and beauty (roses, seeds of roses and beauty spots). Terms of endearment appear throughout the text; in line one of Song 1 we find "dear one," and, in lines three and eight of Song 2, we read "oh you delicately grown one." Song 2 shows that Palestinian society openly celebrated both lust and female beauty. In Song 2 not only are love and physical beauty mentioned but the physical appearance of the beloved is described in detail; she is tall with golden teeth. These examples indicate that the central concerns of the song are romantic love and desire to possess the beloved. That was when they were living in their homeland. Unfortunately, after being forced to immigrate from their village in 1948, the oral literature of the Tirawi people tells us that their forced migration altered not only their material circumstances but the group identity of the whole community. Concomitantly, a state of mourning expressed in the form of religious piety has been used to censor language relating to wine and physical beauty. Additionally, a general atmosphere of sorrow purveys the contemporary texts as we repeatedly encounter the theme of lost place as a literary trope signifying the loss not only of a geographical location and its accoutrements but also the loss of family, friends and lovers (El Salman and Roche, 2011).

Mülinen continues to state his opinions rather than facts in observing that the people in el-Tire do not eat pork and do not keep pigs because they do not like it. However, this was due to Qur'anic instructions. He justified this because some people might drink wine in these villages. According to him (p.37), pigs were not held in the villages; the general abstention from pork is not so much based on the Quranic instruction – as this is often avoided when it comes to wine – but from an abhorrence of pigs impressed upon the Muslims since childhood as they are considered to be filthy animals. First, unless people are so affected by what the Qur'an states, they will not consider pigs filthy animals (they do not say that about cows, for example). In addition, few people drink, and, if so, they drink secretly because it is forbidden in Islam. In addition, it was impossible to openly have wine in the Tirawis' houses at that time, as I heard from many of my interviewees in 1991. At that time, wine was also kept secretly. Therefore, to state that the people of et-Tire did not eat pork because pigs are filthy animals and not because of Qur'anic instructions is merely an opinion.

This continues when Mülinen suggests that the cats of Mount Carmel differ from the cats of Europe. The cats of these villages were also tame and found in the houses. Yet he could simply not differentiate between cats living in houses (as in Europe), and some cats that were stray cats. Stray cats were also normally found in areas similar to these villages.

He even claimed that the horses there were not a good type. Many sources state that Arabian horses are known to be of high quality and are thoroughbreds.

Ultimately, and regardless of the misleading errors that Mülinen made, I must acknowledge and appreciate his great effort to study the area in these details.

المراجع/References

1-محمود السلمان (1991). طيرة حيفا ما بين 1948-1900. قدسية للنشر والتوزيع-إربد

2-عبدالصمد أبو راشد (1993). طيرة الكرمل الأرض والإنسان. إربد-الأردن

3-أحمد الباش (2001). طيرة حيفا كرملية الجنور – فلسطينية الإنتماء. دمشق: دار الشجرة للنشر

4- Mahmoud El Salman, "The [q] Variant in the Dialect of Tirat Haifa," Anthropological Linguistics, Indiana University, USA, Douglas Parks Ed., Vol. 45, No. 4, Dec. 2003

5- Mahmoud El Salman And James Dickins, "The Tirawi Dialect in Damascus." A published paper at the Newcastle University Conference, England. The paper is also published in The Journal of Humanities and Social Sciences, Vol. XVI No. 2, 2008, 67-79

6- Mahmoud El Salman and Thomas Roche, "Change in the Language of Tirawi Wedding Songs," Languages and Linguistics, No 28, 2011.

7. **Mahmoud El Salman and Eid Al Haisoni, "Arabic Dialects Used in the North West of Saudi Arabia: Shamari Arabic (Hail)," Languages and Linguistics, No 31, 2013.**

8. **Mahmoud El Salman, "The Use of the ts Variant in the Bedouin Dialects," International Journal of English Linguistics, Canada, Vol. 6, No. 1, 2016.**

9. **Abdel-Jawad, H. (1981). Lexical and phonological variation inspoken Arabic in Amman. University of Pennsylvania PhD. dissertation**

Contributions to
The Knowledge
of
Mt. Carmel

By
Dr. E Graf von Mülinen

With
2 Tables and 122 Images

Separate printing from the Journal of the German Palestine Society, Vol. XXX (1907), pp. 117-207 and Vol. XXXI (1908), pp. 1-258.

INTRODUCTION

An extended stay at Mount Carmel gave me the opportunity to wander about the mountain in all directions. In doing so, I convinced myself that, from many aspects, this area needs to be treated as though it were unexplored; I have still only visited some twenty ruins, the majority of which are ruins of Crusaders' castles that have yet to be marked on a map. Following the advice of a friend, I thence decided to come forth with my observations to direct the attention of interested parties to this part of the Holy Land. Though I do not have the necessary resources to help me, specifically the lack of a library, making a strictly academic approach to the subject impossible, I, nevertheless, intend to present a most versatile portrait of Mount Carmel and its inhabitants which would also be of interest to Non-Orientalists. Thus, in the following account, I have restricted myself to the indicated region and only dealt with the western coastline which stands in close mutual relation to the mountains.

A sole prerequisite, with the exception of Baedeker and Ritter[1], is knowledge of the *Survey of Western Palestine*. This work, which is very useful in its topographical material, is the only one which exists at this time and should therefore serve as a foundation for all relevant work. While comparing the following information and the English map with the *Memoirs* and *Quarterly Statements*, I felt there was necessary cause for me to depart from this source.

I have good fortune to thank for the locating of many ruins, such as the prehistoric site of cult worship of *'arāq-ez-zīghān*. In particular, I gained Mahmud el-Badawi from *et-tīre* as an excellent local guide.

---

1   Ritter, Geography (Erdkunde). Vol. VIII. Second Part. The Sinai Peninsula, Palestine and Syria; second portion, first and second parts: Palestine and Syria. Thenceforth cited as Palestine I –III. (Graf v. Mülinen, Carmel)

Figure 1. Mahmud el-Badawi from *el-tīre*.

The given sketch[1] of the area aims exclusively at rendering the most important local names at their correct locations as determined by myself. The sketch also records the numerous ruins and the available springs. Other more specific information as well as names not documented on the map can be found in the text.

The heights given for Mount Carmel are based on three different methods. The determination of the Karmelheim was conducted using the precisest of methods by measuring the gradient from the seashore to the resort house, also known as the Luftkurhaus, along the street with a leveler. Dr. Schumacher was so good to determine the height of the *juneidiyye* by recording the angles from there of two points by the ocean, the lighthouse in Old Haifā and foot of the tower in 'Atlīt, with a theodolite. These are most likely correctly marked on the English map. He has confirmed that *qambū'at ed-durziyye* is the highest peak of Mount Carmel, likewise imparted by the theodolite. The remaining figures are based on readings from two aneroid barometers and were calculated in the most commendable way through the kindness of Professor Hess in Freiburg, Switzerland.

---

1   Translator's Note: This possibly refers to a sketch that the author himself made of the area. Unfortnately, this sketch was not included in the copy of the original text I used.

While professing my deepest gratitude to Dr. Schumacher in Haifā, director of the department of planning and building and an expert in classical studies and topography in Palestine, for his ever ready assistance and never failing advice and to Mr. P. Kandler, the religious director of the German Borromeans in Haifā, for his botanical knowledge, I would like to express the hope that within the foreseeable future the still remaining systematic studies will be undertaken on Mount Carmel in order to bring its many hidden treasures to light.

Luftkurhaus Karmelheim (health resort house in Carmel), July 1906.

I.

General Section

A. Preliminary Remark on Linguistics

The predominant dialect on Mount Carmel is the Arabic Fellāheen ("peasant") dialect of Middle Palestine which actually differs among the towns and villages but still creates a unique middle group between that of the urban population and the Bedouins. In order to observe to the required consistency in the reproduction of the sounds, the example of the people from *et-tīre*, whose fields lie on the larger portion of the mountain, is taken as a basis.

As the following account should occupy itself more with real facts, a study of the dialect is not a focal point here. However, a few general comments have been allowed which seemed necessary for understanding the background for this study.

The accent of the local Fellāheen is not as clear as, for example, that of the Druses in Lebanon. In particular, the emphatic sounds (such as *t* and *s*, both with a dot underneath) are sometimes difficult to discern from the non-emphatic (*t* and *s*). Among the consonants, *q* (ق) is always articulated; *t* (ث) and *d* (ذ), such as in the place name *'atlīt* and *dib* (wolf), are often mistaken for the old sounds. On the other hand, the Arabic letter "*jeem*" (ج) suffers a softening into a sibilant which resembles the French *j*; in return, the *d* (د) when in the final position is often hardened into a *t*, e.g. *jāwīt* (أجاويد, the good), *khlunt* (خلد, mole), and *zā'it* (*zā'id*, increasing). The letter *z* (ظ) has lost its old sound; it is pronounced either as *d* as in *dahr* (back) or as *z* as in *zarīf* (gentle, tender, sweet).

The vowels fluctuate lightly as in general in Arabic; one hears *mahraqa* but sometimes *muhraqa* and *mughāra* (cave) right beside *maghāra*. Even the name Carmel itself always sounds like *il-kirmil* with two distinct *i*'s. The word *kafr*, or *kefr*, which means village, (often *kfer* before a place name in Lebanon) is always pronounced *kufr*, as in *kufr lām, kufr es-sāmir*. It is quite possible that a local etymological reference

1

to *kufr* (unbelief) [1]exists, as *kufr*, at any rate, always denotes places or ruins which date from pre-Islamic[2] periods. When consonants seemed too many or too close together, a Fellāh slips in an auxiliary vowel, often an *i*, such as in *safḥat esh-shēkh ʾslīmān*. Such auxiliary vowels are often used when a word's own vowels are dropped: *ibrēghīṯ* instead of *barāghīṯ*; rather than *as'ad*, one always hears *is'ad*, just as *ishqar* for *ashqar* (red). The classic feminine ending *atun* sounds like a high, clear sound between *i* and *e*, yet leans towards *i*, as in the article *il*.

In ceremonial formulas, one occasionally discerns the classical nunation in the nominative case not with *damma* but with *kasra*: *niḏr(in) 'aleyya* (a solemn promise is bearing down on me).

The intonation of the two place names *rushmaya* and *'usufia* exhibits a peculiarity. The first is pronounced in Lebanon as *rushmia*, and *'usufia* is regarded as derived from (affix) *'assāf*. Both words place the stress not on the always long derived ending as often in Arabic but on the first syllable: *rúshmia* and *úsufia* (*'úsᵘfia, óˢfia*).

The predominant use of the preposition *bi* instead of *fi* is striking among the urban population; thus, one always hears *mā bish* instead of *mā fish* (there, or it, is nothing).

This brief description of the dialect of the people of *et-tīre* [3]is in complete concordance with that of the people of *'aṯlīṯ* and for the most part with that of *beled esh-shēkh* and *el-yādshūr* in the north, as well as *'ain hōd*, south of *et-tīre*. The Druses in *'usufia* and *ed-dālie* also use a similar dialect, though they still preserve certain idiosyncrasies.

---

1   El Salman's Note: *kufr* does not mean unbelief as Mülinen has noted in this context. *Kufr* means *baldat* (town). Thus, *Kufr lam*, for example, means the Town of Lam.

2   Translator's Note: The author Mülinen uses the word "pre-Mohammedan" rather than pre-Islamic as is was common in his day to refer to Islam as Mohammedism and to Muslims as Mohammedans. This, however, is a misnomer as Muslims do not worship the Prophet Muhammad, may Allah's peace and blessings be upon him. In each instance of this use, I have replaced it with Islam or Muslims in an effort to use correct and appropriate terminology.

3   El Salman's Note: Et-Tire, unlike the rest of the villages except the two Durz villages, namely Osffyya and Al Dalyyah, use the uvualr variant /q/ variant of the /Q/ variable in their vernacular (El Salman, 2003). The rest of the villages: Balad al-shekh, 'ain Hod and Ijzim use the /k/ variant of the /Q/ variable.

They, like the Metawile in Lebanon, pronounce the long *i* at the end of words as a drawn out *èi*, i.e. *'alèi* and *wādèi* instead of *'ali* and *wādi*.

Opposite this northern group, which displays the strongest influence of urban speech, one finds a convergence to the Bedouin dialect in that of the inhabitants of the southeastern village *umm ez-zeināt* as a result of its nomadic environment. This is evident through the compression of the *k* to *tsh* before light and dropped vowels and the softening of the *q* to a guttural *g*.

The dialect of *ikzim* and other villages on the southern side of Carmel and on the coastal plain takes a middle position. The letter *k* is also compressed, even before a long *a*, pronounced with *imāle*, as in *tshān* (he was). The *q* does not quite become a *g* but also does not remain a strong *q*, making it then difficult to discern from *k* when it precedes a heavy vowel, such as *o* and *u*. Furthermore, the Arabic letter *jeem*, always without softening into *j*, is articulated with a distinctly audible *d* before the sibilant, as in *ija* (he came) and *jebel* (mountain).

The influence of the dialect of *nābulus* is already making itself noticeable in the *khushm* in the south in a rounding of the long *ū* to a long *ō*.

The pronunciation here is strictly rendered from listening. As the language often changes, especially that of the unschooled Fellāheen, even from person to person, the reader should not be surprised at the apparent inconsistencies which appear in this report. For example, the villagers pronounce the word *ne̲dr* (oath), sometimes as *ne̲dr*, or sometimes as *ni̲dr* or *ni̲dir* or even adapting to the urban dialect, as *nedr* or *nidr*, or *nidir*.

The Arabic characters have only been added in parentheses when the dialect form deviated so much from the classical that it was difficult to recognize the latter in its transcribed form.

B. Geographical Location
Orographical and Hydrographical

Mount Carmel presents itself as a special part of the Holy Land. It rises abruptly from the middle of the Palestinian coastal stretch, making it visible from afar both from the sea as well as from the lowlands and elevations of the mainland.

The area covered by the mountain takes on the shape of an almost right-angled isosceles triangle, whose acute angle juts out northwestwards into the ocean[1] from where it protects the roadstead of *haifā* against the south wind. The adjoining eastern arm of the triangle, bounded by the Jezreel Valley (once known as the Plain of Esdraelon, or the Zir'in Valley in Arabic), is roughly twenty-three kilometers long and levels off at the southeastern end where the chapel of the *muhraqa* is located. This is where the right angle is formed as the deep Salt Valley (*wādi 'l-milh*), gently rising from the Jezreel Valley, divides Mount Carmel from the low, watery and fertile yet treeless plateau of the *rūha*. The *rūha* does not consist of steep rocky slopes but rather synclinal drops.

The boundary to Mount Carmel to the south is more difficult. After an almost straight line, which extends from the *muhraqa* to the West, the mountain lowers itself into declining hills southwards until it meets the wide plain of *ikzim*. The vertical formation of the ground passes there along the eastern side into the plateau of *rūha* without significant change while, in the west, the hills which slope down to the coastal plain extend far into the south. This eventually creates a ledge protruding out into the ocean between *tantūra* and *qaisārie* (Caesarea) which is called *khushm* (The Nose).

One would be tempted to mislay the southern boundary of Mount Carmel on this east-west line, beginning approximately where the rocky *wādi 'arāq en-nātif* which flows into the Salt Valley climbs steeply. Then the boundary of the small ridge would be crossed. This separates this *wādi* from *wādi 'n-nahl* (The Valley of the Bees). Lastly, the boundary lowers itself to the plain of *ikzim* from where it would gain a plain through the *wādi 'l-mughāra* (The Valley of the Cave). Mount Carmel would then distinguish itself from the surrounding plains, more precisely, from the plateau of the *rūha* and its western foothills, as a rock mountain.

One must, however, object to assigning such a geographical boundary as a large area south of the imagined east-west line still belongs to Carmel when one considers their beliefs and parlance. This is not only the case for *ikzim* and *umm ez-zeināt*, which are located directly on the line, but also for places much further south. The western coastal hills until *el-fureidīs* and *zummārīn* on the *khushm*

---

1   Thus, the expression from the Old Testament (e.g. Jos. 19:26): "Carmel by the sea" in contrast to Carmel in Juda.

primarily come into consideration here, and after that a series of points in the east. These points form an almost straight line running southwest: it begins at the upper reaches of *wādi 'l-milḥ* which extends until *umm ez-zeināt*. The village *umm ez-zeināt* is still considered to be part of Carmel, but the nearby ruin *el-harāmis* with *bir el-harāmis*, the well for *umm ez-zeināt*, are considered to belong to the *rūḥa*. Subsequently, the ruin of *qumbāze* belong to Carmel as well as the ruins of *umm qubbi* and *hanāne*, whereas the ruins of *qotteine* already lay outside the boundaries. This line meets with *wādi 'l-fureidīs* between the two Isreali colonies, *shefēya* and *umm ej-jimāl*; the latter of which is considered to be part of the *rūḥa*. After which lies *zummārīn* on the *khushm* within the boundaries of Carmel which reaches southward to *umm el-'alaq* until *nahr ez-zerqā* (the "crocodile brook" or "blue river"). With respect to hydrography, the small valleys with springs of *wādi 'l-metābin*, along with several side affluxes to *wādi mādi*, intersect this line at *umm ez-zeināt*. The line then follows along the small hills which separate *wādi mādi* and *wādi 'sh-shuqāq*, both of which flow into *wādi 'l-fureidīs*. This occurs west of the small drop *wādi 'z-zibriyye*. From this it is clear that the system of valleys does not wield any influence over the demarcation line. This line orients itself neither according to the path through the valley nor initially to the watershed, and where it does follow the watershed to its end, it is only an insignificant elevation between two wadis which belong to the same system of valleys.

When the parlance is determined in relation to the given Carmel boundary, irrespective of the lacking differences in the form of the soil, there, however, still exists a reason for this which naturally does not lie solely in geographical areas. If one simply follows along the mentioned points from *wādi 'l-milḥ* to the *khushm*, one finds ferrous "red earth" (*'ard hamrā*) all over the western side of the mountain, while the settled *rūḥa* in the east exhibits white or yellowish-white soil (*'ard bēdā*) by virtue of its strong marl additives mixed into the lime-stone. The dividing line can be easily followed as it can be identified in the sunlight through the radiance of the red earth beside the duller marl hue. Scattered masses of red soil in the east and white terrain in the west do crop up along the border though in small intermittent areas which are not taken into consideration in drawing a dividing line.

Thus, the difference is of a geological nature. It is determined through the striking difference in the vegetation; Mount Carmel is home to a thriving tree and brush culture, whereas the *rūha* is lacking in this. As a result, many cultural differences are associated with this. For example, goat herds rather than sheep herds are kept on Carmel while sheep are by far the predominant animal in the *rūha*.

In contrast to the north and the west, where Mount Carmel stands out against the red soil of the Jezreel Valley and the coastal plain through its vertical height, thereby drawing an orographical boundary, the borderline in the south is a geological-cultural one according to the precedent. This has long been a standard perspective of the natives. From *wādi 'l-milh* at the *muhraqa* until the *khushm*, this border measures roughly twenty-three kilometers which is approximately the same as the northeastern line from the Stella Maris Monastery to *wādi 'l-milh*; this stretch can be considered the southeastern leg of the Carmel triangle.

At thirty-four kilometers, the western coastal plain presents itself as the hypotenuse of the triangle.

The mountain, in its vertical formation, offers a beautiful, majestic view, despite its low altitude. This view has inspired the singers and prophets of the Old Testament to poetic comparisons (Song of Solomon 7:5; compare with Jeremiah 46:18). As with all mountain ranges in Western Syria, Mount Carmel rises slowly and steadily from the ocean coast towards the east, dropping steeply to the Jezreel Valley. One finds a low plateau only at the northern peak; a second adjoins in the east and is even lower in the surroundings of *rushmia*. Thus, the highest points can be found along the ridge stretching east. Generally, from *rās abu 'n-nidā* until over the *juneidiyye* and *'usufia* until the *muhraqa* this ridge remains constant at the same level of roughly 500 meters. The highest peak, the *qambū'at ed-duziyye* (قاموعة الدرزيه, The Peak of the Female Druze), at 547 meters above sea level, is located here; it is a half hour's travel from *'usufia*. Besides that, only the *seq'ab* at *shellāle* almost reaches the ridge's height.

It seems explicable under these conditions that the numerous, longer and more important valleys turn themselves westwards towards the ocean, and the eastern slope, with the exception of the valley of *rushmia*, exhibits a few steep ravines. Thus, all western valleys which are on the ridge create a path which circumvents the main road for the whole mountain.

It is perhaps worth paying closer attention to the hydrological and orographical relations, particularly the language of the mountain's inhabitants which have given form to relevant aspects which may not completely come up elsewhere in this application.

At any rate, Mount Carmel apparently lacks water; the available springs are scattered about: sometimes lying close to the surface (*'aēn*, or *'ain* when it comes before a name), and sometimes have their source in a well-like recess (*bīr*). Thus, they are frequented by shepherds from afar, just as the case with possible troughs in lime-stone in which the rain water survives longer in the springtime. A larger trough of this kind is called *ruhrāh*, pl. *rahārīh*; its presence has served in the construction of place names on different locations on the mountain. The water, which drains from an underground reservoir only after previous rainfall, is called *nezzāze*. Albeit, many springs trickle down through the layers of rock and first emerge in the valleys or on the coastal plain, even partially into the ocean. The little water produced this way is completely exhausted by the Fellāheen for their own purposes or for that of their herds as well as the irrigation of the fields. It can be thus concluded that nearly all valleys are dried out for the majority of the year and their rivulets only contain water in the winter; nevertheless, sudden eventuating downpours can fill them to a dangerous level. Apart from these winter brooks (*widiān ish-shittawiyye*), only *wādi fellāh* by *shellāle* along the short stretch of 200 meters and after that again by *dustrē* actually have a perennial course (*nahr jāri*) on Carmel. In the south, the rivers *nahr ed-difle* and *nahr ez-zerqā* also run deep in the summer.

Let us follow such a valley from the mountain crest to the sea; at the end of this, the typical mountain formation would best present itself. Whether rising from a projecting peak (*rās*), a greater hilltop (*dabbe*), or a smaller hill (*tell*), the valley forms a gently dropping slope (*khalle* or *shulūl*[1]). A mountain torrent often flows sideways into a steeply dropping off ravine which becomes a waterfall (*shāghār*) in winter and spring that bores a deep hole in the rock (*ghadīr*). Sometimes the spring appears further down; then the valley rushes off to the foot of the mountain (*ābāt*), often widening to a *wādi* through connecting with neighboring valleys. At this point, thickets of brush (*'uqdi*, pl. *'uqad*) are located in places; predator animals stay in these thickets. Arriving at the coast, greater courses of water create

---

1   In praxis, both words have the same meaning; *shulūl* prevails among small valleys named by the Muslim Fellāheen, *khalle* among those named by the Druses and Bedouins.

an inaccessible point (*zōr*) or even a swamp (*bassa*), such as by *'aṭlīṭ*. Inertly, they then creep past the dunes that have been built up by the ocean until they, usually joined by others, break through them and flow into the sea.

Figure 2. *'Arāq ez-zīghān.*

The mountain ranges lying between the valleys lower themselves down from the crest in long ridges (*fersh*), where they sometimes split into smaller ridges (*qōd*). Should the mountain face drop steeper, a *safḥa* (pl. *isfāḥ*), an incline of small boulders is formed, called *sīfār* (pl. *sayāfīr*). A single imposing boulder is called *shaqīf*. However, high abrupt rock faces (*'arāq*, pl. *'urqān*, Fig. 2) with large caves (*maghāra*, pl. *mughr*) often rise above the valley, especially at lower reaches. As in former times (see Amos 9:3), these caves serve as hide-outs for the hunted. Particularly wild natural groups are also called *qal'a* (fortress) on account of their mountain-like character. The area located above the *'arāq* is called *saṭh* while the area below the steep escarpment is called *shéfā*. Such areas are now being cultivated in increasing dimensions whereas, previously, everything was wilderness. Here, one differentiates the parts of the region according to whether it is only strewn with stones (*naqqār*) or overgrown with shrubbery and trees (*wa'r*). A small developed area on a *fersh* is called *idrā'* (دراع). Such areas as well as the gentle slopes of a *fersh* were covered with terrace grounds (*rub'ān* or *rbā'*, pl. *rbā'āt*) throughout the mountain in earlier days. These were separated by embankments (*kitif*) and are still discernable today through the former garden walls (*sinsile*, pl. *sanāsil*) even in the most untamed areas. Rather than planting vineyards or orchards (*karm*, pl. *krūm*) as previously, the Fellāheen are now converting the wasteland (*ard 'atl*) to farmland (*ard felāha*) for the purpose of cultivating grain. If tobacco or vegetables sprout from the soil, then the area is called *hākūra* (pl. *hawākīr*) or *meshtel* (pl. *meshātil*). Ultimately, *merj* means a smaller plain mostly planted with olive trees, and *sahil* refers to a larger plain. It is well known that the coastal plain is called *sāhil*.

In conclusion, we turn to the path that leads through the mountain today. As foot paths and mule tracks, they usually have the standard names of *derb* or *tarīq*; an especially narrow mountain trail is called a *misrāb*, an empty passageway is called a *khanūq* or *zārūb*. Aside from those on the coastal plain, the navigable street (*derb 'arabāye*) is to be found only on the northern side of Mount Carmel.

One negotiates the river on the coastal plain by means of a bridge (*jisr*) and the brook in the mountains simply by means of a ford (*makhāda*), which is called a *rsīf* (literally, cobblestone, or a Roman road) when the crossover is made easier through laid-out wooden beams or logs or stones.

C. Geology[1]

Geologically speaking, Mount Carmel is primarily composed of lime formations of varied thickness. For the most part, the surface consists of Senonian rock (*hajar nāri*), the softest type which comes after the degrees of hardness of *hajar sultāni* and *hajar meleki*; both of which are well suitable for building purposes. Cenomanian rock (*hajar yābis*) lies under this as the hardest layer, and sometimes under the *nāri* lies a layer of soft white chalk (*háwwar*). One finds hornstone (scilica) disseminated with the limestone nearly everywhere. The natives call this *suwān* (صوان) and use it as flint.

One occasionally sees delicately flaky, shimmering, yellowish lime spar shining through as well as yellow hard crystalline quartz with

---

1   Compare with Philippson's "Mittelmeergebiet" (The Mediterranean Region) for this section and the next. Translator's note: this possibly refers to Alfred Philippson's "Das Mittelmeergebiet," Leipzig, 1904.

clear crystal features. On account of a certain similarity to the halite, or rock salt, the Fellāheen call both *hajar milh* (literally, salt stone).

Furthermore, it is important to mention the presence of iron (*hadīd*) which is sometimes stored in small pieces of limestone as by *abu suweid* and sometimes detected in such great amounts as by *ikzim* that the extraction of it is only worthwhile by means of opencast mining. In other areas of the mountain the limestone boulders have taken on a resolute reddish coloring due to the iron content. The reddish hue in the soil also comes from the iron, which, as illustrated above, serves as a characteristic feature of the Carmel region in determining the boundary. According to the accounts of the residents of *ikzim*, copper (*nuhās*) was once also mined there.

Near the spring *'ain qatf ez-zukūr* by *et-tīre* as well as at the *merjet ez-zerā'a* in *wādi fellāh*, a porous formation of a yellowish or reddish hue is present. It is used by the Druses in *ed-dālie* as *trāb el-merāmil* (sing. *murmāli*) in the production of clay vessels.

Many areas, namely by *'usufia* as well as *wādi abu jā'* by *et-tīre* and, further, in the soft chalk of the *jebel 'īd* by *ikzim*, fossils from marine creatures appear. Their presence indicates the mountain's rather recent, geologically speaking, emergence from the salt water's tide.

On the other hand, one comes across crystal geodes of the most unusual forms on *fersh iskender* by *'ain es-siāh*. They frequently have the shape of a melon but often take on the shapes of other fruits; they are called *battīkh* (melon) by the locals.

In the caves of the rock face which are in abundance on the mountain, one frequently sees stalactite formations (*natūf*); the natural recesses in these grottos hold a sodium bicarbonate containing water, which is enjoyed by herdsmen and animals despite its bitter taste.

An old dune which is decreasing in the north while rising in the south accompanies the beach of the coastal plain; this dune is formed out of the sand from the shore which has hardened into solid stone under the influence of the weather. This is even the same stone that was used in earlier times for the construction of houses as evidenced through the old quarries found there. The Fellāheen called this *hajar ramle* (sandstone) when in actuality this is limestone debris. The medieval castles on the shore consist, for the most part, of this formation as in the village *et-tīre* today, while the villages at higher altitudes are naturally built out of the limestone found there.

D. Climate

Already slightly elevated from the sea, the climate of Mount Carmel differs greatly from that of the coastal stretch. For example, when the oppressive heat of the summer is weighing down on *haifā*, the temperature on the mountain is mitigated by the almost constant west wind. Consequently, the summer heat usually rises first in August to about 27 or 28°C in the shade; however, temperatures reached 32 and 35°C in the shade on the hot sirocco days in October, 1904. At times, the thermometer sinks below zero in winter, and this can lead to the formation of ice which is called *qazāz*, i.e. glass, by the mountain's residents.

The currents of air carried in from over the ocean produce a great amount of humidity in the atmosphere which becomes distinctly perceptible at increasing altitudes. At the hotel by the Karmelheim, Mr. Pross and later Pastor Schneider have recently taken measurements of the annual rainfall. The following table illustrates the quantity of rain in millimeters according to these measurements:

Rainfall on Mount Carmel at 290 meters sea level

	Jan.	Feb.	March	Apr	May	Jun	Jul-Sep	Oct.	Nov.	Dec.	Total
1903	169.0	133.6	82.0	–	–	–	–	4.0	65.5	73.2	526.8
1904	148.6	37.2	56.4	17.2	5.4	–	–	88.5	184.0	180.0	717.3
1905	81.0	95.5	50.9	20.6	6.9	0.5	–	53.5	57.8	261.9	628.6
1906	137.5	81.9	36.6	50.5	29.3	–	–				

The following summery can be made according to the rainy season (October through May, respectively June):

Winter 1903-04: 407.0
Winter 1904-05: 707.9
Winter 1905-06: 709.0

Studies of the dew precipitation, which appear to be entirely abnormal on Mount Carmel, would, however, be much more interesting than these observations of the rainfall. The rainfall is so strong on many nights that the precipitation runs down the roof gutters. As the year continues, the humidity constantly increases. One experiences clear days in winter on which the view from the elevations of Carmel offers an enchanting colorful picture of the azure ocean beyond the emerald plains and gentle hills of Galilee until the blue line of East Jordan, while from the north the snowy plains of Hermon and Lebanon shine until the other side of the *sannin*. One can even see every snowy field beyond the darker Galilean foothills by moonlight during the especially cold season. The view does not penetrate so far in the summer, and, in the fall, the mountain is often draped with a thick yellowish fog, particularly due to evaporation of the Nile, when the sirocco does not illuminate the air. The west wind (*gharbi*) prevails in the summer though it does blow throughout the year likewise as with the more seldom south wind (*qibli*). In late fall, the southeastern wind begins, often bearing rain; this is referred to as *zerrā'i* because it coincides with the sowing time. The north wind (*shimāli*) is feared due to its harshness, though the east wind (*sharqiyye*, often with the addition of *sammiyye* "poison wind", the sirocco or simoom) is feared even more. It can bring great destruction to villages and seeds over the mountain. This wind is also frequent in winter; one finds it most irritating in early summer and in fall when its latent blazing heat impairs the thriving of the plants, animals and people.

The impact of the extraordinary humidity affirms itself in the great fertility of the soil and in the fact that there is constant plant growth throughout the year. Plants which elsewhere do well only on account of artificial irrigation thrive here alone through the plentiful dew precipitation. The soft limestone quickly weathers under these influences and produces good humus. Even today, the mountain is also suitable for cattle breeding under these circumstances, just as in former times (Jeremiah 50:19). However, persons who have a rheumatic predisposition suffer in this climate while, on the other hand, the climate is praised as having a healing effect on malaria fever.

E. Flora
Wild and Cultivated Plants

Mount Carmel has lost its former abundance of timber; only a few areas exhibit the remains of groups of trees which are either on private property or are protected through old sacred tradition. On a daily basis, the trees fall victim to the growing demand for heating in *haifā* and the many lime ovens; the numerous goat herds prevent natural fertilization from taking root. The century-long neglect has also had its share in contributing strongly to the destruction and is, for the most part, responsible for giving the mountain its characteristic as a stony wilderness. At points where only shattered masses of limestone can be found today and no cultivatable land exists, preserved traces of garden walls prove that crops flourished in ancient times.

Despite this, the local flora is one of the richest in all of Syria. A botanist conducting research is surprised by the countless species and subspecies. The rich cloak that unfolds over the creation that is continuously renewing itself across Mount Carmel even now stirs delight in any nature lover, just as it did in the time of the prophets of Israel (Isaiah 35:2, 33:9; Amos 1:2; Nahum 1:4).

The image that these floral decorations offer is, however, a very different one depending on the season. During the rainy season, particularly towards the end of it, radiant flowers full of rich colors on tender stems sprout forth everywhere. The small white crocus is the first, followed by it bluish-red sister a month and a half later. Almost simultaneously with the first, the daisy (*Bellis perennis L.*, *suffari beda*) and the golden yellow *suffari safra* (*Taraxacum officinale*) appear. Immediately after these come the daffodil, or *jerunjus* (نرجس, *Narcissus Tazetta*), and the frequently sometimes white, sometimes rosy or soft violet cyclamen, called *sabūnet er-ra'i* (literally, Shephard's soap, *Cyclamen latifolium L.* and *S.*), as well as the meadow saffron (*Colchicum Steveni Kunth*) and the fragrant white blooming creeper clematis (*Clematis, ghāshi*). The scenic picture becomes even more splendid in its hues through the shimmering silver *Ornithogalum montanum* of the hyacinth family (*abu suweyy*) and the magnificent anemone (*Anemone coronaria L.*, *berqōq*) in white, blue, mauve, and a rich red. At the same time, the lily species *basūl* and the bulbous plant *khusalān*, which initially blooms in the fall, stretch out their long, almost blue iridescent leaves. The mandrake, called *tuffāh emjenn*, (تفاح مجن "the daze-inducing apple," *Mandragora officinalis L.*) which unfolds into a flower runs wild across the ground; the fragrant Egyptian rue (*Ruta chalepensis L., fèjam*) turns green; one eats this with olives. There is also the tasty fennel (*Foeniculum officinale Al., shōmar*) and the broad-leaved *lūf* that is edible when cooked. In February, grape hyacinth (*basal ferk*) and charming orchids appear. Near the time of Thursday of the Dead (*Khamīs al-Amwat*) in Easter, the many-colored ranunculus, called *berqōq el-khamīs*, blooms. The Fellāheen often do not differentiate among these charming offspring of the plant world by using specific names. A query after the names is almost regularly answered with the same expression "*teshkīl*" (i.e. flowers, as though one gathered many different kinds together in a bouquet). If one returns in the summer, one is amazed at the change. Unlike in the desert which completely loses its colorful splendor of spring by summer, vegetation is hardly lacking on Mount Carmel. Due to the ever-present moisture, the ground is covered in plants just the same. However, these plants are of another kind. The fragile growth of the wildflowers (Saftkräuter) has withered away. The summertime flora has armed itself against the heat with wood stalks and hard leaves. Spikes and thorns appear everywhere on them, and the aromatic odors of many plants protect them against withering. The prevailing color is an indefinable green that shifts into yellow or gray but infrequently towards blue. Only these wood plants survive the summer until they also die in order to let the flora of the rainy season again take precedence in the cycle of rejuvenating nature.

The *sindyān* (the Holm or Holly Oak, an evergreen oak, *Quercus ilex*) is important to mention amid the wild-growing larger trees which only crop up at greater distances from each other. This tree, amongst others, forms the well-known group of the shrine of the forty martyrs. Rarer is its relative the *mell*, the deciduous oak, which prefers the bottoms of the valleys. There are likewise two types of pine trees; the so-called Carmel pine (the Stone or Umbrella pine, *Pinus Pinea L.*, *snōbar berri*, Bedouin dialect: *tagg*) once formed the principle content of the mountain's forests. In recent times, it has had to give this position over its cousin, imported from Lebanon, the *Pinus Halepensis* (the Aleppo pine, *snōbar juwwi*). Its growth is more beautiful, and its tasty kernels are relished. The *'abhar* (snowdrop bush, *Styrax officinalis*) occurs frequently; its berries are used in catching fish. Once thrown into the ocean, the berries become prey to the fish which then die after consuming them; the dead fish that swam on the surface are collected and are then served as food. The terebinth, or turpentine tree, (*Pistacia terebinthus, butm*) can also be found in large numbers. The wild Greek strawberry tree (*Arbutus Andrachne, qēqab*) is less frequent, and more seldom is the *summāq* (sumac, *Rhus coriaria L.*) which produces tannin. The Judas tree (*Cercis siliquastrum, jezārūq*) exists only in smaller specimens.

Among the shrubbery, the so-called Carmel rose (rock rose, *lubbēd*) prevails with its white or red blossoms (*Cistus salviaefolius, Cistus villosus* or *Creticus*) as well as sage (*Salvia controversa, merhamiyye* or *meryamiyye*) and thyme (*Thymus capitatus, za'tar fārisi* زعتر فارسي). They, often together, cover large areas of the mountain and fill the air for miles around with their fragrances. In the valleys, the existence of blackberries (*Rubus, 'ullēq mōy,* عليق ماء) indicates the presence of water. Further along there is the reed (*qasab*), the myrtle (Fellāheen: *bersīm*, urban dialect: *rīhān*) which blooms pleasantly white in the summer, the noble laurel (Fellāheen: *rīhān*, urban dialect: *ghār*, Bedouin dialect: *rand* or *rond*) and, finally, at the onset of the coastal plain, the oleander (*difle*). On the coastal plain itself, there are specimens of *halfa* existing in the *zōr* and a great deal of types of reed grass and rush. Alone in the valleys of *'ain es-siāh*, the bushes of a species of spurge (*Euphorbium antiquorum*), which is called *haleb lebbūn* by the inhabitants there, grow upwards into small trees. They offer a magnificent view with their tender green, contrasting with the yellow blossoms, in the spring, but, of course, their small stems look miserably brown in the summertime. In other valleys, one finds *murrān* (Bedouin dialect; Fellāheen: *sfēra*) with leaves similar to an orange tree, white blossoms, and red berries.

At higher altitudes, one finds many low shrubs such as mastic (*Pistacia lentiscus, serrīs*) and *berze*, a stunted version of the oak, as well as species of teucrium, *izwētīni* (*Teucrium rosmarinforium*), and *'ushbe murra* (literally, bitter herb) used in medicines. The *qrē'a* is important for the Fellāheen as they take its bast and used it for tinder (*qadha*) when they do not use the bast of the root (*fartōsh*) from the *mell* or *kharrūb* for this.

The black thorn, or sole, (*suwēd*) and the hawthorn (*Crataegus, za'rūr*), although they are tree-like plants, bring us to the thorny herbs and weeds and thistle plants which especially dominate in the summertime. Among the first mentioned here are the *shōk qabbār* (caper bush, *Capparis spinosa*) whose berries are valued as a cooking spice, the *mussīs* (spiny molucca balm, *Molucella spinosa*), the thorny green creeper *Smilax aspera L.* (Italian sarsaparilla or Mediterranean smilax, *'ullēq shejar* علّيق شجر), and the *'awarwar* (*Verbascum Tripolitanum*). The leaves of the butcher's broom (*Ruscus aculentus*, *'annāb berri*) serve as a tea for kidney illnesses. Among the thistle plants, the most wide-spread from amongst them is the *khilli* (khella, Bishop's weed, or toothpick weed, *Ammi Visnaga L.*), which supplies the entire Orient with toothpicks, as well as the blue *qursa'anni* (قرصعنه, eryngo, *Eryngium Creticum Lam.*). Even the broom is thorny here as the green *himbel* (Cyprus broom, *Genista sphacelata*) and especially the spiny broom (*Calycotome villose*, *qandōl*) illustrate. For lighting a fire, a Fellāh often uses the *billān* (*Botarium spinosum*). The Galium species *dherji* and the Carthamus species *qūs* should bring this brief summary list to a close to which only the examples of cryptogam family are added: the mushroom *fúqu'*, amongst them the white edible *ftirri*, and the moss species *'ushriq*.

Of the cultivated plants, one is surprised that the date palm (*nakhl*), which is the most typical cultivated plant in Syria, can be found only in very isolated points on Mount Carmel. Its growth does thrive, but this local date as a commodity is so far behind the Egyptian variety that one refrains from planting greater amounts. In former times, the most important agricultural crop was the grape vine (*dāliet 'aneb*) as still evident by the countless grape presses (*midbise*) spread over the entire mountain. It seems that, probably under the influence of the Quranic prohibition on wine, the cultivation receded, although the Muslims enjoy the honey (*dibs*) extracted from the grapes. The Stella Maris Monastery had once held a high regard for the tradition of cultivating the juice of the grape, though it is recently through the German settlers that the cultivation of the grape vine, which turns out an excellent product here, has been expanded again. The olive tree (*zeitūn*, Fig. 3), which frequently reaches a significant size with a girth of seven to eight meters at the chest height of an average man and a height of up to thirteen meters, forms expansive stands in the proximity of all larger villages and towns. It has a lucrative yield. Wild species can also be found at higher altitudes. Similarly, the almond tree (*lōz*) formerly was so prevalent across much of the valley of *et-tīre* that this village was known as *tīret el-lōz*. Fewer still are the walnut tree (*jōz*) and the sycamore (*jummeiz*) while the carob tree (*kharrūb*) occurs more often. If this tree is cultivated, it bears fruits that contribute to the local trade. Aside from that, the beans are still used today, as in ancient times, by the locals as a standard for small weight quantities. On the plains, one finds the mulberry tree (*tūt*), likewise the fig tree (*tīn*), only in more protected areas, often alongside the pomegranate tree (*sejaret rumman*). Apple (*tuffāh*) and pear trees (*njās*) grow both wild and cultivated as *berri* and *juwwi*. In gardens, one plants quince (*sfarjal*), apricots (*mishmish*), and peaches (*khōkh*) but seldom limes (*leimūn halu*) and lemons (*leimūn hāmud*). Oranges (*bortuqāl*) are not planted. Although the *'unnāb*

Figure 3. *Zeitūne* (Olive tree) from the outskirts of *et-tīre*.

(*Zizyphus*) is an old tree native to the mountain, the Japanese medlar (*kidunia*, from the Turkish *yenidunia*, i.e. new world) has been first imported in the time of the present living generation.

The cactus (*sábir*) has secured an absolute right of residence for itself as it surrounds most of the villages in hedges and is found as high as 500 meters. After removing the needles, the cactus fruits are laid in water and offer a pleasant refreshment through its sour flavor. Albeit, the cactus hedges form a common hide-out for the chicken thieves, the Egyptian mongoose.

Legumes, specifically, lupins (*turmus*), the vetch types *kursenni* and *jilbāni* or *fellāha*, the broad or fava bean (*fūl*), dwarf or French beans (*lūbiā*), and the white kidney beans (*fasūliā*), are planted in greater quantities. In addition to that, there are lentils (*'ades*) and chickpeas, or garbanzo beans (*hummus*). Among the vegetables in gardens, one sees cucumbers (*khiār*), the favored zucchini (*kūsā*), another type of cucumber known as *yaqinti*; also, the eggplant (*bedinjān, Melongena*) and okra (*bāmie, Hibiscus esculentus*) which, along with the tomato (*banadōra*), are certainly the most prized garden fruits. Peppermint (*na'ni*) and primarily garlic (*ṯūm*) along with onion (*basal*), which is also cultivated in open fields, are used as spices. The same planting conditions are needed for watermelon (*battīkh ahmar*) and sugar, or muskmelon (*battīkh asfar*).

One recognizes barley (*sha'īr*) and wheat (*hinta*, commonly *qamh*, i.e. kernel) among the varieties of grain. Both are frequently planted and are chiefly used in making bread, though barley is sometimes used as horse feed. One also cultivates durra (*idrà*) for the purposes of making bread. Sesame (*simsim*) is significant for trade; tobacco (*dukhān*) has been very rarely planted since the formation of the administration.

The harvest seasons for the most important crops are the beginning of August for grapes, the months of September and October for the early type of olives, and January for the later olives. As for the grains, whose seeds are sown at the beginning of the rainy season, barley is harvested on Pentecost, or Whitsun[1], and the wheat three weeks after that. Legumes are also planted in the fall but gathered three weeks before Pentecost. Durra and sesame are planted in the spring and are both harvested in August.

The Fellāheen observe a certain crop rotation in that they annually alternate planting cereals and legumes or even watermelon on the same field.

The existence of purely ornamental plants is hardly worth mentioning. Aside from the gardens of the European settlers, one rarely encounters them as a Fellāh does not tend to them. Nor do many of them know the names of these plants, among them the rose (*werd*), stock (*qurunful*), and basil (*habaq*).

---

1   Translator's note: Pentecost, also called Whitsun, falls seven weeks (49 days) after Easter Sunday according to the Christian calendar, thus falling in mid- to late May.

F. Fauna
Wildlife and Livestock

The most dangerous of wild animals (*wuhūsh berriyye*) is the predatory animal, the panther (*nimr*, fem. *labwi*), with a white underside but otherwise covered in a yellow-brownish spotted coat. The panther hides itself in inaccessible caves during the day so it can pay its visits to the herds at night. Just as with the lion elsewhere, the panther has a reputation for magnanimity about which the Fellāheen can tell many tales. Closest to the panther is the red-gray panther ozelot (*fāhid*) and the relatively smaller wildcat (*shīb*) who is feared for its courage. The wolf (*dīb*, fem. *jrēda*) has also not yet been wiped out, and the jackal (*wāwi*) as well as the hyena (*dābi'*, pl. *idbā'*) is even frequent. One seldom encounters a badger (*ghrēri*) and fox (*hsēni*[1]). The weasel (*nims*) and the Egyptian mongoose (*nisnās*, pl. *nasānīs*; in '*usufia* it is called *jurr batnu*, i.e. "belly dragger") are known as chicken stranglers. In comparison to these animals, the *dabbāha* seems yet to be researched. It is a small gray-haired animal similar to a cat with which the shepherds eagerly occupy their imaginations. The otter (*zābir*) occasionally appears in the spring streams of the Crocodile Brook (*nahr ez-zerqā*).

The Carmel gazelle (*ghazāl*, pl. *ghuzlān*), roedeer (*wa'l*, pl. *wu'ūli*) and a small type of deer to which the natives also give the name *wa'l* belong to the other type of wildlife. As with both deer and goats, the male (buck, respectively ram) is called *fahl*, the female (doe) '*anze*, and the young (kid) *sachil*, fem. *sachli*. The wild boar (*khanzīr berri*) occurs in *ghōr*. One finds hares (*arneb*, pl. *arānib*) here and there but not rabbits. The porcupine (*nīs*, pl. *niās*) and the *ubwēri*, which is possibly identical with the daman (*Hyrax syriacus*)[2], are often hunted for their

---

1   The vernacular, which loves to use poetic expressions at any time, has taken the name *abu 'l-husein* (father of the small fortress) from the Arabic animal tales and used in the term *hsēni*. This is similar to the case in our own culture in the story of Reinecke who is the master of his own fortress, the Malepartus. The classical name, also common among the urban population, *ta'leb*, is incomprehensible to the Fellāheen.

2   Translator's note: According to the Latin term for the species given here, Mülinen refers to a daman, or cony, a small herbivorous mammal of the genus Hyrax, though the German term he gives "Klippdachs" is a rock badger, or Procavia capensis.

meat. The porcupines also live in hollows, and their quills are often found. The jumping mouse (*jerbō'a*) is unknown on Mount Carmel.

Among the other mammals to list are hedgehogs (*qunfid̲*, pl. *qanāfīd̲*), rats and mice (*firān*), which are never amiss from any place, as well as moles (*khlunt*, خلد) and bats (*shawátwat*).

The mighty eagle (*ríkhame*) and the nisr (pl. *ansūra*), which feeds on carrion, are considered the kings of the birds of prey. With wings that are black on top and white underneath and a white body, the vulture (*shūha*, pl. *ishwāh*) is significantly smaller; it also snatches up live chickens. As harriers, the *'aqāb* (pl. *'uqbān*) or *bāshiq* and the *abu masas* appear; the *abu 'l-hayāya* (literally, snake father) and the *zrēqi* belong to the sparrow-hawks. One often sees ravens (*ghurāb* or *qāq*) just as much as crows (*zāgh*, pl. *zīghān*). The screech owl (*būm*) sits on trees and walls of ruins; according to wide-spread superstition, its cry summons death (*el-būmi tiz'aq bil-kharāb*).

Among the edible wild foul, the partridge (*hajal*), whose occurrence is unusually frequent, shall to be mentioned first; after that, there are the snipe, or woodcock (here *dujājet wa'r*, otherwise usually *dujājet ard*), the quail (*firri*), and a type of fieldfare (*summan*), and furthermore, the lark (*kurrāgh*). There are many different types of wild pigeons, but those that are shot at most are the wood pigeon (*ruqtiyya*), the common wild pigeon (*hamām berri*), and the *dalam*. In the water, one finds the small wild duck (*batt berri*) and the coot (*ghurr*) with a patch of white on its forehead.

The *qatā*, also called *qatā tatabōz* here, prominent in Arabic poetry, is about the size of a pigeon with a white body, wings that are white on the upper surface and blue-black underneath, a blue-black upper-body, and a delicately small crest on its head. This bird, as well as the magnificent green and blue shimmering *sheraqraq* (possibly a roller), is equally well-liked as fare. Also enjoyed are Solomon's messenger, the hoopoe (*hudhud*), the *abu humār* (pl. *abu hamīr*), a type of song bird, its blue-breasted relative *lāmi*, and the *warwar*. The starling (*zarzūr*) appears in great numbers; the thrush (*shahrūr*) is also frequently found.

The nightingale (*bulbul*), the blackbird (*sawwadi*), and the bright-feathered *'arus et-turkmān* (i.e. the Turkmen's bride), roughly the size of a sparrow, fill the night air with their sweet sounds. All smaller birds are, after all, killed and eaten, such as the yellow hammer (*suffara*), the goldfinch (*qumhiyye*), the buffy hummingbird (*hnēni*), and the dainty white, yet characterized as black, *sa'diyye*. The number of species is so great that not all can be listed here, particularly since their identification presents difficulties. It would be sufficient to name the sparrow (*'asfūr dūri*) and the crested lark (*'asfūr zer'i*) as the most common of all the birds.

Most of those mentioned constantly stay within the region. The migratory birds, which return in the summer, are the following: *ríkhame* and *shūha*, *hudhud*, *abu humār* and *lāmi*, and, furthermore, *sheraqraq*, *warwar* and *ruqtiyya*. The winter guests are *qatā*, *zarzūr*, *hnēni*, and *sa'diyye*. In spring and fall, one sees the wild goose (*wazz berri*) and the stork (*hawwām al-khamīs*, i.e. "the air glider of Thursday of the Dead") are seen passing through without stopping to stay.

The turtle (here *qurqa'a*, elsewhere *zilhiffe*), of which there are smaller and larger species, is to be mentioned among the amphibians. Toads and frogs are lumped together under the name *difda'*, whereas the Bedouins make an exception for the tree frog which they have termed *wirji*.

Reptiles are very numerous. On *nahr ez-zerqā* on the southern border of the Carmel region, crocodiles (*timsāh*) still exist today; the admittedly harmless *rudda'a* is called a skink, a type of lizard. It resembles a green snake though it is equipped with feet and can be up to two feet long. Among the common lizards, the *hardōn* takes the first position, followed by the small *sahliyye* and *umm ibrēs*. Interesting is the case of the chameleon (*hirbāye*) in its ability which takes on the color of its surroundings in a form of mimicry in order to avoid its enemies and feed on its prey consisting of smaller insects. Women and children use this color change to test their luck[1]. The most-feared of the snakes (*hayyi*, pl. *hayāya*) is the *abu qara'*.

An incredible amount of invertebrate and insect species are represented. Sea crabs (*sarta'ōn*) make their quick sideways steps

---

1   In Syria, the chameleon is also vulgarly termed *birbakhti* and addressed in the rhyme *birbakhti shūf li bakhti* (*birbakhti* see me my luck). On Mount Carmel, the women and children cover the chameleon with their headscarf, or *tarbūsh*, and say to it:

yā hirbāye bint ukhti	oh chameleon, daughter of my sister
ballāh iftahī li bakhti	by God, open up my luck for me!
huwa ihmar walla ibyad	is it red, or white?
walla akhdar walla 'smar.	or green or black?

Then one lifts the cover and looks to see which color the chameleon is showing. The first three colors bring luck but black is an evil omen.

on the ocean beach, while the scorpion (*'aqrab*) and the millipede (*arba'īniyye*) can be found everywhere and compete with poisonous spiders (*'ankabūt*) in dangerousness. Other harmless spiders are called *shábaṭi*. In spring, one frequently comes across snails (*buzzēq*, بزّاق); the wells are often inhabited by leeches (*'alaq*) against which the livestock must be protected when drinking from them.

The native inhabitants often do not differentiate among the frequent and wide array of numerous different species of butterflies (*farāsh*), under which the spurge hawkmoth, elsewhere called *beshīri* (messenger of luck), is included, though they make a distinction between the small *jindib* and the destruction-bearing migratory *jerrād* from among the locusts. In apprehensive euphemism, the praying mantis, or *faras esh-shītān* (devil's mare) is called *faras il-melāik* (angel's mare) by the Fellāheen. Aside from the bee (*nahl*), which is found both in the wild building its honeycombs in the hollows of trees and caves and is kept in the villages, the Fellāh is acquainted with the hornet (*dabbōr*) and the wasp (*zúqurta*). All possibly larger beetles are labeled with the word *tazzīz* (pl. *tazāzīz*), among which is the rose chafer, known as *tazzīz fadda* (silver bluebottle). *Sarsūr* is also a rather indefinite term; sometimes it aligns itself with the cricket, sometimes the cockroach, while *sarsūr ez-zibil* is the name for the dung-beetle. On pleasant May and June evenings, the fireflies (*sirāj ghūli*, "the ghostly light") swarm about like a glowing point in the darkening space. In July, the glow worms radiate only on the ground.

With ants, one distinguishes between the large wood ant (*némil*) and the small *darr*. Both are the chosen prey of the ant-lion which bores its holes (*jōret iblīs*, devil's pits) in the sandy portions of the rock groups whereupon it is also referred to as *iblīs* (devil). Flies are altogether called *dibbān* and horseflies *zēraq*. The irritating mosquitoes (*hishis*, urban dialect: *nāmūs*) are never absent, though one is spared from these common small pests in the houses of the Germans. The livestock suffers much from ticks (*qarād*) which hang on blades of grass and shrubs; camels suffer from the small *feshsh*.

The Fellāheen are not very knowledgeable concerning fish. According to him, the best ocean fish is the large white *sulbi*, followed by *samak gharīb*, about the circumference on an arm, and the overall favored reddish *sultān ibrahīm*. The *bōri* is the same fish which is held in a pond by Saint Anthony of Padua in Tripoli. Otherwise, the Felläheen only know the flat white shimmering *serghōs* and the inedible *burraqa*.

The domesticated animals can be divided into large livestock, small livestock, horses and donkeys with their crossovers, dogs and cats, and fowls. Pigs (*khanzīr*) are completely absent from Mount Carmel, and buffalo (*jāmūs*) are only found in the marshes of *nahr ez-zerqā*. Large livestock, consisting of camels (*jamal*) and cattle (*baqar*), are not represented in large numbers; the former are used as pack animals when traveling through the mountain or kept by the camping Bedouins for the production of milk and wool. Cattle are likewise used for producing milk but also for tilling and threshing; otherwise, they are sold to *haifā* for slaughter. The small livestock is much more important for the Palestinian Felläheen; this consists of *ghanam*, specifically the "white small livestock" *ghanam bēda* or *kharūf*, which is here often the white, fat-tailed sheep, and the "black small livestock" *ghanam sauda*, or *ma'ze*, the long-eared goat. One does not see sheep[1] on Mount Carmel itself as the many thorny plants irritate their fleece greatly. The goat herds are larger; they provide the inhabitants with coats of hair and leather as well as milk and meat for consumption, though they are, of course, a danger to the plant life. The horse (*khēl*) is usually only found in the possession of the wealthy and rarely of good breed; one almost only finds thorough-bred animals by the Turkmaniyye Beduoins. The mule (*baghl*) is valued and is used for carrying loads and riding as well as for plowing, whereas the hinny (*naghl*, literally half-breed) is not to be found on Mount Carmel. On the other hand, the donkey (*humār* or *ihmār*, pl. *hamīr*) is the Felläheen's favored animal. The Felläh rides it wherever he can and uses it as a carrier for frequently substantial loads. There are two breeds of dogs (*kelb*) to consider. One is represented through the common yellow village dog which lives, ownerless, in the small alleys in a half-wild state, as is the case all over the Orient. The other breed, often with a white coat and of a larger stature, serves as a guard for secluded houses and Bedouin tents. Actual hunting dogs (*slēqi*) are only in the possession of the few rich. Cats (*bsēni* or *bissi*) are found almost exclusively in houses and gardens, where they, rarely fed, go

---

1   El Salman's Note: This is incorrect. The people of Et-Tire did not keep sheep (*aghnam*) on the mountain because sheep are heavy and unable to climb the montains as goats can. Goats are lighter, and they can better adapt to life on mountains, as they move more easily (El Salman, 1991: 22).

after vermin and mice with such an eager devouring, without ever becoming as tame as they are in Europe. Almost all Fellāheen possess chickens (*dujaj*); they often spend the night in their rooms. Pigeons (*ḥamām*) and turkeys (*ḥabesh*) are much more seldom. Tame goose and ducks are completely absent in the villages. Aside from the previously mentioned bees (*naḥl*), the silkworm (*dūd il-ḥarīr*) also exists as a working animal; the only one used for the purposes of producing silk is in *el-yājūr.*

G. The People

The preserved works of pre-history will be discussed in reference to their locations in the section specific to the descriptions of places. Also, other historical information will be left aside here as this account should express only personal observations. It is impossible to obtain new pieces of historical information from the Fellāheen themselves because they are lacking in every tradition. They live for the day and do not have songs, as the Bedouins, celebrating the feats of their forefathers which are then passed from one generation to another.

Thus, it would perhaps be of interest to describe the living conditions under which the natives of Mount Carmel still live. If the same are not as primitive as that of the Bedouins, then that is because they are often taken from ancient times. To this day, the Fellāh, for example, carries with him his fire steel (*znādi*) and his small piece of tinder (*qadḥa*) with which he catches the sparks from the flint, the first best piece picked up along his way, to prepare the necessary fire.

However, a change in these conditions is imminent. The rational agricultural holdings of the Germans serve as a model for the Fellāheen. The port city *haifā* continues to expand and draws the majority of its workers from the Carmel villages. These workers then acquaint those who remained in the villages with the new achievements of civilization. Soon the Muslim villagers will probably likewise embrace the desire taking hold of those in Lebanon to emigrate to the new world, and thereby, create a complete transformation of the milieu.

a. Ethnicity

The native Carmel population is primarily composed of two groups, the resident peasants (Felláheen) and the nomadic Bedouins (*bedu* or *'urbān*).

The Bedouins, which are an estimated maximum of 300 people, are small branches of larger tribes, who lead a miserly life isolated in dirty black tents (*khíyam*) in *wa'r*. They often tend only goat herds and possess some camels but seldom horses. The women, who only practice the weaving of goat hair for the Bedouin industry, are covered in blue-black tattered clothes. The men wear an *'abā*, the *keffiyye* with the *'agāl* around the head. Occasionally, one finds Negro slaves among them.

When their stays are prolonged, the areas on which they set up their tents receive the name *minzalet* (settlement) with an appendage of the name of the resident shepherd, e.g. *minzalet il-būbān, minzalet 'ayyād*. The Iswētāt from *bilād bshāra* which lies to the north camp by *el-khrēbi*. The Qazalni (Bedouin dialect: *gazālni*) from the Ka'biyye tribe from *merj ibn 'āmir* and the *ghōr* can be found by *shellāle* and in *wadi 'l-milh*; other Ka'biyye are by *bostān* from *ed-dālie*. The Semniyyīn, who come from the *merj*, are met on *jebal 'aqqāra* and by *sheikh ibrāq*. The Sa'eidi, who also come from *merj*, are in the surroundings of *bostān*. Bedouins from the small tribe of el-Hilf stay at *sheikh ibrāq*. Turkmaniyye under Sheikh Mahmūd el-Halef camp on the *merj* between the *rūha* and *wadi 'l-milh*. In winter, many of these tribes return to grounds that are protected as much as possible in *wadi 'l-milh* or to the *shejarāt abu saqr*, many to *'aqqāra*. At the latter, they have a larger burial ground, which is, however, little used today because they now bury the majority of their deceased in the cemeteries of the Muslim villages such as *et-tīre* or *beled esh-shēkh*. The graves of the Bedouins, as with all Muslims, are oriented from east to west; they are identifiable through an oblong oval formed by boulders stuck into the ground. At the western end, the head end, an upright stone rises. Here and there these stones bear the tribe's symbol (*wasm*), namely two vertical lines, the so-called *shuhūd*.

Two hundred years ago, they were the lords of Carmel; it was so reported to me that their Emirs (chiefs) from the Tarabīn tribe of that period have, however, long since moved to the region near Gaza. Their predecessors, the Emirs of the Hawārit family, whose memory is still preserved in *et-tīre*, continue to flourish today as shepherd princes in *nāhiet esh-sha'rawiyye*, east of Caesarea, after they have since given the eastern end of the Jezreel Plain near *zer'īn* the name *bilād hāriti*.

Universally, Bedouins are considered to be robbers and thieves, and an old ancestral rivalry prevails between them and the Druses. Individual Bedouins have become settled and been absorbed into the peasant population.

It is indeed difficult to pass judgment on the origins of the Fellāheen because over time many conquering tribes have moved across the native population. One needs only to consider the invasion of the Crusaders who occupied Mount Carmel with their many fortresses for almost two centuries. All the same, can one really differ between two different types of Fellāheen: one large, strong, relatively coarser, often blond and one smaller, well-proportioned, darker with more defined facial features and petite limbs and extremities. Of course, alone the color of skin and hair is not decisive since the mountain residents are on the average blonder than the peasants in the plain in all of Syria. Also, among the latter a significant number of individuals are fair in their childhood but darken later. Nevertheless, one finds, for example, dark people in *et-tīre*, whereas a reddish coloring prevails in *ikzim*, as confirmed by a proverb that will be cited later. In most cases, however, the two types have been mixed, so that striking varieties can be detected within the same family.

Purely comparatively, the Catholics, who are perhaps the remnants of ancient centuries, and the Druses have resided in the mountains, at least for the past centuries. Both, along with the recently settled Persians, will be discussed in the following section.

The ruling Ottoman race is not represented in the Carmel region as there are no officials stationed there.

The Arab gypsies (*nawar*) characterize a special type of ethnic group. They occasionally roam through the Carmel region and are considered to be Muslims of doubtful orthodoxy. Aside from Arabic, they still speak their own language brought with them from their Indian homeland, the so-called *nawari*. As is the case everywhere, they know all about mending pots and pans and making music.

The Germans, aside from the monks of the Stella Maris Monastery who are primarily recruited from Spain, are almost the only foreigners to be mentioned. The majority of the Germans is from Swabia and belongs or once belonged to the religious community of the Temple. They settled in *haifā* in the beginning of the seventies of the previous century. From there they have extended their property on the northern side of Mount Carmel and on the coastal plain towards *et-tīre*.

On the southernmost part of the mountain, the *khushm*, the European Israelites under the aegis of Rothschild have formed different colonies among which the largest is called *zummārīn*; they own the fields of *'atlīt* on the coastal plain as well. Native Jews, if they are represented at all, can only be found occasionally in one or two villages.

b. Religion

Muslims, Druses, Persians, Catholics, Protestants, Israelites.

The dominant faith is orthodox Sunni Islam; the prevailing school of thought (*medheb*) is Hanifi whereas there are a few followers of Imām Shāfi'i and scant followers of Imām Malik. Indeed, the local religion is interspersed with many unlawful, old indigenous superstitions through the Fellāheen's lack of knowledge as will be later illustrated. Men who have thoroughly studied Quranic sciences exist only in a few villages. One frequently travels to Egypt for these purposes. After taking an exam (*ijāze*), the scholars return to their homelands to enjoy a high standing there with the honorific title of *'ālim*. The Dervish are present here and there; they live on their own and consider themselves dependent on work by their own hands or alms. They belong to the orders of Rufā'iyye, Sa'diyye, Qādiriya, and Bedawiyye and always perform their *dikr* on the evening before Friday. Shādiliyye do not live on Carmel although there is a cave near *rushmia* where the adepts of *haifā* once gathered. Incidentally, they were not considered a proper order by other Dervishes but rather as a religious entity for mutual support.

The Druses represent a Muslim sect. Their settlements on Mount Carmel are on the southernmost foothills of the fifteen communities in Galilee. They are associated with the latter both through familial relationships and mutual subordination under the spiritual leader, the *shēkh aql*, in *jūlis*. They were previously in possession of more villages on Carmel; among them were *el-khrēbi*, *shellāle*, and *bustān* which were destroyed seventy years ago by the Egyptian Ibrāhīm Pasha. At present, only their settlements in *ed-dālie* and *'usufia* remain to which *jelamet l-mansūra* and *jelamet el-'asāfni* are added as dependence villages. It is well known that their religion is a product of the propaganda of the Fatimid caliph el-Hakim bi-Amr Allah (ruler though Allah's command) who they call el-Hakim bi amrihi (ruler by his own command) as an incarnation of a deity. This is a guarded secret; children and the majority of adults considered to be *juhhāl* (the ignorant) are excluded from discovering the deeper knowledge of this. The religious leadership of the community is entrusted to the hands of a small privy of inductees (*'uqqāl*) who have sworn to abstention of spirits and tobacco. The *'uqqāl*, who also include women, can be broken down into three rankings: beginner, advanced, and perfect, or complete. These figures choose a religious head, the *shēkh ed-dīn*, from among themselves for each village; this person exercises far-reaching power though his due authority of excommunication (*hir'm*). This sentence bears with it the sinner's complete expulsion from contact with their fellow believers as a grave consequence, and this can only be lifted by the *shēkh el-'aql* in *jūlis*. The *shēkh ed-dīn* acts as *qādi*; particularly, marriage contracts and dowry certificates are drawn up by him. He also takes on the role of *khatīb* in the direction of the religious services and conducts lessons for the children in winter. Children from the age of five are sent together, but lessons are not regularly attended. The Druses do not have mosques but rather *khalwe*'s which are small cube-like, windowless building in remote areas to which they betake themselves, led by their *khatīb*, on the evenings before Friday and Monday to "read" together. Marriage is monogamous although a divorce (*talāq*) is easy to obtain; after which one can remarry at any time. Each of the two villages chooses two *mukhtāre* for worldly affairs.

The Carmel Druses, like those of Lebanon and Haurān, are frequently blond though one does not find so much beauty among them as in other areas. One recognizes the men from afar by their beards and traditional costume. A white turban (*leffi bēda*) adorns the head; the upper-body is clothed with a shirt (*qamīs*) over which a short smock, called a *bisht*, or sometimes an *'abāye*, is worn. This is replaced with a *qumbāz* on festival days. The legs are often covered in white pants. The women cover their heads with a long white veil (*hrām abyad*) swirling down their backs; by the appearance of an unknown man outside of the house, this veil is held together around the face by their hands. A small cap or bonnet (*nqāf*) lies under this, and a kerchief (*'asbi*) often holds this together on the head. The women's shirt is called *ṭōb*; on weekdays, a *jellāye*, open at the neck, is worn over this, and a *qumbāz* is worn on holidays. The Druses are possibly the most industrious agricultural workers; they, however, have a reputation of great slyness and mendacity with the Muslims.

In recent years, Persians of the Babi sect have settled on the northern slope of Mount Carmel, directly above the German colony in *haifā*. The tomb of Beha Allah, the father of the sect's current leader, 'Abbas Effendi, is located there in *'akkā*. Although the appearance and the lucrative propaganda, namely in America, of this denomination may stir up much interest in respect to religion, it will not be discussed in depth here in light of its insignificant impact on the Carmel region.

Native Christians live only in *'usufia* in the midst of the Druses. They are originally Greek Orthodox and became Uniats to preserve their oriental rite under Rome. Thus, they are in general referred to as *kātūlīk*. They are attended to by a *khūri* (priest) in the church who is subordinate to the Greek-Uniat archbishop in *'akkā*. They choose their own *mukhtār*, who is recognized by the Turkish *qaimmaqām* in *haifā*, for the worldly affairs of the community. They maintain a school for boys and girls with one male and one female teacher. The Christians are about 150 in number which composes about a fourth of the population of *'usufia* from which they are also entitled to a corresponding portion of houses and villages fields as well as the dependence village *jélame*. The dress of the Catholic men is no different from that of the Muslim Fellāheen. The women cover their heads with a veil (*hrām*) just as the females Druses do; however, theirs is colored. Over it, they wear a black kerchief, which they call *zurbend*.

The northwestern peak of the mountain is crowned by the famous Latin Stella Maris Monastery which belongs to an important complex there. It includes the area of the St. Brocard Church from the Middle Ages further on in *'ain es-siāh* and the chapel of the *muhraqa* on the southeastern peak.

The German Swabian Templar and their former coreligionists who have returned to the evangelical regional church have obtained a beautiful property on the northern side of Mount Carmel. This will be discussed in closer detail in the following. They founded the Neuhardthof colony on the coastal plain south of *haifā*, and they operate steam mills in *et-tīre* and *jeba'*.

The members of the Rothschild Israelite colonies on the *khushm* all belong to the Ashkenazim (Jews of Northern European tradition).

c. Culture

Economic. Private and Family Life. Local Beliefs and
Festivities. Poetry. Relations among the Villages.

1. Shepherds and Farmers

The village population is composed of two, albeit not markedly
separate, classes: the shepherd and the quintessential farmer.

While the typical Bedouin shepherd leads a purely nomadic life,
the village shepherd (*rā'i*, pl. *ru'āt*) can be characterized as a half-
nomad. He wanders through the region with his goat herds encircled
by dogs, whereby one hears him emitting a variety of singular sounds
of nature in the form of mating calls (*biyāhi*). Should he arrive at an
area for pasture, he enjoys sounding out his melancholy tune on the
flute (*nāy*), the *mijwiz* (double flute), or the gently resonating *shubbābi*.
In winter, he dwells in the large caves found in the rock face; in
summer, he mainly stays on the coastal plain and seeks shelter from
sunburn under a flimsy shack. The shepherd also owns a house in the
village in which the family resides while individual members of the
families are watching over the herd. The most important yield from
the latter for the shepherds, aside from the hair, leather, and meat
sold in the home village or in *haifā*, is milk; the uses of which will be
discussed further in the section on food.

The original Fellāh is completely settled and owns a house in the
village as well as property that he cultivates. Should he work as a
leased hand on other people's terrain, he is called a *harrāt* (plowman).
The lease contract (*muqāsami*) grants him a continuous portion of
the fruits, which is measured differently depending on the conditions
of the contract. For example, the landlord in *el-khrēbi*, the el-Khuri
family of *haifā*, only supplies land for cultivation and an admittedly
well-built house and takes one fifth of the harvest in return. The cost
for seeds and tools as well as a tithe is the burden of the leased hand.
Impoverished people who do not own property and are not capable of
leasing work for day-wages (*shaghīl bil-yōmiyye* or *bil-fā'il*) and receive a
hissa, a portion of fruit harvested themselves, as payment.

The status of the Fellāh is clearly sinking into poverty. In *et-tīre*,
where the cultivated community fields are completely divided into
private property, one section of the expansive olive plantations after

another is being passed into the hands of people in *haifa*. Through this, the residents are being restricted to the still undivided community property in the mountain wilderness where every individual acquires that which he cultivates. Because the treasury office, however, uses this wilderness as *mīriyye* (feifdom), the issuance of a property certificate from the official land register is denied the Fellāh because he does not fulfill the necessary requirements. Thus, an uncertainty in the property relations arises which seems unbearable for us, but is not considered quite as difficult in this region. In other localities, the population has felt compelled to sell all of the fields. Hence, the region in *el-yājūr* was purchased by the el-Khuri family in *haifa* and that of *'atlīt* by Rothschild.

A particular phenomenon, which certainly occurs in mountain regions of other countries as well, has been observed in *'usufia* and *ed-dālie*. The fields of both places are so vast and encompass such a significant portion of the Kishon in the Plain of *'akkā* that they can not be cultivated by the mountain villages. This, therefore, resulted in the need for the establishment of dependence villages to which the Druses move down during the plowing and harvest seasons. These areas otherwise remain empty (*jélame* for *'usufia* and *mansūra* for *ed-dālie*). Because these dependence villages are desolate for the greater part of the year, they are referred to by a term usually used for ruins, "*khirbe*." Despite its large population and its extensive fields, *et-tīre* does not possess such a dependence village; in place of this, there are various actual ruins, such as *khirbet es-sahalāt* and *khirbet yūnis*, which are arranged as needed.

2. Appearance and Design of Villages. Particular Buildings and Economic Establishments.

The villages are situated in as healthy a location as can be, whether it is in the altitudes, at the entrance to the plains lower in the valleys or somewhat elevated at the foot of the mountain. They offer a continuous picturesque view from the distance. In particular instances, this gains a special appeal with the huts made of leaves (*'arīshe*, pl. *'ursh*) built in the summertime on the flat roofs of the houses. The villages usually lie in the midst of gardens (*bustān*, pl. *basātīn*) or fruit orchards (*karm*, pl. *krūm*) fenced in by cactus hedges, from which, as in *et-tīre* and *ikzim*, the olive orchards significantly expand. Outside of the village, the simple cemetery is located as well as, depending on the need, one or more threshing floors (*bēdar*, pl. *bayādir*) which are firmly trampled grounds for threshing grain. One sees large masses of unused manure (*zibil*) which often create entire hills in all villages.

The material used for building is almost exclusively unpolished rock; the rock used is, to be precise, limestone provided by the mountain, or, as in *et-tīre* and the coastal plain villages, *hajar ramle* which is broken off from the dunes. Wood is only used for internal furnishings and for supporting the roof. The baking oven is usually built out of clay; though one also observes small clay houses and sometimes a clay surface over a stone construction in the poorest villages, such as *umm ez-zeināt*.

Almost constantly one-storied, the Fellāheen houses bear a flat roof, which only recently, namely in *tantūra*, has begun to be replaced by tile roofs in new buildings. The buildings of the poor, which are sometimes consolidated around a courtyard, often contain only a single room in which the family sleeps with their fowl while the donkey is tethered in the courtyard. Furnishings are minimal: the raised floor behind the door hides mats. During the day, niches left in the walls accommodate blankets, which serve as covers at night, as well as the few cooking and eating utensils, and the clothes that are not currently being worn. One or two pillows are, however, always present for the seat of honor for a guest. The more well-to-do have additional rooms, but larger buildings are seldom found.

An inhabited portion of a former Crusader castle still stands in *et-tīre*, and in *ikzim*, the Mādi family has preserved the castle-like houses. All other medieval castles have either completely fallen into ruin or, at most, serve as stalls, as in *'aṭlīṭ*, or as backing for the attached stone houses of the villagers, as in *kufr lām*.

The mosques, which the Fellāheen do not call *masjid* due to the lack of a minaret, are instead given the nicer sounding name *jāmi'*. The village of *et-tīre* has two mosques; *ikzim*, *beled esh-shēkh*, *surfand*, and *jeba'* each have one. They are stone constructions which, in some cases, once served as Christian churches. There occasionally are small rooms on the mosque courtyard which are used as *zāwie* or *menzūl* to accommodate strangers. In villages which do not have a mosque, an ever-present *manzūl* also serves as a gathering place for the worship service. The Dervish cloister (*tekkiyye*) is unknown on Mount Carmel.

As previously mentioned, *khalwe*'s exist in the Druse villages; aside from that, *'usufia* also holds a Catholic church which houses a wooden bell tower. The Stella Maris Monastery likewise holds a church and several chapels. In addition, it includes the lovely chapel of the *muhraqa*. The light of a lighthouse rising next to the monastery is visible from afar, providing a signal for the ships at night. A glass distillery modeling the European prototype was built in *tantūra* by the Israelite colony of *zummārīn*. As a result of difficulties which ensued with the government during the construction, the beautiful buildings, however, have been empty for several years.

The mill (*tāhūn*), likewise built out of stone, is still to be mentioned among the remaining buildings. Because its operation requires perpetual running water – there are no windmills in the Carmel region – and the only one of its kind exists in *wādi shellāle*, such a mill rose solely in that location from which the ruins alone are visible today. The demand for flour is primarily met today by *haifā* or supplied through the steam mills (*bābūr*) of which there is one each in *et-tīre* and in *jeba'*. There are also horse mills (*tāhūnet baghl*) in *ed-dālie* and *'usufia*; however, their wheelwork is set in motion by mules.

A similar system is exhibited by the pump station which serves the purpose of irrigating the gardens; it is well-known as *nā'ūra* and called *bayyāra* in Jafa, *hannāne* in the Carmel region. Still more primitive is the *shellāf mōy*; built over a well, it consists of a gallows of two vertical posts (*qa'ādāt*) which are bound by a revolving stick (*khashabet esh-shellāf*) on their upper ends. In the middle of the latter a long pole (*tārūh*) projecting out on either side of the stick is perpendicularly fixed. A boulder is attached to one end of the pole as a weight (*hajar esh-shellāf*) and a bucket (*delu* if made of leather, *satl* if of metal) on the other end. Through hoisting the stone, the pole is set in motion, and the bucket sinks into the well; if the stone is released, the bucket is raised, and its contents can be emptied. This kind of *shellāf* is found rather frequently in the Carmel region, e.g. in *beled esh-shēkh*, *el-yājūr*, in *'ain hōd*, *'ain en-nakhle*, *'ain el-bēda* by *ed-dālie*, in *mākūra* by *ikzim*.

Elsewhere the wells (*bīr*) are outfitted with stairs which lead down to the water level. One lowers a bucket by hand into the cistern (*sīh*). The cisterns are frequent on Mount Carmel due to the lack of springs and were more numerous in earlier times. Carefully cleaned and kept pure, the cisterns provide healthy and delicious water. The cistern-like cavities in the rock, known to us as silos, which are used for storing grain, are called *bīr*. Sometimes old burial chambers or caves are also used for this.

One finds the grape presses (*midbise*, pl. *madābis*, Fig. 4) of a previous culture just as often as the cisterns. As a result of the fall of vine production, the presses now serve as containers for storing water for the shepherds and the Fellāheen. The *midbise* consists of a flat square basin cut into the stone that slopes slightly downwards (*mustabi*). The grapes are crushed here; the juice then flows through a canal (*qanāt el-midbise*) that is equipped with a removable sieve (*misfà*, مصفاة) into the filtering basin (*birki*).

The olive presses (*ma'sira*, pl. *ma'āsir*) are found in large caverns, often under houses.

Figure 4. *Mustabi* of a *midbise* (grape press) on *rās el-khirbe* by *rushmia*.

Inside, a large round stone (*hajar farshi*), hollowed out in the middle on its surface, lays horizontally. Another large round stone (*hajar bedd*), positioned vertically, rotates by means of a pillar. The olives are spread out on the *farshi* where they are ground (*bidrushā*) by the *hajar bedd*. The mass (*drīs ez-zeitūn*) produced by this is then placed in a basket (*quffī*) onto which a cover (*'ishsh*) is pressed so that the liquid contents flow through the openings in the basket into the settling basin (*bīr ez-zēt*). The oil (*zēt*) is collected here above the residue (*mōye* or *'akr zēt*); the oil is skimmed off, and the *'akr* disposed of. The thick mass (*jift*) remaining in the basket is used as fuel.

One sees beehives (*jurn nahl*) built out of clay in many villages. The beehives are about one and a half meters tall and have a large opening, often stopped-up, for removing the honeycomb. There are many small holes through which the bees swarm in and out.

Every settlement has a baking oven (*furn*, often *tābūn* in the country); it is a hollow cone constructed out of clay which is roughly one meter in height and one meter in circumference at the floor surface. In several villages these ovens are, however, larger and often cubic; they are made of stone and covered with a layer of clay.

Lime ovens also exist in large numbers, and they present a danger not only for the tree population but also for remains of ruins. The larger ovens are called *tūn* (اتون) and the smaller *kabbāra* (pl. *kabābīr*).

There are recesses (*jōret milh*) which collect the seawater on the beach for the purpose of extracting salt. After the water evaporates, the salt remains. Since the sale of salt was transferred as a monopoly to the administration of the public debt, or mortgage, which also keeps the beach under surveillance, the Fellāheen have arranged such places further in on the mainland to which they bring the salt water.

As previously mentioned, one still sees the traces of a mine once operated by means of surface, or open-cast, mining in *ikzim*. It is now deserted though abundant iron ore still exists in the earth. The dunes contain a great amount of quarries (*miqla'*, pl. *maqāli'*) although they are also present in many other places. The ancient and medieval quarries evoke our admiration in the precision of their work which is illustrated in the acutely hewn stone walls. In contrast, the mines in use today are distinguished by the preferred disorder of the quarrymen through which considerable material is lost.

Gardens are partitioned off by stone walls (*sinsile*, pl. *senāsil*). Smaller piles of stones are also called *sensōl*, whereas a larger one is called *rujm*.

That bridges (*jisr*) are only found on the coastal plain has also previously been mentioned. It is regrettable that most of the bridges built for the journey of the imperial

Figure 5. Old quarry (*muqtā'*), named *ed-derejāt*, near *shellāle*.

husband and wife in 1898 lay in ruins. The only one from among these still in good condition is the bridge over the Crocodile River.

At last, the burial chambers are discussed. Instead of the beautiful rock chambers of ancient times (*nāmūsiyye*, pl. *nawāmīs*, ناووسيه) which even stretched into the time of the Crusades, the Fellāh builds a low, long catafalque out of stone or clay with a stone post at both the head (*rās*) and foot ends. Holes for floral decorations are often fixed into the surface of these catafalques. One never sees inscriptions on them. If a saint is buried in a grave that

Figure 6. *Maqām* of Shēkh Khalīl in *et-tīre*.

one visits to ask for mediation, it is called *maqām* (Figure 6). It is frequently covered with a four-cornered building with a domed roof; the roof bears flags and cloths, and there are small tin or clay plates for incense donations surrounding the catafalque.

3. Labor

The main occupation of the Fellāheen, agriculture, is still practiced using traditional methods. After the first abundant rainfalls in late fall, one begins the plowing (*hirāṭi*). The plow (*'ūd hrāṯ*), pulled by animals, is a simple wooden frame with an iron tooth (*sikki*) which leaves only surface furrows (*tálim*) behind it. The farmer, who holds the handle of the plow, drives the animals with the prod (*minsās*, مساس) held in his other hand. The Arab farmland is dispersed with many stones and as such is certainly a wondrous image for European eyes. However, it is not to be overlooked that these stones have intentionally not been removed from the earth altogether in order to sustain the necessary moisture within the earth.

The seeds are simply sown (*ibḏār*) by hand. The harrow was first introduced by the Europeans, and the Fellāheen have until now not yet begun to put it to use.

In harvesting, one uses a round hand sickle (*minjal hasīdi* or, for short, *minjal*) which is guided by the right hand while the left holds together the stalks to be cut. Through this management, an idiosyncratic expression heard in the harvest season is explained. Namely, when a wayfarer passes the reapers, he calls to them, often with a left arm raised high, "*shimālak*," i.e. (give me what you have in) your left hand. This is a plea for charity which, then again, is also passed out to seemingly wealthy passers-by by the harvesters. Upon hearing this for the first time, this expression strikes one as even more curious considering in what far-reaching extent the use of the left hand in general contact with others is otherwise taboo in the entire Muslim world.

The scythe is known to the natives here through the Germans and is therefore called *minjal almāni* or *brūsiāni*. The *hashūshi* is similar to the *minjal* yet smaller and is used for cutting plants used as fodder. Forage grass and herbs, as well as dried hay, are uniformly called *hashīsh*.

After cutting, the sheaves of grain are brought to the village threshing grounds (*bēdar*) and separated into piles (*'urmi* or *qōm*) for threshing. Here and there this task is still carried out by means of animals trampling through (*khafesh*); however, a threshing board (*lŭ̈h idrās*) is often used in this. The board is a wooden plank bent slightly upwards at the front; sharp stones are clamped onto the underside. The threshing board, upon which one frequently sees a young boy, seldom a girl, sitting, is moved around the piles by the harnessed animals. The stalks glide under this to be crushed by the stones.

One observes a perfected threshing board only in *el-fureidīs* and *el-mezār* where it is called *nōraj*. Instead of a plank, this mechanism consists of a wooden frame that encompasses several parallel running rollers. On these, thin sharpened iron discs hang from the edges in order to shred the grain. The frame holds a seat which is fixed on by means of four stakes on their ends. From this seat, one steers the cattle harnessed to the *nōraj*. Even the well-known method of winnowing (*darāwi* or *ḍarāwi*) is used to separate the grain from the chaff as mentioned in the Bible. After this, the grain kernels (*qamḥ*) are collected while the chaff (*tibn*) is swept together to be used as fodder for the livestock. At the end of the harvest season, the image of the girls sitting on the heaps of straw in the evenings while weaving (*taqshīsh*) long blades of straw (*qashsh*) into small dishes (*sīniyyi*) creates a lovely sight. The women also cut the chaff; the name of the milky way visible in the night sky, called *tarīq et-tabbānāt* (The Female Chaff Cutters Trail), is derived from this custom.

Apart from the steam and horse mills mentioned in the previous section, the kernels of grain are ground through the use of a hand mill (*tāhūnet 'al-īd*, طاحونة على اليد) in the country. This consists of two flat stones laid upon each other; of which the upper is called *el-fōqa* and the lower *et-tahta*. The upper stone is fixed with a vertical handle (*īd*) on the side and a hole (*halqa*) in the middle through which one slides the kernels in order to grind them between the two stones.

The ground-up grains (*thīn*) are filtered by means of a sieve (*mūkhil*) by the women; the flour that falls through is called *thīn en-nā'im* and what remains *nkhāli* or *khushkar*, or bran. This is fed to the livestock. The women knead (*bit'adjinu*) the *thīn en-nā'im* in a through (*bāti* if made of wood, *lejen* if of tin or metal) into a dough (*'ajīn*), adding water and salt.

The dough is baked in the previously described baking ovens (*furn* or *tābūn*) after the women have pressed it flat and weighed it on their arms (*bitruqqū 'l-khúbiz*) which they do with masterly dexterity. A layer (*ruduf*) of clay or small stones is placed on the fire first; one places the dough on these and covers it with an earthen or iron lid (*ghátá*). One piles a layer of *jift* (olive marc) or *zibil* (manure) on the lid itself to accelerate the baking process by creating more heat. The various sorts of bread produced by the women shall be listed in the following section on food. Baking is done in every household according to the needs of its members; only recently have occupational bakers (*khabbāz*) begun to settle in the villages. There is a well-known proverb throughout the region: *a'tī khubzak lil-khabbāz wain yōkul nussu* (give your dough to the baker, even though he consumes half of it). This means, one should always appeal to the responsible people with one's affairs, even if these people charge high fees.

The preparation of honey is operated with few materials but with great success in many villages. The Carmel honey is clear, sweet, delicious and fragrant and is in no way inferior to the European products.

The preparation of olive oil and the extraction of salt which were described in the previous section are among the usual activities of the Felláheen. Outside of the harvest season, the Fellāh enjoys making his way up the mountain on his donkey in order to chop wood whereby he unsparingly clears trees, bushes, and roots. The firewood gained, if not needed by him, is sold in *haifā* bringing him, on average, a day's income of five to seven piaster (about one to one and a half Franks). The burning of lime required for use in building is equally as ruinous to the growth of trees.

On the coast, fishing is still practiced applying the primitive method of using a small net (*shabaki*). For this purpose, the fisherman (*siyyād*) with his shirt gathered up to his chest goes so far into the water until he catches sight of his prey. With rapid swings, he then throws the net, seldom missing its target. Every Fellāh in possession of a rifle surrenders himself to hunting with pleasure. Young boys are content with birds as prey using a decoy (*fakhkha*) made of switches or rods. In the case of partridge hunting, one uses the *wujh hajal* (decoy) in several regions. This consists of a creme-colored cloth painted with black rings that is stretched over two rods crossed over each other. It measures one and a half meters square; there are two larger holes just above the middle through which the person wearing it, who hides behind it as though behind a sign, has a complete view. Experience has taught that the partridge is not suspicious of this sight which enables the wearer to approach the partridge and easily shoot it through one of the openings.

Weaving (*hiyāki*) wool or goat hair is no longer performed in the villages as one can buy it cheaper in town or from one of the peddlers. In contrast, spinning (*ghazl*) is a still practiced custom. One even comes across men with a spindle (*ghazāli*) in hand.

An industry that has maintained itself until today is the production of mats (*hasīri*, pl. *husar*) not through hand weaving, such as a wickerwork, but through weaving with a shuttle (*'an-nōl*, على النول). This is called *hiyākat husar*. In *et-tīre* this is performed as a trade by a Dervish but in other smaller villages by the women. The varieties of grass and rush, such as *halfa*, *samār*, *si'id* and *zbēbi*, found in the marshes or swamps by *'atlīt* and growing on Kishon serve as material.

Pottery (*fukhāra*) still thrives yet only among the female Druses in *ed-dālie*. For this, they use clay (*trāb el-merāmīl*) from *merjet ez-zerā'a*. They first wet the clay with water and knead until it attains the desired plasticity, then mould it into a variety of simple vessels by hand without the use of a potter's wheel and fire it in their ovens.

In every village, the women tailor the simpler garments though the *'abāye* is frequently bought ready-made.

4. Food

The Arab farmer, like many people of the Mediterranean, does not tend to overindulge in food. He only drinks water in great quantities and also is not averse to alcoholic drinks, forbidden to him through his religion, when offered to him.

Unlike in Europe, the meals [1]are not held at certain times with the exception of the evening meal, taken shortly after sunset. One enjoys a little snack after waking, likewise sometimes around nine in the morning, and occasionally at midday. Only during harvest season does breakfast become a standard in the mornings; it is called *sabūh el-hassādīn* (breakfast of the reapers).

---

1   El Salman's note: In et-Tire, as in the other villages, there were indeed three separate meals, *fotor* (breakfast), *ghada* (lunch) and *'asha* (dinner). In a different context, Mülinen also noted that, at the dinner meal, people used to gather.

The main food items are bread, milk and, if possible, meat; in addition, there are eggs (*bēd*) which are eaten raw (*nei*), soft-boiled (*brisht*), or hard-boiled (*maslūq*). Nature in its generosity offers a great variety of additional kitchen items. Aside from the numerous fruits and garden vegetables listed in the section on flora, several wild growing herbs which appear in spring are cooked, such as *farfahīne, khubbēzi, 'ilit, 'akkūb, lūf,* and *sayyādi* as well as the thistle plant *qursa'anni* when its leaves are still tender. On the other hand, the lettuce variety *khass* is preferably eaten uncooked and lightly salted. In addition, there are the edible mushrooms as well as the red *fúqu' el-wa'r* and the white *ftirre*.

Bread (*khúbiz*, as a single piece *rghíf*) is often prepared from *qamh* (kernel, i.e. wheat), and the following kinds of bread exist among the farmers. *Khubiz khāmir,* the common sour bread, is a thicker round of bread while the paper-thin, delicate round of bread is called *marqūq* in town and *'āwīs* by the Fellāheen. *Kmāj* are circular, thicker cakes; the same form is called *melātīt* when some oil is added to the dough. On festival days, milk is added to the dough for the preparation of cake (*ka'k*) and O-shaped bread (*zarad*). Much sought-after is the *ftīr* which is made out of several layers of *'āwīs*, soaked in butter fat (*semen*). In town, ground meat, onions, and pine nuts are also placed in between the layers. The poorer peasants make their *karādīsh*, a cake in the form of *kmāj*, out of barley and durra.

One drinks milk (*halīb*) either warm from the udder or cold in its raw state. When boiled (*tafwīr el-halīb*), the cream (*zbīde*) is skimmed off for making *semen* (fat) and then the milk is also drunk in this state. *Leben* is considered a refreshment; it is made from boiled milk which is left to stand for at least six hours so that it becomes sour. The acidification is helped by adding a small dose of earlier-prepared *leben* (*khamīri*). From the *leben*, one makes *lebeni* by hanging the sour milk in a bag and letting the water drip from it. The remaining curd is frequently shaped into balls and preserved in olive oil. The white, quick-drying cheese (*jibin*) made from goat milk is preferred above all other easily transportable food stuffs by the shepherds and farmers.

When the means present themselves, the meat (*lahm*) of the livestock, that is the sheep, goat, cattle and camel, is eaten. Pigs[1] are

---

1   El Salman's note: This is perhaps more an expression of an opinion than anything else. Pigs were not eaten because, in Islam, it is forbiden to eat pigs. Even if someone drinks alcohol, the person does it secretly because, socially and religiously, this is not allowed. Thus, in general, people do not

not held in the villages; the general abstention from pork is not so much based on the Quranic instruction – as this is often avoided when it comes to wine – but from an abhorrence of pigs impressed upon the Muslims since childhood as they are considered to be filthy animals. Among the wild animals, which are cut at their throats with a knife, letting them bleed, primarily the gazelle, deer, hare, and porcupine are considered edible as well as chickens, various types of pigeons, duck, partridge and most smaller birds. The fish species were already listed in the section on fauna. The meat dishes are prepared by boiling the meat in water, baking in oil or fat, or roasting. Boiled meat is referred to as *maslūq*; if the meat is first ground (*lahm mafrūm*), the dish is called *ṯrīdi* or *yákhnit lahmi*. If baked in oil, the meat is called *mahyūs* and, if in fat, *maqli bis-semen*. Fish[1] is also well-liked when baked in oil. In the villages, meat is roasted (*mishwi*) in ovens but on a spit (*'as-sīkh*) or on a grate (*'al-musabba'*). A whole lamb, stuffed with rice, grapes and pine nuts (*kharūf mahshi*), is roasted on a spit for large festivities.

From the remaining, frequently-assembled dishes (*tabīkh*), *sahleb*[2] is the most important; this is boiled milk with some flour and sugar (*neshe*). There is also *bahti*, boiled milk with rice, and *burghul*. The *burghul*, which is called *smīdi* in the villages, consists of wheat and fat (*semen*). If this is mixed with ground meat and shaped into balls, it becomes the popular *kubbi*. Fish with *burghul* or with rice and an addition of pine nuts is well-appreciated as *sayyādiyye*. Likewise enjoyed are *waraq ed-dawāli* (grape leaves stuffed with meat and rice) and the other varieties of *mahshi*: cooked *kūsa*, *badinjān*, or tomatoes stuffed with rice, meat, and pine nuts. One uses the wild-growing fennel (*shōmar*) as a garnish for these dishes. Olives are readily served with rue (*fêjam*) leaves.

One prepares *ftīri bijibni* out of dough; the cheese is wrapped in thin dough soaked in fat and cooked in oil or fat and sprinkled with sugar. Further, there is *mughrabiyyi* (in town it is called *maftūl*) which

---

openly perform what they know is prohibited by Quranic instruction.

1   El Salman's note: In another context Mülinen said that the people were not very familiar with fish and only ate what it is inedible. Here he appears to suggest that they knew how to cook fish and especially enjoyed it when baked in oil. Then he added that it is enjoyed with burghul or with rice and an addition of pine nuts as *sayyādiyye*.

2   El Salman's note: *Sahleb* is not (*Tabkh*) as Mülinen has written here. *Sahleb* is considered something sweet, and it is offered after meals.

is dough with meat and *'asīdi* which is dough with fat and sugar or honey cooked in water. The *luzzāqi* (called *basami* by the Bedouins) consists of fine flour with fat and honey and is cooked on a form whereas the *zelāba* consists of the same ingredients but is baked in oil in a deep dish. Sweets are generally favored by all Arabs; *'asal* (honey), *dibs* (grape honey), and *dibs kharrūb* (carob paste) as well as date paste (*'ajwe*) which is, in turn, sometimes baked in the holiday cake. Sweet dried figs (*qottein*) are very popular, and adults and children enjoy chewing sugarcane stalks (*qasab mass*).

The *khshāf* (ﺁﺏ ﺧﻮﺵ), prepared from *zbīb* (raisins) cooked in water, offers a refreshing drink. Lastly, one cannot forget coffee which plays such a great role in the reception of a guest.

5. Dress

The traditional attire of the Druses has already been described in the section on religion. One frequently sees the *kuffiyye*, a cloth which is bound by a cord made of camel hair or sheep wool (*'aqāl*), as a head covering among the Muslim Fellāheen. Recently, the fez (*tarbūsh*) has gained favor. Should a Fellāh be wrapped in a white turban (*shāsh*), then one is in the presence of an *'ālim* (Quran scholar) or an individual given to the Dervish lifestyle. While the Bedouins let their hair grow long so that one can hardly distinguish

Figure 7. Woman in festival dress from *et-tīre*.

young boys from girls, the Fellāh's hair is closely cropped. Often the head is shaved and only the forelocks *qdelli* (قذال) are worn long.

The farmer wears an *'abāyi* (a short-sleeved coat) or a *qumbāz* over a long trailing shirt (*qamīs*); merely a short smock (*bisht*) is worn over the *qamīs* when working in the field. Clothing for legs is very seldomly seen. The shoes (*merkūb*) are similar to our own coarsest leather slippers; sometimes they are only a piece of untanned leather cut to size and held together by a few stitches. Should a villager traverse through the region, he makes a proud appearance by arming himself with an old muzzle-loading gun. The *tarbūsh* of young lads is decorated on top with a smooth silver ornament (*qurs fadda*) on festival days.

Figure 8. Girl in festival dress from *et–tīre*.

Women wear a dress (*fistiān*) [1]bound rather tightly around the waist; at times, they wear a *qumbāz* (Fig. 7) on festival days. While girls (Fig. 8) wear their hair uncovered in the front – the veil, otherwise common in Muslim countries, is rather unknown here in villages – and wrap a head scarf only around the back of their heads, married women take great care in their head coverings. The *sma'di* frames a woman's face in *et–tīre* as well as in *beled esh-shēkh* and *'ain*

---

1   El Salman's note: In all of the neighboring areas, the word for dress is pronounced "fostan" except in Et-Tire where it is pronounced "fustian". Et-Tire has very unique dilect. This is why I feel it was a poor choice to use the dialect of et-Tire as an example of the dialects of the other villages.

hōd. This is a row of strung-together silver coins; it is often a part of the dowry from the groom. A silk cloth (*'asbi*, pl. *'asāib*) is drawn over the forehead, knotted in the back of the head, and a second cloth (*shúmbar*) is drawn under the chin. The jewelry of the finer sex is perfected through a necklace (*qabbiyyi*) of glass beads (*kháraz*), earrings (*halaqāt*), bangles (*suwāra*), finger rings (*khātim*) and a silk cloth (*mendīl*).

6. Private Life

Village life elapses in a very monotonous manner. People work hard during planting and harvest seasons, but otherwise one readily resigns oneself to *kēf* (a sense of well-being, i.e, doing nothing). Given the mild climate and generally modest life, the farmer does not feel strongly driven to earn money, although he is, on the other hand, marked by great frugality. This is currently being pushed aside only by the true Arab inclination to shine above others.

After the sun sets, at which the beginning of a new day is calculated, the family gathers together for the evening meal; one or two hours later one retires in order to, of course, rise very early in the morning. The monotony of these activities is, however, broken by the duties of hospitality, regarded as inviolable, and religious festivities. Both shall be discussed later; only the celebrations which strictly belong to family life will be mentioned here.

The entrance into this world is only celebrated when it is the birth of a male child; girls do not seem to be worth such great commotion. If several daughters are born to one father, it is even a tradition to give such a poor creature the name *temām*[1] (completion, i.e. now that is enough). Incidentally, there is no special ceremony tied to the bestowing of a name; only the word *bismillah* (in the name of Allah) is spoken by the father before giving the child its name.

Children grow up in complete freedom as soon they no longer need initial care. One often sees these groups of relatively unkempt youths standing together in the villages, and a foreigner is surprised

---

1   El Salman's note: This is an unusal claim which I have never heard before. I know many people from the area who are old enough to have experienced et-Tire. These people had many sons and also had daughters whose names are Tamam. Therefore, I conclude, this is not a realistic reflection.

to see the same games that he knows from his homeland. Counting rhymes are very popular. A few examples are listed here:

Khudruj, budruj temmet tudruj
Min telāte qurqu hummus fish.

Khudruj (a girl's name), *budruj* (chosen for the same sound), it has rolled away.
Of three, *qurqu*[1], chick peas, nothing!

Hadāye badāye menājil tayye
Telāt 'azūr ma'a zarzūr

Divine guidance, beginning, sharp sickles
Three excuses with a Staar (cataract?).

As one sees, these rhymes do not make much sense, and perhaps that is why they are such a pleasure for the youth.

Once a father has the necessary means, a boy is often circumcised in spring by traveling surgoens from Aleppo; a celebration is held on this account. Later, the boys attend a school for reading Quran, and the girls assist with the house work until both can be included in the lighter field work.

At the age of fourteen and fifteen, girls are considered marriageable; the age is sixteen and seventeen for boys. However, the necessary monetary affairs must first be arranged for this, and then the woman is, as in all Arab countries, bought[2]. Among the simple

---

1   The meaning of the expression *qurqu* could not be explained to me.

2   Translator's note: It must be noted that Mülinen has used an inaccurate term here. Women in Muslim societies are not "bought." The dowry (al-mahr) is given to the bride as a gesture of respect and a recognition of her importance within Islamic society. Her consent to marry someone shows a willingness to shoulder responsibilities as well as difficulties. It is a method of giving order to things, such as the dynamics and roles within a family. Based on this, it is not infrequent that families accept a dowry as little as one dinar, for example, although both families may be wealthy. If someone were to take advantage of this dowry in the wrong way, then this reflects a cultural custom rather than an Islamic one as Mohammad (may Allah's peace and blessings be upon him) was very clear when he stated, "The lower the dowry is, the more the woman is blessed by Allah."

peasants, her price stands at roughly 300 to 400 Franks, but it is sometimes also less. This sum sinks to two or three Napoleans, i.e, French gold coins, among the very impoverished. From this dowry (called *fēd* in the villages, *máhir* in town, and *siāq* by the Bedouins), which is often given in money but also paid in livestock, the father of the bride receives half. Of the other half, two-thirds (as *fēd mutqaddim*) are given directly to the bride; this is usually done in the form of her apparel which includes the *sma'di*, at a value of 400 to 1000 piaster, a *qumbāz*, and jewelry. The remaining third (*fēd mut'akhkhir*) is guaranteed through the issuance of a certificate (*sened el-mut'akhkhir*). Should the wife be disowned by the husband, she can reclaim her *fēd mut'akhkhir* on the basis of this certificate which must be shown to a *qādi*. If she were to leave the husband, then she must abandon the latter. Should the groom be greedy or not wealthy but has a sister or daughter who appeals to the bride's father, the father can then give the girl under his authority in marriage to the latter instead of taking his half of the dowry. This is called *bedel juwāz*, or exchange in wedlock. In any case, the bride's half may not be curtailed.

The betrothal occurs through the conclusion of a contract before a *qādi* or an *'ālim* as his representative. For the bride this transpires through a proxy. At this time, the *sened el-mut'akhkhir* is issued.

The wedding itself is celebrated with a great deal of pomp; in long processions, the relatives and friends of the bride bring her to the house of the groom where he has prepared a meal with music for the guests.

As well-known, the *sheri'at* law permits the Muslim men marital relations with Christian and Jewish women, but the Muslim women may not marry Christian or Jewish men. This rule is strictly observed here in respect to the Muslim women. Beyond this law, one then also adheres to the confession concerning Muslim men following local custom. The reason for this is simply that Christian and Jewish women here do not willingly enter into a marriage with Muslim men. In the rare cases in which a Muslim man weds a Druze woman on Mount Carmel, the woman must give up adherence to her sect. Marriage between a Druze man and a Muslim woman are ruled out here, though they do take place in Lebanon, yet however seldom.

While the wife is depicted as a carefully protected luxury object in the Muslim cities, she is truly her husband's life partner in the villages. She works by his side in the fields and shares in his joys and sorrows. This worthy position of the woman is due to the conditions that the women and girls of the flat land go about unveiled despite the Quranic ban as well as the general poverty which results in monogamy. It is well-known that the Turks in Constantinople now detest polygamy; perhaps in consequence of the Christian-Occidental influence, the custom has civilizingly taken over the religious provision. The Arab Fellāh has remained unmoved by such ethnic views; the well-to-do villager who can afford the costs of a courtship for a second bride and a double household, is much more an object of envy on the part of the remaining men. With unconcealed amazement, I was told the tale of a wealthy man in *et-tīre* who could even name four legitimate wives, the maximum number permitted by law (*sheri'at*), as his own.

The Fellāh spends his life, from marriage until his life's end, in these unchanging conditions if military service does not wrest him from his surroundings. Since he does not know anything of our European rush towards work and pleasure and, like most Arabs, is provided with an inherently cheerful character, he spends his existence with little contemplation and without complaint. Discontent with his fate is something unknown to him. Even a weak ray of poetry and music shines upon his life; these especially illuminate his festivities. The description of which shall include some samples of his simple art.

When death occurs, the summoned *khatīb* prays by reciting the *fātiha* (the beginning sura of the Quran) over the corpse, which is then washed and dressed. Should the deceased be a woman, the body is first washed and dressed by an elderly woman after which the *khatīb* arrives and prays. After the deceased is laid in the coffin, the funeral procession (*ajīr*) is set in motion while the *khatīb* intones with the others repeating after him:

> *Lā ilāha ill 'Allāh, dāim bāqi wujhu 'llāh*
> *Lā ilāha ill 'Allāh, Muhammadur rasūlu 'llāh.*

There is no God but Allah, eternal is Allah's countenance
There is no God but Allah, Mohammed is the Messenger of Allah.

The dignified strides of the men and the rhythmic euphony of the solemn chant always make a gripping impression on a stranger sensitive to such things.

If the burial takes place on a Friday morning, the coffin is first transported to the mosque. There the *khatīb* annonces: *asalli rik'atēn 'a hadjenāzi lillāhi te'ālā. Allāhu akbar* (I will pray two rak'at to Allah the Exalted over this body. Allah is the Greatest.); he then recites the prayers of the two rak'at while remaining standing without making prostrations. Once one reaches the cemetery where the women, who followed the procession at a distance, sit separately, the deceased is lowered into the grave. The *khatīb* takes up a handful of dirt, prays over it, and leads it to his right eye whereby he throws it in the grave. As those present, with the exception of the relatives, cover the coffin with earth, the *khatīb* speaks:

> *Yā "Abdallah" yerhamak allāh*[1]
> *Ifham inna 'l-mauta haqq wa inna 's-sirāta haqq*
> *wa inna 'n-nuzūl bil-qabr min ba'd el-maut haqq.*
> *Ifham yā 'Abdallah an yinzal 'alēk malakēn*
> *wa yis'alak mā dīnaka wa mu'tiqādaka*
> *elli mutt 'alēh; terudd 'alēh bilisān il-fasīh:*
> *inna 'l-qur'ān imāmi wal-muslimīn ikhwāni*
> *wa ana hayēt wa mūtit 'ala qaul esh-shihāda:*
> *ashhadu an lā ilāha illā 'llāh wa ashhadu*
> *anna seyyidnā wa nebiyyunā muhammad resūl allāh.*
> *Ifham inna hādā 'l-yōm auwalu min iyyām*
> *el-ākhiri wa ākhiru min iyyām ed-dunyā.*

Oh, 'Abdallah, may Allah have mercy on you!
Know that death is true and that the Sirat bridge is true
and that entering the grave after death is also true.
Know, oh 'Abdallah, that two angels will come to you in the grave
And will ask you of your religion and your faith
on which you died. Answer this in an eloquent tongue:
Verily, the Quran is my Imam, and the Muslims my brothers, and I lived and died on the profession of faith:

---

1   The rendering of the classical form of the word remains incorrect when pronounced by the Fellāheen. This prayer for the dead (*talqīn*) which is spoken by the grave diggers in town is further developed there. The name *'Abdallah* is only chosen to represent the actual name in the above and is replaced by *Muhammad, 'Ali,* etc. depending on the individual situation.

I bear witness that there is no God but Allah, and I bear witness that our master and prophet Muhammad is the Messenger of Allah.

Know that today is the first of the days of the Hereafter and the last of the days of this world.

'Abbās	Ḏīb	Kishk (Bedouin)
'Abdu	Fādi	Latīf
'Abd Allah	Fādil	Mahmūd
"el-Bāqi	el-Fāhid	Mahrūs
" el-Bāsit	Fā'id	Mansūr
"ej-Jelīl	Fā'iz	Ma'rik (Bedouin)
"el-Fettāh	Fālih (Bedouin)	Mas'ad
"el-Ghāni	Fāris	Mas'ūd
"el-Hādi	Fellāh (Bedoiun)	Mfaddi
"el-Hūda	Fu'ād	Mu'dād
"el-Hafīd	Fūzi	Muflih (Bedouin)
"el-Haqq	Ghānim	Muhammad
"el-Hayy	Ghannām	Muhammad 'Ali
"el-Latīf	Glīkh (Bedouin)	Muhammad el-'Ali[1]
"el-Mu'ti	Haidar	Muhammad Sa'īd
"el-Muttalib	Hakīm	Murshid
"en-Nāji	Hamd	Mūsa (Moses)
"el-Qādir	Hamdān	Musbāh
"er-Rahīm	Hámid	Mushhim (Bedouin)
"er-Rahmān	Hasan	Nāji
"er-Rā'if	Hasanēn (the two Hasan = Hasan and Husein	Nā'if
"es-Selām	Hassān	Nāsir
"el-Wahhāb	Hsēn (Husein)	Nassār
"el-Wāhid	Hmed 'Ali (Ahmed 'Ali)	Nejīb
el-'Abid	Hseyyān (Bedouin)	Nimr
Abu Bekr	Ibrāhīm	'Omar
Abu Hméd (after the grandfather)	Ihlāl	'Otmān

---

1   This means *Muhammad* son of (the) *'Ali*.

Abu Mudawwar (Bedouin)	*Ihsēn (Husein)*	*Qasim*
Ahmad	*I'leyyān* (Bedouin)	*Rādi*
'Alēwa	*Ilhāni*	*Rāshid*
'Ali	*Īsa* (Jesus)	*Retīb*
Amīr	*Is'ad* (for *As'ad*)	*Rhayyim*
'Amr	*Ismā'in* (for *Ismā'īl*)	*Ridwān*
'Antar	*el-Ismar* (for *el-Asmar*)	*Rīm* (gazelle)
'Āqil	*Kāmil*	*Sabbāh*
'Āsi	*Kemāl*	*Sabri*
A'wad	*Khadr*	*Sa'd*
Bekīr	*Khālid*	*Sa'īd*
Bekri	*Khalīfī*	*Sakrān*
Beshīr	*Khalīl*	*Sālih*
Bishr	*Khrēwij*	*Sha'būn*
Dahūd (for *Dā'ūd*, David)	*Khurshūt* (for *Khurshīd*)	*Shēkh*
Sherīf	*Semāh*	*Yūsif*
Selāmi	*Slimān (Suleimān)*	*Zā'it*
Selīm	*Ya'qūb*	*Zāmil*
Selmān	*Yūnis*	*Zarīf*

Therewith the ceremony has come to an end, and the grieving return to their homes. The women, of whom the closest relatives have dressed themselves in black (*haddu 'al-miyyet*), begin, as previously in their homes, the lamentations, pull at their hair and strike their chests; even unknown poor women join them in hopes of receiving alms. Professional lamenters (*neddābe*) do not exist in the villages. On the following evening, the relatives bring an animal for sacrifice (*debīha*) and rice to the grave, eat from it themselves, and pass it out to the poor (*'ashā 'l-miyyet*, عشاء الميّت, evening meal for the dead), whereby alms (*hasane*), up to two and three pounds in whole and half coins from the wealthier, are also distributed to the poor. This is also common among the Bedouins on the seventh day after the burial (*sbū'a miyyet*). We also observe another remnant of ancient sacrifice for the dead rites here. Furthermore, the women in particular visit the grave every Thursday evening. Those who could not follow the funeral procession later bring the family a *ajriyye* (funeral gift), often a coat or cloak, to express their sympathy.

Appendix: Names and Families

Perhaps it is of interest to individual readers to find an index of the most common forenames and personal names in *et-tīre* added as a conclusion to this section.

It should be noted in advance that the name and epithet of the Muslim prophet *Muhammad* and *Mustafa*, furthermore all derivations of the root word *hamd*, such as *Ahmed*, *Mahmūd*, *Hamd*, *Hāmid*, *Hamdi*, as well as the names of the members of the prophet's family and of the first caliphs are only held by Muslims in the entire region. Names unique to the Christians are *Qēsar* and *Qostánti*, as well as the female names *Seyyidi*, *Jelīli*, *Bēki*, and *Maṯīl*, whereas the name of the Muslim saint *Khadr* is also used by the Jews. Noticeably, one does not find any women named *Fātima* among the Druses.

It is popular in all circles to give names derived from the same root word within the same family. So it is that two sisters are named *Khushfi* and *Khshēfi*, or *Nūf* and *Nāifi*, or a pair of brothers *Ghānim* and *Ghannām*; another Bedouin family consists of the siblings *Fālih*, *Fellāh*, *Muflih*, and *Felha*.

1. Male Names
2. Female Names

'Afífi	*Haniyyi*	*Nōf* or *Nūf* (=*Temām*, Bedouin)
'Ā'isha	*Hasni*	*Nūkha*
Akābir (Druze)	*Hējar*	*Nūr*, *Nūriyyi* (*nawar* = gypsy)
'Áliyi	*Helāni*	*Qamra* (also *Qamar* as *laqab*)
Anīsi	*Hilmi*	*Qrúnfli* (stock)
'Āqila	*Hind*	*Rābi'a*
Āmini	*Húda*	*Rádā*
Amīni	*Hukmi*	*Rahīl*
'Amra	*Hus̓n*	*Rahmi*
'Ayyāshi	*Ibdūr*	*Ra'ífi*

Báhji	*'Īdi*	*Rīhāni*
Bahījhi	*Izbēdi* (cream, *Zobeida*)	*Rīmi* (gazelle)
Bedawiyyi (as *laqab*, byname)	*Kāmli*	*Sábha*
Bedra	*Karma* (Bedouin)	*Saddīqqa*
Bekriyyi	*Karmella* (after the Stella Maris Monastery where the parents lived)	*Sa'di*
Belqīs	*Kātbi*	*Sādqa*
Dalli (small coffee pot)	*Kerīmi*	*Safiyyi*
Durra (parrot)	*Khadīja*	*Sáfyi*
Etreyya (*Tureyya*, Pleiades)	*Khádrā*	*Sálha*
Fáhdi	*Khōla*	*Sālima*
Fārha	*Khshēfi*	*Sámha*
Fātima	*Khushfi*	*Sāra*
Felha (Bedouin)	*Khuzrān*	*Shēkha*
Gháda	*Jemīli*	*Shemsi*
Ghantūsi	*Latīfi*	*Sherīfi*
Ghazāli	*Lebībi*	*Sēda*
Ghubni	*Mansūra*	*Sēkra*
Hádbi	*Nā'ifi* (= *Temām*, Bedouin)	*Su'ād*
Halīmi	*Na'īmi*	*Temām* (complete)
Hamāmi (pigeon)	*Násra*	*Turkiyyi*
Hamde	*Nejmi*	*Umm es-Su'ūd* (after the grandmother)
Hánā	*Nefīsi*	*'Urūt*
Hanīfi	*Nezha*	*Wādha*
Ward (rose)	*Záhra*	*Zeinab*
Wardi (rose)	*Zarīfi*	*Zeini*
Yúsra	*Zehiyyi*	*Zuhūr*
Záhir		

3. Surnames[1]

Dār ʾAbbās	Dār ʾAmmūra	Dār Muslimāni
ʿAbdallah el-Hāji	ʿel-Báttal	ʿQbēʾa
ʿAbd el-Qādir	ʿel-Bédawi	ʿRayyān
ʿAbd es-Selām	ʿBedr	ʿSaʾd ed-dīn
ʾAbu Dīb	ʿBedrān	ʿSālih
ʾAbu Ghábin	ʿBekīr	ʿesh-Shibli
ʾAbu Ghanāʾim	ʿDerbās	ʿSellūm
ʾAbu Ghēda	ʿHājir	ʿSelmān
ʾAbu ʿĪsa	ʿHsēn (Husein)	ʿet-Tāhir
ʾAbu ʿl-Leil	ʿTʾtéyim	ʿel-ʾŪbdah
ʾAbu Rāshid	ʿKāʾid	ʿYaʾqūb
ʾAbu ʿŪdi	ʿel-Khatīb	ʿZébin
ʾAbu Yūnis	ʿJerbūʾ	ʿez-Zewāwi
ʾAbu Zarīfi	ʿMansūr	ʿZīdān
ʿel-Abwāni	ʿel-Mdérdes	
ʿAllū	ʿMesʾūd	

Only the most well-known families in *et-tīre* have been listed above; in actuality, the personal names under the settled Arabs are as equally widespread as in Europe even if one must frequently ask after them to learn them.

Fellāheen families are also ranked according to their status within the society which strongly influences the courtships. A long-standing residence of the family, greater possession of property and herds as well as a reputation for generosity and hospitality give the bride's father claim to a higher *fēd*.

A genus (*mashāʾikh*) regarded as noble no longer exists today in *et-tīre*, yet one does find such a family, *Dār el-Mādi*, outside of this

---

1   El Salman's note: Mülinen did not transcribe the family names correctly here. In this context, *dar* means family. For example, Dar Ammoura means the Ammoura family. Many surnames Mülinen mentioned are not separate families but belong to the same core. The main core is the family (Dar) and the rest are branches of it. Thus, the names he mentioned (for example, Abdilsalam, Abdel Qadir) are not surnames but branches of the main family (Dar) Ghanayym.

village in *ikzim*. Previously, in the history of the region, this family had played a distinguished role. *Et-tīre* and *'aṭlīṭ* belonged to the family. Aside from their tribal homes in *ikzim*, they still have a summer residence in *el-mezār* as well as different houses in *jeba'*, *tantūra*, *'akkā*, and *haifā*. Two members of the genus occupy high positions in the Turkish magistrates in *'akkā* and *beirūt*. With respect to status, *Dār Abu 'l-Hēja* in *'ain hōd* follows the *Mādi* family. They come from *kōkab abu 'l-hēja* (also called *kōkab el-háwā*) by *saffūriyye* in Galilee. Two branches of this genus are also prosperous in *haifā*. The offspring of the local saint *Shēkh 'Abdallah es-Sāhli* (سهلی) occupies the highest rank in *beled esh-shēkh*. Thereafter, the *Sadaqiyye* family from *umm ez-zeināt* follows at relative distance. The house of *Shēkh 'Abdallah ej-Jum'a* in *el-yājūr* can be mentioned in this context. Among the Druses, the members of *'Ā'ilet Dār Hassūn* and the *el-Halebiyye* family in *ed-dālie* and *Dār Abdallah el-Yūsif* in *'usufia* are highest in rank, whereas the genus *es-Sābā* comes in second.

7. Hospitality

The relationships amongst the individual families stand under the protection of hospitality, regarded as a natural law by Arabs, which bridges the barriers of race and religion. Even in the case of secret enmity, which is not rare among the Fellāheen, the house owner is not freed from the duties of receiving guests, although, on the other hand, it seems natural that one asks his enemy for reception only when in adversity. Incidentally, the Arab, who attaches so much importance to his outward dignity, knows how to control his emotions and gives the impression of being on good terms with everyone.

When the Fellāh is traveling, the friendly greeting is sounded at every encounter even among unknown persons. The formula *es-selām 'alēk* (peace be upon you) is only used among the Muslims. If a Druze addresses a Muslim in this manner, he must acquiesce in the response *'alā 'l-mūminīn es-selām* (peace be upon the believers) rather than the customary answer *wa 'alēk es-selām* (and peace be upon you also). Christians are often addressed with *allah ma'ákum* (may God be with you) or *el-'awāfi* (health) while Europeans are generally greeted with *nahārak sā'id* (نهارك سعيد, may your day be pleasant) and evenings with *lēltak sā'ide* (سعيدة, may your evening, respectively your night, be pleasant). By all confessions, one frequently hears *márhabā* (actually, distance or complacency) and *marhabtēn* (doubled complacency) as a response. A special greeting is common when one meets another at work in the field in which case the wish resounds: *sahh bedenhu* (fem. *sahh bedenhā*, pl. *sahh abdānhum*, fem. *sahh abdānhun* may his, respectively her, person be healthy)[1]; the answer is *bedenhu ysallimu*, respectively *bedenhā ysallimhā* and pl. *bedenhum (bedenhun) ysallimhum* (*ysallimhun*, may God keep his, respectively her, person healthy).

Upon arriving in a village, an unknown visitor is guaranteed a dignified reception if he does well to inform himself beforehand whose house is the most generous (*mīn el-akram*). If he enters the house of his choice, then the seat of honor on a pillow is offered to him to which cigarettes (*sukkarāt*), more seldom a narghile (water pipe, *shīshe*), are added. At the same time, one serves, when wanting to show the weary traveler a kind gesture, lemonade until the popular beverage, coffee, is ready. The coffee beans are lightly roasted and then ground in a mortar (*jurn*) with a pestle (*īd*) where with skillfulness is deployed in dropping the pestle in rhythmic strokes (*daqqa*). This cadenced sound serves the purpose of calling the neighbors attention to the presence of a guest at whom they hurry to have a look. As the room fills with their figures, the coffee is brought to a boil in a small pot (*rikwe* or *dalli*) over the coals. The spice *hān*, favored among the Bedouins, does not seem to be used by the Fellāheen. It is common to sweeten the drink with sugar for Europeans and, in the case that a guest is especially honored, spice it with cinnamon (*qirfe*). Poured into a small cup (*finjān*), the coffee is first tasted by the host and then passed to the guest who drinks it and returns the cup with the words *dāimā bil-afrāh* (may you always be in a state of joy) whereupon the host wishes him a long life. Thereafter all present are provided with coffee according to their rank, the host being last, whereupon the rounds begin again one or two more times with the traveler repeating the same expressions each time. During which the cross examination of curious questions bring the guest into great distress from which he can best be saved by a jesting word. When the visit ends, all present rise after the traveler does, and upon expressing his gratitude to the host and bidding farewell, he is wished safety on his journey. Should the guest spend the night or stay for a meal, then the best room and best food to be found are offered. Payment for the accommodations

---

1   The use of the third person pronoun rather than the expected second person is regarded as a rare expression of respect (للتعظيم) in the Arabic colloquial but was however the rule in older letter writing.

to the attendents or a small gift for the children is frequently not rejected. Incidentally, native travelers, who wish to stay in the area for a prolonged period of time, are provided for through a *menzūl*, a room for lodging which is often located near a mosque, in almost every village.

The hospitality comes from the heart, and the friendly nature, expressed with the words *ahlan wa sahlan* (you have come to your people and to comfort, i.e. may you feel at home with us) not only warms the tone of the speaker but also radiates from his eyes. Generosity, a fundamental element of the Arab character, is closely related to exercising this social duty; this generosity is directly refered to as *maruwwa* (male virtue). Nonetheless, vanity, which seeks its liberation in the unfolding of a grand display which often exceeds the pecuniary means, binds itself almost always with this generosity as a less pleasant, national element. Here and there, the hospitality is also not free from some expediency.

8. Religious Celebrations, Holy Sites, and Local Beliefs

It is well-known that Islam intends to penetrate the existence of its adherents whereby it regulates their behavior in every particular matter through its prescripts. Admittedly, one does not follow the religious obligations so strictly in the villages. Nor are the prescribed prayers – the recurring five daily prayers as well as the Friday prayer, the prayers on the two major festival days, and the *terāwīh* prayers in Ramadan - held as regularly as in town, nor is the fast of Ramadan, from which, incidentally, small children are completely exempt, observed precisely, or are the alms taxes paid. Pilgrimages to Mekka occur only rarely, and one has not heard talk of religious wars in a long time.

The two major festivals, the feast of sacrifice at the time of the pilgrims' arrival in Mekka (*'īd el-qurbān* or *'īd ed-dahiyye*) and *'īd el-fitr*, or *'īd es-saghīr*, at the breaking of the fast at the end of the month of Ramadan, find greater favor. Since these occurrences, based on the sharī'a, the divine law of Islam, are sufficiently well-known and do not differ here greatly from the events in other Arab regions, a discussion of them should be unnecessary.

Among the festivals to be mentioned is the *'āshūra* festival on the tenth of Muharram, called *'awāshīri* here, which is not a legitimate, but a traditional Muslim festival. It is celebrated separately in each family with a meal (*tabkha*) to which neighbors, poorer relatives, and acquaintances are invited. The main portion of the meal consists of chicken prepared with rice, tomatoes and sour milk. The following adage applies to this:

idbahū djājkū ulāqū hujājkū

Slaughter your chickens, so you will find your pilgrims again.

It is namely the beginning of the time in which the pilgrims who have gone to Mekka, of whom so many do not return, could arrive again.

The origin of this festival, which is often associated with Husein's martyrdom in Karbala but also with Noah's rescue from the flood, is already shrouded in darkness. However, even more uncertainty prevails over the age of other celebrations surrounded by just as much religious nimbus from the people which do not follow the alternating Muslim lunar year but rather the fixed solar years. Indeed, one is dealing with originally native, certainly pre-Islamic festivals here. Similar is the case of the custom we observe of coloring eggs for Easter and striking them against each other whereby the owner of the undamaged egg wins the ownership of the broken one.

The Wednesday of the Greek Holy Week is called *arba'at eyyūb* (Job's Wednesday) and is likewise a festival sanctified through convention. On this day, one proceeds to the ocean where one bathes and takes a meal. According to the tradition, this happens in remembrance of the Prophet Job who washed himself to cure his boils.

While the women, often accompanied by a Quran-reading *khatīb*, visit the graves of the deceased every Thursday of the year as mentioned in the description of the funeral, a special celebration takes place on the Thursday following the Greek Palm Sunday (*had esh-sha'nīne*) which is called *khamīs el-amwāt* (Thursday of the Dead). The men also proceed to the cemeteries on this day to recite the *fātiha* for the salvation of the souls of his deceased ancestors and hand out alms (*hasane 'an amwātna*, alms for our dead). One would not do wrong to trace this practice back to the time of the once ruling ancestral cult; however, the determination of the date, which is identical with the Greek *khamīs el-ghusl* (Thursday of the Foot Washing), which also represents the eve of Good Friday, may be dependent on Christian influence. The day coincides with the traditional pilgrimage to the *qubbet es-sakhra* in Jerusalem (*ziāret el-quds*).

Furthermore, there are other celebrations bound to fixed days of the solar calendar: three Muslim celebrations attended by the inhabitants of the Carmel region and two Christian celebrations also considered sacred by the Muslim population. Among the first, the pilgrimage to *nebi mūsā* south of Jericho takes place during the Greek Easter and begins in Jerusalem. The *'īd en-nebi sālih* (Festival of the Quranic Prophet Sālih) is celebrated in *ramle* in the spring, and the *'īd en-nebi rūbīn* (Festival of the "Prophet" Ruben) is primarily celebrated by those living in the surrounding area of Jaffa on the *rūbīn* river in September. Among the Christian holidays, *'īd mār ilīās* (Festival of the Holy Elijah) at the Stella Maris Monastery on the twentieth of July according to the new calendar is the largest celebration in the region with which we are concerned. Thousands of Christians, Muslims, Druses, and Jews gather together there and camp in and outside the Monastery in droves. A market is held there. Already on the preceding evening, one, dressed in his best, proceeds there on foot, by horse or donkey, or by cart; he spends the entire festival day thereat under all kinds of *fantaziyya* and returns home on the following day. On this occasion, there often are brawls as the villages are frequently at odds with each other; the day seldom passes without severe injuries, murder, and manslaughter. The other great celebration, *'īd dēr el-mukhallis*, occurs on the day marking the Transfiguration of Jesus, the sixth of August according to the

Figure 9. Stand of oaks from the *shejarāt el-arba'īn*.

new calendar, and is held in the Greek-Uniat Monastery of the Holy Redeemer by *saida*. The pilgrims for this leave from Mount Carmel. The monastery has a reputation for working miracles with all natives, including Muslims. To prevent the disputes that always occur at the festivities, the monastery has, however, remained closed in recent years on the festival days.

The five last-mentioned festivals, as well as the *ziāret el-quds*, are, as illuminated through the above, not only related temporally to certain days but also spatially to particular places. This leads us to the examination of sites considered sacred by the people. Among them, there are two categories to be distinguished: holy stands of trees, partly with a

Figure 10. *Mihrāb* in the *shejarāt el-arba'īn*.

consecrated well, and the tombs of saints, or holy persons. The shrines of both categories are visited at any time; specific festival days are not attached to them.

Among the sacrosanct tree groups, the *shejarāt el-arba'īn* ("Trees of the Forty" Saints, Fig. 9), called "Trees of the Forty Martyrs" by the Christians, enjoys the greatest repute. The site consists of a larger stand of beautiful old *sindyān* (evergreen oaks) between *el-khrēbi* and the climb to *juneidiyye*, eastwards, relatively underneath the ridge of Mount Carmel. A *mihrāb* (prayer niche, Fig. 10), an approximately one-meter high half circle built into the slope of rough boulders, is located in the shadows of the trees. Previously, a form of alter also stood there; it was a chunk of crag with steps cut into it which were, however, transported to *haifā* for the construction of the home of Selīm el-Khūri, the property owner. According to local belief, the spirits of the saints gather here, like on Temple Mount in Jerusalem, on a Friday of the year; the date of which is shrouded in secrecy. The trees are under their protection, and their punishment of every violation to the shrine is just as merciless as it is sudden. The legends which report such revenge are numerous. Only recently, so it is said, a wood cutter who wanted to chop off a branch there was first punished with the death of his donkey and then his own. Another Fellāh who wanted to use a branch for the roof of his house was struck dead along with his family when the roof collapsed over their heads. Should someone want to set the trees on fire, he would be unsuccessful as they do not catch on fire, but, however, would be consumed by the fire himself. Nevertheless, it is permitted to take a small twig as a blessing (*barakiyye*) for the home. This beautiful group of trees has this superstition to thank for its preservation. This superstition also has other charitable consequences: tools or other objects placed in the *mihrāb* of the shrine are guarded against being stolen and one shies from breaking oaths sworn on its grounds. Also, vows pledged on this site must be carried out, if one does not personally want to insult the saints. Who the persons, or deities, behind the forty saints really are, remains an open question? One thinks of the forty Christian martyrs who were martyred under Emperor Licinius in Sebaste (Sivas) in Armenia. Their Memorial Day falls on the seventh of Ides (the twenty-fifth of February according to the old calendar = the tenth of March according to the new). This view, however, seems to contradict the fact that the *shejarāt el-arba'īn* is visited by the Muslims and Druses but not by the local Christians. At any rate, the Muslims have claimed the saints, and one encounters many places in all of Syria named after them and revered by the Muslims. The "Forty" have their place in the holy hierarchy of Muslim mystics, which are composed of one *ghūt*, two *qutb*, the "Threes," the "Seven," the "Forty," and the

Figure 11. *Bīr-fádil.*

"Thousand." One is probably dealing with the remnants of ancient local heathenism; similar cases will immediately be reached for discussion.

The *bīr-fádil* (Fountain of Excellency, Fig. 11) is also protected by the spirits of the saints. The fountain containing excellent water is surrounded by four *sindyān* trees, and it lies on the upper end of *wādi bīr fádil*, a side valley of *wādi missilli* south of *et-tīre*.

The third sacred group of trees at which, like both previously mentioned sites, vows are offered consists of several *mell*, deciduous oaks. It stands by the ruins of *es-sitt khádrā* east of *shellāle*.

Among the shrines of the second category which are related to certain persons and are often considered to be their graves, the *maqām* of the prophet *el-khidr* (pronounced *el-khadr* here) occupies a special position as his soul is considered to be immortal on earth after he tasted from the waters of eternal life as related by the commentators of the Quran. Because he disclosed his revelations sometimes here and sometimes there, shrines to him can be erected everywhere. Among these *maqām*, the most important within the entire region is the one found at the foot of the Stella Maris Monastery near the ocean. The shrine consists of a spacious cave; the entrance to it is through the gate of a building which houses, in part, the home of the custodian and, in part, accommodations for the visitors. A palm tree stands in the courtyard; beside it there are several apartments of anchorites cut into the rock from an earlier era. The cave itself displays, aside from a *mihrāb*, several flags and old graffiti on the walls, a niche in which the Prophet Elijah is supposed to have sat and conducted lessons based on his prophethood. Elijah is namely identified with *el-khidr* here, whereas in other places, the Christians see Saint George in *el-khidr*. The site is regarded as holy since ancient times as will be later explained in the description of the Stella Maris Monastery. According to Christian tradition, the Holy Family rested in the Cave of Elijah on their return from Egypt. During the Middle Ages, it was in the possession of the Stella Maris Monastery but for several hundred years has been a *waquf* of the Muslim family of Dār el-Hāj Ibrāhīm which holds a hereditary title to the office of *qiyyam* (custodian) for the site. Muslims and Jews carry out vows on this site with fondness for which small offerings and donations are given to the custodian. The current *qiyyam*, however, complains that the Jews here only present offerings and reserve their donations for their holy rabbis in Tiberias.

The more or less historical graves of saints visited by the inhabitants of Mount Carmel are numerous, scattered throughout all of Palestine. From among them, only the most notable are listed.

Aside from the previously mentioned *nebi sālih* in *ramle* and that of *nebi dā'ūd* (Prophet David) in Jerusalem, the *maqām* of *sīdnā 'ali ibn 'alēm*, praised for many wonders, on the coast north of Jaffa is the most well-known. The *maqām* of *nebi hushān* by *shefa 'amr*, that of *shēkh ibrēk* in *merj* (The Plain of Jezreel), and, not far from that, that of *abu shershūh* by *qīre* all lie in Galilee. The small Mount Hermon bears two *maqām*: that of *nebi dáhi* and of *seyyid el-bédawi* on the descent to *endōr*, the latter of which enjoys several veneration sites as in the case of *khidr*. Particularly from *'ain hōd*, one travels to *shēkh abu 'l-hēja* on the *kōkab* by *saffūriyye*. *haifā* also holds the *maqām* of *shēkh 'isa*, which had to make room for that of the *sitt iskēni* (سكينه) on account of the increasing need for traffic. *shēkh ibrāq* is located on the southern coastal plain on the dunes north of *surfend*; *shēkh 'abdarrahmān el-mujērimi* is in *tantūra*; *shēkh ahyā* by *mezār*; and *shēkh 'amēr* by *jeba'*. Mount Carmel itself exhibits, aside from *el-khadr*, the tomb and the adjoining *maqām* of *shēkh sálihi* by *beled esh-shēkh* and even five *maqām* in *et-tīre*: *shēkh slīmān* is located on a hill east of the village and the graves of the shēkhs *khalīl*, *rebī'a*, *idrār*, and *el-ghureyyib* are found within the village itself. *hāj hamād* and *shēkh ighnēm*, found under a dome, are revered in *el-fureidīs*; likewise, *shēkh ishhādi* is found under a dome in *'ain ghazāl*. *Ikzim* is also rich with *maqām*; *shēkh kashkūsh* lies in the upper portion of the village, *shēkh isfār* and *shēkh ightāsh* are found in its midst, and *shēkh yāqūt* and *shēkh mahmūd* are by the mosque. Besides this, the village also presides over the grave of a holy enchanter (*qabr el-mejdūbi*) whose name has fallen into oblivion.

The Druses venerate their *abu ibrāhīm* in *ed-dālie* but visit the festival of *nebi sh'īb* (*shu'aib*, Jethro) in *qarn hattīn* with great pomp.

The Christians offer vows and offerings to the Stella Maris Monastery (*mār iliās*) and on the *muhraqa*, while the Jews make a pilgrimage to the previously mentioned *nebi hushān* as well as to Elijah (*khidr*). From the previously-mentioned facts it follows that the veneration of saints, or holy persons, does not differ significantly in observation among the adherents of the various religions of Palestine. It flourishes just the same among the Muslims, Christians, and Jews. This respect, which is especially enjoyed by the Prophet Elijah, will be returned to again in specific portions in the section on the Stella Maris Monastery.

This holy cult is, as Goldziher has conclusively proven in his *Muhammedanische Studien* (*Muslim Studies*), an element not only foreign to Islam but contradictory to its deepest fundamentals. It characterizes itself as a regression to atavistic views against which the 'ulema are unsuccessfully fighting. Eventually, they found themselves compelled to make a compromise by allowing the people to do as they like provided their superstitions are cloaked in a robe of orthodoxy. Specifically, for Syria and Palestine, the beings of the holy persons (*weli*, pl. *auliya*) can generally be traced back to ancient local deities according to Curtiss' *Ursemitische Religion* (*Primitive Semitic Religion*), though it can also be admitted that in individual instances historical personalities have obtained hero-worship status. The fact that the famous traveler of Arabia, J. L. Burckhardt from Basel, who converted to Islam, occupies a *maqām* at *bāb en-nasr* in Cairo presents an interesting picture. In Cairo, he still performs many wonders today as *shēkh ibrāhīm* as I was assured.

Thus, Islam has not overcome ancient heathenism neither on the flat land nor in the mountains. It has, on the contrary, increasingly transcended the national religion, whereas the Fellāheen, however, do not cease to regard themselves as good Muslims because expressions of this have been sanctioned. Even fanaticism does not remain foreign to them.

That the ancestral cult, reaching back into grey antiquity, has left traces which are still detected today has already been indicated above in the description of the funeral rites as well as in the mention of Thursday of the Dead. The worship of local deities, also prehistoric, as expressed in the reverence of consecrated groves and benedictory sources as discussed above, is of an earlier date. The reserve about entering certain caves in which the spirits reside belongs to this context. A variety of such caves exist in the Carmel region: the most well-known is the *maghāret el-mārid* (Cave of Ghosts) along the way from *et-tīre* to *wādi missilli* where the spirit appears at night in the form of a blue column reaching up to the sky. Apart from that, for the superstitious Fellāheen, the area is filled with all sorts of spirits who namely perform their mischief at noon and when darkness falls. Indeed, it is not to be denied that the existence of the *jinn* plays a large role in the tradition of the Arab prophet, but this may only prove that Muhammad could not completely free himself from the old inherited views despite his knowledge of God as one. Singularly, he was successful in completely eradicating the further development of heathenism, which manifested itself in the pictorial, or sculptural, depiction of a deity, from his community.

The sacrifice (*debīha*) and the vow (*nedr*, pl. *nudūr* and *nudūrāt*) are still to be added here to the forms rooted in the ancient local beliefs in which the religious need finds its content. The Palestinian custom of sacrifices, which seems to be practiced more among the Bedouins than among the Fellāheen, has been recently described in detail[1] therefore it will not be dealt with in detail here. In contrast, the second tradition will be thoroughly described as it is still observed today on Mount Carmel. Thus, the following will summarize the vow.

For the moment, we will discuss a type of vow intended for a deity and not a saint: the *nidr liwujhi 'llāhi te'āla* (vow before the countenance of God, the Most Exalted). It takes place in the house of the vower (*fī bēt en-nādir*) and aims at achieving the blessing of Allah through feeding, or, respectively, passing out money or clothes to the poor. Once the proclamation has been made several days preceding, "*bil-yōm il-fulāni tefaddalū, ileikum 'azīmi, btahdarū tsherrifūni*" (on such and such a day have the kindness, to you goes an invitation, to gather together to honor me), the invitees appear at the given time,

---

1   *L'immolation chez les nomads á l'est de la Mer Morte* by Père A. Janssen in the Jerusalem Dominican *Revue Biblique* Nr. 1 from 1 January, 1906, p. 91 et seq.

mornings or towards the evening, for a meal (*it'ām*). A lamb, goat, or cow, eventually a camel for a larger group, is slaughtered for this. After coffee and cigarettes are passed out with the usual formalities, the host leads the meal with the invitation, *"tafaddalū yā jāwīt"* (have the kindness, you nobles). Upon taking their leave, the guests express the wish that the vow is accepted (*maqbūl en-nidir*), recite the *fātiha*, and depart with the customary farewell.

The remaining vows are offered to a holy person (*weli*) as intercessor often on the evening before Friday; the poor perform the *nidr il-bakhūrā* (incense vow) or the *nidr il-istār* (vow of the veil). Both should prevent a calamity or bring about the realization of a hope; such instances are an illness in the family or the happy return of an absent person. The *nedr* is offered by the head of the family and, if prevented, then a relative, even a young girl. In executing the *nidr il-bakhūrā*, the vower proceeds to the tomb of his preferred saint, kisses the *maqām*, recites the *fātiha* as best he can, and says:

> *nidr(in) 'aleyya; 'n tāb il-'ayyān* (respectively, *rawwih il-ghāib bisselāmi*)
> *ajīb lak bakhūrā yā sīdī ; yā sīdī iqbal nedrak lillāhi te'āla.*

I have taken a vow; in case the sick is cured (respectively, the traveler returns safely),
I bring incense to you, oh, my master; oh, my master, accept your vow for Allah the Most Exalted.

Then he places a small plate (*sahn*) out of metal (*tenek*) or clay (*fukhār*) with incense before the *maqām*. He lights the incense, and to this he places a small lamp (*sirāj*) with oil (*zēt*) and a wick (*fitle*) which is likewise lit. Before departing, he kisses the *maqām* again.

The *nidr il-istār* (نذر الستار) is performed in connection with or in place of the *nidr il-bakhūrā*. After purchasing a green veil (*bāz akhdar*) the length of one or two cubits from a trader, one kisses the *maqām*, binds the veil at the top of the stone posts at the head end of the grave (*rās el-maqām*). The words spoken while performing this are the same as in the *nidr il-bakhūrā* save that the passage *"ajīb lak bakhūrā yā sīdī"* is replaced with the form *"ajīb lak istār yā sīdī"* (I bring you a veil, oh, my master).

These two vows are so frequent that one seldom sees a *maqām* not encircled by small plates and lamps and decorated with green veils.

More well-to-do, or even rich, persons offer a sacrifice vow combined with greater monetary expenditure with the *nidr ez-ziāra* (vow in connection with the visit of a shrine) in more important instances, such as an appeal for the birth of a son. For this purpose, the vower visits the *maqām ez-ziāra* with his family, women and children included, as well as friends, all forming a ceremonious procession dressed in their festivity clothes. The head of the family strides forward with the men; they are followed by a young man or boy on horseback, who is referred to as the groom (*'arīs*; the procession itself is called the groom's procession, *zeffet el-'arīs*). The women follow behind them and, to be precise, the unmarried women who walk two or three to a row while covering themselves with a single large black coat (*hasāwiyye*, coat out of *hasā*, a type of *'abā*). The end is formed by the married women, likewise in twos or threes, yet often without a coat. Such a *ziāra* always takes two, or, if the location of the *maqām* is further away, three days. Upon the arrival of the procession there on the evening of the first day, the *'arīs* dismounts from the horse, and the vower kisses the tomb, or, in the case that there is no tomb, as with *khadr*, the *mihrāb* of the *maqām*. Then he recites the *fātiha* and offers his vow:

> *Yā sīdī nidr(in) 'aleyya; bāji azūrak.*
> *ida kān allāh 'ntānā[1] sābi,*
> *bajīb wāhid debīha u kīs ruzz.*

> Oh, my master, a solemn vow is bearing down on me; I have come to visit you.
> If Allah grants us a son,
> I will bring an animal for sacrifice and a sack of rice.

Thereupon he kisses the *maqām* again; the party slaughters, cooks, eats and drinks and absorb themselves in pleasures. One proceeds again to the revered site on the second day; then one abandons oneself to the varied amusements summarized in the word *fantaziyya*. The last day of the *ziāra* begins with renewed visits to the *maqām*. In the presence of the *'arīs*, the *nādir* places a small sum of money at the foot

---

1   *'ntānā* is dialect in the sense of *a'tānā*; thus, always *banti* = I give.

of the grave whereupon the *zeffe* returns to their home village. The monetary donation goes to the *qiyyam* of the *maqām*. At such places, such as the *shejarāt el-arba'īn*, where there is no guardian appointed, the poor are allowed to take the donations but only after kissing the *mihrāb*.

9. Amusements. Dance and Poetry.

The pleasures in which one indulges at the just-described festivities (*fantaziyya*) are based on the cultivation of dance and poetry and are often accompanied by music. One differentiates among *raqsa*, *dabki*, and *sahji* in the dance styles; the men and women always dance separately in the Carmel region.

For the *raqsa*, the people sit in a circle and clap their hands to the beat (*yaduqqū bil-kaff*); a flutist (*zammār*), either sitting in the circle or standing near the center of the circle, plays a melody while one or two dancers (*raqqās*) perform in the center with cadenced movements. They hop, turn themselves around, and swing a sword, a pistol, or a veil (*mahrami*).

The *dabki* can be divided into two subcategories, the *dabket il-mijwiz* (i.e. with the double flute) and the *dabket el-matlū'*. The *dabket il-mijwiz* is performed by a number of people holding hands while the musician stands in the center. They form a half-circle and move to the right around the musician. The person on the right begins while the others follow (*yihdi 'd-dabki*); he swings a shimmering veil and is called *lawwāh*. There is no song for this dance. The *dabket el-matlū'* occurs with or without instrumental accompaniment. Those present form a much larger enclosed circle in this dance. All are standing and holding hands; the leader (*el-hāshi*) stands in the middle and sings (*bihdi 'l-matlū'*). The others give the beat with their right feet and repeat the leader's song, line for line.

The *matlū'* performed is a song which consists of a number of rhyme verses which often follow each other in pairs. As already mentioned, the repetition of the chorus is characteristic of the *matlū'*. Two examples of this follow:

Matlū' 1[1]

---

1   El Salman's note: The older songs contain numerous lexical items relating to romantic love (wishes, besotted, and waiting), and beauty (roses, seeds

1. *Leia u leia yā habībi u leia*[1]
2. *Lasbur walau jār ez-zemān 'aleyya!*
3. *Yā zāri'īn il-ward mā khallētū,*
4. *Wa bdār*[2] *'and en-nās mā khallētū.*
5. *Mirhabā bikum in jītum u tallētū!*
6. *'Allamtūna durūbi jihil ghasbiyya.*
7. *Yā zāri'īn il-ward (b)bāb ij-jarra,*
8. *Uzzein sūsáhnī u tili' barra.*
9. *Ya zāri'īn il-ward bil-'arīshi,*
10. *Uzzein sūsáhnī bishúrb esh-shīshi.*

1. (Come) to me! And to me, my darling, and to me!
2. I must endure when the time is pressing down on me!
3. You who planted the rose, you have neglected nothing,

---

of roses, and beauty spots). Terms of endearment appear throughout the text; in line one of Song One, we find "dear one," and, in lines three and eight of Song Two, we read "oh you delicately grown one". Song Two shows that Palestinian society openly celebrated both lust and female beauty. In Song Two, not only are love and physical beauty mentioned but the physical appearance of the beloved is described in detail; she is tall with golden teeth. These examples indicate that the central concerns of the songs are romantic love and the desire to possess the beloved. That was when the people were living in their homeland. Unfortunatetly, after being forced to immigrate from their village, the oral literature of the Tirawi people tells us that their forced migration altered not only their material circumstaces but the group identity of the whole community as expressed in oral literature. Concomitantly, a state of mourning expressed in the form of religious piety has been used to censor language relating to wine and physical beauty. Additionally, a general atomosphere of sorrow purveys the contemporary texts as we repeatedly encounter the theme of a lost place as a literary trope signifying the loss not only of a geographical location and its accoutrements but also the loss of family, friends and lovers.

1   *Leia u leia* is a popular song beginning for the *mauleyya* genre; one uses the words as a joyous exclamation when meeting loved-ones. In general, it is very difficult to obtain intact texts from the villagers, and thus these songs present some unclear points which cannot be eliminated through the Fellāheen. In the context of this work describing the Carmel region, a discussion of this must likewise be abstained from as a prosodic examination and improvements of the texts would require particular work. These examples should only give a general idea of the poetry of the Fellāheen.

2   *bdār* according to the urban pronunciation for *bḏar*.

4. And you have not left grain with the people (you have sacrificed nothing).
5. Welcome to you, when you arrive and approach!
6. You have taught us the ways of foolishness against our will.
7. You who planted the rose on the opening of the jar,
8. And the ornament has bewitched me and has gone away.
9. You who planted the rose by the leaf huts,
10. And the ornament has bewitched me with its narghile smoking[1].

Matlū' 2

1. *Mūjina bi mūjina*[2]
2. *Mā yamūt illā 'lladi 'umrah dána.*
3. *Yā zarīf et-tūl, 'aini, yā zarīf,*
4. *Ladummak damm el-habaq bihwādi rīf.*
5. *Yā zarīf et-tūl yā sinn ed-dahūk,*
6. *Yā mrábbā bidalāli ummak u abūk,*
7. *Yā akhbār esh-shūm yōm in talabūk,*
8. *Sha'r rāsi shāb u dahri 'nhánā.*
9. *Yā zarīf et-tūl, yā abu 'sh-shāmatein,*
10. *Tíswa min haleb lihadd esh-shāmatein.*[3]
11. *Nidr(in) 'aleyya min*[4] *massēt esh-shāmatein,*
12. *Láhjum 'al-bārūd lau 'umri dána.*

1. *Mūjina* with *mūjina*
2. Only he dies who has approached his life's aim.
3. You delicately-grown one, my eye, you delicate one.
4. I want to encircle you the way basil is surrounded in the flowerbed rows of the watered garden.

---

1 The short song ends with a harmless punchline with an intended comical effect.

2 *Mūjina* is a corruption of *mijana* which is known in Syrian poetry as ميجانا, however, is correctly written as ميجنه. The *mijana* songs, like the previous example, are based on the category of the *mauleyya* songs, initially in the *basīt* meter.

3 *Esh-shāmatein*, the two Damascuses, is a hyperbolic expression (مبالغه) as the Arabs especially enjoy it using in poetry.

4 *min* stands for *in*, when.

5. You delicately-grown one, whose teeth are smiling,
6. You who were raised under the caresses of your mother and father,
7. Oh, the message of misfortune on the day on which your departure was called for.
8. My hair whitened and by back curved.
9. You delicately-grown one, you with the two beauty moles,
10. You offset (everything) from Aleppo to the two Damascuses!
11. I take a vow: if I can kiss the two moles,
12. Then I will throw myself at the powder (against the enemy shotgun), in case my life's aim also approached.

The most popular of the dances is the *sahji*. A circle is not formed here but rather a long row in a straight line (*saff sahji*). The *hāshi* stands before all, giving the beat and performing a song (*bihdi hadādi sahji*). After every line of the song (*haddāwiyye*, pl. *hadādi*)[1] which is characterized as a form of *qasīde* with a single continuous rhyme, the people answer with the refrain *yā halāli yā māli* "oh, you, my rightful property, my possession." This is an expression of joy as brought on by the enjoyment of one's legitimate possessions.

Before the performance of the *haddāwiyye*, the *hāshi* begins with a preamble (beda', بدع) in which he sings while swaying back and forth:

> *Seirū yelli*
> *Yā abu qdelli*
> *et-tāiha*
> *kull id-dinyi rāiha!*

> Oh, you (people) march,
> Oh, man with the forelock,
> which hangs down,
> the whole world is going there!

Then he stands still and calls:

> *Habīs yamma lil-qōm?*
> *Yā khayyi 's-salā was-sōm,*

---

1   *Haddāwiyye* is a song that one uses to drive the camal but also to encourage others to dance.

Yā khayyi 'l-'atab wal-lōm,
Ghazāli mā r'eitu 'l-yom,
Ghazāli bifeyy id-dōm,
'Ayūnu sāhi lin-nōm.

(Am I) a prisoner or (do I belong) to (you) people?
Oh, my brother in prayer and fasting.
Oh, my brother in rebuke and reproach!
I did not espy my gazelle today,
My gazelle is in the shadows of the Dōm tree[1]
Whose (soulful) eyes (as though) letting itself go to sleep.

After that the *haddāwiyye* begins. Two examples from this poem genre are also given here:

Haddāwiyye 1

1. *Isma' el-qaul el-béda' mir rās[2] ilsāni sarrábha!*
   Refrain: *yā halāli yā māli* is repeated after every verse.
2. *Qūlū liz-zeini titla' el-leile, leilet tarábha!*
3. *Allah yajīrak yā Mahmād[3], kull il-badāwi hārábha,*
4. *Táwwa' bilād el-'āsi welli mā tā'at kharrábha;*
5. *Mā yirkab illā 'l-abāyi; el-'ūja yirmi 'asábha.*
6. *Mā lbūsu ghēr il-hasāwi; 'al-kitif yilma' qasábha.*
7. *Bint il-abāyi jelāha[4], taht es-serāya nasábha.*
8. *Yōm in bihjim 'ala 'l-qōm mélik yōm in birkábha.*

1. Hear the unusual song, the tip of my tongue lets it flow down!

---

1   According to Ritter (Palästina I p. 508), the Dōm tree is the *nebek* (*Rhamnus napeca*) found in Syria and throughout Arabia.

2   The grammatical construction is unclear here.

3   "*Mahmūd*" is used here in place of the name whose bearer is extolled by the *hāshi*.

4   *Jélā* or *jelw* is the dance performed by the bride on the wedding night; standing in her jewelry, one of her friends steps up behind her back and causes her to delicately move her head and torso so that she can be seen in all her grace. The friend who parades the bride thus is called *jalat el-'arūs*. The comparison of a young noble mare to a bride cannot be conspicuous in the naïve poetry of the Bedouins.

2. Tell the ornament, she wants to come out tonight, the night of her pleasures!
3. May Allah protect you, Mahmūd, he has waged war on all (other) Bedouins;
4. He brought the land of the rebels to obedience, and he ravaged those who did not obey.
5. He only mounts the noble mare; he destroys the tendons of the lame ones.
6. He alone wears the coat from Hasā; golden threads gleam on his shoulder.
7. He parades (like a bride) the mare's filly; he has tied her up at the palace below.
8. On the day he lunges at the people, he is a king on the day he mounts her.

Haddāwiyye 2

1. *Ghāfil wahhid khalīlak! yā ghāfil salli 'an-nébi*
   Refrain: *yā halāli yā māli* as above.
2. *Tobannā yā tobannā, 'amūd el-khēmi tobannā[1]*
3. *Wahna laulā jahannā[2] mā jina u dashsharnahénna.*
4. *Jīnā ndáwwar 'ala z-zein, wa tāri' ez-zein 'andahenna.*
5. *'Abidi abu barātim rīhit abātak musinna,*
6. *'Umrak mā jibti qlī'a wa lā 'l-bīd ahmedinna.*

1. You, drowsy one! Praise the oneness of your friend (i.e., Allah)! You, drowsy one, pray to the prophet!
2. Our flock, oh, our flock, we have secured the pillar of the tent.
3. And we, when we are not committing folly, we would not have come and we would not have neglected them.
4. We came to prowl around the ornament, yet, see, the ornament (stayed) with them.
5. My slave with swollen lips, the odor from your armpits is foul;

---

1 The explanation heard by the Fellāheen is reproduced in the translation; in accordance with this, *tobannā* stands for *tabannā*, our flock, in the first two cases whereby it is understood as a verb at the end of the verse. The "pillar of the tent" metaphorically means the chief of the flock (the tribe).

2 *Jahannā* for *jahilnā.*

6. All your life you have not gotten prey, yet the white (women) celebrate (you) in song.

During the men's *fantaziyya*, the women likewise enjoy themselves with *raqsa*, *dabki*, or *sahji* but without a flutist when they do not want to listen. The woman leading the song is not called *hāshie* but rather *qawwale*; those responding are called *tejāwibūha*. With fondness, however, the women pursue the *tehlīl* (through emitting the sound *lu lu*) which is also referred to under the general term *ghanāni*, but specifically *zughretiyye* in the Carmel region.

Even the time when one is not abandoning oneself to the passion of dance is often filled with music and the performance of songs which are usually accompanied by the *nāy* (flute), the *mijwiz* (double flute), and the drum called *deff*. One most frequently hears the so-called *'atāba* verses, popular throughout Syria, within these songs:

> *Hála biqdūmhiṃ walfein sahla!*
> *R'eit ed-derb laḥn dall sahla!*
> *Yā zāri' jneini b'ard sahla,*
> *Udakhlak lā zīd b'nā 'aḏāba!*

Your arrival is welcome, your health two thousand times!
Oh, if only the path remains easy for them!
You who plant a garden on level ground,
Have mercy, do not let the torment last longer for us!

> *Hála bitārish muqbil alēna!*
> *Rīqhu 'asal hal muqbil 'alēna.*
> *Ya sīdī nrūh wallā ndall héna?*
> *Dakhīlak rudd la'abdak jewāba.*

Welcome to the newcomer who is walking to us!
He whose kiss[1] is sweet as honey, who is walking to us.
Oh, my master, are we moving away or staying here?
Have mercy, give your slave an answer!

As evidenced here, the main motif of the Fellāheen poetry is love; this is the only sensation that stirs up the ordinariness of their daily

---

1   Literally, saliva.

life. Therefore, these poems take a back seat to those of the Bedouins whose frequent feuds give them an opportunity to arouse their enthusiasm; without which true art is inconceivable. The two examples of *haddāwiyye* songs given contrast sharply from the usual; the first of them, in particular, is distinguished through its poetic momentum. These two songs originated among the Bedouins and have gradually found their way to the coastal plain. Only the beginning verse of the second has its origins among the Muslim Fellāheen but frequently serves as an introduction for the *sahji*.

10. Relations among the Villages

It was made clear in the previous section on hospitality that, outwardly, the Fellāheen seem to be on best terms with each other. Their conduct upon meeting is always appropriate, and every house is open to visitors. There is absolute security, namely for wayfarers and strangers, on the mountain during the day; women especially enjoy the protection of the custom which declares any injury committed against their decency strictly taboo. Stealing is also considered dishonorable whereas one tends to regard the overreaching of his neighbor as a sign of intellectual superiority. At the most, sheep and goats are purloined here and there by poor shepherds.

However, under the guise of general respectability, feelings of hate and envy sometimes slumber. Discord between individuals and entire families exists in many instances and can degenerate into dangerous quarrels. It is, for example, enough that a Fellāh should make a secret find in an ancient grave on his property to cause his neighbor to report this to the authorities in *haifā*. Thereupon, the *zabtie* (local constable) arrives, and the delinquent is handed over to the punishing branch of the Turkish law.

We find similar relationships with regard to the villages. There are often disputes about the village field boundaries causing villages to be at odds with each other as is the case between *et-tīre* and *beled esh-shēkh*[1]. Sometimes old inherited enmities come to new outbreaks on

---

1   El Salman's note: This is highly unlikely. I have never heard from older Palestinians about any dispute between et-Tire and Balad al Shekh. Indeed, most of those who came to et-Tire at that time for an engagement ceremony were from Balad al Shekh. One was Al Sheck Al Sahli from the Al sahli family from Balad al Shekh.

occasions such as the major celebration of *mār iliās* or elsewhere. Such excesses are quickly suppressed by the administration which obtains the proper respect. The heated emotions immediately cool in the face of strict penalties imposed by the authorities, and everything returns to the previous state. In general, one can describe the peace in the Carmel region as undisturbed. Feudal conditions from the Middle Ages as they occasionally prevail in northern Lebanon between individual communities are completely unknown here. At most, the old inherited hostility between Druses and Bedouins expresses itself occasionally in attacks on wanderers even outside of the festival season. Sometimes one hears of robbery near the Israelite colonies on the *khusm*.

The reputations the villages have are best characterized by the proverbial expressions (*mu'nā*) which circulate about them. The same shall have its space here. It should be noted that only those from the coastal plain or localities nearby will be distinguished in this way.

> *Kebīr esh-shāsh tīrāwi*: The people from *et-tīre* wear a large headband, i.e. a thick head hides under it.

> *Kebīr et-tuhli 'atlīti*: The man with a swollen spleen is from *'atlīt*; because frequent fever prevails in *atlīt*.

> *Dīk el-mezābil surfendi*: The rooster on the dung is from *surfend*. The highest elevation in this village is namely a large manure pile on which the notables gather in the evenings.

> *Kufr lām, úfrush u nām*: *Kufr lām* (regarded as hospitable), unfold your beds and sleep.

> *Tantūra umm el-'atūra*: *Tantūra* is the mother of perfuming, i.e. pleasures, because there are many affluent young people located in this village who pass their time with pleasures.

> *Sabbāb el-'asal jeb'āwi*: He who buries much honey in sweets, i.e. the hospitable one, is from *jébā'*.

Ishqar el-lihya kazmāwi: A red-bearded man is from *ikzim*.[1] One is reminded of the hadith of the Prophet with this expression: *lā khaira fil-ashqar*: there is nothing good in redheads[2].

Jīnā 'alā 'ain ghazāl, talabnā 'l-ghádā ghaddūnā, talabnā 'l-mōy mā saqqūnā: We went to *'ain ghazāl* and requested a breakfast and were given breakfast; we requested water but were given none. This refers to the fact that there is no water to be found in *'ain ghazāl*.

One tells a great deal of further stories about the inhabitants of *'ain ghazāl*. It is not to be denied that these stories have a certain similarity with the known escapades of a simpleton.

d. Administration

State and Municipal Ordinance. The Villages and Division of the Fields.

The Carmel region and the adjoining western coastal plain are within the jurisdiction of *qadā haifā* which belongs to the vilayet *beirūt* (province) as a portion of the *mutesarriflik* (district of) *'akkā*. All administrative affairs of great importance are brought before the *qāimmaqām* in *haifā* where both a *qādi*, a judge responsible for matters of religious jurisdiction, and a territorial force major for exercising military sovereignty preside.

Permanent state organs do not exist in the villages with the exception of the tax collector in *tantūra* and the small military post in *'atlīt* which consists of one *onbashi* (corporal) and two soldiers. Some necessary state functions are carried out through commissioners or through the community government under special state instruction.

The interests of the state primarily refer to two points: charging taxes and recruitment to military service. The collection of taxes transpires with the cooperation of the municipal government. The most oppressive tax, through not so much because of its high rate but

---

1 El Salman's note: It is written and pronounced Ijzim

2 Translator's note: This is not necessarily an authentic hadith. It is also said that *ashqar* refers to blond hair rather than red hair.

rather due to the type of levy, is the tenth which amounts to about 12.5 % of one's salary. This is namely leased to the highest bidder, and the leaseholder (of the tenth) seeks to extort a far higher sum from the peasants through all sorts of vexations. In recent years, the residents of *et-tīre* have protected themselves from these further demands by leasing the tenths themselves through negotiation with their *mukhtāre*. For the purpose of recruitment, a military commission under a *mufettish* (inspector) proceeds twice annually through the villages: the intents of these visits are to find young men fit for service (*aqlama*, from the Turkish *joqlama*) in the spring and to conduct the physical (*mu'āyene*) performed by a military doctor after the harvest. Those required to appear are informed of the date of their enlistment after the latter. The village *mukhtār* is consulted in the decisions of the commission to which he adds his seal. The Turkish military service is highly unpopular among the rural population. Hence, wealthier Fellāheen purchase immunity from this with a legally standardized ransom of 50 Ltq. (approximately 1140 frs.). Those unable to do this seek various excuses, frequently even through fleeing, to evade the service. During the recent revolt against Yemen, the troops recruited from Palestine are believed to have proved a failure.

A record of the population (such as births, marriages, and deaths) is not kept as the female births are not of consequence to the state. However, in the fall of 1905, a population census was carried out in the entire *qadā haifā*. The result of which is taken into account in the following.

As the *qādi* of *haifā* does not visit the villages, he appoints one of the few *'ulema* (Quran scholar) in the larger municipalities as a representative for practicing religious jurisdiction. This person holds a special seal and the specific title of "*ālim*." The marriage contracts are namely conducted by him; he charges fees for this in his own favor, whereby he allots higher fees to wealthier villagers. The *imām* or *khatīb* (clerics appointed for the mosque) has only religious and no state functions. Among the Catholic (Greek-Uniat) Christians in *'usufia*, the religious jurisdiction is performed by a *khūri* (priest) who stands subordinate to the Archbishop in *'akkā*.

The organs of the community administration are the village mayors (*mukhtār*), one for every *qarie*, and one each for every quarter (*mahalle*) of larger localities. They are chosen by the inhabitants, confirmed by the *qāimmaqām* in *haifā*, and provided with a seal for their post. The Catholics in *'usufia* have their own *mukhtār*.

The schools within the Muslim communities are only for boys, and they are not state institutions but rather Quran recitation schools established according to tradition and appointed by the communities. They are under the direction of a *khoja* (teacher) who often instructs while at the same time looking after all the youths entrusted to him in his apartment whereby physical punishment makes up an important method of schooling. The lesson proceeds as follows that on one day the *khoja* recites (*ders*) together with the boys a section which the boys must recite aloud. To relieve the *khoja*, the advanced students help teach the beginners. Lesson subjects are Quran recitation (*qirā'a*), writing (*kitābe*), and arithmetic (*hindi*). The boys usually stay four years in the school without winter or summer vacations. Brighter students can, however, take their final exams (*imtihān*) as early as the end of their second or third year. The results of this education are, incidentally, not of long-lasting effect as one rarely finds someone among the adult villagers who has a great command of reading and writing. There are two of these schools located in *et-tīre*, one in *ikzim* which was installed as an extension to the mosque, and one each in *beled esh-shēkh*, *'ain hōd*, and *'ain ghazāl*. The Christians in *'usufia* have their own school under the auspices of the *khūri* in which girls are also instructed. The Druses send their children either to the latter institution or to one of the schools held during the winter months.

The government calendar (*sālnāme*) of the vilayet *beirūt* from the year 1322 (1902 A.D.) contains a list of the places approved of by the state as a *qarie* (village community) within *qadā haifā*. The villages which come into consideration for the Carmel region have been taken from the list and entered here. The numbers recorded next to the village names are based on a statistical record of the population from the previous year.

مزجا	*Ikzim*[1]	1519
امالزنيات	*Umm ez-zeināt*	630
بلد الشيخ	*Beled esh-Shēkh*	350

---

1 See the last paragraph in the second specific section for the spelling *ikzim* rather than *ijzim*. The same is explained in the discussion of the village *ikzim*.

جبع	Jeba'	406
دالية الكرمل و ام الشقف	Dāliet el-Kirmil and Umm esh-Shuqaf	744
سوامر	es-Sawāmir[1,2]	-
صرفند	Surfend	220
طنطورة	Tantūra	737
طيرة	et-Tīre	2435
عين حوض	'Ain Hōd	283
عين غزال	'Ain Ghazāl	883
عسفيا	'Usufia	595
عتليت	'Aṭlīṭ (most likely an overestimated population count)	100
فريديس	el-Fureidīs	297
كفر لام	Kufr Lām	136
مزار	el-Mezār	79
ياجور	el-Yājūr	153

It should be noted that in the Turkish population census the numbers, in general, seem to be underestimated because many individuals seek to flee from the census out of fear of the military and tax burdens. Nevertheless, the results listed here should be approximately correct as the statistical record was conducted with extraordinary stringency and accuracy in *qadā haifā* in 1905. Thus, according to this, there is a sum total of 9567 persons for the region discussed here, excluding the *khusm*. From this, 1193 of the native population are located on the coastal plain, and 8374 are on Mount Carmel itself. In addition, there is still the Israelite colony Mayer-shefeya (شفيا), lying in the Carmel region, with 30 inhabitants, whereas its twin village *umm ej-jimāl* (ام الجمال), or *bath-shelōmō*, is considered part of the *rūhā* and is therefore not taken into account here. On the *khusm*, *zummārin* (زمارين), or *zikhrōn ya'qōb*, has 536 Israeli colonists to

---

1   *Es-Sawāmir* by *'ain ghazāl* is only ruins today and must, therefore, mistakenly have been kept in the government calendar listing of previous times. *Es-sawāmir* is then logically passed over in the population statistics.

2   The Turkish listing left out the article "*el*", which is added again in the transcription, in the place names *es-sawāmir, et-tīre, el-fureidīs, el-mezār,* and *el-yājūr*; the Turkish bureaucracy has adopted the urban pronunciation *'atlīt* (عتليت) for the name *'aṭlīṭ* (عثليث).

which the *el-merāh* and *el-burj* settlements south of the *nahr ez-zerqā* belong. Likewise, the Arab villages *umm el-'alaq* with 45 residents and *shūne*, or *miamās* (ميماس), with 15 residents lie on the *khusm*, as well as *brēki* (بريكة) with approximately 100 and *sindyāne* (سنديانه) with 600 persons in the east.

The village fields will be more precisely cited in the specific portion covering the individual villages; a brief summery of the division of property on the mountain is sufficient here. The region of the Stella Maris Monastery occupies the northwestern slope; the portion of the town of *haifā* joins it to the east of which the first northern plateau belongs to the Germans. The landholdings of *et-tīre* stretch out towards the west, south of the Monastery region; those of *beled esh-shēkh* are in the east adjoining the fields of *haifā*, and south of that those of *el-yājūr*. The Druse villages *'usufia* and *ed-dālie* lie on the elevations; both of which reach down into the Jezreel plain with their plots of land. The southeastern peak of the mountain occupies the terrain of the *muhraqa* belonging to the Stella Maris Monastery. *Umm ez-zeināt* adjoins it to the south. *'Ain hōd* borders it west of *ed-dālie* and, in turn, is separated from the ocean by *'atlīt*. Lying south of here, mostly at the foot of the mountain, are *el-mezār, jeba', ikzim, 'ain ghazāl* and *el-fureidīs*, followed by *surfend* and *kufr lām* parallel to the coastal plain and *tantūra* on the ocean. The Israelite colonies on the *khusm* form the conclusion there with the recently named Arab villages. It should be noted the Monastery properties as well as the Germans' plots of land on the northern plateau are dismissed from the organization of fields among the villages.

Appendix on Folklore

One obtains the best insight into the customary mentality of the Orient when one listens to the popular folktales. They reflect the prevailing views, and one recognizes the ideals of the individual tribes in the traits attributed to the characters portrayed. The art of story-telling is, nevertheless, at an even lower niveau than the poetry in the Carmel villages. Nowhere did I find, as in the cities, a man possessing the talent for illustration otherwise inherent to the Arabs who could gather around him a circle of listeners to teach and entertain with his treasures of knowledge. Despite this, two "tales" (*hikāye*) are offered which aside from several linguistic peculiarities also incorporate odd content. The first text is an animal fairy tale and portrays the magnanimity of the panther in an equally clear light as the character of the fox. The latter, as in the majority of similar Arab tales, is depicted as sly but falls into inconvenience through the application of greater cunning. The jackal who appears at the conclusion takes on the role of the detached third person in a nuance of irony. The second example deals with a religious question, and, to be precise, the age-old Tannhäuser motif. The somewhat barbaric solution is surprising for us, in which the precept mitigatively introduces the notion, that the woman's injury is the greatest wretchedness.

Hikāyet el-hsēni wu 'n-nimir

Iltaqa 'n-nimr w̆ 'l-hsēni bil-khála. Háka 'n-nimir ma'a 'l-hsēni; qāl lu: 'ala ēsh dāir, yā abu 't-tahsan? Qāl lu: dāir adawwir 'ala nasībī. Qāl lu: enti mā bta'rif itsīd? Tá'a tā ḏallimak es-sēd. Qāl lu: 'allimni, yā abu 't-ténmar. Mishi huwa u yāh. Bī͟ haiwānāt bir'ū bij-jebel; wúqif il-hsēni wu 'n-nimir sáwa. En-nimir bidrub ḏēlu 'ala dahru, qāl lu: kīf 'aneyyi yā abu 't-tahsan. Qāl lu: 'aenēk humr mit̲l en-nār. Biqūm en-nimir yerūh 'al-haiwānāt, bilbid, binutt, bimsik wāhid min el-haiwānāt, buqtilu biqūl: ta'a, kul. Biji 'l-hsēni bōkil tā yishba', biqūl lu: kattar khērak, yā abu 't-tenmar. Qāl lu bta'rif itsīd mit̲li? Qāl lu bat'allam. En-nimir deshsher el-hsēni; el-hsēni biddu yitsayyad lahālu. Dār bil-berriyyi, lāqā jamal nā'ikh. El-hsēni biddu sīd ej-jamal mit̲l mā kān en-nimir sād el-báqara. Ája 'l-hsēni lij-jamal, rabat ḏēlu bidēl ej-jamal hattā yōkhudu 'ala mōkaratu, shadd ḏēlu bidēlu. Qām ej-jamal wuqif 'ala ijrēh; sār el-hsēni marbūt bij-jamal fōq. Dār ej-jamal yir'ā 'as-séjar, mu'allaq el-hsēni bidēl ej-jamal. Mīn lāqāh? El-wāwi. Qāl lu: 'a bāb allāh, yā abu hasan? Qāl lu: bidēl hal-khīy̆ r.

The Fox and the Panther

A panther and a fox once met in solitude. The panther spoke to the fox and said, "Where are you running to, oh, father of the fortification?[1]" He answered, "I am going (around) out on my lot (what

---

1   The words *tahsan* and *tenmar* are formed after the Arabic names of animals but at the same time carry the given meaning. Further on, *tahsan* changes to a new word play with the similar sounding name *hasan*.

I get to eat).” Then the panther asked him, “Don’t you know how to hunt? Come, I will teach you how to hunt.” He said, “Teach me, oh, father of the spotted-existence.”

They went together. There were animals (livestock) grazing on the mountain. The panther and fox stopped and stood there together. The panther hit his back with his tail and asked, “How do my two eyes look, oh, father of the fort?” The fox answered, “Your eyes are as red as the fire.” Then the panther rises to go after the animals. He crouches low; he jumps and seizes one of the animals. He kills it and says, “Come, eat.” The fox comes and eats till he has had his fill; then he says, “Thank you, oh, father of the spotted-existence!” Then he asked him, “Can you (now) hunt as I do?” He answered, “I will learn to.”

The panther leaves the fox, and the fox will now go hunting alone. He went around in the wilderness; then he found a camel kneeling (sleeping). The fox would like to hunt the camel just as the panther hunted the cow. The fox approached the camel. He bound (in order to do the job very well) his tail to the camel’s tail. Then the camel rose and stood on (literally: on both) his feet. Now the fox was bound onto the top of the camel. The camel walked around and grazed the plants, and the fox hung on the camel’s tail.

Who met him? The jackal. He asked him, “(Where to) in God’s gate (wherever are you going), oh, father of Hasan?” The fox answered, “On the tail of this noble (i.e. this depends on his nobility).”

Hikāyet esh-sháqī

Fī qadīm ez-zemān kān wāhid sháqi qātil tis’a u tis’īn nefs min el-minādamīn, biddu yetūb ‘an esh-shaqāwi. Rāh lil-khatīb, kallam ma‘a ’l-khatīb, qāl lu: yā sīdnā ’l-khatīb. Qāl lu: na’am yā ibni? Qāl lu biddi ªshūf ākhírtī kīf, qatalt tis’a u tis’īn nefs.

El-khatīb khāif min esh-shaqi, qāl lu: yā ibni, bitghuzz ‘asātak bil-maqbara, idā kān bitsabbigh khadra bi’lam allāh bi’amalak. Akhad el-‘asā rāh al-maqbara tā yaghuzzhā. Wujid insān bāhish ‘ala miyŷti tā yatūlhā min el-qabir. El-miyŷti rabbnā hatt er-rūh fīhā hattā itdáfi’ ‘an nefshā, bas et-tim mā bihkīsh. Aja ‘sh-shaqi ‘al-mukhābata, qāl lil-insān: itla’; lammā tili’, qatalu; wal-miyŷti rāhat rūhhā ‘and rabbnā. Dafan il-miyŷti u dafan il-insān elli qatalu bighēr mutrah. Ghazz el-‘asā ‘ala qabr il-hurmi u rawwah ‘ala bētu.

Es-sub̯h 'ala bukra rāh shaf il-'asā elli ghazzhā 'al-qabir, lāqāhā sejara tāli'a khadrā. Ista'jab, rāh lal-khatīb qāl: yā sīdī ta'a shūf el-'asā. Rāh el-khatīb shāfhā; qāl: yā ibni shu 'imilt el-lēli? Qāl: ana kunt qātil tis'a u tis'īn ul-lēli kammalthin 'al-miyye u hakā lu hikāyet el-hurmi. Qāl lu: yā ibni, allāh 'afā d̯unūbak bihēt̯ innak sattart 'ala hal-hurmi.

The Sinner Condemned to Hell

Long ago there was a villain ripe for hell; he had killed ninety-nine people from the race of Adam. Now he wanted to proselytize from his malice. He went to the Imām, spoke to him and said, "Oh, our great Imām." He said, "What is it, my son?" He answered, "I want to see what my hereafter looks like; I have murdered ninety-nine people."

The Imām was afraid of the villain and said (to evade the answer), "My son, you should thrust your staff into the cemetery (grounds); if it turns green, then Allah knows of your behavior. He took his staff and went to the cemetery in order to put it (there). He found someone there who was digging up a corpse to raise it out of the grave. Yet concerning the deceased, Our Lord (Allah) had brought her spirit down to her so that she could defend herself. Only her mouth could not speak. The villain approached the scuffle and said to the person, "Come out of there!" And as he was coming out, the villain killed him, and the spirit of the deceased went to Our Lord. Then he buried the deceased and (also) the person he had killed (but) in a different place. Whereupon, he thrust his staff into the earth covering he grave of the woman and went home.

Early the (next) morning, he went, saw the staff he had thrust into (the earth by) the grave and found in its place a plant that had turned green. He was astonished, went to the Imām and said, "Oh, sir, come see the staff." The Imām went and saw it. He asked him, "Oh, my son, what did you do last night?" He answered, "I had killed ninety-nine persons, and last night I completed one hundred." And he told him the story of the woman. The Imām then said to him, "My son, Allah has forgiven you your sins because you protected this woman."

II

Specific Section

DESCRIPTION OF MOUNT CARMEL AND ITS RUINS

This specific section pursues the aim of serving as a guidebook for a visit to Mount Carmel as a secondary purpose without thereby replacing the indispensable native guide. Therefore, the most important paths through which the guide leads one are included in this description of the mountain. The amounts of time noted here have been measured according to the steps of a rusty pedestrian unless nothing else particular is cited, as on the plain where a cart ride is used as a basis.

1. The Stella Maris Monastery[1][2]

The northwestern peak bearing the Stella Maris Monastery (Fig. 12) is the most frequently visited point on the mountain. It is venerated by the native Christians, Jews, and Muslims as a shrine and has been idealized through religious benediction for many European pilgrims.

Even in ancient times, Carmel was considered to be a sacred mountain as, aside from the works of the authors of antiquity, is still evidenced today in the ruins from *a'rāq ez-zīghān* and the previously described holy sites. The people continued to sacrifice on the mountain even in later generations, and Tacitus (*Hist.* II, 78) mentioned that "the

---

1   The historical facts given here were, in part, gathered from Baedeker and Ritter (Palästina III, namely, pp. 705-722), and occasionally from two works published by Carmelites: *"Le sactuaire du Mont-Carmel. Notice historique par le R. P. Julien de Sainte Thérèse,"* Marseille 1876, and *"Le Mont Carmel. Description de la montagne, histoire abrérée des Ermites et du Sanctuaire d Notre Dame du Mont Carmel,"* Franciscan press, Jerusalem, 1890.

2   Translator's note: The Monastery is also often referred to as the Carmelite Monastery.

god of Carmel" issued an oracle in a temenos in which only an altar but neither an image of an idol nor a temple stands.

The Israelites built Yahweh an alter on the mountain during the time of the cult of high places which later fell into ruin (1 Kings, 18:30). Mount Carmel, however, owes its greatest reputation to the prophet Elijah. His struggle with the idolatrous royal house of Omri occurred here and has been immortalized for all time in the account in the first Book of Kings in the Bible. While the miracle of his sacrifice described there has been identified as the *muhraqa* square on the southeastern peak of Mount Carmel by the church, tradition places another portion of the prophet's activity on the northwestern peak near the Monastery. The previously mentioned Cave of Elijah (*el-khadr*) is located at the foot of the latter and is also called the Prophet's School. An additional cave also ascribed to him is hidden under the main alter of the Monastery, and the source of the Spring of Elijah is in the *wādi 'ain es-siāh* not far from here. A grotto above the Cave of Elijah is dedicated to Elisha, Elijah's disciple and successor, who likewise lived on Mount Carmel (2 Kings, 2:25, 4:25). Another grotto nearby has been dedicated to the "children of the prophet."

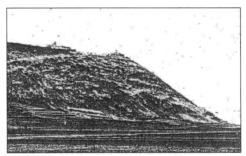

Figure 12. Northwestern peak of Mount Carmel with the Stella Maris Monastery and Lighthouse; *maqām el-khadr* at the foot of the mountain.

Thus, the memory of the mighty prophet is closely bound to Mount Carmel. The Carmelite order traces its founding back to him, and today the entire northeastern peak, as far as the property of the Monastery reaches, is still called *jebel mār iliās* (Mount of the Holy Elijah) in Arabic.

Following the earlier remarks on the holy cult among the Muslim Fellāheen, a few words about the reverence of Elijah among the native Christians shall be permitted. The focal point for the reverence is on Mount Carmel but spreads throughout all of Palestine and Syria, indeed all of Christianity within the Arab world. The Prophet holds the epithet *el-hayy* (the living) because he was taken to the heavens without experiencing death, and he is considered to be, if not one of the most powerful, then certainly one of the most feared of saints. One often hears the affirmation *wahyāt el-'adrā* (by the life of the Holy Virgin) reinforced through the vow *wahyāt mār iliās* (by the life of the Holy Elijah), and this glorious intensification is completely all right as the Virgin, in all her mercy, willingly grants the requested forgiveness which is not to be expected from Elijah, the destroyer of the priests of Ba'al. Herein lies the typical characteristic of the saint. He is the avenger[1]; full of zeal, he punishes wrongs, particularly when his name is needlessly called or his shrine is violated. In the latter instance, he can also be dangerous for Muslims. Volney illustrates this in his work *Etat Politique de l'Egypte* in which he discusses the 1776 death of the Mamluk ruler Mohammed Bey. "The Syrian Christians", he writes, "are convinced that this death was a punishment from the Prophet Elijah whose church he desecrated on Mount Carmel. They

---

1   This popular opinion is expressed in many legends; only those are mentioned here which seek to explain the existence of the earlier listed melon-like crystal geodes by *'ain es-siāh*. Elijah, so the story goes, was strolling through the garden there and requested some of the beautiful fruits, but he was turned away with an explaination from the gardener that what he sees are not fruit but stones. "Well, then," returned the incensed saint. "They shall become stones in reality." From that moment on, the fruits were transformed into stones. – The same version is symbolized through an old painting in a Greek-Uniat church in Beirut. Elijah stands there in a dark cloak with a long beard and sinister features; his left hand seizes the head of a sinner and is cutting his throat with the sword in his right. For the knowledge of this picture, I thank Mr. Georges Dimitri Sursock, the dragoman at the Emperial Consulate in Beirut, who has also imparted much information to me that has been used in this work. It must be added that, according to the customs of religious jurisdiction, it is permitted that the opposing party be requested to swear by the Holy Elijah rather than the common court oath on the Bible before the native priests and bishops. I learned from the other side that a Lebanese immigrant to America recently spent a large sum of money to transport a wooden image of the saint *mār iliās el-hayy* found in *anteliās* near Beirut across the ocean for his pending litigation in New York. – A specific study comparing the relevant opinions with the older and later Jewish traditions about Elijah may reveal the most interesting information.

even say that [Bey] saw the same in the form of an old man many times during his death throes, and that he incessantly called, 'take from me this old man who besieges me and frightens'." The keen observer continues, "If one were to write the (current) history of the Syrian and Egyptian Christians, one would find it just as filled with miracles and phenomena as the past." Under these conditions, it is not surprising that many Christians, from the outset, seek the protection of the powerful saint; it is namely a tradition that the parents praise the prophet at the first hairs of their sons. By doing so, they place the children in his care. Consequently, one lets the hairs grow on the dedicated boys until they are four or five years old; thereupon they are shorn with festive ceremonies which are combined with even greater pomp when it takes place on Mount Carmel.

While we have not learned about the holy site from the late Jewish epoch, the veneration of Elijah drew many believers in the Early Christian period according to church records as the prophet stands in multiple relations to the New Testament, particularly with respect to John the Baptist (Matt. 11:14, 17:12-13). According to tradition, he received revelations from the Mother of God who also appeared to him in the ascending rain clouds after a long drought. The Holy Family is supposed to have rested in the Cave of Elijah during their return from Egypt.

Before long, Mount Carmel was, in effect, a gathering point for pious hermits living in the many caves; a chapel rose by the Elijah Spring. It is reported that Saint Helena erected a church which enclosed an old chapel in 326 AD supposedly near the current monastery. In the beginning of the nineteenth century, numerous Greek inscriptions from this era were found but have, for the most part, now disappeared. The hermits were subjected to the rule of Saint Basil by John II, bishop of Jerusalem, in the year 400.

No information is given to us about Mount Carmel from the following epoch of Islam; the Crusaders reawakened the memory of the holy mountain. After the conquest of the land, the monk Berthold de Malifaye retired here and united the followers of the same faith around him. His successor, Saint Brocard, obtained a rule of sixteen articles from the then Latin Patriarch in Jerusalem, Albert, which was confirmed by Pope Honorius III in 1224. The thus founded order was called *Ordo Beatae Mariae de Monte Carmelo* and soon spread throughout the Holy Land. Their first settlement was located in the valley of *'ain es-siāh* where the ruins of the then constructed St. Brocard Church are still referred to as *ed-dēr* (the church) by the native population. Soon, though, a convent was also to be built near the current Stella Maris Monastery as can be assumed from the ruins found there.[1]

St. Brocard Church was, however, devastated in 1238 by the again advancing Muslims whereby the monks were either butchered or drowned in the pool of the Elijah Spring. The order therefore then began to migrate to Cyprus and later to Europe where they primarily settled in Mediterranean countries and in England. In 1245, the Prior General Simon Stock brought about a reform which was recognized by a bull from Pope Innocent IV. After Saint Louis of France also visited the convent on Mount Carmel in 1254 in order to thank the Mother of God for his rescue from a shipwreck near *haifā*, the building was destroyed in connection with the conquest of *'akkā* by the Mamluks.

As this is not the place to discuss the history of the order in detail, it should simply be mentioned that John Soreth, named General of the Carmelites in 1451, founded a female branch which was reformed by Saint Theresa in 1562. A settlement of female Carmelites, living under the strictest of rules and cut off from the outside world, is located by *haifā* near *rās el-krūm*. This reform, with the collaboration of Saint John of the Cross, also embraced a portion of the monks who now called themselves "Discalced Carmelites" (*Carmes déchaussés*) to differentiate from the previous "Calced Carmelites."

Among the latter, Father Prosper returned to Mount Carmel in 1631 to regain the old home for his order. At that time, a "Prince Tarabé" (possibly the Emir of the Bedouin tribe of the *tarabēn*) was ruling the mountain; after this prince issued an edict dated Jumādā[2]

---

1   This convent was certainly fortified as were all Crusader monestaries as well as the St. Brocard Church. The Arab geographer Yāqūt, who died in 626 Hijra and lived during the Crusades, mentions a castle (*hisn*) on the mountain towering over Haifā in his *mu'jim el-buldān* (*s.v. Kirmilu*). By this, he could only mean the fortified convent as there was no other castle standing in direct proximity to Haifā. He later states that the location was known as under the name mosque (*mesjid*) of *sa'd ed-daula* in the earlier times of Islam; thus, it was considered to be a sanctuary before the time of the Crusades.

2   The works published by the Carmelites do not inform if this took place in the first or the second month of Jumādā. The beginning of the first month of Jumādā fell on the 25th of November, 1631 during the cited year of Hijra.

1041 Hijra (November 1631), Prosper took possession of the Cave of Elijah where he celebrated mass. The new founder of the Monastery permanently established himself in the land in 1634. As he was, however, exposed to much persecution by the Dervish residing by *el-khadr*, he relocated his chapel to the so-called Grotto of the Prophet's Children in 1636. In 1761, the Monastery was destroyed by Dāhir el-'Omar from *'akkā*[1]. Rebuilt on its current location on the mountain due to a royal firman from Constantinople in 1767, the Monastery was pillaged by the Mamluk Mohammed Bey as early as 1775. General Bonaparte used it as a hospital during the siege of *'akkā* in 1799; after his retreat, the remaining patients were massacred by Jezzār Pasha'a troops and the Monastery was ravaged. Father John Baptist came to Mount Carmel in 1816 for the purpose of restoring it, but 'Abdallah Pasha of *'akkā* carried out a complete destruction in 1821 using its bricks for the foundation of a summer residence near the current lighthouse. Equipped with a new decree issued in 1826, Father John Baptist could lay the foundation stone for the current cloister in 1827. He dedicated his life to overcoming the many difficulties that opposed his task. In 1853, the Monastery was completed.

The Monastery is under French protection. The monks here, united under the vicar, who is also the mission's superior, number

---

[1] The most well-known men from *'akkā* during the last century and a half are the Arab Dāhir el-'Omar (1750 – 1776) and the Bosniak Jezzār Pasha (1776 – 1804). Ismā'īl Pasha seized the city after the latter's death and laid siege to the gate of Khaznedar Ibrāhīm Pasha according to orders. After which the city was handed over to Suleimān Pasha (1804 – 1819), a former Mamluk under Jezzār. After his demise, 'Abdallah Pasha, the son of one of Jezzār's mamluks, was named wali to *saidā* with its seat in *'akkā*. His violent rule led to an intervention by Mehemet Ali of Egypt in 1831, whose son Ibrāhīm Pasha conquered *'akkā* in 1832 and took 'Abdallah Pasha captive (according to Volney, Jabarti, Dr. Ibrahim Effendi Nadjar's *misbāh es-sāri*, and Tannūs Schidiāq's *kitāb akhbār el-a'yān fi jebel libnān*). Ibrāhīm Pasha governed Syria with a strong hand in the name of his father, and the country flourished in an extraordinary way. In 1840, he forced the majority of the major Europaen parties to retreat to Egypt whereupon Syria was again taken possession of by the Turkish troops. As a result of the reform work of Sultan 'Abdulmejīd, stricter centralization appeared in the country while the former dictator stood partially in simple nominal subjection to the portal and partially in open revolt against the divan. The Palestinian Fellāheen therefore calculate the effective government of the Ottoman Sultan as first beginning in 1840.

roughly twenty. They exert an extensive hospitality and, in part, occupy themselves with gardening and agriculture. Furthermore, the well-known "Carmelite Spirit", or "Spirit of Melissa," and a first-rate liquor are extracted from the aromatic Carmel herbs. The current superior, Father Cyrillus, is an energetic German.

The major celebrations observed by the order take place on the 14th of June (Feast of Saint Elisha), the 16th of July (Feast of Our Lady of Carmel), and the 20th of July (the major Festival of Elijah).

The extremely strong and imposing monastery building (Fig. 13) at an elevation of 170 m above sea level[1] is a two-story oblong rectangle with a sixty-one-meter-long facade and and is thirty-two and a half meters in depth. A gently ascending carriage path leads directly from the German Colony in *haifā* to here within about a half hour. A church is located in the center of this rectangle. The first floor rooms in the west and south wings are for pilgrims, and the east wing holds a library as well as great halls and the living quarters of the members of the order.

The beautiful church, built in superior Italian Late Renaissance style and with a dome visible from afar, forms a rotunda on the plan of a Greek cross. On the right of the cross ends, an alter to Saint Simon Stock stands; an alter to the patron Saint Joseph stands on the left with a lovely painting that depicts Saint John of the Cross and Saint Theresa. A painted

Figure 13. The Stella Maris Monastery (photo by J. H. Halladjian).

wooden image of Saint Louis is mounted above the confessional box to the left of the door. The elevated choir, at an ascent of twelve steps, supports the massive main alter bedecked with an excellent bas-relief.

---

1   The height indication is taken from Baedeker.

Above this, a marble structure encompasses a statue of the Mother of God between four Corinthian columns in front of a niche. She holds the child Jesus in her left arm and the scepter and the scapular (shoulder dress) of the order in her right. A vestry is attached to the left of the choir, and the chapel of the Saint Joseph containing a wooden statue of Elijah stands to the right. Under the choir, one descends to the grotto dedicated to the prophet where the altar consists of a rock on which, according to tradition, Elijah used to sleep. An old wooden carving of the prophet rises up behind it. The mass is celebrated here; this site is considered to be a shrine for Muslims as well.

From the twenty-meter-high, flat roof of the Monastery one enjoys a splendid view. The blue ocean tide stretches out to the west which is bordered by the beautiful bay of 'akkā and the projecting rās ennāqūra in the north and by the even shore line running against 'aṭlīṭ in the south. The regularly-built German Colony, shaded by trees, and the city of haifā are at the foot of the mountain below while the view curves to the right across Galilee until Mount Hermon.

A garden is located in front of the Monastery in which, among other things, plants are grown which the monks use in preparing the Carmelite spirit. A simple memorial to the butchered patients from Bonaparte's army built in 1876 by Baron Grivel, the commander of the war ship Château Renaud, rises in the middle of the garden.

A terrace joins it on the north side which bears a column with a gilded statue of Our Lady of Carmel. It was donated, as the inscription reads, in 1894 by the Republic of Chili to honor the saint "as patron of the army and special guardian to her domestic herd."

The terrace was closed off during the reconstruction of the former qasr 'abdallāh pāshā, now called "Palais des Arabes," as the lodging house for the Levantine pilgrims.

The lighthouse looking far out into the sea rises behind this. Its white light circles in a period of two minutes.

One reaches the chapel of Saint Simon Stock, which is partially hewn into rock, and the "Grotto of the Prophet's Children" by the descent leading down to el-khadr from the terrace. The chapel of Sacré Coeur lies in a turret beneath the lighthouse; it bears the name mār jiryis (Saint George) in Arabic.

Large commerce buildings stand south of the garden next to the cemetery and the Chapel of Saint Theresa. The Chapel of John the Baptist (mār hanna) is located on the left, slightly secluded. It is to the east on the navigable road which leads over the elevations to the large Carmel road. The Chapel of the *Immaculata Conceptio*, called *tubyānu* by the Arabs, lies nearby.

The new superior let an economy way be laid out which also made it possible for wagons to reach the western coastal plain over *khallet et-tin'ame*. He is in the process of building a better road through the elevations via the just-mentioned navigable way. It would meet up with the large Carmel road. He has, in addition, surrounded the entire monastery region by a wall about nine kilometers in length.

The fields of *haifā* border the monastery region to the west, north, and east, and the German Carmel colony borders it to the south. In addition, it stretches out in a tip emitting southward to the fields of *et-tīre* by *wādi 'l-ghamīq*. The special map of the northwestern end of Mount Carmel offers a survey of this (Table III).

One sees old burial chambers and caves next to the road leading directly to the Monastery buildings from the German Colony in *haifā*; a large quarry lies above it to which the megalithic landmarks of antiquity once found there have fallen victim. The short but deep and fertile *khallet bustān ed-dēr* sinks to the plain between the Monastery and the lighthouse. An additional small valley, *khallet el-yawākhīr* (Valley of Stables), stretches southwards out to the coast where it merges with *wādi 'j-jimāl* running almost parallel to it. Even further south there is a significant ruin called *khirbet et-tin'ame* located on a ridge protruding westward from which, among other things, water installations are still preserved. According to the statements of the Fellāheen, it once reached *tell es-semek*. The *khallet et-tin'ame* is named after this and runs eastwards past an antique grape press against the elevation where it takes on the name *khallet er-rahārīh*. Still further south, one encounters *khallet abu rīsh* with a small offshoot sideward, *khallet es-serj* (Valley of the Saddle). Between *khallet abu rīsh* and the valley parallel in the south, *wādi 't-tatar*, lies the olive tree stand *zeitūnet abu rīsh*. *Wādi 't-tatar* divides nearby. The northern branch, likewise called *khallet es-serj*, reaches the ridge here by the new monastery wall where the road leading to the German Colony makes a sharp curve to the southwest. The main valley ends after a curve to the south near the Karmelheim. Many ancient so-called orthostatic walls run through the terrain north of *wādi 't-tatar*; this land also contains various cisterns of which the opening stands out due to its still well-preserved rendering. Its fine square opening, carefully rounded on the edges stemming from the Roman Period is also striking. The orthostatic walls and memorials found namely between the two in a small valley known as *khallet es-serj* shall be discussed in connection with the similar pre-historic structures of *a'rāq ez-zīghān* in the fourth section.

At last, *wādi 'l-ghamīq* (The Deep Valley) follows southwards and likewise leads up to the Karmelheim. There is still evidence of ruins where it enters the plain; the ruins possibly once stood in relation to *birket ghēṭ*. Until this point and still somewhat further along until *wādi 'ain es-siāh*, the path running along the monastery wall at the foot of the mountain, bending off from *tell es-semek* at the coastal road, is navigable for wagons only in case of emergency.

The Latin rectory in *haifā* maintains the Monastery and has two annexes on Mount Carmel: the old St. Brocard Church[1] and the chapel of the *muhraqa*. The latter will be dealt with in its own individual section (9). The St. Brocard Church, however, shall be immediately discussed because it is in the immediate vicinity of the Monastery although it proves to be an enclave within the region of the village of *et-tīre*.

The Former St. Brocard Church in Wādi 'Ain es-Siāh

Wādi 'ain es-siāh is the valley parallel to *wādi 'l-ghamīq* in the south. It originates in three small ravines south of the Karmelheim and stretches westwards between the *kebābir* in the north and the *fersh iskender* in the south where it forms the highly fertile, well-irrigated valley floor *bostān 'ain es-siāh* before its entrance into the plain. Several, partially half-underground Fellāheen huts stand below this. The small *wādi hayā* (Valley of Life), entering from the northern slope of *fersh iskender*, merges with the valley here.

The most comfortable route there leads directly from the Karmelheim past the houses of *mezra'at el-kebābir* in steep descents to the *'ain es-siāh* spring in a solid half hour. This

---

1 Translator's note: Mülinen refers to this as the St. Margaret Church.

Figure 14. The Spring of Elijah, *'ain es-siāh*.

Figure 15. Ruins of St. Brocard Church.

spring is called "Hermitage Spring[1]" which is considered to be the Spring of Elijah (Fig. 14) by the Christians based on old church traditions. It actually consists of two springs; one spring trickles down through the rock layers from the elevations while the second spouts forth from under the boulders. Their waters run together in a large basin cut into the crag which irrigates the *bostān 'ain es-siāh*.

---

1   The word *sā'ih*, pilgrim, sometimes also hermit or monk, forms the plural *siyyāh*; since the local pronunciation of the Arabic name for the Elijah Spring, strictly speaking, is *siāh* or *siyāh*, it is perhaps the case of a verbal substantive *siāh* in the sense of *siāha* (hermit's life, hermitage) rather than these plural forms. The cave immediately to be mentioned proves the existence of ancient eremite settlements in the valley.

One reaches the site of the St. Brocard Church (Fig. 15), dating from the Middle Ages, by traveling up the valley over several steps carved into the shining white limestone. The castellated ruins bear witness to the former strength of the structure. This site, still called *ed-dēr* (the monastery or cloister), is walled by a new wall. Old boundary walls extend upwards to the west and the east towards *fersh iskender* where they are connected by an old wall which still stands. The order, which administers the region, had built a small chapel here approximately forty years earlier. A wooden statue of Paul the Apostle with sword and book stands on an altar erected on the western side. It is now considered to be an image of Elijah. The spring *'ain umm el-faraj* (The Mother of Liberation Spring) has its source in the rock slightly eastwards; this is prepared as a well (Fig. 16). Various, now partially destroyed caves and an old wine press lie on the slope.

An interesting two-story cave (Fig. 17) is located opposite this on the northern side of the valley. The lower cave, carefully carved out, exhibits several niches as well as mangers dug into the stone. Indeed, once a Greek Lady Chapel, it must have later served as a stable whereas it is now occupied by Fellāheen in the wintertime. From here, one climbs to the upper story by means of a hidden staircase which was protected against attacks through this layout.

Further upwards, the substructures of an old tower which once protected the eastern corner of the monastery region stand where the valley divides. Now a lime oven has found

Figure 16. *'Ain umm el-faraj.*

Figure 17. Two-story cave by *'ain umm el-faraj*.

accommodation therein. One can return to the Karmelheim by taking the ravine on the left.

Figure 18. Coat of Arms of the Stella Maris Monastery.

2. The Northern Slope belonging to the Fields of Haifā

The portion of the fields of *haifā* that come under consideration here stretches out south of the town of *haifā* until the edge of the first northern plateau of the mountain and is bordered by the Monastery region in the west and the fields of the village of *beled esh-shēkh* in the east. The mountain slope was still overgrown with shrubbery and small trees in the time of previous generations; now it has been completely deforested. Yet one is beginning, also on the Arab side, to again submit the land to agriculture by laying out terraces for the purpose of cultivating grapes following the example of the German colonists.

The ancient Cave of Elijah, *maqām el-khadr*, described in the listing of holy shrines, is located near the ocean in the west. It lies at the foot of the mountain beneath the lighthouse. A road constructed by the Germans leads from the colony to the elevation east of the road leading to the Monastery; it winds itself around the building, which has been determined as the grave of the former leader of the Persian Babi sect Beha ullah. The road then surrounds the Monastery region and leads, leaving *fersh es-snōbar* (The Pine Ridge) on the left, to the German Carmel. Three small rivulets sink down to the town *haifā* from the mountain slope; all three are united under the name *wādi 'n-nisnās* (Valley of the Egyptian Mongoose). The *fersh es-snōbar* continues in *qōd umm ez-zbāli* in the east. Two steep footpaths branch off from here; one path leads towards the colony and the other towards *haifā*'s old city. East of the latter, a small depression with a lovely walled-in well spring, the *neba'at el-qazaq* (Spring of the Cossacks), shaded by carob trees, stretches towards the outlet of *wādi rushmia*. One encounters various works by stone carvers in the rock there which hint to previous inhabitation; the arrangement gives the impression of hermit residences. The lower portion of the *wādi rushmia* supplies *haifā* with the majority of its building stones; the Hejaz Railway laid down tracks here for the transport of this material. At this point, *haifā*'s fields follow the projecting *fersh es-sa'ādi* at the foot of which the springs *'ayūn es-sa'ādi* (Springs of Happiness) have their source. The springs are abundant in water but marshy and surrounded by rushes (*si'id*). Above this, one catches sight of the small *khirbet es-sa'ādi* of which only several stone remain can still to be seen. Caves and burial chambers in the rock face, which were recently opened, lie a bit higher in the northwest. This yielded, among other things, a good lead sarcophagus. Ancient orthostatic walls appear nearby as they will be described in the section on *rushmia*. *Fersh abu mudawwar* joins with *fersh as-sa'ādi*; *fersh abu mudawwar* concludes the *rushmia* valley system and runs eastwards to the wild *el-hawwāsa* ravine. The fields of *haifā* end here, and the region of *beled esh-shēkh* begins.

3. The German Carmel

With respect to economics, the so-called German Carmel, namely, deserves special treatment; here the Swabian colonists from *haifā* offer the native population an example of how to regain the mountain's plant culture after centuries of neglect. They achieve this through their rational methods of operation, a ceaseless diligence otherwise unknown to the area, and, specifically, how they have reintroduced viticulture.

The German Vice Consul Mr. Keller, among others, is most deserving of the profit from the establishment. In a process of several years with the Monastery which lays claim to this portion of the mountain without the evidence of a certificate, Keller and fellow settlers successfully contended for the beautiful property. In this, he had the generous aid of a German woman and the firm support of the Imperial Embassy in Constantinople. The Karmelheim (*jebel es-sitt* in Arabic which means The Lady Mountain, Fig. 19) forms the core of the settlement at 290 meters at sea level.[1]

The border of the German property begins at the first northern plateau of Mount Carmel by the newly built wall around the Monastery region and first runs eastwards along the northern slope, *fersh es-snōbar*, until it meets *qōd umm ez-zbāli*. It then descends towards the headwaters of *wādi hajar el-qālib*, encircles *fersh el-bhēri* until the southern fork of *wādi 'l-'ullēq*, and thereafter turns back to the Karmelheim following the Ridge Path. From here, it accompanies the southern border of *wādi 'l-ghamīq* westwards until the point where it touches the Monastery property. At this border, it merges with *wādi 't-tatar*, surrounding its upper portion, in order to head back alongside the Monastery wall to its starting point.

The 4.8-kilometer-long road laid by the Germans leads from the seashore through the colony by *haifā* to the Karmelheim in five quarter hours. After one has overcome the ascent, one sees the first German houses on the plateau which are placed next to each other in individual nascent villas on either side of the street. The Imperial Square (Kaiserplatz) is on the left of *fersh es-snōbar*. The Imperial majesties were led here on the occasion of the Palestinian journey on October 25, 1898 to enjoy the magnificent view of the German colony

---

1   The threshold of the health resort house lies at 290.41 meters above sea level according to the levelling taken for the purpose of this work.

haifā, the bay of *'akkā*, and the Kishon in the Plain of Akko with the Galilaen hill country lying behind it. Lebanon pines have now been planted on the site which has been designated for a community establishment belonging to the Germans of *haifā*. In the northeastern corner of the German area before *qōd umm ez-zbāli*, a summer resort has been built in the German Borromeans' ward in *haifā* for the admission of patients. Nearby, the two footpaths mentioned in the previous section lead down to the old city of *haifā* and the German colony.

Figure 19. The Karmelheim.

Figure 20. The Carmel Hospice Resort (Recreation Home).

After taking a sharp right on the road, one thereupon arrives at the blooming property of the Karmelheim, surrounded by several country houses which adjoin the continuing new settlements. A hotel, now a Christian hospice (Figure 20), and a climatic health resort (Luftkurhaus) which serves as an institution for Germans seeking relaxation stand next to this. A pine plantation belongs to the latter; it received the name "The Empress Augusta Victoria Grove" on the silver wedding anniversary of the Imperial couple on February 27, 1906. Near the hotel, one finds several Roman graves in the upper end of *wādi 't-tatar* and an ancient winepress in the garden of the Karmelheim itself. Recently, a good road, following the southern border of *wādi 't-tatar*, has been built from the Karmelheim to the western coastal plain. From the health resort, the oft-trodden path stretches further south across the ridge of Mount Carmel.

Aside from the fruit and grain commodities, the German Carmel produces an excellent wine which increases in exportation with each year. The German Carmel can look forward to a thriving future as a relaxation and summer resort for the residents of the rapidly growing port town of *haifā* who are joined by visitors from all over Palestine and Egypt.

4. Wādi Rushmia

At not much more than a solid half hour's distance from the Karmelheim, the ruins of the Crusader Castle *rushmia* rise to a dominating elevation in the middle of a large, almost circular hollow which warrants a thorough portrayal, topographically and archeologically, although it belongs to the fields of *beled esh-shēkh*. Five valleys on the Carmel Ridge, springing from gentle slopes which are the sources of several small rivulets, gouge deep, romantic-looking ravines in limestone masses after short distances in order to unite themselves under the name *wādi rushmia* and to cut between two rock reefs in a cannon-like outlet north of the path to the Tel Kishon. A small plateau forms the border of the valley system only in the southeast; this plateau descends towards *beled esh-shēkh*. The names of individual localities do not need to be listed here as they are apparent in the specific map sketch added here (Table II).

A mule path leads from *haifā*, winding around *qōd umm ez-zbāli* and then passing by the valleys *hajar el-qālib* and *wādi 'ain el-ullēq*, to the castle ruins in one and a half hours and from there another half hour to *a'rāq ez-zīghān*. Another mule path crosses the spillway of *wādi rushmia* that enters the plain. It climbs *fersh es-sa'ādi* and likewise reaches *a'rāq ez-zīghān* in two hours. From this point, one can either turn southeast towards *beled es-shēkh* or travel south across *qōd halqat el-kharrūbi* to reach the Carmel Ridge by *minzalet il-būbān*.

The Karmelheim, however, offers the best starting point from where one can choose from three routes. One needs an hour, give or take, to reach the castle when one immediately descends the *el-laghwa* slope and follows the course of the valley until coming across the first of the previously mentioned mule paths from *haifā*. A large fallen block of stone (*hajar el-qālib*), which lent its name to the valley, once stood there; recently, however, it has disappeared since it can be utilized as good meleki rock in the construction of houses. A cave is located here behind a stone hut; nearby, hewn rocks testify to an old settlement, and a *midbise* (winepress) is still preserved. If one follows the mule path coming from *haifā* further and ascends to the *minzalet il-'ayyād*, one soon catches sight of a cave with a niche on the left which may have indeed served the hermits. After one passes by *wādi 'ain el-ullēq* (Blackberry Spring Valley) not far from the spring, one climbs the castle hill leaving behind an additional cave on the left.

Another path merely demands a solid half hour; it leads to *fersh el-bhēri* by following the ridge and, on the other side of this, turns left towards the southern fork of *wādi 'ain el-ulleq*. Crossing over this fork, one finds the small ridge which connects *rushmia* with the Mount Carmel Ridge. This point holds an extremely large number of old oil and winepresses, graves, cisterns, water basins, and caves which give evidence to the region's intensive development in earlier times. Soon after this, one encounters the locality's ruins themselves which were protected by the castle. In recent times these ruins have fallen victim to the nearby lime ovens as well as the increasing cultivation of the land at a rapidly progressing rate. This route is particularly recommended for the return.

The most comfortable route, only slightly longer, leads out, following the ridge road, across *fersh el-bhēri* to a second elevation, *fersh abu hassān*, from which the mule path to *et-tīre* branches off to the right twenty minutes away from the Karmelheim. After crossing this elevation, one has the upper reaches of *wādi rushmia*, *khallet el-a'dām* (Valley of Bones), on the left.

Two parallel rows of piles of stones accompany the ridge route here on the right side. Dr. Schumacher was so kind as to call my attention to these noting that they represent the remains of an ancient, certainly pre-Roman road. I have followed this road and have found them again at many other points on the mountain. It is not the same sight overall. One often finds an enclosure formed by large limestone boulders (Fig. 21), often placed vertically in the ground. These are so-called orthostates, which today still frequently tower more than one meter above the ground. Elsewhere, one sees clearly (Fig. 22)[1] that a wall ran on both sides of the road. Then these walls appear again now as simple stone ramparts, often partially or completely covered by undergrowth. Only a single road boundary remains at many points; at others, the road has completely disappeared and can only be found again by following the more-or-less straight-lined trace left by it. The current industrious cultivation is eliminating this and lets it exist only if the modern-day route runs through it.

From the condition of the points where the road is still best preserved, one can form an image of the appearance of the road before the century-long continuous destruction by weathering and human hand began. On both sides, the walls rose at 1.25 – 1.5 meters thick

Figure 21. Side view of an orthostatic road.

---

1   The wall site in this image seems to have been somewhat restored by the Felläheen a few years ago since it should have served as a terrain border; the superficial restoration has, however, done nothing to blur the character of the wall.

Figure 22. Side wall of the pre-historic road.

and were more than one and a half meters high. These walls were formed by orthostates on both sides; the space in between was filled in with smaller stones. The height measured more than the width at the orthostates; only where the base consisted of a rock slab was it necessary to choose limestone blocks with a larger base. The use of any binding material such as lime cannot be proved in its current weathered condition; traces of carving are as usual not clearly visible. Several overturned stones which have remained intact in their more sheltered position do, however, exhibit strikingly flat surfaces on the wider surfaces that can only be explained by the handiwork of humans. Such a great quantity of naturally smooth-surfaced stones as required for the construction of the walled roads could not have been found. The area between the walls that was the actual road was leveled but not paved. Its width was, on average, six or seven meters; depending on the terrain to which it conformed, it also reached eight meters or was narrowed to five. At individual locations, one finds the same construction with a smaller width of three to four meters. As previously indicated, the trace was often marked out in a straight line. Thus, this was also the case when considerable gradients were to be overcome so that it led remarkably steeply upwards to many elevations. Due to its size and stability, the road may have served as protection for armies passing through; at certain locations where it opened up to possible settlements, it most likely simultaneously functioned as a fortification. At other locations, they are not doubled roads but rather simple boundary walls which illustrate the same orthostatic type. It should not go unmentioned that even today the walls on Mount Carmel are still built in a similar fashion by inserting smaller stones in between two rows of limestone blocks. However, there is a fundamental difference between the old and new walls in that today the blocks are laid horizontally and not placed in the ground orthostatically. The same road construction was already noted at the *ma'īn* ruins in Moab in 1818 by the English travelers Irby and Mangles without, however, mentioning their origins.[1] There is no doubt that the road is pre-Roman and certainly ancient. I will return to discuss the presumed era of this construction at the conclusion of this section; for the time being, it will be referred to as pre-historic.

One branch of this pre-historic road turns into *wādi rushmia* where it, however, soon disappears and is recognizable only at a few points. The main road ascends to *rās el-madābis* whose crest it reaches on the other side of the uppermost end of *wādi 'amr*. The two walls part at this point; one follows the ridge in a straight line, and the other descends at a right angle to the previous direction to the right towards the *es-sahalat* ruin. A settlement may have stood at this point.

Now following the above-mentioned branch and descending to *wādi rushmia*, one catches sight of a large round stone resembling a column drum on the left side of the rivulet after ten minutes. It rises one meter above the ground and has a circumference of one and a half meters. The flattened surface, inclining down towards something near the edge, exhibits an artificial cavity in the center that is roughly twenty centimeters deep and just as wide which is why it is called *hajar el-maqdūh* by the natives. It holds another name, *jurn el-hadd* (Boundary Hollow), among the residents of *et-tīre* due to the circumstances that, in their opinion, their village fields, reaching beyond the ridge here, stretch to this point. In opposition to them, the *es-sahli* family of *beled esh-shēkh* occupies the entire *wādi rushmia* up until the ridge. Despite the occurrence of weathering on the surface, I could discern several primitive sketches of trees as well as

---

1   Compare with Ritter, Palästina I, p. 580, "Soon therafter, a road was found which was not paved with stones like the *viae stratae* of the Romans, but rather only bordered with stones, which seemed to lend it an even older appearance."

a cross potent, or crutch cross ✛, carved into it; the latter, of course, must first date from the Middle Ages. Mr. Oliphant has already

Figure 23. Limestone blocks from the pre-historic road.

Figure 24. Column drum from *khirbet hanna*.

taken note of this stone and raised the question to its intended purpose; he believed it to be an altar. This must be objected to because blood grooves are always dug into a burnt offering altar slab. Such blood grooves are absent here. Also, the column which bears the altar slab does not require a cavity as the blood runs down the outside of the column. An incense altar, as far as we have learned, would furthermore not have reached such significant dimensions if it even was composed of stone. Due to its excessive thickness, it could not have served as one of the three large stones of an oil press, namely *hajar bedd*, *hajar farshi*, or *lekīd*. In addition, the name used by the Fellāheen, *jurn* (drinking trough), does not lead to any information as the cavity is too small and too far from the edge for a drinking trough. I found similar stones by several ruins which undoubtedly date back to the Roman Era; the largest of which is in the *khirbet hanna* which is anticipated here in this illustration (Fig. 24). Both the height and width of the last column drum measure approximately one and a half meters.

Only somewhat further down the valley, on the opposite slope heading south, situated slightly higher, a beautiful ancient burial chamber[1] with a vestibule and three loculi under acrosolia can be seen

---

1   In an effort to simplify the terminology used in the later section of this description of Mount Carmel, the ancient graves found locally in this region will be briefly characterized. According to the language of the native inhabitants, they can be divided into burial chambers, also called tomb chambers (*mughr*, singular *maghāra*, essentially cave), and into *qubūr shemsiyye*, "sunlit," i.e. graves which lie on the surface. The latter are, similar to our graves, buried from above in the surface of the ground but not in the loose dirt but rather in horizontal rock slabs. Their depth is, on average, two to three feet; all remarkably small, they often exhibit a carving for supporting a cover on the upper edge. They are always individual graves which, however, lie next to several others in certain locations; the orientation, even in such gathering places, differs, sometimes east to west, sometimes north to south, and sometimes seemingly in any direction. A *qabr shemsi* of this type is located in the eastern surroundings of *ed-dālie*; it is, however, not in the ground but rather in a massive free-standing stone slab with a raised edge which possibly once held the cover.

The burial chambers were built into vertically sloping rock face and are reachable from the outside through a side entrance. They partly contain single graves or also double graves separated by a narrow, unharnessed space between them on the floor which are designed like the *qubūr shemsiyye*. They often have no lock from the outside; yet its only entryway, usually small, is sometimes high above the earthen ground, and one must climb though it in order to reach the grave below.

In part, they are, however, family tombs. Its arch–shaped grave portal carved into the rock was sealed by a large stone which could be pushed into a hollow on the outer side of the grave in order to open it. In individual cases, one reaches the doors only after descending a vertical shaft. The family graves all contain an empty room with a square floor area in the center, the so-called vestibule; the actual graves lie to the sides of this room. Depending on the type of arrangement of the latter, a further differentiation is made. Long, narrow cavities into which a corpse can be pushed in the rock run out from the floor of the vestibule at right angles to its sides, respectively at acute angels to the corners; one calls these *kōkīm* (Hebrew, sing. *kōkā*) which is usually regarded as Jewish. According to P. Vincent, these date as early as the Maccabean era. One often counts nine *kōkīm* in larger grave chambers; this means three on each side of the vestibule whereas the entrance side remains free of *kōkīm*. The orientation varies but the entrance is frequently on the north side.

If the graves are, however, laid lengthwise parallel to the sides of the vestibule, one speaks of loculi, and the arches carved into the rock above them are referred to as arcosolia. These loculi are either recesses which, like the *qubūr shemsiyye*, descend from the niveau of the vestibule floor into the rock, or they resemble troughs with a front wall rising one half or three-quarters of a meter up from the vestibule floor whereas the back wall and the narrow side walls, sometimes hinting at a border, were built through the vertical rock. One frequently finds three loculi in one chamber; in this case, there is one loculus for each side of the vestibule. It is determined that the construction has Roman origins, particularly when several steps descend from outside towards the chamber portal. The entrance is variably oriented, more often from the north or south than from the east or west. The extremely large number of burial chambers with trough graves ceased to be used for a very long time particularly as the very considerable production costs could only be met by the nobility or the rich. One would not be wrong to assume that these types of graves continued into the Byzantine rule after the Roman Era and extended into the Mediterranean despite the Arab invasion. It can also be learned from further evidence that the Roman culture was still a foundation for private living conditions throughout the centuries.

The graves of the Crusaders' are therefore often difficult to discern from the ancient burial chambers with such trough graves. Frequently, though, two or three troughs lay here under one single arcosolium; the troughs are separated by a narrow corridor and stand at a right angle to the vestibule side. The prevailing orientation of the entryway from the east as well as a further extension of the burial plots in accordance with the higher stature of the corpses to be buried from the members of a larger race can both be viewed as additional characteristics. An unmistakable mark of identification is, nevertheless, simply the Crusader's coat of arms affixed to the cover of the grave.

On Mount Carmel, I did not come across a combination of several graves, accessed through a common front hall, such as an atrium, as occurs in Jerusalem; on the contrary, each has its own special entrance here when several chambers lie in a single face of rock. I did not find grave inscriptions in a small escarpment. Aromatic maidenhair fern (*Adiantum Capillus Venris L.*) runs rampant in this.

After descending the valley in the direction of *'ain rushmia* for seven minutes, one reaches a well, partially carved into the rock and partially walled. Steps lead down to its water level. A trough (*jābi*) for the animals to drink from stands above. The spring has good perennial water but is, however, poorly collected thus a large quantity of water is lost to the ground.

From here, one climbs a short, steep incline to the castle hill. The path, which presents itself as the continuation of the mule path coming from *haifā*, first passes by eight old olive trees and caves inhabited by the Fellāheen locatyed above on the slope.

The knight's castle of Rushmia, with a dominating position that can only be truly appreciated on the spot, forbade the Carmel passage from the western end of the Kishon Plain to the Crusader settlements in *et-tīre* and *'atlīt* during the Middle Ages. It is the first link in a dense chain of castles which, as we will see, guarded the northeastern slope of Mount Carmel. It occupied a significant area with its barbicans and was encircled by wide terraces corresponding to castle grounds known to us in the west. The northernmost barbican where several ruins and cisterns can still be found offers a splendid view into the deep-cut wild valley ravine which holds a massive cave, *maghārat wādi rushmia*, inhabited by goat herders, further to the north.

The once solid castle is in complete agreement with the buildings of *'atlīt* in its construction; smaller stones, clay, and debris for obtaining the necessary wall thickness are embedded in between large, oblong ashlars set in good mortar which cover the walls on both sides. Today only one portion of the donjon still stands as well as the portal to it with a beautiful, unfortunately half-demolished pointed arch with steps

---

anywhere; even sculptures on the grave portals are seldom as Tauruses, or bulls, and bull heads are considered to be heathen, hexagrams Jewish, and the egg-and-dart motif Roman. Individual deviations from the basic type mentioned here will be discussed later. I have distanced myself in the above characterization from the graves of the Israelites, Canaanites, Egyptians, and Stone Age people, known through recent research and discussed clearly in P. Vincent's just published work *Canaan* (1907). These graves, which lie lower in the earth, can only be determined through excavation which was not a viable option for me. Individual caves, which have an air shaft (today called *rōzane*) attached indicating this early time of origin, and several related structures and aspects shall likewise be discussed later.

and embrasures (Figs. 25 and 26). One observes an almost submerged cistern with a double opening next to it. Eastwards, somewhat lower, a large rectangle of stones enveloping a depression is located; it was most likely the dungeon of the tower constructed there. On this spot, as at so many ruins, the lush growth of a fig tree thrives. Northwest from here, in the slope of a terrace, there are burial chambers and caves; above their entrance, there are two gullies gouged in the rock carrying away the rainwater which flows down. The largest of these caves, now often sought out by goat herders, has three entrances and a cover artificially flattened above it. It is called *maghārat esh-shādili* and earned its name from the fact that the members of the religious society of the *shādiliyye* from *haifā* used to hold nightly gatherings here several years ago. In a depression called *khallet et-tīne*, northwest of the castle, Fellāheen have settled in the ruins of a barbican. Ascending from there, one reaches the remains of the locality which lay in the protection of the castle. The multitude of basins and presses which, as already mentioned, covered the entire hill ridge, stretches still further to the northwest.

Even if the majority of clay and glass shards lying around the castle terraces date from the Middle Ages, the settlement must be of a much earlier date. Copper coins point to the Roman Era; finds of silver coins reach back to the Diadochi. The ancestral leader of the *es-sahli* family from *beled esh-shēkh* seems to have distinguished himself in the conquest of *rushmia* by the Mamluks. The recent chief is still in possession of a *hudje*, a certificate of possession, according to which the entire castle region, the so-called *ard rushmia*, was

Figure 25. The knight's castle in *rushmia*.

Figure 26. Portal of the knight's castle in *rushmia*.

handed over to this religiously zealous fighter and his descendents as a *waquf* (family endowment). This region encompasses nearly the entire valley system of *wādi rushmia* and reaches from *a'rāq ez-zīghān* on the slope descending towards *beled esh-shēkh* as far as *khallet esh-shēkh* in the east.

If one wants to hike from the castle to *a'rāq ez-zīghān*, which takes a solid half hour, one returns to the spring from where he follows the mule path eastwards. The latter winds itself past several now disappearing caves or burial chambers around the foot of the *abu suweid* hill (Father of the Blackthorn). Above ancient, narrow garden embankments, the hill provides an area on which a limestone block terrace, four to five feet in height, rises like an island. The peculiar flat spot suggests a sacrificial altar to many visitors; traces of carvings can still be recognized. It has already been mentioned in the geology section that there are small pieces of iron ore scattered in the stone.

The mule path crosses a low col on the other side of the southern *wādi abu suweid* which again exhibits evidence of the trace of the pre-historic road to an experienced eye, which henceforth accompanies us; at this point it passes the *khallet el-ghamīqa* (The Deep Valley) and ascends to an additional col which crosses the *qōd abu mudawwar*. Looking back, one has a view of the small side valley, *rbā' abu basali* (Terrace of the Onion Father), with the double spring *'ain es-suwāniyye* to the southwest. The spring displays the seldom phenomenon that it, flowing only in winter, has also continued throughout the entire summer for the past five years which may be singular in respect to the change of the mountain's water conditions in historical time. On the elevation of the col, one observes several hollows to the left and a *midbise* whereas the northern continuation of *qōd abu mudawwar* accommodates several ruins, supposedly originating from a *muntār* (watchtower), on the peak. On the col, we leave the mule path which leads away to the right, heads to the Karmelheim across the *halqat el-kharrubi* (Carob Tree Circle), and marches straight towards the southwest. We are poised to enter the extensive grounds of the cult site of *a'rāq ez-zīghān*, which has remained unknown until now.

A'rāq ez-zīghān (Crow's Rock) is a rock precipice, twelve to fifteen meters high, in the direction of the North and East (Fig. 27). It is located between the united small valleys

Figure 27. *A'rāq ez-zīghān.*

Figure 28. The niche in *a'rāq ez-zīghān*.

khallet el-bersīm (Myrtle Valley) and *khallet es-serrīsi* (Mastic Valley) in the west and *khallet el-'abhar* (Storax Valley) in the east. The rock gained its name from the crow's nests in its cavities where today other birds of prey have settled. A small plateau stretches out before this; it descends slightly in the direction of *wādi abu mudawwar* in order to rise again slightly on the other side of this towards *fersh abu mudawwar. Khallet es-serrīsi* nearly disappears in this inclined area; it finds its continuation there in the western fork of *wādi abu mudawwar.* Directly opposite *a'rāq ez-zīghān*, the natural, uniquely round-shaped lime hill *tell abu mudawwar* rises. The plain is bordered in the East by the bay of *khallet el-'abhar* which flows into the wild stone ravine *el-hawwāsa* (Turning), the western conclusion to *fersh abu mudawwar.* From the rock face, one observes the Bay of *'akkā* on the other side of *fersh abu mudawwar* and a portion of the Kishon lowland to the North and a still greater area of the plain beyond the dip of the *hawwāsa* in the Northeast. Today a spring does not exist in the nearest surroundings; *'ain es-suwāniyye* lies approximately twelve minutes away. The entire region is now overgrown with undergrowth and is a popular pasture ground among the herders of the Ka'biyye Bedouin tribe.

The area overview is illustrated in the sketch in Figure 29.

A niche is seen in the rock face (Fig. 28) which perhaps originated naturally but has been well-defined by human hands; it is shaped like a parallelogram standing upright with a height of 1.30 meters. The interior walls are only primitively flattened;

a knob in the middle, still evident in photographs, has since been knocked off, possibly by the shepherds. The floor of the niche which stands twenty-three centimeters above the ground has likewise been smoothed by the simplest of methods; this was perhaps achieved by merely rubbing with a hard stone. The niche hollow, measuring only fifteen centimeters at the top, increases towards the bottom where it measures twenty-five centimeters. The width of the hollow also increases from the top (seventy-three centimeters) to the bottom (eighty centimeters). The thus achieved extension of the area in connection with the artificial smoothing suggests the notion that the niche was once designated for holding or storing an item. Its orientation, like

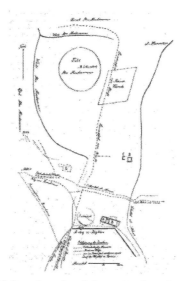

Figure 29. Map sketch of the ruins by *a'rāq ez-zīghān*.

its appearance, has similarities with a Muslim *mihrāb*; it is pointed southwards with a slight deviation of 5° towards the west. Thus, its opening looks out almost directly northwards; the visitor's view, turning his or her back on the opening, is confronted with the peak of *tell abu mudawwar*. The open sea stretches out towards its two sides west of *rās en-nāqūra*.

A large boulder lies at a distance of five meters from the niche though it protrudes at a relative slant; another such boulder lies next to it both to the right and the left. It seems questionable whether these masses fell down from the rock face or whether they represent the remains of a gallery which perhaps once partially concealed the niche.

A cromlech, a circle of stones (Fig. 30), is located fifteen meters from the niche; its larger southern section still survives and often rises up to two feet from the ground whereas the smaller northern half reveals only a few individual ruins. Its dimensions, almost sixty meters in circumference, are much greater than other similar monuments commonly found in the area. It was composed of two rows of massive orthostatic stones which were often one and a half meters wide and three quarters of a meter thick. A path of flat stones leads through the center of the circle; perhaps this is a *via sacralis*.

The ruins of a building (Sketch A) lie east of the cromlech; it consists of two rooms of which the second is again divided. The first room forms a square with thirteen-meter-long sides; the second is nine meters wide and fifteen meters long. The smaller chamber within it measures nine by four meters. The partition between both rooms has a thickness of one and a half meters whereas the chamber wall is one meter thick. The outer wall is equally 1.35 meters thick on every side. Just as the plan of the building was not constructed at perfect right angles, there is no discernable standard principle for the orientation. The western wall points towards the East at 25° rather than directly towards the North. One could call the design, as illustrated in Figure 31, cyclopic or polygonal to use a modern expression. The material used here consists of larger and smaller blocks which are stacked up on large stone block foundations.

Not far from the building's south wall, I found a large stone lying on the ground, measuring 1.63 meters long and sixty centimeters thick which was rounded in the most

Figure 30. Cromlech by *a'rāq ez-zīghān*.

Figure 31. East wall of Building A by *a'rāq ez-zīghān.*

primitive way, apparently without iron tools, and slightly tapered at one end. If this point included a cavity, it can no longer be determined today. On a later visit to the site of the ruins led by Dr. Schumacher, he found an additional building lying directly at the southwestern corner and a stone treated in a very similar fashion (Fig. 32) overgrown with undergrowth which we had then cleared. It seemed to have survived intact as it measures two meters long and sixty-two centimeters thick. I later saw a third similar stone close by; it measures one and half meters long and sixty-three centimeters thick as it suffered more damage from weathering. These stones were undoubtedly meant to be erected; they exhibit an ancient form of steles although already submitted to artificial methods which can be found within the entire Arab region and in Europe all the way to the Atlantic. Commonly called menhir, the stones are frequently referred to with the Biblical term *massēbā* in Palestine.

Adjoining Building A, one sees the ruins of a second larger building with more rooms (Sketch B) already halfway up the slope of *khallet el-'abhar.* The current condition of this building did not permit me to record more accurate measurements without excavating. The purpose of these lines is indeed only the signaling not, however, the scientific investigation of the ruins for which we appeal to the field experts. The design, in general, agrees with that of Building A; only the partial use of larger orthostatic blocks is striking. Figure 33 depicts such a block which has possibly remained from the building's gate. A primitively rounded column like the just-described stele also lies here; next to it, I, however, found two further steles of nearly similar dimensions yet these are carved into squares, and therefore must date from a later era.

Traveling north from here, one crosses a long boundary wall running west to east through the entire plateau in the manner of the earlier illustrated pre-historic road walls; it crosses over the rivulet of the *khallet el-'abhar* and continues eastwards towards *khallet esh-shēkh sahli* as will be read in the section on *beled esh-shēkh*.

Figure 32. Stele on Building A by *a'rāq ez-zīghān*.

Figure 33. Orthostatic block of Building B by *a'rāq ez-zīghān*.

117

Further northwards one encounters two buildings also near *khallet el-'abhar*. The first of these (Sketch C) has been all but destroyed, as seen in Figure 34. Only the foundation walls remain which almost give the impression of natural rock masses and prove to be man-made only upon closer inspection. The other building (Sketch D) is a nineteen meter long

Figure 34. Foundation walls of Building C by *a'rāq ez-zīghān*.

and seventeen-meter-wide square, including the walls, and lies on the slope of the creek bed; it is similar to Building A in its design. It even corresponds with Building A in the thickness of the enclosure walls at 1.35 meters.

Finally, one arrives at a massive four-walled structure in the North; its sides are nearly 190 meters long. I am not clear as to what its purpose was.

Tell abu mudawwar bears a small ruin on its peak; the Bedouins call it *muntār*. The few carved stones that lie around between the jagged lime cliffs do not lead to any conclusions about the former meaning of these ruins. Nevertheless, the location is fitting for a watchtower or a small fortification; the building, however, may have been related to the rock niche which stands opposite it.

Returning from the *tell* to the rock face, one passes by a smaller wall after the four-walled structure which extends to the ruins C and D; then one comes across the large boundary wall which cuts through the entire plateau. If one follows this wall westwards, one reaches a hill with an additional ruin (sketch E). It measures twenty meters on the eastern side; the northern side is thirty meters because another smaller building connects to the main building in the west. Little has been preserved from this building. On the other hand, the position, protected by several walls, seems solid, and, according to the ruins which are several large lime blocks, the construction also has a distinct orthostatic style.

In addition, the hill was surrounded by walls. The rampart forms the already named boundary wall in the south; a wall descends from this on the eastern side towards *wādi abu mudawwar* while another wall likewise descends on the western side ahead on the slope of *qōd abu mudawwar*. Near the corner, which is formed by the latter and the boundary wall which ends here, it meets in an obtuse angle with the pre-historic road coming from *wādi rushmia*. This road loses its southern wall border here; the northern of which, however, continues in the rampart previously referred to as a boundary wall. The southern boundary also appears again far beyond *khallet el-'abhar* in the East.

A cave is located on the slope of *qōd abu mudawwar*; admittedly, the cave has nearly been carried off by stone carvers lately. There are recognizable traces of orthostatic structures underneath this cave. The grounds exhibit an unusual flat area there which extends like a ribbon towards the hill with the ruin E. One can perhaps assume that a road was here which was related to the *via sacralis* of the cromlech.

The constructions of *a'rāq ez-zīghān*, for the most part, have been destroyed while the remaining portions have almost sunken into the ground, and thus have been completely forgotten yet they rebuild themselves before the mental eye of the wayfarer. They were covered by undergrowth, and neither the Fellāheen nor the Bedouins know their names. The native inhabitants refer only to the rock face and not the ruins with the name *a'rāq ez-zīghān*; they do not take notice of the existence of the ruins. Alone my question about the niche is answered as *'alāme* (mark of human hand) by the Bedouins. One gains the best view of the field of ruins from the terrace above the rock face. From here the stones seem to be growing up out of the ground from the viewer's perspective as the passers-by do not see the stones. Thus, one can make out the outline of the building more distinctly.

It has been made clear through the already sketched general outline of the sites that, despite the partial view of the ocean and the Kishon Plain, this can not be considered an actual "height" in the sense of a cult as is the case with the shrine of the *nebi tātā* on the *khushm* which will be described later. On the contrary, the small plateau lies almost half-way up the slope between the plain and the Carmel Ridge, and, furthermore, one needs only a quarter of an hour from the latter to reach the peak of *abu 'n-nida* which offers a lovely panoramic view. It is further noteworthy that there is no sign of graves presented to the traveler limited to observing from the ground and that there is also no spring flowing today in the immediate vicinity. The site cannot ultimately be considered a municipal shrine because the present ruins only come from larger individual scattered buildings, and a village-like settlement seems to be ruled out of the question. At the most, it should be declared that *tell abu mudawwar* or the orthostatic ruin E could have been fortified points. All the aspects which would normally accompany the setting of a cult site are consequently absent. Nevertheless, perhaps precisely with respect to the uniqueness of the site, one would not turn away from the assumption that the site has an exclusively sacral character. The existence of the niche, the cromlech, and the steles seem to warrant this; after this, one is allowed to look into the buildings at the most convenient temple.

One would also not ascribe a very old age to the monuments as with the majority of megalithic and orthostatic witnesses of the past. One can perhaps even distinguish two eras. One could transfer the niche, the cromlech, the orthostatic ruin E, and the round steles to the older era; the more recent would then be represented by the steles carved in squares, the buildings with polygonal style, and the *via sacrilis* of the cromlech. I am authorized to put the decision of the question to a knowledgeable person of to which strata of the pre-Israelite population (the Canaanites, the early Semites, or even their predecessors) the construction of these structures can be attributed. I am, however, permitted to introduce a reason for its pre-Israelite origin supported by my observations made on Mount Carmel. I am adding this indication primarily for the non-experts since, with the darkness which still embeds the ancient Israeli culture, the possibility is not actually ruled out that, also on this point, the Israelites, as in many other respects, had copied the architecture of the former local inhabitants. Thus, it is said of Jacob (Genesis, 28:18 and 35:14) that he set up a massebe (stone pillar) for God in Bethel.

The ruins of *a'rāq ez-zīghān* are in closest connection to the oft-mentioned pre-historic road. Because this not only runs right through the field of ruins, the road is even almost included in the sacral site as the rampart wall of the orthostatic building E where it agrees with one section of the orthostatic design. Thus, one must justify both types of structure as having the same origin. The walled road is no longer discernable not only at many points on Mount Carmel but also on the western coastal plain, e.g. by *khirbet el-khuneizīre* south of *ʿaṯlīṯ*. Because the road is found in Moab, it must have once run through the entire land of Canaan. Works of this kind can not be dated to a temporary conquest by foreign nations; it must have been undertaken by a people permanently settled in the region. When one acknowledges the archaistic construction method, only the Israelites, the Canaanites, or the people displaced by the latter come as such into consideration. According to our recent knowledge, the origin of the walled road can not date back to the Israelite monarchy. On the other hand, it is highly unlikely that such massive structures which include the walled road although one only envisages the remains preserved on Mount Carmel, taking many years, indeed decades, were created in their turbulent reign. Consequently, only the Canaanites and their predecessors remain as the presumable originators of the road. Certain Bible passages are in complete agreement with this; according to the reports from the Book of Numbers 20:17 and 21:22, roads ("king's highway" in the Hebrew text) already existed in the land of Canaan before Joshua's entry. In the connection between the walled road and the ruins of *aʾrāq ez-zīghān*, one would, nonetheless, also see proof of pre-Israelite origins with respect to the latter, just as an archaeologist, whom I led to the site, undoubtedly saw in the general character of the structure. This archaeologist recognized the traces of an ethnic group in the megalithic-orthostatic ruins. This race occupied the region after the Troglodytes but before the Semite immigrants. Systematic excavations on the plateau by Crow's Rock could reveal more noteworthy results since comparatively few monuments of this kind have become known in West Jordan Land until now.

The monuments found in the Monastery region, mainly between the two small valleys called *khallet es-serj*, have one characteristic in absolute agreement with the walled roads; their existence was already indicated in the first section. An orthostatic stone enclosure was kindly brought to my attention by two Beirut professors, P. Ronzevalle and P. Bovier-Lapierre. On a visit to the site near the Monastery taken together with the latter professor we thereupon still found the ruins of a row of buildings which deserve a more precise description. The stone enclosure stood here, where the newly added road from the Monastery to the upper Monastery wall gate meets with the lower *khallet es-serj*; a sketch of the enclosure is shown in Figure 35. Four orthostates, smoothly hewn on their long sides, of different lengths and heights, varying from eighty to ninety centimeters, rise upwards from the ground. The inner room measures 1.10 meters on the south side then the walls diverge slightly towards east and west so that the inner room reaches a width of 1.25 meters at its widest point. It is to be assumed that the walls approach each other again towards the North, and one could give the structure an approximate length of two meters. The orthostates are reminiscent of the well-known dolmen in their arrangement; at that point, it was, however, surrounded by a rampart which consisted of a doubled circular row of large limestone blocks which have now partially disappeared into the ground or been carried away. The rampart had a thickness of 1.75 meters. The work is not executed very exactly, as the varied lengths of the orthostates display; the carving was apparently done without iron tools. The orientation is not accurately directed according to the cardinal points.

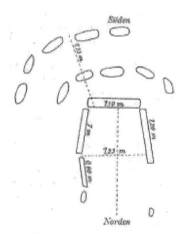

Figure 35. Stone enclosure at *khallet es-serj*.

Returning on a later visit on the path towards the northwest, which shall be replaced by the newly added road, I found the traces of a round tower, five meters in diameter, left of the path. The tower leans against a wall. It is severely damaged so that little can be said about it.

The terrain exhibits many orthostatic walls at this point; the majority of which run north-south and parallel to each other but hereto stand partially at right angles; their orientation is also not exact. At a distance of approximately thirty meters southeastwards, an additional tower, now still rising 1.20 meters, is located; it joins with a wall. Its appearance today is like that of an irregular square: the north side measures eight meters, the east side six and a half meters, the south side seven meters, and the west side again almost six meters. The southwestern corner has been damaged and now seems almost rounded. An entrance formed by orthostates is located on the north side. It is fifty centimeters wide and leads to a pear-shaped inner room hollowed out from the ground plan. The latter is 3.70 meters long and 2.20 meters at the widest point according to my estimates; incidentally, one must remove the fallen masses of ruins in order to obtain more precise results. A wall from the stonework is discernable on the partially uncovered east side of the inner room; the remaining visible portions of the structure consist of orthostatic blocks with smaller stones inserted between them. The inner room is not oriented precisely towards the North; it diverges 15° eastwards lengthwise towards the entrance. The tower walls encircling the inner room are two meters thick east- and westwards but three meters southwards.

Crossing an expanse of an area of twenty-four meters with several rows of stones running north-south through it, one arrives at a round tower southeast-southwards. The tower stands on a wall running east-westwards. It has a diameter of six and a half meters and a wall, two meters thick, built out of three rows of large limestone blocks. This wall likewise encircles a hollowed-out inner room. The latter's entrance does not seem to be on the North side but rather the east side. Lengthwise, the inner room also does not seem to point to the cardinal point; it diverges 25° to the south. On the ruins obstructing the hollow, a four-cornered, smooth-sided stele rests; the stele was carved without the aid of iron tools and seems to be more tapered at one end than at the other. It measures 1.20 meters long, twenty-five centimeters thick, and forty centimeters wide at the widest point. The wall, two meters thick, flanks the tower and meets a rampart in the East; this rampart is three meters wide and stretches out to both sides. It forms the west side of a large square, enclosed by ramparts, measuring sixty-seven meters long by thirty-one meters wide. The area thus enclosed is crossed by five parallel rows of blocks in the direction of north to south. The two outer rows are separated from the ramparts at a distance of seven meters; the three inner rows lie only three meters apart from each other and from the other rows. The pre-historic walled road well-known to us is visible from the other side of the east wall. A lime oven rises further eastwards which may likewise have been an old tower. The entanglement of the wall continues on all sides.

As the means for excavations were not at my disposal, I have distanced myself from making a sketch of this region in order to avoid errors. Though subject to the investigation to be later carried out by experts, it can still, at least, be recognized from what has been said that the terrain bore a settlement. This has been confirmed by the presence of numerous, if however crude, though not to be doubted, flint artifacts[1]. The congruence of the structure located here with the walled road and the ruins of *a'rāq ez-zīghān* illuminates both from the imprecise orientation of the constructions and their orthostatic character as well as the carving of the stones executed without iron tools. We previously saw that the race who built these monuments laid roads and possessed shrines; we will make the observation in the sixth section that their terrace-like vineyards were not unknown; here we encountered one of their settlements protected by broad walls. I have thus accordingly searched for the remains of residences yet did not find any. Perhaps these people lived in tents, branch huts or wooden buildings for which the forests of the mountainous region of that time would have provided sufficient material (compare Joshua 17:15). The just-described round, respectively four-cornered towers and the formerly depicted stone enclosures, which were also encircled by a round stone rampart, could not possibly have served for residential purposes since the extension of the hollow inner room was not sufficient for this. One could easily see these latter constructions better as the graves of chiefs; such a use seems to best correspond to its megalithic character. It is not surprising that they were built above ground, in contrast to the underground burial sites of the autochthonous Troglodytes, and perhaps only contained a substratum buried low in the ground. The Pharaohs of Egypt were also interred in pyramids built above ground. It remains unknown whether these megalithic people used additional graves in pure dolmen conformation

---

1 P. Bovier-Lapierre collected a number of Neolithic weapons here; among these, a handsome little flint hatchet especially aroused the admiration of those surveying his collections. Bovier-Lapierre has already discovered several Stone Age depots in the vicinity of Beirut and has, namely, verified a whole series of tool workshops south of *rās beirūt*.

without a stone rampart aside from these. Most of the monuments in West Jordan Land have been destroyed; to want to make a conclusion about their original nonoccurrence based on the current absence of dolmen would be an argumentum ex silentio.

5. Et-Tīre

a. Field Boundaries. – b. The Western Coastal Plain. – c. The Northern Section of Mount Carmel's Western Slope up to the Village *et-tīre*. – d. The Village *et-tīre*. – e. *Wādi 'ain et-tīre* with its Branches. – f. The *fersh ez-zellāqa* [1]Ridge of Mountains. – *jebel maghārat abu rāshid* [2]and the *lūbie* Ruin. – g. *Wādi missilli*. – h. The Most Southern Portion of the *et-tīre* Region.

By wagon, one and a half hours from *haifā* to the village *et-tīre*; by foot, from the Karmelheim, beginning over the Carmel Ridge, one hour and twenty minutes.

Et-tīre is the most significant community of Mount Carmel, and its region covers a large portion of the mountain as well as the western costal plain. Along with the smaller scattered settlements belonging to it, it counts 2435 residents.

a.   The field of *et-tīre* once stretched from *tell es-semek*[3] in the North up towards *dustrē* and from the ocean in the west until the

---

1   El Salman's note: It is *alzalqa*. It was called *alzalqa* (but pronounced *ez-zalqa* from the verb *zalaq*) as people used to go down from this hill to the ground through a very slippery path. Thus, *zalaqa* means very slippery, so when you travel down this hill, you are likely to slip. My family (El salman) and some people from the Ammoura family lived on this hill. It is located in the southern part of Et-Tire.

2   These caves were named after the surname of the Abu Rashid family who are from Et-Tire (see also El Salman, 1991; Abu rashid, 1993). The Abu Rashid family is known to have so many goats and cows. These caves were used by the Tirawis' families to hide their cows and goats. Another important *maghara* (cave) in et-Tire was named *magharat al Baqarat*. It was used for the same purpose (El Salman, 1991)

3   The assumption may be addressed here that the name of the old town *Sykaminum* has been preserved in the reference "*tell es-semek*" (Fish Hill). The omission of the ending (*inum*) frequently occurs with Greek or Roman

wilderness on the Carmel Ridge (*min il-bahr lil-wa'r*). Once the northern section of the coastal plain was acquired from the people of *haifā*, the border begins at *wādi 'l-ghamīq* today and, circling the *mezra'at el-kebābīr*, reaches the ridge somewhat south of the Karmelheim but excludes the Monastery region in *wādi 'ain es-siāh*. Then running along the ridge, in general, the march bypasses *el-khrēbi* which belongs to *el-yājūr*, turns to the *juneidiyye* southwest of the peak *esh-shēkh jebel*, and then extends across *ard abu mudawwar* and *ard el-mughrāqa* on the upper end of *wādi 'ain abu hadīd* to the course of *wādi felāh*. [1]It also partially encompasses *fersh musakkir bābu* south of the latter and then follows *wādi felāh* up to *dustrē*. The ocean still forms the border in the west.

b.   The coastal plain between the dunes on the seashore and the foot of the mountain is consistently cultivated and, for the most part, bears cereals and legumes, and frequently also sesame. Vegetable gardens have been planted where water is present whereas orchards, frequently olive tree plantations but also carob trees, are located near the mountain. Fig tree orchards are more seldom. *Birket ghēt* is first to be mentioned immediately after passing *wādi 'l-ghamīq* when one, coming from *haifā*, follows the road which stretches along the beach. It is a small, murky pond that is half

---

place names; incidentally, it is a well-known passion of the local residents to Arabize foreign words. Thus, a Franciscan settlement *terra santa* becomes *dēr es-santa* (Santa Monastery), the German male personal name Dück is construed as *dīk* (rooster) and Gottlieb is transformed into a *dīb* (wolf). An occasionally applied means to reach this purpose is shifting the consonants in a syllable, also otherwise commonly occurring in modern Arabic, such as *renjīs* or *jerunjus* for *nerjīs* (narcissus) or *fortēka* for *forkhetta* (fork). The transformation of *Sykam* or *Sikam* to *semek* could just have easily followed as the presence of fish, when it involves a place on the seashore, offers a compellingly obvious association of ideas for the Arabs. The ruins of *tell es-semek* have a very considerable expanse which indicates it was once a larger town, and the many beautiful marble columns found there attest to its period of prosperity. Incidentally, van de Velde has already placed Sykaminum at this location, and de Saulcy proved the identity of Sykaminum with the ruins of *tell es-semek* in his work *"Numismatique de la Terre Sainte"* (*s. v. Sycaminos*) based on the old itineraria.

1   El Salman's note: *Wadi Fallah* is very important in Et-Tire. There were many quaries in this valley. The cartian stones are found in this valley and Tirawis used to extract the cartian stones from this valley (El Salman, 1991: 22).

dried-up in the summer. After crossing *wādi kufr es-sāmir*, one comes across the well, *bīr ebtēne*, where a pathway branches off to the left which leads to the eastern gate of Neuhardthof and further to *et-tīre*. The main road leads past the western side of Neuhardthof, a small Templar colony recently founded in 1898, which bears the name *bāb en-nahr* (River's Gate) in Arabic from the nearby western outflow of *wādi rīshi*. One catches sight of the beautiful Crusader well, *bīr el-kniese* (Fig. 36), with a pumping station hidden in the tower on the beach beyond *shulūl el-wa'āwi* (Jackal Valley) through which *wādi abdallah* flows into the ocean[1]. The well is often visited by herdsmen and is connected to *et-tīre* by a direct route. The hill *khallet 'ali 'z-zīdān* which adjoins it in the south bears the ruins of a knight's settlement, a small fortress, which probably enclosed a church as the name *el-kniese* [2](the small church) seems to imply. It measures 150 meters from the north to the south and seventy meters from the east to the west. The majority of the building stones, namely the marble blocks, is cracked and, as I was told, has been transported to *haifā* not long ago. I was also shown the location of the gate at the

Figure 36. The Crusader Well, *bīr el-kneise.*

---

1   El Salman's note: Mülinen used the word ocean instead of the sea (the Mediterranean). The people of the area use the word "sea" and never used the word ocean.

2   El Salman's note: *kniese* is the diminutive of *kanisa* (church). It is said that it was abandoned when the people converted to Islam (Abu Rashid, 1993:17).

southwestern corner which has disappeared. Nonetheless, several round columns and a square column pedestal are still preserved on the surface, and, aside from this, the debris may hide much more. One observes a plastered stone hollow that is twelve meters deep next to a cistern; many castle ruins contain such a structure which the Felläheen commonly call *sīh*. Whereas the walls of these underground basin-rooms otherwise fall vertically, the basin in this case expands downwards. The people of *et-tīre* give this special construction the name *el-habs* (the jail). As with most knight's castles, graves lie outside of the fortress wall on the southern continuation of the dunes. Smaller individual open basins are next to the graves. *Wādi 'l-musrāra* attains its connection to the ocean through the break in the dunes, *bāb ej-jurf* (Notch Gate), located to the south not far from here. This *wādi* is the valley's lower course from *et-tīre* and takes its name from *ard el-musrāra* which stretches out between the village and the dunes. *Ard el-musrāra* is a terrain where many small stones (*sarār*) are found. Such sun-bleached groups of stones on the ground always indicate ruins. In fact, aside from ruins, at *ard el-musrāra* one comes across another large column drum furnished with a hole at the top, as described by *wādi rushmia*. After one passes the small dune rise, *tell ʾkhres*, one reaches *mellāha*[1] which is filled with water in the winter. At this point, *wādi missilli* [2]merges with several northern and southern Carmel valleys to flow into the ocean. As the name (*mellāha*, salt production) implies, the people of *et-tīre* fulfill their salt needs here. Up on the dune hill, *tell el-aqra'* (Bald Mountain), visible from afar, one reaches the ancient well *bīr el-bedawiyye* (Well of the Female Bedouin) carved into the rock at the outflow of *wādi ibn esh-shibili* [3]with a new

---

1   El Salman's note: The people of Tirat Haifa (Et-Tire) used to call this area *almalaha* (the land of salt) because they used to make big holes in the ground in order to fill them with seawater. They then let the water sit in there for some time until the water evaporated, leaving the salt in the hole.

2   El Salman's note: Mülinen wrote this word as missile. Indeed, it is pronounced *misslyah*. The last letter is important as it is a word that refers to a feminine noun. (See also El Salman, 1991:9 where the word is written this way in the map of et-Tire before 1948.)

3   El Salman's note: *Al shibli* (pronounced esh-shibili) is a name of a family in et-Tire. This family is a branch of the biggest family in et-Tire known as

pumping station opposite it. The more immediate surroundings of the site deserve to be examined more precisely. Shortly thereafter, one reaches *dustrē* where *wādi felāh* has gouged a path through the dunes that is constantly filled with water. A wagon ride from *haifā* to this point requires one and a half to one and three quarters hours.

c. The western slope of Mount Carmel until *et-tīre* is crossed by numerous valleys and ravines. The declivity, gently sloping westwards, was well cultivated in ancient times and is also used in most recent times for considerable cultivation.

The following valleys are listed from north to south with the hill ridge lying between them: *wādi 'l-ghamīq*; the settlement *mezra'at el-kebābīr*; *wādi 'ain es-siāh* with the southern *wādi hayā* flowing into it; the ridge *fersh iskender*; *wādi kufr es-sāmir* with three larger forks with *fersh ej-jambūr* between the second and third; the small crest *qōd el-khushshe* (Crest of the Small Stone Hut) which ascends to a hill summit, the northern portion of which is called *miqtal abu sakrān* (Site of Murder of *abu sakrān*) while the southern portion is called *dabbet rīshi*; the *qōd el-khushshe* is bordered by the small valley *khalāil es-sa'bi*; the rivulet *khallet abu ghábin* reaches upwards to *miqtal abu sarkān* from the plain; *wādi rīshi* is south of *dabbet rīshi* with two springs and three larger forks, the northernmost of which is referred to as *shulūl er-rīhān*; *wādi 'amr* with three forks; *fersh es-sahalāt* with the *es-sahalāt* ruin and the rock drop *a'rāq el-masālima* projecting towards the plain; the large valley *wādi 'abdallah* [1] with different branches: first the *shulūl hajali* northwards, then *derb es-sahalāt*, southwards *wādi 'n-nezzāze* and *khallet el-mifqa'a* (Discovery Site of the Mushroom); afterwards, the large northerly ravine touching *minzalet hamid* on the Carmel Ridge with the spring *'ain w. 'abdallah*, then two smaller ravines, likewise reaching to the Ridge, with *fersh el-berze*, *fersh abu dīb*, and *fersh 'ali zebin* lying between them, hereupon the large ravine on *rās wādi 'abdallah* opposite *khallet es-serrīsi* which finds its end, and

---

Hamolat Alhamolah to which I myself belong (see also El Salman, 1991: 11; Abu Rashid, 1993:304)

1   El Salman's note: Wadi Abdullah is also called Wadi El-Tire. The people of et-Tire used to take the Sultani stone from this wadi (valley) (El Salman, 1991: 23).

an additional smaller ravine which branches off to the southeast; the wide, round ridge *fersh el-beled* across *et-tīre*, the eastern continuation of which is called *el-mifqa'a*.

From the Karmelheim, one reaches *mezra'at el-kebābīr* in twenty minutes. According to the name, it is a new settlement between lime ovens. Several Fellāheen from *ghazza* [1]settled here in eight small houses thirty years ago; two palm trees stand near by. On the way there one follows the oft-mentioned pre-historic road on the other side of *wādi 'l-ghamīq*. An ancient ruin also stands at the site of the *mezra'a* itself; its name has since been forgotten but large cubic blocks of stone are still visible. A circle of orthostatic blocks with a circumference of five meters is located two hundred meters northwest of the *mezra'a*. The pre-historic road leads northwestwards from here to an orthostatic square, measuring four by five meters, and then descends steeply to *wādi 'l-ghamīq*.

From *mezra'at el-kebābīr*, one looks southwards down upon *wādi 'ain es-siāh* which was discussed at the conclusion of the section on the Stella Maria Monastery. *Fersh iskender* rises on the other side of this.

One needs a short half hour from the Karmelheim to visit *fersh iskender*. This ridge is especially celebrated by pilgrims because they collect the oft-mentioned melon-shaped crystal geodes at the site referred to with the poetical name of "Elijah's Garden." Incidentally, it is crossed by the old orthostatic wall as well as the recent wall, and a wall also borders the Monastery region *ed-dēr* in *wādi 'ain es-siāh* which ascends to the plateau. The foundation walls of the building stand in the middle of the *fersh*; a mostly destroyed wall, several meters wide, descends northeastwards towards *'ain es-siāh*. Directly above the western corner of the Monastery property, I found a small orthostatic building that was comparatively better preserved measuring 2.50 meters long and 1.70 meters deep. The lime blocks used for the walls are still seventy centimeters high; the walls are one meter thick. The entrance opening is in the North and measures a half meter wide. Another orthostatic building stands at the western corner; however, its stones were used in constructing a local Fellāheen house. The western and southern slopes contain good Meleki rock, and the quarry, which

---

1   El Salman's note: This group came from Gazza and belong to the Abu Rashid family as it is said that this family is originally from Gazza (Abu Rashid, 1993: 302).

is often used, illuminates far into the region. Six years ago, this point was declared strategic and seized by the Turkish military treasury.

The extensive ruins of *kufr es-sāmir* lie at the southern foot; this is the once significant place *Castra Samaritorum* which is known in the Talmud under the name of *Castra* as a town of Samaritans and heretics. Aside from several carved-out caves and burial chambers, numerous remains of structures lie on the surface; among them is a water conduit which empties into a spa. I also saw several *midbise*, some of which contained a lovely mosaic floor, and a smaller column drum such as displayed in *wādi rushmia*. The coin and grave finds mostly date from the Roman and Byzantine Imperial periods. Some cut stones are of strikingly crude craftsmanship; individual caves are used today by herdsmen and coal burners from *et-tīre*.

Aside from the beautiful view, the route from Karmelheim to *et-tīre* has little to offer that is worth remarking upon. First following the ridge, one turns right towards *dabbet rīshi* after twenty minutes. The hill ridge is covered with ancient terrace walls like almost all similar places on Mount Carmel; further westwards, somewhat north of the route, the foundation walls of a large building can still be made out on *miqtal abu sakrān*. It was

Figure 37. *A'rāq el-masālima.*

Figure 38. The Village *et-tīre* from the South.

possibly a temple to which one made a pilgrimage upwards from *kufr es-sāmir*. Ascending to *wādi rīshi*, one walks through the olive tree gardens of *et-tīre* which already begin here. A *midbise* stands on the other side of *wādi 'amr* at the foot of the mountain which the local superstitions claim is populated by *jinn*. Soon one catches sight of the imposing castellated rock drop *a'rāq el-masālima*[1] which takes its name from the *muslimāni* family in *et-tīre* (Fig. 37). Large, partially artificially hewn caves offer protection to the herdsmen and their herds during the rain season. On the mountain ridge *fersh es-sahalāt* which connects this protrusion with the Carmel Ridge, after a half-hour ascent one encounters *khirbet es-sahalāt* with a large cistern and ruins of buildings next to a Fellāheen house surrounded by old orchards. However, instead of climbing up this, one passes through the lower reaches of *wādi 'abdullah* and soon arrives at the village of *et-tīre*.

d.   The village *et-tīre* (Fig. 38) is of old origin and is generally constructed with *hajar ramle* (so-called sandstone) from the dunes. It must have played a significant role in the Middle Ages. It was once called *tīret el-lōz* on account of the former almond

---

1   El Salman's note: A'raq almasalma became a'raq abu Hamda after the name of a man from et-Tire called Abu Hamid who owned this land (El Salman, 1991: 7).

tree plantations which gave the prior travelers cause to the most wonderful alteration of a name.

Entering from the North, one passes a Muslim cemetery with the simple *maqām* of *shēkh el-ghureyyib* near a threshing floor. A parallel eastern entrance passing by is more interesting; it lies a bit closer to the foot of *fersh el-beled*. One notices the remains of the pre-historic orthostatic road next to it and a larger number of *midbise* and ancient graves further on. At the point where one reaches the village here, a *dēr kufri* (Church from the Time of the Unbelievers) is supposed to have stood according to the account of the residents. Somewhat westwards, a wall made of large lime blocks built atop smaller blocks extends itself. Dr. Schuhmacher judges that this wall dates from the Canaanite era as it exhibits a later style than the orthostatic or even the essentially cyclopean walls. A small village path beginning there contains a stone slab with the coats of arms of Crusaders (Fig. 39). Still higher up on the mountain, not far from several caves, the domed *maqām* of *shēkh el-khalīl* rises; within the village itself, two additional sacred graves, that of *shēkh rebī'a* and *shēkh idrār*, lie. Likewise on the slope of *fersh el-beled*, still further southwards and in the East of the village, one observes many beautiful *midbise* with deep, in part plastered basins with stairs leading down to them. One of these *midbise* was not a wine press but was intended for the preparation of *dibs* (grape-honey) as proven by the round stone hollow next to the four-cornered *birke* which one calls *bīr el-midbise* in Lebanon. Next to this, one finds two

Figure 39. Stone slab with Crusaders coats of arms in *et-tīre*.

mihrāb-like artificial niches in the crag which, however, point north. Above this point, large caves reach into the mountain; among these, one, called *maghārat esh-shaqīf*, arrests attention. Aside from the side entrance, an air shaft, a so-called *rōzane*, namely leads to it from above. This arrangement is indicative of an ancient grave such as were uncovered in the lowest layers in the most recent Palestinian excavations. In fact, two large earthenware jugs were found there as a credible source informed me. One jar contained a carob fruit kernel while the other, however, contained *tibr* (gold sand) which was cast aside due to lack of knowledge.

Other than the so-called small mosque (*jāmi' es-saghīr*), a former church with its arches still intact lies on the main road running through the village from north to south. It is the Crusader palace (Fig. 40 and 41) which is called *dār ibn esh-shibli* today. It was not constructed as a castle but rather as a city palace; today it still appears solid and stately although only two of the four towers which once formed a large square stand today, one at the northeastern corner and one at the southwestern. The first, nevertheless, supports an Arab structure on the upper level but the latter is still intact. Underneath the lovely dome, it contains the palace chapel on the first floor which is still recognizable as such in its construction and ornamental painting. The joints of the arches form a cross which is accentuated by black hues. Medallions are located next to it; the space in between is

Figure 40. The Crusader Palace in *et-tīre* (Northeast).

decorated with various ornamentation among which are two lilies. A German steam mill has now been added to this tower. The still inhabited section of the palace exhibits rather crude late Arabic adornment in the rooms and on corridor walls. According to an uncertain village tradition, the building was once affiliated with the *el-hāriṭi* Bedouin family which was powerful during the time of feudalism. They held possession of the location before the *el-mādi* family. The Crusader building has perhaps this notion to thank for its preservation.

Figure 41. The Crusader Palace in *et-tīre* (Southwest).

Figure 42. Inscription over the door of the Great Mosque in *et-tīre*.

The great mosque (*jāmi' el-kebīr*) stands next to the palace in the southwest. It is formed by a courtyard with outbuildings and the actual prayer room. Here two marble columns with dark late-Romantic capitals support the ceiling arch. A stairway leads from inside to the flat roof. The following Arabic inscription (Figure 42) can be read above the entrance to the prayer room:

بسم الله	bismi 'l-lāhi
الرحمن الرحيم	'r-rahmāni 'r-rahīm
امر بعمارة هذا	amara bi'imārati hādā
المكان القبارك الامير	'l-makāni 'l-mubāraki 'l-amīru
عساف ابن نمر باي سنه ٩٨٧	'assāfu bnu nimr bāy sanata 987.

"In the name of Allah, the Most Gracious, the Most Merciful. Emīr 'Assāf, son of Nimr Bāy. ordered the construction of this blessed place. In the year 987."

The inscription has been well preserved but is not executed very skillfully. I read the second name in the last line as Nimr but one could also just as easily think of 'Omar[1]. Likewise, the year 687 (1288 A.D) could have been meant rather than 987 (1579 A.D.); the fact that the practice of rendering the date with numerals rather than written-out words was not yet predominant during the era of the Crusades speaks contrary to this version. This practice became common during the Turkish Era. The unartistic style of the script also points to this late period. Bāy is the old Arabic form of writing the Turkish title "Bey." According to tradition, Amīr 'Assāf was a member of the above-mentioned Bedouin family Hāriti.

Apart from this, et-tīre has two zāwie [2]for accommodating travelers and two Quran schools. Several large oil presses in underground caves date from earlier times; here and there, one finds columns with capitals dating from the Middle Ages in houses. The lovely village well, bīr 'ain et-tīre, stands in the East; its water comes in

---

1   El Salman's note: The name is, in fact, Nimr and it is not Omar as Mülinen suggested. I myself heard it from many Tirawis as Nimr. Among those informants was the last mukhtar of Et-Tire who is my uncle, Abdullah El Salman, and whose house is now used as a police station in the center of et-Tire. Abdullah El Salman was born in 1885 and he saw what Mülinen described. As a mukhtar of et-Tire (mukhtar means chosen by the people), he is considered to have the best knowledge about the area.

2   .El Salman's note: zawie means a big house or hall where people who belong to the same group regularly meet. In et-Tire there where two Zawie, and the more well-known of the two was frequented by the Al Bash family (in et-Tire, we use the word family, but it is equal to a clan in the Bedouin traditions).

long, partially underground conduits from the spring *'ain qatf ez-zuhūr.* The oldest village arrangement may be found in the eastern portion of today's village. South of the riverbed, the rocky ridge *dahr en-nawāmīs* (Ridge of Graves) rises there. This ridge contains many rock graves from different periods which are eagerly plundered by the residents. The old castle hill joins this in the East; it will soon be discussed. The numerous grave finds, primarily discharged to tourists in *haifā,* date from the Middle Ages upwards through the Byzantine and Roman periods until the Era of Jewish Kings. A small clay horse, possibly an *ex-voto,* indicates, in Dr. Schuhmacher's estimation, Cyprian origin and, even according to P. Ronzevalle, Mycenaean origin. It may be conclusive for the old age of the settlement.

Characteristic traits of the residents of *et-tīre* (*tīrāwi,* pl. *tayār[i]ni* or *tayárni*) are well-proportioned growth, delicate limbs, and finely-cut facial features; dark hair [1]is predominant among them. The dress, under which the headdress of the woman in particular is striking, has already been described in the General Section in the portion on dress. The residents stand under two officially recognized *mukhtrāe* provided with government seals. In addition, an under-mukhtār (*mukhtār ṯāni*) is associated with them.

The earlier reputation of the people was not a good one as conveyed in the already mentioned adage. Despite their fanaticism, they were considered to be given to consuming alcohol and, furthermore, marauding. They let their friends sell the livestock that they stole in East Jordan Land; for this reason, the spoils of the latter are brought to market in *haifā.* Therefore, one frequently finds individuals among them who have spent a long time in the jail in *'akkā* for stealing or fighting. They are namely averse to military service, and individuals prefer to hide in the many caves of the impassable Carmel ravines for many years. Recently, they, however, seem to have improved these conditions. At least, I did not hear too many complaints from

---

1   El Salman's note: There were, in fact, many families in et-Tire, among whom are AAloh, Hajiir, Bakiir and Amoura, who are known as fair-skinned and have blond and brown hair. In the Al Hamola family, there are branches that are so fair-skinned with red hair that they are called "Dar Al 'asal" (the honey house). I belong to the Al Hamola family which is known to be the largest family (El Salman, 1991, Abu Rashid, 1993, Al Bash, 2001), and all the branches that belong to this large tribe are known to be very fair-skinned with blond or brown hair.

the German settlers who acquired possession of the village fields and employed the Fellāheen as workers. The villagers are moving to *haifā* in increasing numbers where they earn as day workers.

e. The elongated valley of *et-tīre* has an outlet through the coastal plain which is called *wādi 'l-musrāra*. The valley itself is called *wādi 'ain et-tīre* in the vicinity of the village and, abbreviated, *wādi 'l-'aēn*. In its upper course, it takes on the names *wādi a'rāq el-ihmar* and *wādi 'l-murrān*. As *wādi 'l-'aēn*, it is a small, yet very fertile lowland and was once planted with almond trees through which *et-tīre* bears its name *tīret el-lōz*[1]. Further up, it becomes a narrow, jagged ravine in which the path to the valley bed still extends only sporadically. The torrent has gouged deep holes (*ghadīr, jurfet mōy*) in the rock in several places. Lime blocks still lie in these holes which, grasped by vortices, produce the moulin-like cavities. An especially interesting place of this kind where a row of such formations stretches out bears the poetic name *qudrān el-qashshū'*, Kettle of the Forlorn Orphan Boy, which one compares to our German term "Fündling" (foundling). This place is difficult to traverse and lies west of the mouth of *wādi 'l-muntār* off the path which will pursue the tour following later. The narrow southern parallel valley *wādi abu jā'*, which climbs to the elevations after a short lowering in the East, merges with the valley of *et-tīre* below the village in order to extend there in a low depression until *khirbet lūbie*.

On the northern side, south of *fersh el-beled* and its eastern continuation, the *mifqa'a*, two smaller notches, *karm abu hassān* and *khallet abu hassān*, open up, then the side valley, where the spring *'ain qatf ez-zuhūr* lies, and which above is called *wādi 'l-qasab* (Reed Valley) above. The latter contains an additional spring *'ain el-qasab*, reaches eastwards until *rās el-muhellil* on *rās abu 'n-nida*, and acquires two smaller ravines northwards, east of *shulūl khālid*. The rock ridge

---

1   El Salman's note: Though it is true that et-Tire was once called Tirat el-Loz, the most well-known and most commonly used name is "Tirat Hiafa" as it was very close to Haifa, almost 7 kilometers (El Salman, 1991). Thus, the Diwan (the big house or court where Tirawis regularly meet) of the Tirawis which is now in the city of Irbid (Jordan) is called Diwan Tirat Haifa.

north of the latter is called *fersh dār kāid*. Still from the North, *wādi 'l-muntār* (so called because of a supposed watchtower ruin located in its branches) empties thereupon in the valley with several ravines. The westernmost of these, *khallet en-nahle* (Valley of the Bees), is bordered in the northwest by *fersh[1] en-nahle* which follows *fersh dār kāid*; the three middle ravines reaching towards the Carmel Ridge Road do not bear any particular names whereas a smaller eastern ravine is called *khallet il-musrāra*. Eastwards on from the mouth of *wādi 'l-muntār*, the valley of *et-tīre* is accompanied for a stretch in the North by a high rock face *a'rāq el-ihmar* (The Red Rock Cliff) with several caves which lends the name *wādi a'rāq el-ihmar* to the valley here.

The valley is bordered on the southern side first by *dahr en-nawāmīs* and the higher adjoining *safḥat esh-shēkh 'slīmān* which is separated from the imposing rock face *a'rāq esh-shēkh* by a short, shallow depression. This rock face continues eastwards in *a'rāq er-rāhib* which lies opposite *a'rāq el-ihmar*. East of *a'rāq er-rāhib*, a branch of the valley, *wādi 'l-khalāil*, turns towards the south. It sends a ravine up to *khirbet lūbie* westwards and *wādi abu mudawwar* to *ard abu mudawwar* eastwards. Three small rivulets *ashālīl et-trābi* (Small Vallay of the Earth) flow into the latter whereas the middle branch of *wādi 'l-khalāil* finds its end southwards in *ard el-mughrāqa* (The Sinking Ground).

East of the two rock walls *a'rāq el-ihmar* and *a'rāq er-rāhib*, the valley of *et-tīre* first extends in a straight line as a narrow ravine, now called *wādi 'l-murrān* (Laurustinus Valley); northwards, the rock face *a'rāq 'ishsh esh-shūha* (Vulture's Nest Rock) rises above this with interesting caves. After a short distance, the ravine separates: *wādi 'l-murrān* extends further eastwards, *wādi abu khammāsha* flows in from the Northeast. The last-mentioned *wādi* combines six small valleys which come partially from the Carmel Ridge northwards and partially from *juneidiyye* from the East; they are *khallet el-mihdib*, *khallet maghārat el-khrēbi* or, abbreviated, *khallet el-maghāra*, *khallet el-khrēbi*, *hawākīr umm el-hīrān* as well as *khallet er-rīhān* and *shulūl en-nimri* which gains the small *khallet el-bersīm*. Two additional small rivulets, *khallet er-ruhrāh* and *shulūl el-'abhar*, merge with *wādi abu*

---

1   El Salman's note: *Farsh* is a word used to describe the summit of a hill or mountain where the ground is flat enough to live and build on. So we have, for example, *Farsh Al Zalqa* (pronuounced *fersh ez-zellāqa*) where my family used to live before they were forced to immigrate in 1948.

khammāsha from the southeast not far from the spring *'ain wādi abu khammāsha.*

Wādi 'l-murrān continues its course eastwards and is strengthened shortly thereafter by *wādi 'l-qil' el-gharbi* (the western *wādi 'l-qil'*) which enters from the North and comes from the *juneidiyye.* It sends out a side-branch northwards and splits at the *juneidiyye.* Now *wādi 'l-murrān* is surrounded by two low ridges, *wāsit trābe* in the south and *wāsit hukrish* in the North from where the spring *'ain hukrish* originates. Further eastwards, the mountain comes close to the creek bed on both sides, forming a rock portal. One finds *a'rāq khallet et-tūti* connecting with *wāsit trābe* southwards and the rock protrusion with the cave *maghārat el-glīkh* northwards. A path leads from *el-khrēbi* towards *esh-shellāle* across this rock portal.

On the other side, that is, east of the rock portal, *khallet ed-dāmūn* extends southwards past the *maghārat ed-dāmūn* to the large ruins of *khirbet ed-dawāmin.* From the North, first *wādi 'l-qil' esh-sharqi* (the eastern *wādi 'l-qil'*), then the small *khallet el-hūti* (Ravine of the Cleft), and finally three small valleys, *ashālīl zeibaq,* flow into *wādi 'l-murrān.* The middle of these three small valleys contains a winter spring and reaches up to the Carmel Ridge. *Wādi 'l-murrān* ends in the East under the name *khallet abu 'īsā* by *khibet el-matāmīr* which joins with *rās jibb 'usufia.*

The southern parallel valley of the valley of *et-tīre, wādi abu jā',* is bordered in the south by the ridge of mountains *fersh ez-zellāqa* and in the North, however, first by *dahr en-nawāmīs* and then by *safhat esh-shēkh 'slīmān.* Opposite the latter, the small valley *wādi 'd-derej* branches off; it is so named because the natural recesses of the creek bed look like steps above which the rugged natural rock group *qal'at mas'ūd* rises in the east. Southeast of *safhat esh-shēkh 'slīmān, wādi abu jā'* climbs the elevations. On the western edge it stops in a shallow notch as it extends eastwards over *a'rāq esh-shēkh* and *a'rāq er-rāhib* through the rocky terrain called *el-khalāil.* It sends more small branches southwards of which the last, *khallet el-bassūl,* turns towards *khirbet lūbie.*

In order to visit the places of interest in the valley of *et-tīre,* one turns south at the eastern end of the village by the well, crosses over the creek bed and ascends to *dahr en-nawāmīs* and from there to *safhat esh-shēkh 'sīlmān.* This was the old castle hill which is concluded from its position and remains of the fortification. That it was still inhabited during the Middle Ages is recognized through a large plastered cistern and a *sīh*, a deep water basin; the presence of which can be verified at many Crusader castles. Today the hill bears the name of a saint, *slīmān*, whose long, low *maqām* is walled with stone and brushed with clay or mud. Several wooden posts for attaching veils while making vows are fixed in the cracks in the stones at the head end, and a cooking spoon for potential meals for the poor (*tabkha*) is inserted. Next to this one observes a larger watering hole (*bīr*) which is walled at the top. One looks down on the wild small valley *wādi abu jā'* harboring many beautiful fossils to the south and on the insignificant ruins of *mifqa'a* lying opposite this to the north, on the other side of the valley of *et-tīre*.

After a few minutes to the east, the rock face *a'rāq esh-shēkh* can be reached. A rock pillar arches east- and westward there, entwined by yellow blooming *mussēs*, forming a massive portal to a large cave on each side. The eastern cave (Fig. 43) is especially interesting; after a large antechamber one arrives at a hall through a carved portal. From this hall, various holes stretch in into the mountain. One of these is so low that one can only wriggle through by crawling whereupon one again reaches a natural dome in which, according to the impartiings of a credible German visitor, many flint artifacts are to be found. Undoubtedly, the cave served as housing for hermits or Dervishes in earlier times; according to village tradition, it has its name from the previously mentioned *shēkh slīmān*. The imagination of the Fellāheen not only provides the site with apparitions but also with wonders of human architecture. One tells of a hall with a water basin situated in the mountain which is supposed to be surrounded by twelve stone seats. Today large and small birds of prey reside in the crag where herdsmen and their herds have not moved in.

Descending the steep slope, one arrives at the delightful and fertile *wādi 'l-aēn* passing beside carved rocks once used as quarries. On the path leading eastwards, one still recognizes remnants of a road pavement that is possibly of Roman origin. After a quarter of an hour, the small valley with *et-tīre*'s spring opens up; the spring bears the lovely name *'ain qatf ez-zuhūr* (Bouquet Spring). A carefully carved ancient, probably Roman gallery at a length of ten meters leads into the rock to hold the water; an additional gallery extends westwards into the rock. It runs out into an old aqueduct. The latter was half-demolished but was newly built not long ago by the villagers according to the statements of Dr. Schuhmacher. It is partially underground and brings the good and abundantly flowing water to the village well. A second, now shattered water conduit dating from the same ancient period extends upwards in the small valley overgrown with blackberry bushes until the large valley and serves as irrigation there; the water flowing under here trickles freely into the ground. Even today the romantic site, splendid in its lush floral array, is a favored pleasure spot of the Fellāheen, and large goat herds gather almost uninterrupted at this trough. Afterwards they camp in the shade of a great sycamore. The slope opposite consists of the red-yellow formation, *trāb el–merāmīl*, a porous volcanic tuff.

From the spring, one ascends northeastwards to the ruins *khirbet is'ad el-yūsif* which stretches roughly one hundred meters further eastwards and sends its outwork southwards into the valley. Various cisterns, a *kharaze* (an upper stone for an outlet) lying next to one of these cisterns, a *sīh* (water basin), stone door posts, and, further south, a large, circular *jurn* (a boulder carved out for animals to drink from) let one assume in connection with the carving of the stone that we are dealing here with a castle from the Middle Ages. It commanded the eastern entrance to *et-tīre* from a favorable position; the entrance descends from and passes by the Carmel Ridge near *rās abu 'n-nida*. The southernmost outwork, bearing a special

Figure 43. Cave in *a'rāq esh-shēkh*.

Figure 44. Column with notches from *khirbet el-'aēn*.

name today as *khirbet el-'aēn*, hides an upright vertical column in the midst of the stone walls. The column is more than a meter tall and bears four longer, discontinuous notches on its sides (Fig. 44). One comes across this peculiar carving on the columns at most of the ruins of Carmel; incidentally, the respective columns not only date from the Middle Ages but also from antiquity. More details about such notched columns will be found in the eighth section on the Carmel Ridge.

Wandering eastwards, one reaches *wādi el-muntār* (Watchtower Valley). *Khirbet el-muntār* is surrounded by the valley's forks and is located half-way up the Ridge. Although the ruins originate not just from a watchtower but from many buildings, they do not warrant a visit because of the complete destruction. Thus, one should stay in the main valley where one soon arrives at an attractive site. High, craggy rock face constrict the valley here; *a'rāq el-ihmar* (The Red Rock) is in the north, and *a'rāq er-rāhib* (The Monk's Rock) is in the south. The former first contains an easily attainable cave, sought out by the goat herds; a bit further, a row of caves connects with this cave which one penetrates only by climbing vertical walls. The effort of the dizzying tour is, however, greatly rewarded by the view of lovely eremite residences in which they seem to have settled. Well-carved caves with niches served in religious services; the water trickling from the rock into an adjoining cave, which forms small stalactite hollows, tastes only slightly of sodium bicarbonate and provides the necessary refreshment. Via several steps attached to the rock face outside, one can find sleeping quarters situated higher with a stone camp, or storehouse, while a comfortable, lovely carved outer seat awards one a magnificent view down into the valley. Wild bees have made their residence in a hole that lies so high above the caves that human hand can not reach it. The tranquility of the lonely valley is only enlivened by the beating of wings from the *nisr* family nesting further above and sometimes by the short echo (*mujāwabe*) off the opposite-lying rock walls of the resounding call of the herdsmen.

The Muslim tradition ascribes the caves of the still wilder and steeper *a'rāq er-rāhib* to a Christian monk *buhēri*[1] as his residence. Indeed, the name *bhēri* occurs among the Muslim residents of *et-tīre*; because the case here, however, deals with a Christian anchorite, such a name may not come into question. The fanatical Fellāheen would barely have preserved a memory of even the possible monks of the Middle Ages. We are not mistaken that we are dealing here with a localization of the memory of the monk Bahīrā, well-known from the biography of the Arab prophet. His name is linked to many places in the Muslim Orient.

The valley splits east of this rock face. While the main valley, now called *wādi 'l-murrān* (Laurustinus Valley), continues eastwards, *wādi 'l-khalāil* (Valley of the Ravines) extends eastwards while separating the ridge of mountains of *fersh ez-zellāqa* from the foothills of the *esh-shēkh jebel* (One Man's Mountain), located in the East and abundant in cliffs. At the very beginning of this valley, at the foot of *wāsit et-trābe* (Middle of the Ground), I found a beautiful, large *midbise* on the *birke* of which traces of plaster could still be established. A smaller grape press still stands in its immediate vicinity. A jagged rock drop, bearing the name of the lower *qarnīfet el-wāsit* (Tower of the Middle), rises above this. However, the upper *qarnīfet el-wāsit* is still more interesting; it is not far from here and is located higher southwards. In its reefs, I saw a still undisturbed necropolis from the Stone Ages. First, I noticed a split rock slab which contained three artificial holes as can be seen in the added sketch (Fig. 45). The holes are hewn through the rock, apparently without iron tools, under which a cave is located. Westwards of Opening A, located somewhat lower, a side entrance into the cave is affixed, likewise artificially carved, but it is now impassable due to the accumulated soil. Still further

---

1   El Salman's note: Buheri is a name of a branch of the larger family, Al Bash (see also El Salman, 1991:12). Thus, we call this branch Al Buheri Bashia, indicating it is part of this large family (clan). In et-Tire we do not use the word *'ashira* (clan) but *dar* to mean a large family or a clan in this context.

southwards up the valley, a larger niche open towards the western side becomes apparent; next to it is a smaller niche with a double opening, one towards the west and one towards the north. In their style of hollowing-out, both are in accordance with *maghārat es-sammāki* south of *aṯlīṯ*. On the rocks and in its surroundings, one sees several shallow depressions, some goblet-like and some bowl-like, such as those that have been found at several of the oldest burial grounds, e.g. by the rocks at the foot of the Palace of Megiddo. Those are now referred to as *cupulae* (libation goblets); they served the cult of the dead.

According to this, the caves of *qarnīfet el-wāsit* were burial places. According to the prevailing opinion, such caves were used in the most archaic of times by the Troglodytes who reached the inner rooms through a side entrance. In a later era, when progress had already been made in the carving of stones, one found it safer for the peace of the dead to close up the side entrance and to lower to corpses into the caves through the

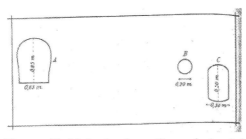

Figure 45. Holes in the ceiling of a burial
cave in the upper *qarnīfet el-wāsit*.

openings which were borne through the ceiling of the cave. These openings could be easily closed by stones laid on top.

While this type of interment leads us back to very early eras, another type of grave, which I found immediately next to the rock slab, thus indicates still more primal relations. They are, namely, not artificial hollows in the ground or in the rock but rather simple, natural cracks in the rock in which the corpse was embedded and covered with a stone slab. What appears very remarkable here is the presence of a *cupula* on the stone slab and larger, bowl-like crevasses in the rock next to it. The existence of an ancestral cult is thus verified for the most primitive periods. Figure 46 shows such a stone slab with a *cupula* that has fallen into the rock cracks next to which the bowl-like depressions are discernable. Several more slabs like this can be seen there; their length varies from sixty centimeters to 1.30 meters. Their width measures forty to fifty centimeters on average, and their thickness measures seven to ten centimeters. I could not research the necropolis further because I abstained from all excavations. – The adjoining regions *wāsit et-trābe* and *ard abu mudawwar* are, for the most part, crossed by the walls of old garden grounds.

Running eastwards on from the outlet of *wādi el-khalāil* in a narrow ravine, *wādi 'l-murrān* is overtaken there in the North by *a'rāq 'ishsh esh-shūha* (Vulture's Nest Rock) which likewise contains interesting caves. Then the valley divides itself anew; the branches of *wādi abu khammāsha*[1] (Valley of the Father of the Female Who Scratches) lead northwards on the Carmel Ridge. Two middle branches extend towards *el-khrēbi*, a branch slightly eastwards and likewise near this point, to the *hawākir umm el-hīrān* (Vegetable Garden of the Mother of Young Camel). The ruins there will be described in Section 8 because they are easier to access from *el-khrēbi*.

One can first follow the creek bed in *wādi 'l-murrān*. It becomes too impassable upon the entrance of *wādi 'l-qil' el-gharbi*, and one climbs up to the elevations slightly to the North. Not far from the path, the spring *'ain hukrish* originates in a small cave; the surroundings are certainly worth researching which, however, is made very difficult by the thick bushes. For a time, the route follows eastwards along the elevation *wāsit hukrish* and then descends again into the valley. One of the most romantic spots on the entire mountain unveils itself to the eyes of the viewer here: the rock portal of *wādi 'l-murrān*. From the north and south, massive stone masses push together between which the torrent forced a passage by leaving deep cavities behind long ago. The jagged mountain *esh-shēkh jebel* (Old Man's Mountain[2]) is in the south;

---

1   El Salman's note: Mülinen's literal translation of *khammasha* does not connote the true meaning here. When a title follows the word *Abu* (father) then it is written in this way. *Khammasha* (scratching) refers to him but not to a female girl who is supposed to be his daughter. To clarify, when we say in Arabic Abu Tawila (the tall man), for example, that does not mean he has a girl who is called Tawila (Tawila litrary means a girl whose name is tawila and tawila means a tall girl). However, when it is preceded by abu, it has the possibility to mean a man who is described to be tall, and it is used humerously.

2   El Salman's note: The correct name here is Jebel El Shekh rather than esh-shekh jebel as Mülinen cited. It is also worth noticing that *el shekh* is pronounced *esh-shekh* as it has what is so called the solar lam, a phoneme that is assimilated to the following esh in Arabic language. In addition,

it sends the wild *a'rāq khallet et-tūti* (Rock of the Mulberry Valley) here. The *juneidiyye* is in the north. A massive boulder with the *maghārat el-glīkh* (Cave of the Bedouin *glīkh*), inhabited by shepherds in the winter, makes itself out to be its foothill. In the middle, one observes the stone groups of the upper *wādi 'l-murrān*, *a'rāq el-qil'*, and *ashālīl zeibaq* (Quicksilver Valleys). Undergrowth of laurustinus, arbutus, laurel,

Figure 46. Grave in rock crack from the upper *qarnīfet el-wāsit*.

Figure 47. Rock Portal of *wādi 'l-murrān*.

the word *el shekh* should not be translated as old man because it could also mean a religious shekh (it is a religious title) and, at the same time, a young person. It could even a be social title, also given to a young person.

summāq, and many smaller bushes cover the valley slopes in the foreground above which the *nisr* nesting in the nearby holes in the rock are almost always hovering. Photography (Fig. 47) is not able to reproduce the powerful view which would be worthy of the paintbrush of a great artist. The site is, incidentally, easy to reach as the path from *el-khrēbi* to *esh-shellāle* passes by here.

This path to *esh-shellāle* shall be briefly described later in Section 10. Here in this section, attention will only be called to a group located not far from it which still belongs to the fields of *et-tīre* and would certainly pique the interest of an archeologist. After scaling the southern rim of *wādi 'l-murrān*, the *wāsit trābe*, one chooses a side path climbing eastwards to the elevation of *esh-shēkh jebel*. After twenty minutes, one has beautiful antique quarries on the left and soon afterwards a *rujm* (stone pile) in front. One still recognizes in this the bulky foundation walls of a tower, forming a square with sides four meters long. It contained an empty inner room, now overgrown with brush, in its center. Opposite the quarries, to the right of the path, an attentive researcher notices a reef on the surface of which a primitive grape press is carved out. Almost all presses still found today in the Carmel region have the construction of two square rock surfaces connected by a conduit which was already described in the first section, part Gc, in the second paragraph. The grapes were stamped on one surface while the liquid running off is filtered on the other. If the set-up should not only be used for the extraction of wine but rather simultaneously for the preparation of grape honey, there is a round stone depression in which the boiled grape honey is filtered again. This type of *midbise* is always in use in South Lebanon as well as in *bilād bshāra*; historically, it can be followed upwards through the Middle Ages until the Byzantine and Roman periods, perhaps even into the Hellenistic Era. The *madabis* of antiquity are characterized by careful and precise stone carving; the best of the Roman Era furnished the walls of the filter basin with a lime finish and the floor frequently with a stone mosaic lining. The preservation of this form is explained in the expediency of the apparatus. This form has endured unaltered over such a long period of time and according to a multitude of specimens numbering in the hundreds is documented alone in the Carmel region. The primitive *midbise* on our rock reef deviates from the described type. Already the attachment of a high stone is something unusual since the later presses were always inset on level ground in the rock; thus, it is not a case of two but rather six rock hollows which together form a chain oriented west-eastwards. The hollows were possibly originally all completely primitively carved without iron tools and only exhibit an artificially smoothed surface of varying size. The first hollow as well as the last three have preserved this characteristic whereas the second and third hollows were rebuilt together in later, perhaps Jewish, times to a proper wine press which, nevertheless, still does not correspond with the classical version. Its *mastabe*, the treading floor, although in the beginning laid out in the shape of a square with 1.25-meter-long sides, is namely not closed by a straight line on the south side but rather by a relatively irregular curve. The slightly smaller square filter basin is deeper and more carefully hewn than the treading floor. The two are connected both by a gutter that is open today and by a conduit in the rock border of the *mastabe* located next to it. We will later meet a very similar occurrence on *shāsh el-qādi* in Section 10.

One does not let the effort of searching further on the split reef of the western slope on *esh-shēkh jebel* discourage oneself. Slightly beneath the *midbise*, one arrives at a square rock carving open to the North with 1.80-meter-long sides; its interior is now partially filled with humus. The south side, which is the most concealed of the sides, is roughly one meter tall and exhibits an artificial niche in the middle. The niche is fifty-five centimeters tall and sixty centimeters wide on the surface. Its walls rise first vertically from the bottom to the top in order to then meet in a pointed-arch at the top. Behind the entrance, the niche widens some and its hollow is rounded. A second niche of the same dimensions stands in the middle on the western side; its top, however, does not form a point but rather runs in the same width as the surface and is only rounded at the upper corners. Without excavating, which would have laid open the floor, I could not determine for what purpose the rock carvings with the niches were used. Thus, the question remains open whether the niches formed entrances to vertical graves, or, what seems more likely to me, whether portable alters were set up before the niches. A similar formation is also present is *esh-shellāle* and will be describe in Section 10. – Standing in front of this rock carving and looking up to the elevation of *esh-shēkh jebel*, one sees several apparently natural niches in the rock as we will later encounter at *bāb et-tantūra*. At an additional, relatively hidden niche which looks like a primitive artificial hollow, stair-like stone carvings are visible. Nearby, there is still another artificial hollow which leads horizontally deep into the smoothed rock face. The western foothills of *esh-shēkh jebel* form a solitary, large, rugged rock pile. A large hollow, only crudely leveled at the bottom, is located on its surface. It is surrounded by broken lime blocks as well as a wall forming three-quarters of a circle. From here, one sees several more deep, very primitively wrought rock hollows with similarly level floors; rough conduits hewn in the stone connecting the hollows prove that they were used as grape presses. Here we have another native type of *midbise* as we have just become acquainted with. The acreage of *wāsit trābe* leaning on *esh-shēkh jebel* was used as vineyards which must have already existed in ancient times as demonstrated by the structural character of the garden walls crossing it. If the vine culture dates from the early period of the orthostatic wall, as will be later introduced in Section 6, one must, nevertheless, assume that grape presses were already carved in stone at this time. The entire region here deserves a thorough investigation by experts whom I would like to advise to use my second guide, Sulaimān Rūhāna, a Christian from *'usufia*, in touring the terrain.

Only a solid half hour from this point, I saw a *midbise* on the western slope of *wādi 'l-khalāil*, westwards, directly opposite the lower *qarnīfet el-wāsit* and above *a'rāq er-rāhib*. This *midbise* is discussed at this point because it depicts the crossover from our primitive grape presses to the later adopted Classical type. The included sketch, kindly drawn by Dr. Schuhmacher, best illustrates its form (Fig. 47a).

A *mastabe* of irregular contours, only two centimeters deep, is located on a larger, gently inclining rock slab which rises from the higher situated terrain by means of a coarsely hewn border: in general, the area is carved as four-cornered and measures 1.22 meters on the western side, 1.61 meters on the northern side, 1.65 meters on the eastern side and, in contrast, two meters on the southern side. Both corners on the southern side are approximate right angles; those on the northern side are clumsily rounded. The surface if the thirty-five-centimeter-deep *birke* is leveled yet it deepens to a cavity for collecting next to the southeastern corner. The side walls are in general vertical but form a ledge protruding by six centimeters at the top with a width of ten centimeters. The carving, apparently executed without iron tools, the imprecise measurements, and the clumsy rounding of the corners executed without the use of an angle measure shift the creation of this grape press to a time long ago.

We will later encounter a *midbise* corresponding in construction and implementation by the ruins of *wādi a'rāq en-nātif* near *umm ez-zeināt*; the latter ruins most likely may date from the pre-Israeli, though possibly from the Canaanite cultural periods.

The wild ravines located behind the rock portal prove less interesting. It should only be mentioned that a grape press is located in the current wilderness at the junction of *ashālīl zeibaq* and *wādi 'l-murrān*. Also, a path leads through the *khallet ed-dāmūn* past the large, inhabited *maghārat ed-dāmūn* on the elevation of the *ed-dawāmīn* ruin which shall be described in the following Section 10.

f.   The *fersh ez-zellāqa* ridge of mountains and the *lūbie* ruin.

The *fersh ez-zellāqa* ridge of mountains which borders the valley of *et-tīre* in the south takes a half hour to climb when coming from the village. The *fersh* juts out further in the North, bearing the shallow depression of *wādi abu jā'* and forms the already mentioned

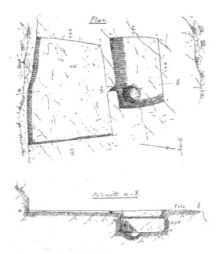

Figure 47a. Grape press above *a'rāq er-rāhib*.

rock precipices *a'rāq esh-shēkh* and *a'rāq er-rāhib*. In the south, it recedes slightly towards the East under the name *harīq el-mu'ammar* (The Built-upon Fire Pit) in order to then lean against *rās missilli* which protrudes afresh to the west. The topographical nomenclature of this group will be immediately listed in the description of *wādi missilli*. The route leads eastwards joined by an old road running next to it towards the cave of *abu rāshid* which gives the mountain the name *jebel maghārat abu rāshid*. One and a half hours after leaving the village, it continues on to the previously unknown *khirbet lūbie* (French bean). The

Figure 48. Roman sculptures from *qubūr el-'arab* by *lūbie*.

position seems to have been created for the edification of a castle or fort; built on a small peak, the ruin looks southwards down into *wādi 'ain abu hadīd* which sends a small ravine upwards to the east as well as to the west. The last offshoot of *wādi abu jā'*, *khallet el-bassūl*, approaches in the north while a small valley similarly rises from *wādi 'l-khalāil* in the west. The ruin covers an area occupying 8000 square meters excluding the outwork pushed very far to the east. The castle wall is still recognizable to the northwest and the west; the gate stood to the right next to its corner. As with many medieval castles, the burial chambers lie westwards and southwestwards outside of the wall. Even the majority of the earthenware shards point to the Middle Ages, possibly to the Crusader period. Dr. Schuhmacher judged there are also pieces of good Roman pottery among these. Somewhat further eastwards there is a site which bears the name *qubūr el-'arab* (Graves of the Bedouins) and was still later used for burying the dead by the Bedouins as evident in the sign of the clan (the so-called *wasm*) carved into the *nasāib*. Here I found a stone slab with handsome, typically Roman sculptures (Fig. 48). This is by far not the only site of this kind. Apart from a *hajar bedd*, a number of sculpted stones are lying around within an, although narrow, extended area which occupies the hill ridge and is encircled by solid walls of large ashlars on both sides of the valley. All of the stones bear a common character as they often reproduce flowers and bead and reel motifs. Some are wall stones; others are columns or column pedestals. Further, a rope-like approach in the boss is noticeable in many of the stones from the arch. No other ruin in the entire Carmel region is so abundant in sculpted decorations; it undoubtedly dates from prosperous Roman times and included a palace or a large villa in addition to a castellated construction. The many cubic *qālāt* (tesserae) lying scattered on the ground as well as the earthenware shards and bricks fit with this assumption. Since I found only one larger cistern here, it can perhaps be supposed that a spring that later disappeared once ran in the upper reaches of *wādi abu hadīd*, in the so-called *'irsh*. The location has apparently not been subsequently overbuilt.

The elevation soon descends to *wādi 'l-khalāil* in the west and to *ard abu mudawwar*; there it merges with the continuation of the elevations of *wādi missilli* which come to an end in *ard el-mughrāqa* (The Sinking Ground, i.e. the marshy area). The mountain rises again towards the east in order to extend between *wādi 'l-murrān* in the north and *wādi felāh* in the south until the Carmel Ridge by *rās jibb 'usufia*. There it forms the massive, wild rock crest *esh-shēkh jebel*; its southwestern branch is called *a'rāq khā'id*. One reaches the elevation *er-ruhrāh* via *khirbet ed-dawāmīn* and *khirbet el-matāmīr* and arrives at *rās ej-jibb* from there.

g. Nearly forty minutes from the *et-tīre* village, one reaches *wādi missilli* by following the foot of the mountain and circumventing *fersh ez-zellāqa*. As already mentioned, the latter forms a receding slope, *harīq el-mu'ammar*, further southwards upon which the mountain again juts forward, however, as *rās missilli*. Three small valleys descend from *harīq el-mu'ammar* to the plain: *shulūl il-merhamiyye* (Sage Valley) in the north, *khallet ez-zeitūn* (Olive Tree Valley) in the middle, and *shulūl il-masri* (Valley of the Egyptians) in the south. The latter of the three continues in a built-up hollow, *el-miflāh*, on the mountain ridge. During the rain season, the waters of these valleys merge with those of *wādi missilli*, *wādi abu taha*, and *wādi abu hasan* in order to flow into the ocean through the *mellāha*.

The path at the foot of the mountain leads through an area that is today also still well-built and, for the most part, planted with olive trees; it must have once been part of a high culture. Coming from *et-tīre*, the traveler, passing by several *jōret milḥ* (salt extraction sites), first comes to an olive tree forest of very old specimens which is called *ard er-rūmi*, i.e. Roman (Byzantine) [1]ground. It is singular that elsewhere on Mount Carmel, similar ancient olive trees are also referred to as *rūmi*. In greater stretches, the ground here contains a vast amount of antique, carefully carved olive and grapes presses furnished with stairs as well as cisterns, graves, and caves. Among the last-mentioned, one cave of large dimensions is known as the Cave of Spirits (*maghārat el-mārid*). *Khirbet missilli* forms the conclusion of these witnesses of the former flourish; it is located at the foot of *rās missilli* and by the entrance to *wādi missilli*. While these ruins most likely stem mainly from the Roman or Byzantine period, a walled well, somewhat westwards on the large path, may date from the Era of the Crusades.

By following the creek bed of *wādi missilli*, which reveals only one wild ravine, one thus reaches the rock face *a'rāq el-bārūd* with two caves after *wādi bīr fadil* flows in from the south after a half hour. The caves are inhabited by Fellāheen in winter. It takes its name from the thick layer of nitrous goat manure covering the cave floor and used by the Fellāheen in the preparation of powder (*bārūd*). The larger cave continues deep into the rock and collapses into larger and smaller hall-like sections which partially exhibit stalactite formations. Climbing upwards from the valley bed which carries the name *wādi 'ain abu hadīd* from here on, one passes *wādi miflih* with *shulūl el-qēqabi* northwards which rises upwards west of *jebel maghārat abu rāshid*. Afterwards, one arrives at the spring *'ain abu hadīd*, a filthy water site, which is surrounded by several carob trees; a short distance further, two small valleys climb up right and left to *khirbet lūbie*. The valley comes to an end under the name *el-'irsh* by *ard el-mughāaqa* which is still assiduously being built.

1　El Salman's note: This does not mean that these olive trees can be traced back to the Roman era. Olive trees do not live more than 200 years. The word is used metaphorically to indicate that these olive trees are very old. Mülinen misunderstood this, and, as a result, he added the word Byzantine, a synonym for Rome although the word Byzantine is not used at all in this context. In other words, olive trees are not referred to as Byzantine olives.

A route leads up from the spring *'ain abu ḥadīd* to the peak *rbā' nāsir* (Terrace of the *nāsir*), a ridge of mountains, which borders *wādi 'ain abu ḥadīd* in the south by beginning in the west at *a'rāq el-bārūd*. It runs to *tell ez-za'rūr* (Hawthorn Hill) opposite the peak under the name *madābi'* (Sites of the Hyenas) and *qutta* in the East. Today the site is tilled; the stones of the ruins were used in building a new small house for Fellāheen although I still observed damaged cistern, several hewn caves, the traces of two buildings, and a large, deep *sīh* (basin). An orthostatic wall is visible next to it, and the remains of the pre-historic road were evident along the way from the spring *'ain abu ḥadīd* to here.

The rise of *rbā' nāsir* descends southwards towards *wādi bīr fadil*; in the upper portion of this, at the foot of the *madābi'*, the *bīr fadil* well is located. It belongs to the *esh-shellāle* region and was already listed in the General Section among the sacred shrines. One descends a rather primitive staircase to the surface of the spring which is considered to be sacred on account of its quality and otherwise blessed attributes. A *jābi*, a trough for the livestock, stands next to it and is also frequented by the wildlife and countless birds. The lower course of the *wādi* extends westwards through a built-up area called *ard el-khuzriqa* where the course creates a barely perceptible notch until it turns northwards towards *wādi missilli*.

From *et-tīre*, one needs one and a half hours to arrive at the spring *'ain abu ḥadīd* and two hours to *bīr fadil*. Upon returning, one can take the route across *harīq el-mu'ammar* [1] leading out of *wādi 'ain abu ḥadīd* through *wādi miflih* and the *miflāh*. A visit to *bīr fadil* can be conveniently combined with a visit to *khirbet yūnis* which will be immediately mentioned.

h. The southernmost portion of the mountain region of *et-tīre* forms a row of wild groups separated by rocky ravines towards the western coastal plain. South of *wādi missilli*, the rock wall *a'rāq el-mintaq* (Rock of the Climb) rises and ends with *wādi abu táhā* in the south; similar to *wādi bīr fadīl*, the latter drains *ard*

---

1 El Salman's note: It is known as Muammar, not al Muammar. Proper names are not followed by definte articles in Arabic unless it is a surname. Muammar is proper name here. It is said that it was land owned by a person called Muammar, and then his land was burnt so the Tirawis started to call that area "hariq (fire) muammar (the burnt land of Muammar)."

el-khuzriqa yet it does not touch on the rising mountain heights further eastwards. Following southwards thereafter, we find *wādi abu hasan* which likewise stretches a short way on the plateau in two smaller branches called *en-nezzāze*. *Wādi ibn esh-shibli*, the southernmost parallel valley lying before *wādi felāh*, takes a similar course though it no longer sends out its waters into the *mellāha* as the former but rather into the ocean at *bīr el-bedawiyye*. *Wādi ibn esh-shibli* finds its source in three ravines in the elevation which collectively bear the name *wādi 'l-khawānīq* (pl. from *khānūq*). The site located slightly lower than their junction is called *'uqdet el-khirwi'* (The Laurel Thicket) and divides into archaeologically interesting hills. The northern hill, *tell el-batta* (Duck Hill), is crowned by an ancient castle site of more significant dimensions which nears the orthostatic constructions in character. The southern hill bears a four-walled structure in ruins with fifteen-meter-long sides which is known under the reference of *qabr el-faras* (Grave of the Mare). It possibly stems from a tower. Not far from here a cistern half-filled with rubble is located; due to its archaistic, irregular square carving with clumsily rounded corners, its opening merits attention. A plateau stretches out above the western slope; its northern section, *ard el-khuzriqa*, has already been mentioned. A bit to the south and situated higher, between the beginning points of *nezzāze* and *wādi ibn esh-shibli*, the *khirbet yūnis* (the Jonah Ruin) stand in the open; aside from piles of rubble, several cisterns, caves, and graves are present. From this ruin, one can access *bīr fadīl* via *fersh es-sīh* or the elevations running eastwards a bit to the south; among these, only *tell ez-za'rūr* will be mentioned. From the latter, one has a lovely view of *wādi felāh* with *esh-shellāle*. Southwest of *khirbet yūnis*, an additional small group of mountains, located on the other side of *wādi felāh* on *fersh musakkir bābu* (the mountain ridge which closes the portal to the *wādi*), belongs to *et-tīre*.

A comfortable route leads along the foot of the mountain south of *khirbet missilli* until after *'ain hōd* which meets *rujūm el-qarānīf* (Stone Piles of the Tower), a small ruin, by *wādi abu tāhā* and the antique *khirbet shīha* by *wādi ibn esh-shibli*. The western adjoining portion of the coastal plain until *wādi felāh* bears the same feature as the portion north of *et-tīre*.

6. Beled esh-Shēkh

From the Karmelheim, two and a half hours across *a'rāq ez-zīghān* by foot; from the German colony at *hafiā*, three-quarters of an hour through the Kishon valley by wagon.

The village field begins in the North by *hawwāsa* where it borders on the region of *haifā*, encircles the valley of *rushmia*, runs along the Carmel Ridge across *rās el-madābis, minzalet hamid, rās wādi 'abdallah*, and *rās abu 'n-nida*, and then descends into *wādi 't-tabl* which forms the border against *el-yājūr*. In addition, it stretches out over a segment of the Kishon plain. The western portion of the fields, i.e. *ard rushmia* until *khallet esh-shēkh*, is *waquf*-property, and the remaining portion belongs to the villages.

East of *a'rāq ez-zīghān, khallet l-'abhar* empties into the *hawwāsa* where it gains two branches of the *khallet esh-shēkh* issuing from four ravines. The short, rocky ravine *el-khānūq* lies south of the *hawwāsa*; south of this, yet north of the village, *khallet esh-shēkh sahili* turns first southwestwards and then northwestwards and there drains two branches of *khallet el-harāmiyye* (Robbers Valley) and two branches of *khallet en-nūriyye* from the south. The mountain ridge, *qōd beled esh-shēkh* or *qōd el-beled*, stretches between *khallet esh-shēkh sahili* and *wādi 't-tabl* sending out three small valleys, *khalāil el-beled*, to the village. Above the village, an olive tree stand, *zeitūnāt es-sa'diyye*, is situated; above this in the northwest, a rock group, *balātat el-mils* (The Smooth Stone), lies.

The path first leads across *khallet el-'abhar* leaving from *a'rāq ez-zīghān* and then across *khallet esh-shēkh*. Where the traveler crosses it, its incision disappears almost completely into the narrow plateau in order to first enter further again into two ravines. The parallel boundary walls of the pre-historic road coming from *wādi rushmia* accompany the path again here; they later disappear anew. Aside from this, one comes across various old garden walls from terrace grounds (*senāsil*) in the region; their existence on the now craggy terrain must evoke our amazement. It provides evidence that in earlier times the cultivation on this site was profitable, and the terrain attained its current appearance only through neglect under the influence of rain showers and weathering. Likewise, its orthostatic design is, however, also worth noting; this lies close to the theory that several peoples of Mount Carmel already submitted to a controlled cultivation in antiquity. Hereto one compares the account from the Book of Numbers in the Bible (22:24-26) according to which vineyards already existed in the region during the time of Balaam. The paths, straitened by the vineyard walls at sections, ran through the region. What is mentioned there, nevertheless, refers to the regions on the other side of the Jordan, east of Moab, yet it can be assumed so much more justifiably that the same is true for the Carmel region which was created by nature for vine cultivation. After one has followed *khallet esh-shēkh sahili* for a stretch, the path turns northwards and then descends northeastwards on a steep path leading down to the plain where one meets the road from *haifā*.

When one, coming from *haifā*, passes the *hawwāsa* on the road leading to Nazareth, one sees shortly thereafter the last parallel, the *khānūq*, a short cut in the rocky slope. Soon afterwards, one reaches the point where the footpath across *a'rāq ez-zīghān* enters the plain. Passing several of the previously mentioned pumping stations, called *shellāf,* one reaches the olive tree forests of the village below which the creek bed of *khallet esh-shēkh sahili* and the humble *maqām* of the village saint next to his grave are barely visible.

The village *beled esh-shēkh* takes its name from the local saint *shēkh 'abdallah es-sahli.* It counts 350 residents (*sahili,* pl. *sahiliyye*) and lies agreeably at the foot of the mountain before the well-cultivated Kishon plain (Fig. 49); it even makes a picturesque impression with the flat-roofed houses built for the summertime and leaf huts (*'arīshi,* pl. *'ursh*) used as sleeping quarters. However, the residents are known to be fanatical, and

Figure 49. View of *beled esh-shēkh* from Mount Carmel.

Figure 50. *Hajar farshe* in the wilderness by *'ain jūbie*.

Europeans can easily expect an inhospitable welcome. Upwards in the village, the mosque stands with, in part, handsome architectonic ornamentation; in its current form it dates from the eighteenth century. It contains the cenotaph of the village saint and the graves of his sons whose descendents still command the village regiment today and own several larger houses near the mosque. In addition to this, the village contains a *menzūl*, e.g. overnight lodging for Muslim travelers, and a Quran school. In the southeast, a well stands by the road and provides the village with good drinking water. Ancient graves lie at the foot of the mountain; they are supposed to have yielded a rich treasure of antiquities. Nearby, the pre-historic walled road is visible at various points.

7. El-Yājūr

One hour by wagon from the German colony *haifā* by way of *beled esh-shēkh*; twenty-five minutes by foot from *beled esh-shēkh*.

Encircling *wādi 't-tabl*, the village field extends out to *rās abu 'n-nida* on the Carmel Ridge where it still takes in *el-khrēbi*. Thereafter it follows the ridge path across *juneidiyye*, leaps by *maghārat 'aqqāra* via *wādi 'aqqāra* and descends north of *dabbāt berjas* to half of the mountain's height. *Dabbāt berjas* accompanies it along *wādi abi hayyi*. Rather than enter the plain with the latter, it passes over the rock ridge which separates the same from *wādi 'sh-shōmariyye*, also jumps over this valley, and descends first on the other side, by the *jurn el-muhādade*, into the lowland. Significant stretches are still part of this in the Kishon plain. The region can thus be divided into three different sections: namely, *wādi 't-tabl* with all its branches, Mount Carmel's steep northeastern descent from *wādi 't-tabl* until *wādi 'sh-shōmariyye*, and the plain. The latter section will be refrained from here as it does not belong to Mount Carmel.

Wādi 't-tabl, bordered in the North by *qōd beled esh-shēkh* and the adjoining *qōd el-harāmiyye*, extends upwards until *rās abu 'n-nida*. There it gains two small valleys, both of which are called *jōret yāsīn*, and *khallet el-khūriyye* (Valley of the Pastor's Wife) east of here. The ravines, now heading southeast, already run into the side valley *wādi 'aqqāra* coming from the East; they separate into two groups. The first group, originating near *el-khrēbi*, consists of six small ravines: namely, *khallet tell el-'ades*, *shulūl shejarāt el-arba'īn*, *shulūl bīr el-khrēbi* (*shulūl el-bīr*), *khallet esh-shīh*, and two ravines called *khallet es-sindyāne*. The second group is made up of *wādi 'ain er-rebī'a* with *khallet ej-juneidiyye* and of *shulūl 'ain el-bēda*. The latter first sends out the small *shulūl maghārat 'aqqāra* next to the cave of *'aqqāra* to the northern slope of the *juneidiyye*; the *shulūl el-qēqāb* follows and then the wide *jibb 'usufia* and *khallet et-tājāt* (Crown Valley) are sent southwards. Finally, it stretches itself southeastwards. While these valleys are concluded south of the Carmel Ridge, the ridge of mountains *dabbāt berjas – jebel 'aqqāra* along with its western continuation, *qōd el-ubweiriyyāt*, encircle the valleys in the North. The steep northwestern descent of *qōd el-ubweiriyyāt* is called *isfāh el-qmēr*.

The *khallet en-nūri* issues from *jebel 'aqqāra* in the North and keeps parallel to *wādi 't-tabl* in the lower reaches.

The small ravine *khallet et-tabāiq* flows down to the village *el-yājūr* on the northeastern slope of Mount Carmel. Further southeast, *khallet idrā' shāhīn* and *wādi abu mustafa* follow this ravine as well as *wādi abu hayyi* and *wādi 'sh-shōmariyye* after *khallet rbā' shtāwi*.

The main valley of the region is *wādi 't-tabl* (Drum Valley), running from the southwest towards the northeast; approximately in the middle of its course, it takes on *wādi 'aqqāra* coming from the East. While the main valley only counts a few side ravines, plenty of smaller and larger valleys flow towards the latter. These valleys are brought together by *jebel 'aqqāra* which protrudes westwards like a bolt and by the adjoining *qōd el-ubweiriyyāt*. As the name of the latter crest implies, the rare, marmot-like rock badgers house themselves in its abundant reefs on the northern side. The northernmost of these valleys finds its origin in the vicinity of the castle ruins *tell el-'ades* (Lentil Hill), the local ruins *el-khrēbi*, and the sacred oak stand *shejarāt el-arba'īn*. These points will be described in the following section as they lie on the Carmel Ridge. From the oak grove, a steep path leads westwards into *wādi 't-tabl* to the filthy spring *'ain jūbie*. Nearby, in the middle of the wilderness, I found the *hajar farshe* (bedstone) of an ancient olive oil mill (Fig. 50). From there, the path continues down the main valley past the lovely spring *'ain el-qasab* (Reed Spring) into the plain that is planted with olive trees. Another path, beginning at *shejarāt el-arba'īn*, first turns eastwards towards *wādi 'ain er-rebī'a* and then northwards into *hāwi 'aqqāra* (the land[1] of *'aqqāra*). Due to its protected location, the site is a gathering point for Bedouin herdsmen in the wintertime; the many graves are evidence that they previously buried their dead there. From here one can either follow the upper course of the valley and arrive at the shrubby spring *'ain er-rebī'a* as well as the large cave *maghārat 'aqqāra* further on. Thereafter one reaches the lovely spring *'ain el-bēda* with the ruin of the same name in the southeast from where one attains the Carmel Ridge through *khallet et-tājāt* (Crown Valley). Or one climbs the descending ridge of *jebel 'aqqāra* northwards. This ridge appears like a corner ledge of Mount Carmel to the hiker coming from the North and bears a path which climbs through *khallet en-nūri* and continues further southeastwards on *dabbāt berjas*; near *qambū'at ed-durziyye*, the path leads to the mule path that guides over the ridge towards *'usufia*. Such a site is particularly favorable for building a castle. Situated half-way up the mountain, one can easily reach the plain from here; aside from the mentioned shortest way from *beled esh-shēkh* towards *'usufia*, this site still commands the entries to *wādi 'aqqāra*, just as *tell el-'ades* dominates *wādi 't-tabl*. Here I actually found a ruin, *khirbet 'aqqāra*, overtaking *hāwi*, which sets its origin in the Middle Ages despite the thorough destruction and the intense weathering of the soft construction blocks. Its expanse measures roughly 200 meters from northwest to southeast but only approximately eighty meters from northeast to southwest. The scattered stones and the ashlars of the foundation wall are, for the most part, of medium size yet one also finds some of more

---

1   The word *hāwi* refers to fertile lowland in which water conjoins; thus, it corresponds, though not etymologically, at least in the usage, to the German locality name "Grund" (land, ground).

substantial volume. Stone door posts on the northeastern corner are still recognizable where the remains of a bastille are also located; in addition, an inner portal lies near the southwestern corner. Burial chambers carved into the rock are placed outside of the enclosure walls at the southeastern corner. To be mentioned among the individual finds are a perforated, T-shaped column, i.e. the *lekīd*-stone of an oil press, and, further south, a large *hajar farshe* (bedstone) with the *hajar bedd* (grindstone) still lying atop it from an oil mill. We will encounter similar vestiges of oil presses by still many ruins undoubtedly dating from the Middle Ages; the style of the wall construction corresponds with this period of origin. Thus, *khirbet 'aqqāra* conforms harmonically to the system of fortifications which crowned Mount Carmel on the northeastern side and led to the strongly protected position of *'usufia*.

We now follow the path leading across *khallet en-nūri* into the plain, and, passing by several stone, red tile-roofed economic rooms of the *el-khūri* family, we arrive at the small village *el-yājūr* after a half hour. It counts 153 residents (*yājūri*, pl. *yājūriyyīn*) and resembles the village *beled esh-shēkh* in its location by a ravine at the foot of a mountain and its array of leaf huts. It does not have a mosque, nor a *menzūl*, yet one is well received by the people, in particular by the *mukhtār shēkh 'abdallah ej-jum'a*. The village field is no longer in possession of the residents who, in fact, still own only their houses; the communal property was bought several years ago by the rich resident of *haifā, selīm el-khūri*, whose heirs efficiently farm the terrain. They have planted a large mulberry plantation on the plain and built facilities for breeding silk worms near the small village. However, a silk spinning mill is not incorporated in this. The small *khirbet et-tabāiq* is located above the village on the ravine of the same name.

The northeastern slope of Mount Carmel, lying south of the village and still considered to be part of it, is an untilled wild mountain slope on which only a few shallow rivulets are apparent until one reaches the outlet of *wādi abu hayyi*. Already issuing from the foot of the mountain, a few minutes south of *el-yājūr*, there are three springs which are called *'ayūn el-bass*[1] by the Fellāheen. *Wādi*

---

1   These springs are known under the names *'ayūn el-werd* in travel literature. This is translated as "Rose Spring". Roses do not bloom at this site but the livestock probably drink from there; the word *werd* is also not translated with the word "rose" but rather "access to the spring." – *Bass* not only means swamp but every ground on which one hits upon groundwater after enough digging.

abu hayyi (Valley of the Snake Father), descending from the western elevations of *dabbāt berjas*, rises its course in a straight line towards *wādi 'sh-shōmariyye* (called *wādi 'sh-shōmara*, Fennel Valley, in *'usufia*). Directly before the site, where it could have entered, it is hindered by a narrow yet rocky crest, which forces the valley to establish an independent connection with the Kishon directly northwards. On the northern border of *wādi abu hayyi* at the height of roughly 100 meters, one sees the ruins of a small settlement; the rock protrusion towers over this with two great caves. The lower cave, *maghārat wādi abu hayyi*, has a significant expanse and is distinguished by long corridors and a high air shaft. The other cave, situated, however, much higher is named *maghārat es-sabra* due to several puny cactus plants and is sometimes frequented by herdsmen. Several minutes above this, one observes the solid foundation walls of a very small ruin, possibly a watchtower. On the narrow space found on the peak, called *rbā' shtāwi*[1], I found a carving in a rock slab on the ground shown in the sketch (Fig. 51). The entire rock slab measures approximately one and a half meters squared; the carving is sixty-two centimeters long. In the image, a pear-shaped illustration with two-centimeter-wide and likewise deep lines is positioned between two circular, cupule-like yet flat holes ten centimeters in diameter. A one and a half centimeter deep, one-centimeter wide line snakes through the pear-shaped image. The contours are too sharply limited and too regular in form to be a simple play of nature; on the other hand, the method of execution is indicative of very primitive tools. An archeaologist, to whom I showed my sketch, has recognized an archaistic sacrificial altar in the rock slab. The investigation of the surroundings revealed nothing notable.

Figure 51

The rocky ridge dividing *wādi abu hayyi* and *wādi 'sh-shōmariyye* bears a small ruin, *khirbet wehb*, on a small plateau protruding northward surround by lushly flourishing *sindyān*, terebinth, and carob trees. The ruin takes its current name from a Druze whose personality we will meet in the description of the village *'usufia*. Among the very

---

1   I was told the previous owner, *shtāwi*, was a Bedouin. He was given his name on account of a heavy rainfall (*shitā*) that occurred at his birth.

solid wall stones thicker than a meter, the orthostatically built portal still towering a half meter is striking; the division into two rooms is still recognizable. The larger of these rooms measures ten by six meters and contains a large stone in the middle, possibly the remnants of a column. Still other walls of cubic carved stones of great dimensions are visible on the slope towards the North. Northeastwards, still further beneath this, the remains of a building also lie. Concluding from the design, the ruin may date from antiquity; the position is admittedly that of a castle yet the type of ruin does not offer cause for such an assumption. Perhaps a temple once stood here to which one made a pilgrimage just ten minutes away from the ancient village at the conclusion of *wādi 'sh-shōmariyye*.

When one circumvents the rocky ridge, one arrives at the outlet of this valley. *Khirbet esh-shōmariyye*, unnoticed until now, lies here, bordered in the south by a portion of the creek bed and crossed in the North by another portion. It measures 300 meters from the south side northwards where an orthostatic wall protects it against the water flowing beneath it, and it measures 200 meters from the west to the east. Over the course of the centuries it suffered from weathering and possibly also from floodings so intense that no traces of carving are visible on most of the stone blocks. Alone the massive blocks used in constructing this suggest the old age of the settlement (Fig. 52). Among these blocks, individual blocks measure more than two meters in length, depth and height. It presented a very lovely view on the winter days I visited it. Fresh green undergrowth strove to rise from the ruins, and countless anemones of all colors as well as white, red and blue cyclamen

Figure 52. *Esh-shōmariyye* ruin.

Figure 53. *Jurn el-muhādade* by *esh-shōmariyye*.

sprouted between the weathered stones. Meanwhile bevies of birds, possibly lapwings or pewits, enlivened the sky, and horses and cows from *el-yājūr* grazed in the adjoining meadows. The dark red rock faces of *wādi 'sh-shōmariyye* formed the background; high above them, a dozen *nisr* circled. Now the ruins are serving the Hejaz railway as quarries.

The field of *el-yājūr* stretches out a brisk walk of several minutes still further southwards. A large hollow, called *jurn el-muhādade* (Boundary Trough, Fig. 53), carved into the rock is located there at the foot of the mountain; it serves as a drinking hole for the livestock.

8. The Carmel Ridge until 'Usufia

Three hours from the Karmelheim to *'usufia*. In order to not go astray, one has to follow the ridge elevation whereby the path branching to the left should be taken in doubtful instances.

The northern and northeastern slopes of Mount Carmel have already been discussed insofar as they are considered to be part of the village fields of *beled esh-shēkh* and *el-yājūr*; the remaining section of the fringe of the mountain shall be described in the following section because it lies on the path to the *muhraqa* leading through the plain. The southern slope has been partially dealt with in the section on *et-tīre*, and it will be partially described as belonging to *wādi felāh*. The description following here can thus be restricted to the Ridge itself and the points located in its immediate vicinity.

Following the ridge path southeastwards from the Karmelheim, one sees the various arms of *wādi kufr es-sāmir* and *wādi rīshi* to the right and several side valleys of *wādi rushmia* which were already listed in the fourth section to the left. After the first half hour, the main valley of *wādi rushmia* opens up towards the North while imparting a lovely view of the castle ruin; the branch leading to *a'rāq ez-zīghān* descends on the pre-historic road here. The ridge path accompanies the pre-historic main road, passing the property of the Fellāheen *ed-duwēri*, climbing slowing towards the elevation of *rās el-madābis* (Peak of the Grape Presses) which also belongs to the affluent widow of Mr. Oliphant in *ed-dālie*. After passing the upper course of *wādi 'amr*, one turns to the right onto a new path which arrives at *et-tīre* via *khirbet es-sahalāt*; it meets with one of the ancient grape presses a few paces after the turn. The press lends this portion of the mountain its name. Rather than pursuing it, one keeps to the left a bit higher whereupon the mule path cuts across the northernmost of the four long arms of *wādi 'abdallah* in its upper course. At the *minzalet hamid*, a newly-built stone house flanked by a black Bedouin tent, one reaches the ridge elevation which now stretches southeastwards in a straight line between *wādi 'abdallah* on the right and several rivulets flowing into *wādi rushmia* on the left. An old structure is visible on the northern side. Straight ahead one encounters wide bands of small stones running through the length of the ridge; one is no longer able to determine if these are from former walls or an ancient road. *Rās wādi 'abdallah* is a peak only approximately twenty meters wide to which the southernmost arm of the mentioned *wādi* from the west and *khallet es-serrīsi* from the East reach. Now the upward climb to a larger ridge begins; this ridge is recognizable from afar by several heaps of stones. A chain coming from *fersh el-beled* by *et-tīre* merges with the ridge here; it is called *fersh khirbet el-amayya* after a small ruin of remnants of buildings and two grape presses only a quarter of an hour away. A second *khirbet el-amayya* lies just beyond this on the path; excluding several carved stones, only four cisterns remain from this, and a Fellāheen from *et-tīre* has set up his summer residence in one of them. On the directly adjoining site, *minzalet il-būbān*, the mule path from *haifā* enters from the North across *qōd halqat el-kharrūbi*. The path extends across *rushmia* and *a'rāq ez-zīghān*. The first high peak, *rās abu 'n-nida* (Peak of the Dew Father, 479 meters above sea level), stands before the traveler; it takes a solid quarter of an hour to climb this but is worth it on account of the magnificent wide view. The mule path bypasses it westwards and crosses the upper course of *wādi 'l-qasab* which is called *rās el-muhellil* (Peak of the One who Praises God) here. On the other side one notices a path winding up over *fersh dār kāid* to the right; it leads from *et-tīre* and descends into *wādi 't-tabl* around *rās abu 'n-nida* in the north. The point of intersection between the ridge path and this shortest connection between *et-tīre* and *beled esh-shēkh* is called *el-musallabi* (The Crossways) and must have once played a role as a strategic point as one finds the remains of an ancient tower now overgrown with brush not far from here. One follows the branch of *wādi 'l-muntār* that ends here southwards to the right and then approaches *el-khrēbi* (Small Ruin).

The path meets a smaller cave to the right; as the name *maghārat et-tib n* implies, the cave served as a storage point for chaff. A larger cave, located somewhat below the path, gave the branch of *wādi abu khammāsha* that reaches up here its name, *khallet el-maghāra* or *khallet maghārat el-khrēbi*. One sees rock slabs on the left in which a handsome antique rock burial chamber, the *nāmūsiyyet el-khrēbi*, several grape presses, and basins carved in the stone are found. A foot path leads through here to the stone economic building visible from afar; the building was built by the proprietress of the fertile site, the *el-khūri* family from *haifā*. A hill, *tell el-'ades* (Lentil Hill) projects northwards behind it; towards *wādi 't-tabl*, the hill is surrounded by castellated terraces. The ground is now cultivated; despite this, the scattered debris stones still lying around imply that a castle once stood here whereto the dominating position passes over *wādi 't-tabl* coming from *beled esh-shēkh*. A burial chamber in the rock that was indeed emptied to be used for storing straw lies outside the ancient enclosure wall. This is the case with so many castle ruins. The ruin of the village which enjoys the protection of the mountain is to be found slightly southeastwards where the ridge path runs through it. Indeed, the site has been built upon; nevertheless, one still sees many stones, individual remnants of buildings, and traces of wide, terrace-like gardens on the western side. The field of ruins measures roughly 350 meters from the northwest to the southeast and 100 meters from the northeast to the southwest. The ruins, considered to be old (*khirbi kufriyye*), are also not

as small as one would like to assume based on the name "Small Ruin."
In connection with the fact that the former place name has apparently
been forgotten, this knowledge suggests the assumption that the name
is concealed in an Arabicized form in the term *el-khrēbi*. Glass shards
found here indicate the Middle Ages.

From the field of ruins, one looks down to the south on a small
valley planted with vegetable crops; the valley is separated from one
of the ravines of *wādi abu khammāsha*, the *qōd er-rīhān*, by a rock reef.
The site is still called *hawākir umm el-hīrān* (Vegetable Garden for
the Mother of the Camel Foal) after a former Bedouin settlement.
I found a large, round column there on the reef. It measures more
than two meters long and one meter thick and is covered all over with
notches. The latter are not executed very regularly; in fact, all run
along the length of the column and are all circa five centimeters deep
and wide yet they vary in the extensions of their lengths (Fig. 54).
This column is suitable for giving us information on the purpose of the
notches on so many of the columns of ruins of which we have already
noted in *khirbet el-'aēn* by *et-tīre*. The great amount of indentations and
their irregular use excludes that they served the purpose of affixing
decorations or including doors. They could only have been used for
attaching the levers, or handles, for transporting the column. That
so many notches are found in the example before us can be explained
in the difficulty of hoisting the stone colossus onto the reef. It is to
be assumed that the column was furnished with a wooden lining or a
cloth after its definitive erection. In direct proximity, two similar, yet
shattered and weathered columns still lie, and the foundation walls of
a small but solid building constructed of large blocks are next to them.
A few paces away from here, one sees a lovely *midbise* and a cave on the
slope of *qōd er-rīhān*. The cave was originally an antique rock burial
chamber as exhibited in the portal carving; the round capstone still
rests in front of it. The cave was possibly later expanded by herdsmen.
Somewhat further above this, building ruins still stand. The location,
which is elevated from all sides, is not fitting for a castle, and the
massive columns are certainly too grand for a private villa. Perhaps it is
not too daring to want to see an antique temple in the ruins.

The beautiful stand consisting of nearly eighty evergreen oaks
of the *shejarāt el-arba'īn*[1] extends on the northern slope of the crest

---

1   The urban pronunciation, also common among the Bedouin, *shejarāt*, has
     been retained for this well-known place name; in *et-tīre*, it is called *sejarāt*.

about five minutes away from the ridge path. This stand of oaks was already cited in the first section of this work among the sacred sites. It offers the traveler, who has now covered roughly half the distance to *'usufia*, an all the more welcome opportunity to rest with its shade and its colorful floral splendor. The traveler can supply himself with fresh water from *bīr el-khrēbi* located not far from here in

Figure 54. Column with notches from the *hawākir umm el-hīrān* ruin.

front of a stand of olive trees. During this pause, the *mihrāb* (prayer niche) of the shrine deserves to be more closely inspected; indeed, it is a common half-circle of red boulders but its orientation will strike the attentive observer. The niche is namely not oriented like every other Muslim *mihrāb*, directly towards the south, but rather to the south-southwest. Hence, the opening looks to the north-northeast, and the visitor's view immediately meets with the peak of Mount Hermon in this direction, towering over the entire vast countryside. It is worth remarking that many of the ancient sites of reverence in Palestine and Syria, such as, for example, those of *blūdān* in Antilibanus, have chosen a similar aim. In the arrangement of the *mihāab*, one may thus see further evidence for the antiquity of the "cult" of the Forty Martyrs.

Now the ascent to the broad mountain peak *ej-juneidiyye*, projecting eastwards, begins. At the outset, a path leads off to the right; after it encounters a *midbise* at the end of *qōd er-rīhān*, the path splits again. The right-hand branch leads to the rock portal of *wādi 'l-murrān* beneath *maghārat el-glīkh* and further towards *esh-shellāle*, but the left-hand branch winds its way between *maghārat el-glīkh* and the *juneidiyye*. It reaches *wādi 'l-murrān* opposite *maghārat ed-dāmūn* from which one reaches the large ruins *ed-dawāmīn*. We, however, remain on the ridge path and climb the peak of the *juneidiyye* which is called *el-matall* (the lookout, the complete name *matall el-khrēbi*, the lookout on *el-khrēbi*) by the Druses in *'usufia*. The peak lies 524 meters above sea level. From now on, the path continues at the same niveau until *'usufia* with the exception of slight drops and inclines. Nearly eighty meters south of the path, shortly before one looks to the left down into *wādi 'ain er-rebī'a*, a deep rock crevice suddenly opens up in the level ground. This is the so-called *bīr el-ḥūti* (Fountain of the Rock Crevice). Soon afterwards, one enters the upper course of one of the *ashālīl zeibaq* to the right of the ridge where the traveler is shown the *ma'sirat zeibaq* in the rock cracks. It is, however, not an oil press, as the name suggests, but rather one of the many *midbise* (grape presses). Nevertheless, the *midbise* are also called *ma'sira* in *'usufia*.

After the path ascends the ridge once more, one observes a new peak, *rahārīh el-matāmīr*, before him towards the south. The elevation of the *ed-dawāmīn* ruin and further the mountain *esh-shekh jebel* merge with this peak in the west. The path circumvents it and sinks into the wide valley *jibb 'usufia* (well, i.e. hollow of *'usufia*) eastwards. The valley flows into *wādi 'aqqāra*. On the other side, the path rises again to *rās ej-jibb*. There one observes an orderly path bordered with small cobbles; this path turns right and soon leads to *wādi 'l-qasab* or *wādi qasab ed-drūz* and further across *merjet ez-zerā'a* towards *ed-dālie*. Mr. Oliphant had the path repaired in order to arrive at his country house there by the shortest route. From here on, the ravines visible to the right of the ridge no longer flow into the valley of *et-tīre* but rather into *wādi felāh*, situated further southwards, with its upper branches reaching far to the East. Presently, one is looking down to the right into one of the ravines of *wādi 'l-qasab*, then to the left into *khallet el-tājāt* (Valley of Crowns) which joins with *jibb 'usufia*. Immediately afterwards a larger branch of *wādi 'l-qasab* opens again to the right; this branch is well formed and is called *maqtal el-'arab* (Site of the Killing of the Bedouins).

One of the few local historical traditions preserved by the people, which will therefore shortly be cited here, is bound to this site. Nearly more than one hundred years ago, at the time of *bin berto el-fransāwi*,

Bedouins camped here. They were from the tribe of *ghureifāt* who still lead a nomadic existence in *merj ibn 'āmir* today. One day a Christian merchant from *shefā 'amr* came to them, as he often did, to trade grain and products made by the Bedouins, such as carpets and the like, for goods from the city. This time he, however, only received abusive words from the sons of the desert for his wares, and when he demanded payment, a fight broke out so that he, badly beaten, could just barely save his naked body. He complained of his misfortunes to the Frenchman who was passing through the land at the time and who also listened. His soldiers encircled the Bedouin camp at night which was taken by surprise at daybreak. Everyone was slaughtered except for the women and children. Since then the site has been called *maqtal el-'arab*. – Not difficult to understand, the memory of Bonaparte has been preserved in the Arabized term *bin berto* (son of Berto) by the residents of the mountain.

On the other side, the ridge path leads past an elevation, *qambū'at ed-durziyye*, lying to the right. It represents the highest peak of the Carmel mountain range at 551 meters above sea level. The foundation walls of a small square building with three-meter-long sides is discernable on the peak; it is difficult to determine if this served as a watchtower or was used in the cult of high places of still earlier times. West of this, located not far from here, a peculiar round knob, approximately seven meters high, rises on an almost horizontal layer of limestone. Its level surface forms a circle with a diameter of five meters, and its circumference measures approximately sixty meters at the base.

The investigation of this building, now overgrown with undergrowth, reveals that is was built out of artificially constructed stones. Only excavations could determine how the building was constructed and, accordingly, in which period it is to be placed. The odd sight gives the impression of a very old age. At any rate, this hill has occupied the imagination of the villagers more than that of the until now unobservant tourists as the former gave it the distinctive name, now transferred to the entire range of mountains, of "Cap of the Female Druze." The headdress of the local female Druses that went out of style nearly forty years ago, the *qambū'a* (قمبوعه), which embodies an analogy to the *tantūr* of the female Lebanese, was an almost foot-high cap made of cloth comparable to an empty sugar loaf. It was tucked over the bare head sometimes from the front, sometimes in the middle, and sometimes at the back of the head. The while cloth veil, *hrām*, hung over this leaving the face free, or the colorful cloth, *fūta*, was encircled around the head by the headband, *'asbi*, and secured.

The footpath from *beled esh-shēkh* enters from the North across *jebel 'aqqāra* and *dabbāt berjas* where one passes the elevation. The ruins of a large square tower lies on the same path only a quarter hour's distance from here. The tower possibly aided[1] *dabbāt berjas* in acquiring its name. It towers eastwards above the slope of *dabbāt berjas*, standing in the middle between the ravines of *ashālīl el-fersh* which hasten towards *wādi 'sh-shōmariyye*. One of these reaches the ridge path only somewhat south of *qambū'at ed-durziyye*. *Wādi 'ain el-hāik* opens to the right opposite the last-mentioned ravine. The valley separates into two small branches above. It takes its name from the spring originating further below, *'ain el-hāik* (Spring of the Weavers). The ruin *khirbet 'ain el-hāik* sits enthroned on a hill above the spring. It measures one hundred meters from north to south and sixty meters from east to west. Little remains of it aside from enclosure walls; yet based on its dominating position, it could have been a castle. The view from here of *merjet ez-zerā'a* of *wādi felāh* is lovely.

After this, one has a new elevation, called *er-rahārih* or *ruhrāh abu 'njīli*, on the right. With 542 meters above sea level, it almost reaches *qambū'at ed-durziyye*. *Khallet hammūd* is on the left; it merges with *wādi 'sh-shōmariyye* through *wādi hassān*. At the point where *wādi abu 'abdallah* now opens to the right towards the *miqtali* of *wādi felāh*, one encounters ancient cobbled paving on the ridge path. The traces of this were already apparent along the previous path yet without being sufficient to ascertain reliably. There can be no doubt in establishing the origin of this paved road that the Roman Imperial Era was the only period which left behind monuments of this kind in the land. It is well-known that the Romans gave the *via stratae*, laid for the purpose of the enduring control over of the conquered province, an excellent substructure; they did this by placing one layer of stone slabs and one layer of stones set in mortar between three cement-like layers. The actual paving was first placed on the uppermost cement-like layer. The

---

1 As *berjas* can not be explained in Arabic, it is possible to derive the name from the Greek word πύργος, tower. The continuation of Greek place names has evidenced nothing remarkable in Palestine with the exception of *nābulus* (Neapolis) and *sebastie* (Sebaste) and still many other examples. Incidentally, this foreign word in the form of *berjās* already occurs in the chivalric novel of *beni hilāl* with the meaning of fortification.

current ridge path seems to move here over the layer of stones set in mortar after the upper pavement had been destroyed over the course of the centuries. Soon thereafter, I could, however, also recognize further traces of the latter on a higher embankment next to the road. That a paved road ran through Mount Carmel during this ancient era may not be surprising in the context of the region's intensive culture of that time which begot so many antique graves because the ridge forms the main route of transportation as previously mentioned in the section on the mountain's geography. This Roman road led forward across *'usufia* towards the East; after its existence was established, I followed it backwards over the *jibb 'usufia* and the *juneidiyye* through *el-khrēbi* and until the *musallabi* on *rās abu 'n-nida*. Here it seems to lead across *fersh dār kāid* towards *et-tīre*. I could not discern if another branch from the *musallabi* led further over the northern ridge.

After one has left *khallet hamdūn* on the left and the small valley of *khallet el-ghamīqa* that flows towards *wādi abu 'abdallah* with its spring *'ain el-'alaq* (Leech Spring), one enters the village *'usufia* (Fig. 55) across a wide area used for the threshing floors. The village's highest point lies 536 meters above sea level; it is in the cemetery built on the eastern side. The village is encircled by cactus hedges. It is primarily built out of stone though the smallest parts are of clay. It offers a delightful view from all sides. It counts 595 residents (*'asfāwi*, pl. *'asāfni*) of whom a quarter are Catholics (Uniert Greeks with Rome) and three-quarters Druses[1]. The division of the houses and the village field corresponds with

Figure 55. The village *'usufia* from the Northwest.

---

1 Very recently, in August 1907, the spiritual leader of the Druses, the *shēkh ed-dīn*, converted to Sunni Islam by taking the Islamic confession of faith before the Qādi in Haifā. Nearly thirty of his former co-religionists followed him.

this ratio whereas, from the three Mukhtāre, one is chosen by the Christians and two by the Druses. The Christians possess a church with an adjoining rectory as well as a school for boys and girls. The Druses have a *khalwe* and a reading school for boys which they attend in the wintertime. In addition, the village contains a number of underground oil presses and several horse-powered mills (*tahunet baghl*). Upon entering from the north, one passes a cylindrical recess in the rock, the so-called old *tannūr* (furnace); there are several ancient burial chambers as well. The current village was newly founded by the Druses who migrated from Lebanon two hundred years ago. *Wehb* was the name of the first settler given to me; he first settled in *khirbet wehib*, already known to us, and later in *'usufia*. Others of like faith soon followed him. Christians also joined them in the eighteenth century. They also lived in the Druze villages, *el-mansūra* and *ed-dawāmīn*, which were founded at roughly the same time but destroyed after 1840. Christians are not present in the Muslim villages of Mount Carmel. I was shown Wehib's house; it contains a handsome arch and displays an old sculpted cross. *'Usufia* was namely once a ruin as demonstrated by the antique graves and the coins, in addition to the previously mentioned ancient *tannūr*, found here dating from the Middle Ages through the Byzantine and Roman Imperial Eras. In general, not only the Druze settlements dating from the eighteenth century but almost all current villages on Mount Carmel are built atop ancient ruins which explains the oft-used expression *khirbi* for a village. The reason for this, with the exception of the generally healthy location where a spring can always be found nearby, may primarily have been the simple procuring of construction materials from the antique debris. - The frequent occurrence of fossils, mostly starfish and sea urchins but also many mussels, has previously been mentioned.

The village field begins on the *juneidiyye* in the west and is bordered by that of *el-yājūr* in the north and the northeast. Entering the plain at *jurn el-muhādade*, the field reaches until *nahr el-muqatta'* (Kishon) which it follows upstream until the mouth of *wādi maghārat umm ahmed*. Here it climbs westwards until the ridge elevation of *rbā'āt el-khurfēsh* in order to descend on the other side through *khallet abu fāris*, and, touching *ruus el-qabāla*, to cut across the *miqtali* until *a'rāq el-wensa*. Then it encircles *bāb el-hawa*, the *merjet ez-zerā'a* and continues to *rās en-neba'*. Intersecting *ashlūl[1] el-munyasa*, it ascends to *esh-shēkh jebel* and descends to *maghārat ez-zembaq[2]* on the other side whereupon it reaches the *matall* of the *juneidiyye*.

In the west, on *rās en-neba'*, the village field meets with the region of *esh-shellāle* which was taken into possession by the people of *'usufia* after its destruction. This region is considered to be separate from the field community of *'usufia* since it has been acquired by Mr. Shukri Mansūr. Because the tenth levied from him is, however, still paid to *'usufia*, its boundaries will soon be included here. They ascend from *rās en-neba'* in the south to *rbā' et-tawīl* on the *seq'ab*, turn towards *khallet ed-dukhān*, and arrive at *mughr ushāh* (called *mughr esh-shiāh* in *et-tīre*) via the *ma'sira*. Crossing *wādi felāh*, they extend across the *bayādat esh-shammās* until *bīr fadil* which they also encompass. They return to *rās en-neba'* from across the *ka'b el-mughrāqa* and the *rbā' faqqūsi* (Terrace of the *faqqūs*, a type of cucumber) on *a'rāq khālid* and finally cutting through *ashlūl el-munyasa*.

Although *'usufia* lies on one of the highest points of the mountain, the view from here is completely open only to the north. Thus, it can not be put on a par with that of *rās abu 'n-nida*, that of the *muhraqa*, or even that of the *seq'ab*. In the foreground, there is the lovely, sprawling olive tree plantation, *merj 'usufia*, to the south in which the small valley *khallet sa'id*, originating directly east of the village, enters. The valley basin extends northwards; the ravines of *wādi abu hayyi* and *wādi 'sh-shōmariyye* merge here. Its western border forms *fersh dabbāt berjas* which joins with the Ridge by *qambū'at ed-durziyye*; the Ridge surrounds the basin in the south. *Khirbet esh-sharqiyye* rises on a hill in the east; situated on the eastern border and bearing *khirbet esh-shimāliyye*, *rās el-ibrēghīt* (Fleas' Peak) extends northwards. It attains the plain with its foot, called *ka'b el-ibrēghīt*. The northern boundary forms the *qōd el-ubweiriyyāt* (Crest of the Rock Badger) from *dabbāt berjas* in the west until the site of *rbā' shtāwi*, already known to us, above *maghārat es-sabra*. In this valley basin, one has the spring *'ain 'usufia* in a valley bottom called *el-khalāil* or *khalāil 'amīra* directly at

---

1   The word *ashlūl* in the *'usufia* dialect corresponds with the form of *shulūl* in the *et-tīre* dialect.

2   The pronunciation *zembaq* denotes the same that is conveyed with *zeibaq* (quicksilver) in *et-tīre*; the *maghārat ez-zembaq* of the residents of *'usufia* is identical with *maghārat ed-dāmūn* known to us through the description of the valley of *et-tīre*.

his feet. The olive trees of the *burtā'iyye* lie slightly westwards; *khirbet el-burtā'iyye*, located on either side of *khallet hamdān*, stretches still further westwards. There is almost nothing left to see of the ruins; several columns are supposedly buried under the farmland. Burial chambers lie further to the Northwest at the foot of *khallet hammūd*; the handsome olive tree stand, *shejarāt abu saqr*, is located at the eastern foot of *dabbāt berjas*. The entire valley, and especially the northern part of *wādi abu hayyi*, is strewn with individual larger *rujūm* (piles of stones) which remain from ancient buildings.

The individual valleys of this basin, listed from east to west, are called the following: *khalāil 'amīra* (the actual spring valley of *wādi 'sh-shōmariyye*), *khallet hamdān*, the lower course of which is called *el-midbise* before flowing into *wādi 'sh-shōmariyye*. Thereafter follow the ravines. Their union is called *wādi hassān* and likewise flows towards *wādi 'sh-shomariyye* where it takes on the name *mashābik wādi hassān*. The ravines are *khashabet el-bedd* (Oil Mill Wood) and *khallet hammūd*. Three rivulets are collectively assigned merely the name *ashālīl el-fersh*; two additional *ashālīl el-fersh* join up here just above *shejarāt abu saqr* and then flow towards *wādi abu hayyi*.

The larger paths leading to *'usufia*, aside from the ridge path on which we came and which merges with the path from *beled esh-shēkh* across *jebel 'aqqāra* and *dabbāt berjas* near *qambū'at ed-durziyye*, are: 1) the path leading through the *miqtali* towards *ed-dālie* in one and a quarter hours by passing through *khallet el-ghamīqa* and *wādi abu 'abdallah* in the southwest; 2) a path in *merj 'usufia* to the south; 3) the path to the *muhraqa* to the southeast from which 4) a path branches off eastwards to *wādi 'sh-sha'īr*; 5) to the east next to *khirbet esh-sharqiyye*, a path into *wādi 'l-a'waj* and into the dependence village *ej-jelame*, or *jelamet el-'asāfni*; and 6) a path leading to *khirbet esh-shōmariyye* in the plain across *rās el-ibrēghīṯ*.

The further surroundings of *'usufia*, including the dependence village *ej-jelamet*, will be discussed partially in the description of the two paths leading to the *muhraqa* in the following section and partially as belonging to *wādi felāh* in Section 10. Nonetheless, several ruins shall still be mentioned here which can only be reached from *'usufia*.

Khirbet esh-sharqiyye (The Eastern Ruin) lies only ten minutes north of the village separated from it by a depression. It is situated on a hill towering 536 meters above sea level which corresponds with that of the burial grounds of *'usufia*; this hill forms the last peak elevation of the west-east longitudinal profile of the mountain range. From here one enjoys a spacious view of the Jezreel Plain towards Galilee and far into East Jordan Land. The steep drop to the east between *khallet el-a'waj* and *wādi 'sh-sha'īr* and the fact that four paths merge here with the ridge path by *'usufia* seem to have been determined for the construction of a castle on this already dominating position. The expanse of the ruins fit with this assumption; however, the building blocks have been primarily used for the construction of the houses in *'usufia*, and the slopes serve as cultivated fields today. Therefore, it appears impossible to more precisely define the ruin today without excavations.

Khirbet esh-shimāliyye (The Northern Ruin) has, as with the former, lost its ancient, unique name. It lies on *rās el-ibrēghīt* on the path leading from *khirbet esh-shōmariyye* towards *'usufia* approximately twenty minutes away from the village. Today the ruins have been completely destroyed, and the soft building stones have endured so much under the influence of weathering that even the traces of carvings have disappeared. Only three plastered cisterns such as found by the medieval castle ruins have been well-preserved. The ruins give the impression of originating from a double castle of the Middle Ages as they are considerably extensive from the north to the south and divided into two parts. The ceramic and glass shards I found there also suggest this epoch. *Ras el-ibrēghīt* approaches the vicinity of the Kishon with its foot whereas the foothills of the Galilean hill country protrude on the northern side lying opposite this. The narrow passage formed here was therefore a highly important strategic point at all times as will be illuminated in the following section. This must have been especially true in the bellicose Crusade Era, and it is, therefore, not surprising that the elevations dominating the passage were strongly fortified. The position of *'usufia* and its surroundings was of even greater importance in this because from Mount Carmel one could easily threaten the Crusaders' landing point in *'atlīt*, the *castellum peregrinorum* of our chroniclers. The consideration of castles built near the *muhraqa* will become even more apparent at this moment. If these general observations are already close to the conclusion that the *khirbet esh-shimāliyye* was a Crusader castle, it thus seems more probable in the manner of the ruins. Just as the *khirbet esh-sharqiyye* commands the East entrance to *'usufia*, the *khirbet esh-shimāliyye* guards the north entrance.

One proceeds southeastwards from *'usufia* to the upper course of *wādi 'sh-sha'īr* (Barley Valley) called *ez-zuhlaq*[1] that is planted with olive trees and then follows the valley course to arrive at *qal'at el menābir* (Castle Pulpit). After a third of the course, one can turn directly southwards and arrive at the destination across *shulūl ej-jisr*. However, we intend to descend still further into the valley until we catch sight of *khirbet ez-zuhluq*, which shall be described in the following section, and then turn southwards at roughly one third of the ridge elevation. Above the slope which is called *miqtal sa'id furru* (Site of the Killing of Sa'id Furru), we pass through an area which exhibits several simple Muslim graves from an older era between the higher lying *wa'rat khalīl hallūl* and *khallet el-maqbara* (Grave Plot Valley) leading into the plain. After we pass through the ravine *miqtal sālih* (Site of the Slaying of Sālih), the lower course of the just-mentioned *shulūl ej-jisr* (Bridge Valley), we arrive at a ridge, *umm el-barāghīt*, which exhibits ancient traces of carving in the rock. A short set of stairs hewn into the stone leads to burial chambers and caves; a larger, basin-like hollow stands next to it surrounded by ruins of large stones lying around which are partially covered by bushes. The slope here is so steep that for these ruins one can not think of a period of origin which was rich in culture and thereby accustomed to greater comfort. Thus, the site may reach back into very ancient times wherewith the primitive carvings coincide. After one also passes through the small *khallet el-menābir*, one stands before the *qal'at el-menābir*. At the foot of the mountain, at approximately one third of the ridge elevation, a peculiar, half-round, rugged rock dominates. It forms three-quarters of a circle above and is connected with the mountain ridge only by a narrow side in the west. This site remained unnoticed although its form must have attracted the attention of the traveler passing the Kishon Plain.

---

1 On Mount Carmel, the word *zuhluq* implies a precipitous location with many boulders or loose gravel on which one can easily slip.

Figure 56. The Castle Pulpit, *qal'at el-menābir.*

Figure 57. Cyclopean wall of *qal'at el-menābir.*

As the name implies, the form is reminiscent of a pulpit (Fig. 56). Like *khallet el-menābir* on the northern side, it borders *khallet el-qal'a* on the southern side where a deep cistern is concealed by a fig tree growing out of it. The now flat surface forms an almost regular circle nearly twenty-five meters in circumference. On the western side where one can more easily climb the pulpit from the mountain ridge, the entry is made difficult by the massive limestone blocks piled on top of each other. This structure is not polygonal but rather actually of cyclopean design; although not of equal size, the blocks are stacked horizontally in layers (Fig. 57). The height of the wall measures 2.25 meters in the middle and more than three meters on either side towards the valley. We may have a pre-historic fortification here before us which can be counted among the megalithic architectural monuments. The ascribing of a time period and race, respectively, should be left to the judgment of the experts on this subject. The *qal'at el-menābir* was marked to still play a small role in the previous century. Namely, as Ibrāhīm Pasha's Egyptian army trekked across the Jezreel Plain in 1831, the pulpit was occupied by the Druses from *'usufīa* who wanted to confront the enemy here. Yet the Egyptians directed the cannons towards this point. The first cannonball, however, fell, as I was informed, to the earth deep below the plateau of the pulpit which caused great joy among the Druses. Although as the second shot came within direct vicinity of the mountain ridge, the company scattered to search for higher and more protected points of the mountain.

Foundation walls of additional buildings can be recognized on the mountain ridge west of the *qal'a* only at short distances. When one has passed the small *khallet el-qal'a* on the southern side, one finds similar foundation walls on a second rock protrusion near *khallet el-iqshar* which possibly gave cause to the plural form of the name (*menābir*, pl. from *minbar*, pulpit). This second ruin bears the term *khirbet umm es-senāsil* (Ruins of the Mother of the Walls); there is nothing noteworthy about it. It takes one and a half hours to reach *qal'at el-menābir* from *'usufīa*.

The visit to *khirbet 'alā ed-dīn* and *maghārat umm ahmed* is very interesting. The route there until *khallet 'amūd er-randa* (Valley of the Laurel Cane) is the same at that to the *muhraqa* and will be described in the following section. One turns to the East on what is called the *khalle* in order to climb the small elevation on which *khirbet 'alā ed-dīn* lies after a one-hour march from *'usufīa*. The field of ruins is very extensive and must date from a very large village which flourished for many centuries. From here, one has a magnificent view eastward of the Jezreel Plain. Large, well-carved ashlars as well as an altar slab (Fig. 58) and then lovely quarries and graves in the southwest indicate the antiquity of the site. The remnants of a castle with medium-sized stone blocks may date from the Middle Ages. A deep, vaulted basin (Fig. 59) from a walled arch is located near these castle ruins. Additional ruins such as several grape presses, a four-cornered *jurn*, several basins, and many cisterns, upon some of which the opening stone (*kharaze*) still lie, have a character which is difficult to discern. The name of these ruins, which were unknown until now, "'Alā ed-dīn's Ruin" must date from earlier times.

From here I continued along a small path possibly begun by Europeans; the path leads southeastwards towards *khallet el-aswadiyye* which is supposedly named after a Bedouin. Artificial *cupulae* are situated there on horizontal limestone blocks on jagged cliffs; they are similar to those present at the stone necropolis of *qarnīfet el-wāsit* in the *wādi* of *et-tīre*. Rather than descend to *aswadiyye*, I turned eastwards towards the rock protrusion over the valley upon which I found an old structure. It runs in a fair extension eastward and then northwards – enclosure walls of a castellated settlement which already stood there in ancient times. In fact, I soon afterwards saw the location of an ancient sacrificial site. The stone slabs that form the ground there showed slight crevasses upon which blood grooves extended and flowed together to an outlet pointing south. Several caves and graves are concealed under high bushes nearby. The site is called *dahr maghārat umm ahmed* and bears the ruins of a four-cornered tower that probably dates from the Middle Ages on a peak situated

Figure 58. Altar slab from *khirbet 'alā ed-dīn*.

Figure 59. Walled arch above a basin at *khirbet ʿalā ed-dīn*.

slightly higher. It forms the counterpart to *khirbet ed-dawābe* rising further to the south. I then followed a path through the cliffs which ascends to *maghārat umm ahmed* (Cave of Ahmed's Mother). This is a large cave with a stalactite formation which is drawn into the rock. It is visited in the winter by shepherds who have set up sleeping quarters and furnaces

Figure 60. Stone Age grave next to the cave *maghārat umm ahmed*.

in the cave. A layer of hard goat manure several feet deep covers the cave floor; wild capers and a plant, unknown to me, with three to four stalks and umbel-like blossoms grow rampant before the cave.

Somewhat beneath the cave, approximately forty paces to the North, I saw to my surprise five Stone Age graves of a type still unknown to me. They lie together on a pile, oriented more or less from west to east so that the western end is a bit higher (Fig. 60). One coarsely smoothed stone slab rests on each of two parallel rows of large, oblong boulders sunk into the ground in an orthostatic manner. This grave differs from the remaining graves in its expanse. Its stone slab measures approximately 1.70 meters long, sixty centimeters wide, and ten centimeters thick. The other graves had stone slabs of like thickness and were fifty to sixty centimeters wide but roughly only one meter tall. Whereas the stone slabs in the west are laid out on the ground, one could observe a small inner room in the east between the foremost stones of the stone walls. These graves are reminiscent of the well-known dolmen which one often encounters in relation to the cromlech. However, the humble size of these dolmens does not permit them to be classified among the megalithic structures. The race which built the latter must have occupied the land for a longer period of time according to the great number of monuments left by them in Palestine, in particular in West Jordan Land. It would not be striking if their architecture had set a precedent. The graves located next to the Cave of Umm Ahmed convey the impression of copies of the dolmens by a later race, possibly smaller in stature. Some forty paces further northwards, I saw a natural niche in the rock face with its opening looking directly to the east. It measures approximately two and a half meters tall, one meter wide, and a bit more than a half meter deep. The side walls conjoin towards the top. The floor of the niche is coarsely leveled and exhibits old traces of a fire that was probably kindled long ago. As the slope before the niche leads rather steeply downhill, thus being inappropriate for a camp, the fire cannot possibly have been stoked by the herdsmen who had previously visited the Cave of Ahmed's Mother. Thus, the notion that the niche once served sacred purposes imposes itself upon the visitor.

Descending eastwards from this point for ten minutes, one arrives at a small plateau where Bedouins often camp. One observes several more Stone Age graves of the just described form on the slope; these are, however, difficult to discern because they are almost concealed by the humus piled up around them. Altogether, they only measure roughly one meter long. I noticed a small circle of boulders laid out at the Bedouin settlement; it resembled a pen. I was told that the very young calves were put in it. Such a circle is not referred to with the usual name for pen, *sīri*, by the Bedouins but rather as *zerb*. I found scatterings of forked branches wedged into rather numerous piles of stones. They are called *shird* by the Bedouins and are used here for fastening the tent ropes where dowels cannot be driven into the ground.

Tell el-wa'r (Wilderness Hill) lies a half hour's hike below towards the plain; it will be discussed in the following section.

9. The Muhraqa

Paths: 1. Five hours from the Karmelheim on the Ridge across *'usufia* (including a break); one hour and forty minutes from *'usufia*.

2. Two hours by wagon from *haifā* through the Kishon Plain across *beled esh-shēkh* towards *jelamet el-mansūra*; from here a steep climb by foot of one and a half hours.

3. Five and three quarters of an hour (including a short break) from the Karmelheim via *ed-dālie*. The key to the *muhraqa* chapel is found with the village shekh in *ed-dālie*. Whoever wants to enter the chapel or its roof must choose this route or let the chapel key be brought to him by a messenger which does not seem advisable. It is better to ask for a second key at the Stella Maris Monastery. The visit to the *muhraqa* is most easily arranged so that one first takes the Carmel Ridge (path 1) by foot or by horse and then returns on the path towards *haifā* through the plain (path 2). The descent from the chapel until *jelamet el-mansūra* requires only three-quarters of an hour by foot or by horse. After *jelamet el-mansūra*, one orders a wagon for the return trip to *haifā*. After reaching the chapel by way of the first path, a good rider can return via *ed-dālie*, the *umm esh-shuqaf* and *bistān* ruins, the village *'ain hōd* and the western coastal plain towards *haifā* or the Karmelheim all in the same day.

The *mesjid el-muhraqa*, the chapel of the burnt offering, or simply *el-muhraqa*[1], crowns the magnificent southeastern peak of the mountain upon which Christian tradition places the reported sacrificial miracle of Prophet Elijah according to the First Book of Kings, chapter 18. The site and its surroundings belong to the Stella Maris Monastery and form the popular destination of many pilgrims and tourists. Sacrifices and vows are made there by local Christians.

1. Descending southeastsouthwards from *'usufia*, one arrives at *ez-zuhluq* to the left of *khirbet esh-sharqiyye* and to the right of *merjet ez-zeitūn*, or *merjet 'usufia*; this location is planted with olive trees and is the highest portion of *wādi 'sh-sha'īr*. An artificial trough, *jurn 'abbūd*, lies among a group of stones to the left of the path. From the next elevation, *el-maqāzih*, which still bears traces of ancient construction, one observes *khānūq smēt*, a small valley, before one to the southwest. This valley opens into *wādi felāh* through *'ishsh ghurāb* (Raven's Nest) and soon follows a second parallel valley, *el-meshālih* (Pillaging Sites). To the left, the grape press, *ma'sirat khēr allah*, is on the other side of a small elevation; a Negro, *khēr allah*, is supposed to have resided here half a century ago. He made the region unsafe and namely took to raping the women. The elevation *ma'sirat el-a'dām* (Wine Press of the Bones), adjoining in the south, takes its name from two additional presses lying further down the path. It bears the ruins of a large four-walled structure made of medium-sized stones on its peak; the structure is separated in the middle by a wall and possibly was originally a tower which does not appear to date from ancient times. The slope that one has just passed is called *karm el-humāra* (Vineyard of the *humāra*, i.e. the jenny). From the elevation beyond this, *umm es-senāsil* (Mother of the Garden Walls), one has a view of the peak of *ruus el-qabāla* (Chiefs in the South, namely from *'usufia*) to the west. It lies 520 meters above sea level and contains several ancient grape presses. To

---

1 The terminology for the site, which the Fellāheen pronounce sometimes *muhraqa* and sometimes *mahraqa*, is understood as *nomen loci* in the sense of "Site of the Burning" and is interpreted as "Site of the Burnt Offering." It is indeed more correct to use the word *muhraqa* in the common liturgical use of "Burnt Offering." Thus, the church does this in which the complete name is *mesjid el-muhraqa*, the Chapel of the Burnt Offering, as given above.

the East, one looks down upon *khallet 'amūd er-randa* (Valley of the Laurel Stalk) which attains the Kishon Plain somewhat south of *qal'at el-menābir* under the name *khallet el-iqshar*. The path branches off eastwards here to the nearby *khirbet 'alā ed-dīn* already known to us. The ridge narrows as the foothills of *wādi felāh*, *khallet abu fāris* and *khallet hamze* stretch upwards until this point. The path winds through bushy terrain that stays marshy long into spring, frequently crossing remnants of broad, ancient garden walls, slightly eastwards towards *khallet el-aswadiyye*, the upper course of *wādi maghārat umm ahmed*. The slope descends eastwards to a small plateau in order to ascend gently on the other side. The *khirbet ghayada*, named after a Bedouin of the same name, lies here at a quarter hour's distance from it. The intensely damaged and not very large ruin may date from antiquity based on the large and weathered construction stones; the presence of a large column drum as we encountered in *wadi rushmia* coincides with this. The column drum here, however, does not exhibit a round depression in the middle of the surface but a square one. The basin of a *midbise* is still found next to it. After a quarter of an hour, coming from *khirbet ghayāda*, one arrives at *khirbet umm ahmed* on the rocky eastern slope of Mount Carmel. It is situated lower, towards the Kishon plain. Northeastwards, one can detect a doubled row of fortification. Beneath each of these, rock burial chambers and caves are located outside of the walls as with so many castles; outworks still lie upwards on the slope. The actual castle stood slightly above on a small plateau which, however, has since been cleared. Still higher, one sees an old quarry. Particulars to be mentioned are: stone door posts, a large *sīh* (basin) with a nearby cistern, a cistern hewn further into the rock but walled along the opening, a smaller basin, a cave with two openings with two adjoining caves, an additional cave which still bears plaster, and, to some extent, very singular rock carvings. Several *qubūr shemsiyye* are supposed to lie further to the south. The graves and carving may partially date from antiquity though the actual castle was possibly built in the Middle Ages. It guarded the entry to the two valleys *khallet el-aswadiyye* and *khallet ej-juneidiyye*.

One sees the remnants of a stone building to the left where the mule path, which we had departed from upon visiting *khirbet ghayāda*, approaches *khallet ej-juneidiyye*, the upper course of *khallet en-na'miyye*. The Fellāheen consider this building to be no more than a *muntār*, yet it is worthy of closer observation. A small tower, which is still almost two meters tall, rises on a square foundation with three-meter-long sides. Today, only the northern side (Fig. 61) and a portion of the western side are still preserved; the rest lies in ruins on the ground. These walls are stone slabs piled atop each other which are hewn but

Figure 61. *Rujm baḥt* by the *muḥraqa*, northern side.

Figure 62. *Rujm baḥt* by the *muḥraqa*, northeastern corner.

not with an iron tool. Similar slabs of approximately the same thickness lie horizontally in stacks almost everywhere. A round stone slab is positioned vertically only at the northeastern corner (Fig. 62); the upper layers bore these stones. Along the path from the *muhraqa* to *ed-dālie*, a half hour from the last location, two such towers still exist which, among the Druses, bear the curious name *rujūm baht*, i.e. rice pudding stone heaps. They are better preserved and still rise up to three meters at most; one can recognize them in that the stone layers go all the way through without leaving an empty room in the interior. One sees a fourth tower of this kind at roughly a quarter hour's distance from the latter two when crossing the small valley *hajar el-bedd* coming from *ed-dālie* on the path towards *umm ez-zeināt*. All the stone slabs are towered horizontally upon each other in each of these three structures. At any rate, these small towers are very old; one would tend to place their construction in the pre-historic Stone Age based on the primitive carvings. Even so, it should be kept in mind here that such work without iron tools remained common for sacral purposes into later periods; according to Exodus (20:25), it was also prescript for Israelite altars. I am also not able to answer the question about the intent of the construction of the towers. Their repeated occurrence at small distances does not necessarily need to contradict their use as altars as, for example, Balaam built seven altars each at three locations according to the Book of Numbers (23:1, 14, 29). However, one cannot quite understand how a priest could have sacrificed upon the altars due to the apparent lack of stairs leading to the tower surface and the relative, yet all the same significant height of the structure. Perhaps they served other purposes such as commemoration like that which Jacob and Laban erected as affirmation of their reconciliation according to Genesis 31:46.

After passing the upper course of *khallet ed-dawābe*, one climbs a ridge with large rock slabs through old terrace grounds where one must beat through thick bushes in order to arrive at the *muhraqa* leaving *khirbet ed-dawābe* on the left.

2. The path through the Kishon Plain; the same has already been described until the end of the field of *el-yājūr* near *wādi 'sh-shōmariyye* in Sections 2, 6, and 7.

The northeastern slope of Mount Carmel from *ka'b el-ibrēghīt*, the foot of *rās el-ibrēghīt*, and on first counts five small valleys: *ashlūl 'arbes, ashlūl 'ammūra, ashlūl el-qattāni, ashlūl es-safhat es-saghīra*, and *ashlūl el-billāni*. At this point, a larger valley, *wādi 'l-a'waj*, opens up. The dependence village of *'usufia, jelamet el-'asāfni*, lies in the valley's lower course. A natural hill with a ruin, *khirbet jelamet el-'atīqa*, lies somewhat ahead of this. When one bypasses the eastern protrusion of the Carmel, one sees *wādi 'sh-sha'īr*; the lower course of which is called *el-zuhluq* like the highest portion of the upper reaches. It lends its name to *khirbet ez-zuhluq*. The small valley, *miqtal sa'd furra*, extends up to it on the eastern side. Then *khallet el-maqbara*, called *wa'ret khalīl hallūl* in the upper course, and the ravine *miqtal sālih* follow; the upper reaches of the ravine are called *ashlūl ej-jisr*. After this comes the small ridge *umm el-barāghīt*. *Qal'at el-menābir* lies between *khallet el-menābir* in the North and *khallet el-qal'a* in the south; the small ruin *umm es-senāsil* is situated on the edge of the last-mentioned *khalle*. *Shulūl el-mizibli* leads to *khallet el-iqshar* which is called *ashlūl el-qar'i* further above and *'amūd er-randa* in the upper-most portion. After the two small valleys *khallet es-sukhsēli* (Valley of Ramps) and *khallet el-murrār*, the short acclivity *khallet et-tell*, or *khallet tell el-wa'r*, extends towards the protruding *tell el-wa'r* which still stands in connection with the mountain only by way of a ridge. On its southern side, *wādi maghāret umm ahmed* leads on past the cave already known to us towards the Carmel Ridge where its upper course is called *khallet el-aswadiyye*. On the other side of the *ghiyāda*, its sister valley, *khallet en-na'miyye*, presents its upper course, *khallet ej-juneidiyye*, already known to us. The ridge leaning on the *na'miyye* in the south is also called *ej-juneidiyye*. Hereupon, *khallet en-nawar* (Valley of the Gypsies) follows; it comes from *jōret el-'abid* (Negro Pit, or old mine) against which the small valley descends and separates *khirbet ed-dawābi* from the *muhraqa*. The dependence village of *ed-dālie, jelamet el-mansūra*, lies on *khallet en-nawar*. *Khallet el-bīr*, or *khallet bīr el-muhraqa*, forms the conclusion of the valleys moving directly towards the Kishon Plain. *Khallet el-manatt* (Jumping Point) follows thereafter and already proceeds southeastwards towards *tell el-qeimūn*; it ends in *wādi 'l-milh*.

The Kishon Plain rapidly becomes narrower near *rās el-ibrēghīt* which borders *wādi 'sh-shōmariyye* while Mount Carmel extends its foot still further into the plain as the last Galilean hills simultaneously push forward in the North. The passage becomes even narrower through the partly artificial and partly natural hills. On the Carmel side, these are the hills with the ruin *jelamet el-'atīqa* and *tell el-wa'r* which still stand in connection with the mountain along with *tell el-'amr* which already rises up the plain. The range with the hill of *harbaj* begins on the other side of the Kishon; the small *tell es-semen* is located next to it. The hill of *el-hāritiyye* then follows, further the small *tell el-'āli* and the hill of *shēkh ibrēk* behind *qurū' esh-shēkh ibrēk* (bare hills of *shēkh ibrēk*). *Tell el-qassīs* is situated on the eastern curve of the Kishon; *tell el-qeimūn* rises in the south by the entrance to *wādi 'l-milh*. The significance of such a strait increases more with the fact that the passage does not merely lead from the Jezreel Plain, actually lying in the East, to the seashore but rather breaks west Jordan Land in two mountainous parts. However, the mountains were always avoided by the conquering army masses or those passing through whenever possible. Thus, even Napoleon Bonaparte explained in his expedition to Palestine that the (Judean and Samaritan) hill country did not lay within his basis of operation. The passage is therefore Southern Palestine's most natural connection with Egypt on one side and with northeastern Syria and Mesopotamia on the other side. Indeed, Thutmosis III passed southeast of Mount Carmel through *wādi 'āra* and the *rūha* towards Megiddo but later generals often avoided such arduous marches. The path of the warring parties was thence the Sharon, or Saron, Plain and its northern continuation until the protrusion of Mount Carmel by the sea. There it turns towards the southeast until the strait from where it leads eastwards through the Jezreel Plain on the Jordan and towards Syria. Conversely, this site was the portal for the swarms of Bedouins and the conquerors from the East who wanted to advance westwards. It is natural that the respective leaders of the land sought to secure a key of this kind. The large number of towers, castles, and fortified sites on either side of the Kishon Plain cannot be noticed by us from there. Aside from the three ruins situated in the North, *rushmia*, *tell el-'ades*, and *khirbet 'aqqāra*, we have already come to know the following on Mount Carmel itself: the tower of *berjas* on the eastern slope, the likewise un-walled *khirbet esh-shōmariyye*, *khirbet esh-shimāliyye* and *khirbet esh-sharqiyye*, the tower of *ma'sirat el-a'dām*, *khirbet 'alā ed-dīn*, the fortification of *dahr maghārat umm ahmed*, the pre-historic *qal'at el-menābir*, and *khirbet umm ahmed*. The remaining ruins are *khirbet ez-zuhluq* at the foot of the mountain, *khirbet ed-dawābe* near the *muhraqa* further southwards, *khirbet el-mansūra*, and the *el-kerak* ruin. The fortified compound of Vespasian near *jelamet el-mansūra* should also be mentioned in this context. The hills positioned on either side of the river on the plain have already been named. Four ruins are still found on the Galilean hills of *ard el-ghābe* (Forest Ground) on the other side of the hill of *el-hāriṭiyye*; they are as follows: *ej-jājiyye* (*ej-jījiyye* among the Bedouins), *bēsūni*, *umm rāshid*, and *sūr tarābulus*. Although these are still unknown, the scope of this work does not permit us to study them.

The first group along the path to the *muhraqa* that travels through the plain from *jurn el-muhādade* in *wādi 'sh-shōmariyye* until *wādi 'l-a'waj* (the Crooked Valley) does not offer anything striking. The dependence village of *'usufia*, *jelamet el-'asāfni*, lies on the outlet of the latter *wādi*; it is a settlement of thirty-one houses that the residents of *'usufia* move into only when they are prompted to during the sowing or harvest season of their fields lying in the plain. A natural knoll which bears the ruin *jelamet el-'atīqa* pushes forward there in the plain. There is little of this that remains to be seen with the exception of several cisterns; most of the stones have broken apart or have been used elsewhere. An old necropolis, however, still survives to a great extent on the rocky northern border of the knoll. Aside from large caves, it contains many handsome tomb groups, namely family tombs with loculi under arcosolia, which may stem from antiquity. *Tell el-'amr* rises opposite the knoll; indeed, it lies on the western side of the Kishon yet it is still on the plain. Therefore, it will not be discussed here.

Two bridges lead over the Kishon at this point; one carries the tracks of the Hejaz Rail, and the other serves as a road. The latter divides into two branches soon thereafter. The road to Nazareth leads eastwards past the hill of *el-hāriṭiyye*, climbing the low hill country known as *el-'abhariyye* (The Storax Forest) which is planted with *'abhar* and *mell* trees. The road to *jenīn* turns southwards. It negotiates the Kishon anew through a ford slightly north of *tell el-wa'r* and then follows the foot of the mountain up until the elevation of *jelamet el-mansūra* where it, leaving behind *wādi 'l-milh* and *tell el-qeimūn* on the right, extends further to the southeast. One can use the wagon on this road when one wants to reach the *muhraqa*. One can even ascend to *jelamet el-mansūra*.

We have, nevertheless, chosen to only stick to the mountain's mule path west of the Kishon on foot or horseback. For this purpose, we separate ourselves from the road by *jelamet el-'asfāni* and circumnavigate the mountain's foot, close to the riverbed. We arrive at *khirbet ez-zuhluq* situated on a low extension of Mount Carmel via the *zuhluq*, the lower course of *wādi 'sh-sha'īr*, or through the short acclivity, *miqtal sa'd furru*, located a bit further southeastward. It is sometimes called *khirbet el-meshātil* on account of the *meshātil* (sing. *meshtel*, actually nurseries, but also vegetable and tobacco crops) planted there. On the way through *wādi 'sh-sha'īr*, one encounters a cave now occupied by goat herds; it is evident through the carved entrance that this is an ancient extended burial chamber. Beneath it, two additional burial chambers with five *kōkīm* and an unfinished chamber are located. Navigating the *miqtal sa'd furru*, one passes by many rock burial chambers on the northern slope as well as a cistern further on; most of these consist of four of five *kōkīm* each incorporated around a vestibulum. An ancient orthostatic wall stretches along the first slope; one observes traces of castle walls of medieval construction on the knoll above this. Among the detail carvings, I found a *hajar bedd* (grindstone of an oil press), a *jurn*, a plastered cistern, and a grape press with a *bīr* which did not serve the preparation of wine but rather grape honey. Although the stones are rather severely weathered, the conclusion that another Crusader castle was built here seems acceptable. The castle dominated both the narrow passage and guarded the entry to *'usufia* through *wādi 'sh-sha'īr*. Thus, the settlement must have bloomed for a long period, from the pre-historic era through the Jewish period until into the Middle Ages.

Again descending to the foot of the mountain and following this southeastward, one sees the pulpit-like rock protrusion in the west which bears the *qal'at el-menābir* already known to us. Soon afterwards, one stands before the protruding Carmel hill, *tell el-wa'r* (Wilderness Hill). From the North, one can climb to the hill via the gently inclined and well-developed *khallet et-tell* (or *khallet tell el-wa'r*) which contains several grape presses and ancient rock burial chambers. One recognizes two different ruins on the peak of the hill; eastwards, one observes a long building stretching forty-three meters from the northwest to the southeast which is well-preserved in its foundation walls. It is seven meters wide. It is divided into chambers according to width; the middlemost chamber was separated off by doubly thick walls. Three enclosed rooms are still located on each side of this central chamber. The walls do not seem to be of very old origin and consist of smaller than medium-sized stones. Similar elongated buildings divided into chambers in other regions from the Middle Ages and the era of Arab feudalism following thereafter are, in part, better preserved while others continue to be used today. Here, they are called *sūq* (market) and elsewhere *khān*; they are rooms for accommodating travelers who stop here. The ruins of the second building, which is not so long, are of an older date. The building was built with larger stones, and its depth, however, comprised of two and, in some places, three rows of rooms. A circle of relatively crudely hewn, rounded stones is discernable in the middle of many of these rooms. It was possible used as a fire pit. One still comes across traces of rock carvings which indicate burial sites on the western side of the hill which is separated from the mountain by a small depression. The imposing rock face with *maghāret umm ahmed* looks down on *tell el-wa'r* from the west. Opposite this, almost directly eastwards, *tell el-qassīs* (Priest's Hill) rises on the Kishon bend. Although no longer part of Mount Carmel, it thus deserves to be mentioned here because, according to the tradition of the church, Elijah slaughtered the priests of Baal after their idolatry was proven fallacious by the miracle of the sacrifice. From *tell el-wa'r*, we arrive again at the road to *jenīn*.

Wādi maghāret umm ahmed empties on the southern border of *tell el-wa'r*; an ancient road, strewn with stones though perhaps never consistently paved, extends eastwards here towards the Kishon. Dr. Schumacher drew my attention to this road. Passing by the *ghiyāda* and the soaring *khirbet ed-dawābe* beneath this, now leaving the road to *jenīn*, one arrives at the small Carmel knoll with *jelamet el-mansūra*. Before we enter the latter, another brief look at the surroundings proves worthy. Dr. Schumacher, who has thoroughly studied this entire region of the Kishon Plain, showed me a stone wall which stretches eastwards from *jelamet el-mansūra*. In doing so, he informed me that they are the remnants of the fortified compound of Vespasian. *Khallet el-bīr* reaches the plain further to the south; it passes *bīr el-muhraqa* which will be immediately mentioned. Still further, on the other side of *khallet el-manatt* which disembogues southwards towards *wādi 'l-milh*, I found the traces of a pre-historic orthostatic road which leads in a remarkably gentle incline up from the plain towards *bīr el-muhraqa* or the northeastern hill of *khirbet el-mansūra* located nearby.

Jelamet el-mansūra[1] is a dependence village of *ed-dālie* just as *jelamet el-'asāfni* is such for *'usufia*; considering the smaller spread of the field lying on the plain of the first village, *jelamet el-mansūra* has fewer houses than *jelamet el-'asāfni*. The residents of *ed-dālie* also descend to their dependence village only during the planting and harvest seasons. Slightly above the village, a new steam mill belonging to a resident of *haifā* stands. The well, *bīr el-mansūra*, is located in its immediate vicinity. A steep path leads upwards from *ej-jelame* which lies directly at the foot of the *muhraqa*; it passes *bīr el-muhraqa* at two-thirds of the elevation of Mount Carmel (Fig. 63). The certainly ancient well, inexhaustible even in dry years, may date from the Middle Ages in its current state. For the most part, it is walled with medium-sized blocks. One reaches the water level by means of a stairway; a

Figure 63. The well *bīr el-muhraqa*.

---

1   The second portion of the name is a reference to the nearby ruin, *el-mansūra*, which will be described shortly. The Fellāheen derive the first portion from the verb *jalama* which refers to the sheering of sheep. However, the place appellation traces back to an old, inexplicable word not stemming from Arabic. In this regard, it is worth noting that the name of a ruin south of *kufr lām* on the western coastal plain is pronounced *ej-jelame* by the residents of *'atlīt* yet as *ej-jelālīm* by those of *kufr lām*. The form *jelālīm* thereby seems to be construed as an (irregular) plural of *jelame*.

Figure 64. The Chapel of the Burnt Offering, *mesjid el-muhraqa*.

stone *jābi* (a trough for watering the livestock) and, furthermore, a wooden trough stands next to the well. The wooden trough is often used by the herds of the Bedouins camping in the surroundings. A long rock slab stretches southwards across the hillside; I could determine small traces of carvings on the slab. An olive tree plantation is located slightly above this to the North; it belongs to the terrain of the Monastery. From here, one climbs the terrace of the Chapel of the Burnt Offering, slashing through thick brush, in the direction of northwest in a solid half hour.

3. Traveling eastwards from *ed-dālie*, one arrives at the *muhraqa* in one and a half hours. After roughly ten minutes, one sees a handsomely round, carved stone colossus, the *tābūt jell fakhr ed-dīn* (sarcophagus in the Garden of Fakhr ed-Dīn) to the left of the path. It shall be discussed at the mention of the village *ed-dālie* with the ancient monuments found nearby. After a short while, one sees a large pond, *birket ed-dālie*, which remains filled with water into the summer. Its effluent reaches southwards, through *khallet ʿāli*, *khallet el-bīr* or *khallet bīr dūbil*, and further *wādi ʾn-nahl*. After a half-hour march from *ed-dālie*, one meets both towers, *rujūm baht*, just listed under the first path, near a small valley, *khallet hajar el-bedd*, which likewise leads to *wādi ʾn-nahl*. After one has passed *bīr el-hūti*, a crack in the rock that opens in the ground to which many legends have been linked, further in

the East, one looks right to the upper course of *wādi 'n-nahl* itself. Soon thereafter, one climbs *fersh el-kerak* which takes it name from the nearby *khirbet el-kerak*. It is here in this wild, stony region, with brush growing only sporadically, where I first saw a *fahid*, a red-gray panther. The long and wide stretches of wall, which divides the region into consistent right angles, are evidence that a civilization once stood in this area. Lastly, one can take the last section of the first path to ascend to the elevation of the *muhraqa*.

The chapel (fig. 64), erected on a small terrace[1], is a lovely new building; it contains a liturgical room with an altar and three bas-reliefs relating to Elijah's sacrifice miracle hanging on the wall. Aside from these, there are also lodging rooms with a kitchen. An upper story is currently being added (1907). One has a magnificent view from here which can be best appreciated from the roof of the chapel. One looks down on the deep *wādi 'l-milh* (Salt Valley) towards the southeast; this forms the border of the Carmel region. The low plateau of the *rūha* (*bilād er-rūha*) lies behind this, stretching southwards; it includes the villages *qīre*, *dāliet er-rūha*, *er-rīhāniyye*, *umm el-fahm*, and *subbārīn*. The Jezreel Plain spreads out in the East; Mount Gilboa (*jebel fuqū'a*), the lesser Mount Hermon (*nebi dahi*), and the lovely round form of Mount Tabor (*jebel et-tōr*) rise behind the plain. The blue lines of West Jordan Land bring the background to a close. Further northwards, one observes the elevations of Nazareth and *saffūrie*, then the *kōkab el-hawa* and the mountain of *safed* over which the larger Mount Hermon (*jebel esh-shēkh*) towers. The Galilean hill country occupies the entire northern side. On clear days, Lebanon beckons from the other side of this. The gentle slopes of Mount Carmel descend towards the ocean in the west. The ocean itself gleams near Caesarea in the southwest. The view is also open to the south. One has the village *umm ez-zeināt* at his feet. The open lay of the land implies that one can see the blazing of the chapel of the *muhraqa* as an emblem of the holy mountain from many locations in Palestine. It, namely, shines as the peak of Mount Carmel from the north, east, and south. The actual highest point of the mountain, *qambū'at ed-durziyye*, is not visible from the east and the south of the countryside. It does not rise clearly from its surroundings at any point.

---

1   According to previous assessments, the terrace lies 514 meters above sea level; my barometric reading, however, only revealed a height of 486 meters.

The terrain, belonging to the chapel and thus under the administration of the Santa Maris Monastery, is an enclave of the village field of *ed-dālie* from which it was separated. A cistern is located next to the chapel; the Bedouins residing nearby enjoy using this cistern. Several economic buildings stand to the Northwest. The terrain, surrounded by a small wall, stretches along the eastern slope of Mount Carmel until near *bir el-muḥraqa*.

Tourists and pilgrims often pose the question as to where Elijah's fire sacrifice stood. The account of the first Book of Kings places the incident without a doubt in the vicinity of the *muḥraqa* as it mentions the peak of Mount Carmel (King 1, 18:42). The Kishon, where the Baal priests were slaughtered, must be nearby (see 18:40). It can also be assumed that it concerns a point on the eastern slope of the mountain where Elijah, who was traveling by foot, could hurry ahead of King Ahab who was returning to Jezreel by wagon (see 18:46). In so far, the tradition may be correct if it adheres to this region. Determining the exact site is, of course, hardly possible due to a lack of precise clues. This remains true even when one considers the site where Elijah built his altar (see 18:30-32) to be identical with that where he bent down to the earth and placed his head between his knees awaiting the advancing rain clouds (see 18:42). It is well-known that the Latin Church places the miracle on the very same peak which now bears the chapel. The local Christians consider the peak rising next to it, upon which *khirbet ed-dawābe* stands, to be the holy site. They often refer to the ruin there as *khirbet ed-dēr* (Ruins of the Monastery); it has also been attempted to interpret that the name *khirbet ed-dawābe* (Ruin of the Melting, or Fusion) is a corruption of *khirbet ed-dawābih* (Ruin of the Sacrifice) - an etymology of which indeed adulterates the place name of local folkllore. The fact that Elijah sent his youths up to look out towards the sea according to 18:43 contradicts both of these localizations. Accordingly, Elijah did not stand on the highest peak. Previously, it could be considered that the site of the *muḥraqa* was the point where the boy saw the small cloud rising from the ocean (see 18:44). As mentioned above, the ocean is visible in the southwest from the *muḥraqa* which is the direction from which the wind frequently brings the rain. Others look for the site of the altar by *bir el-muḥraqa*, almost on the rock slab lying next to it to the south. It seems to speak for this theory that this well, never drying up, could have provided the water that Elijah doused over his altar (see 18:34).

Perhaps one may draw a connection with this that a gently sloping ancient road extends from the well, on the other side of *khallet el-manatt*, towards *wādi 'l-milh* on which Ahab could have traveled up the mountain in a wagon (see 18:44, 45). One could perhaps also draw on the elevation with the northernmost portion of the ruin of *khirbet el-mansūra* in determining the site of the altar. This elevation lies not far from the well and rises above the end of *khallet el-manatt*, and it shall immediately be described. Admittedly, each more precise specification relies on pure hypotheses as the accounts obtained by us do not mention topographical details.

Khirbet ed-dawābe lies on a summit of roughly the same height located more to the North; it is separated from the *muhraqa* only by a small valley. It appears to form a single elevation at some distance from the *muhraqa*. The building which must have undergone complete destruction as well as suffered greatly from weathering extends approximately 250 meters from the northwest to the southeast. Outworks stood on the eastern side and towards the southwest; today Bedouin graves can be found under these. One arrives at the main castle on the northwestern side by passing several simple cisterns and one double cistern. The main castle itself is one hundred meters long and forty meters wide. Its walls indicate a typical Crusader style in which larger ashlars set in mortar, encasing smaller stones in the middle, were used for the outer walls as in *'atlīt* and *rushmia*. Door posts with hinge holes and a cornice overtopping the portal as well as two notched columns can still be recognized. A sarcophagus (Fig. 65) stands on the western slope; it was carved out of the living rock and rises two feet above the earth's surface in the front. It bears sculptures on the narrow front side which are, of course, no longer clearly decipherable today. A large circle occupies the middle. A smaller circle appears to stand in the upper left corner while a star seems to stand in the upper right. The ornamentation on the lower corners cannot be determined. Based on the sculptures, the sarcophagus may stem from late antiquity; later it may possibly have served as a container for water. It is not placed in connection with the current ruins of *khirbet ed-dawābe*. The latter are remnants of a Crusader knight's castle as concluded from its construction. The ceramic and glass shards from the Middle Ages found there fit this assumption. The name *khirbet ed-dēr* (The Monastery) given to the site by the local Christians also suggests a Christian origin. This term is frequently used in the entire region not only for monastery ruins but also for medieval castle ruins.

Situated between the two small valleys *ghurq et-tōr* (the Bull's Sinking) and *khallet esh-shurbēta* on the southern slope and at the same height as *bīr el-muhraqa*, *khirbet el-mansūra* can be reached in twenty minutes from the *muhraqa*. Until about seventy years ago, a Druze village where Christians also lived stood here, but it was destroyed shortly before the remaining Druze villages *ed-dawāmīn*, *esh-shellāle*, *bistān*, and *umm esh-shuqaf*

Figure 65. Stone sarcophagus by *khirbet ed-dawābe*.

by the Muslims from *umm ez-zeināt*. There is almost nothing left from this Druze settlement that cannot be noticed in the structural character of the current Fellāheen villages. We will still encounter similar instances several times; the village *es-sawāmir*, once built to the south on the western slope of Mount Carmel still existed twenty-five years ago, has now completely disappeared except for several cactus hedges. It will be mentioned later. The still visible ruins of *el-mansūra*, mostly dating from an earlier period, lie on three hills. The ruins of the northernmost hill, indeed the oldest, have been destroyed beyond recognition. The middle hill bears the remains of a four-cornered chamber called *el-masbani* (The Soap Factory) by the Druses. It is built on the knoll so that its front side facing east still rises three and a half meters yet the western side, at the same height at the top, rises only seventy centimeters tall. Its walls are only thirty-five to forty centimeters thick and consist of smaller stones. Aside from ceramic shards, the mortar holding them together, curiously enough, still contains small glass slivers. The southernmost hill bears the main ruin, an extensive castle, as well as the remains of the Druze village. Indeed, the castle has been shattered with the exception of its foundation walls. One still finds door posts, several cisterns, and two columns with intermittent notches. The foundation walls consist of stones smaller than that which one commonly finds in medieval castles. Based on this, it is perhaps permissible to deduce that the ruins are the debris of an Arab castle. The name *el-mansūra* (The Victress) may correspond with this. It is a common name for the Arab feudal period which followed the Crusades. The many glass and ceramic shards also suggest the Middle Ages. However, this ruin may possibly not have been the oldest settlement on this site. Burial chambers and antiquities found within at the foot of the hill indicate that a similar settlement already stood here during ancient times.

A brief half hour from the *muhraqa*, on the other side of *fersh el-kerak*, already known to us, *khirbet el-kerak* rises on a small hill. It is surrounded by *khallet el-kerak* which flows into *wādi a'rāq en-nātif*, a side valley of *wādi 'l-milh*. Ascending from the west, one passes by large rock burial chambers, caves and grape presses, a nine-meter-deep cistern, and a large *hajar bedd* (grindstone from an olive press) on the way to a small plateau on the elevation that is surrounded by solid walls. The ruin is better preserved than many others and exhibits a group of large, beautifully carved ashlars. The wall construction that is, as a result, clearly discernable corresponds exactly with that of *'atlīt*. Southwards, on the valley's slope, one observes the extremely massive outworks. One has a lovely view to the south from the elevation. *Umm ez-zeināt* appears close-by; *er-rīhāniyye* and *kufrēn*, already in the *rūha*, are visible somewhat further on. *Umm el-fahm* greets from the east. *Umm et-tūt* is visible before the *khushm* by *zummārīn*; on the other side of this, *khdēra* lies northeast of Caesarea. Ascending to the east, one passes a large pond and a row of basins which suggest a well-arranged water supply. A *hajar farshe* (bedstone from an olive press) with a 1.75-meter circumference lies among the basins. There are countless ceramic and glass shards from the Middle Ages found all over the terrain but particularly on the gentle northern slope. Due to the many glass slags evident among the latter, one can assume that a glass smeltery was also once operated here. There should be no doubt that *el-kerak* was a Crusader castle. According to its position and construction, it is the solidest of all the castles I have seen on Mount Carmel. Thus it rivals in this important respect – if not also with regard to size and significance – with its two more famous sisters in name, the *husn el-akrād* or *qal'at el-husn* which is the *Crac des chevaliers* of our chroniclers between Tripoli and Homs and the extensive garrison castle *el-kerak* to the southeast of the Dead Sea.

The circle of fortresses borne on the eastern slope of Mount Carmel ends here. As we saw, indeed, most of the castles dated from the bellicose time of the Crusades. On the one hand, they threatened the narrow pass; on the other hand, they should have averted a surprise attack on *'atlīt* which was not quite as vulnerable from any other side. The *Castellum peregrinorum* was then protected in the North by Carmel's protrusion on the sea which was crowned by the Monastery of the Carmelites that was certainly fortified as well. In the south, the dune hills extended. Thus, Mount Carmel needed to be transformed into a rampart. The process of this in the North has been previously illuminated. The castle ruins become sparser moving on from *el-kerak*. Perhaps they also no longer formed such a densely closed system. All the same, they must have been sufficient for the needs of the time. *Wādi felāh*, for example, counts multiple castles in the valley and on either side of the elevations. At least, all important points were occupied on the southern portion of Mount Carmel as will be presented in the following sections.

10. Wādi Felāh and ed-Dālie.

Wādi felāh (Valley of Victory, or Luck)[1] is the largest and longest valley of the Carmel region. It empties into the ocean in the west and, after it traverses the coastal plain, climbs upwards to the mountains which it almost completely intersects. Its foothills reach up to the Carmel Ridge which forms only a narrow border between

---

1   It is a peculiarity of the local dialect to often leave out the article before the second word in compound place names although written Arabic would directly demand it. One may compare the village names *'ain ghazāl* (Spring of the Gazelles) and *'ain hōd* (Basin Spring). New names, however, have the article in this case, such as *beled esh-shēkh*. Equally, one finds it constant when the second word is a plural form such as with *umm ez-zeināt*.

'usufia and the *muhraqa* descending towards the Kishon Plain. The valley system is more than thirteen kilometers long from west to east while its streams simultaneously drain a region from north to south which is more than five kilometers wide at its widest point between *rās jibb 'usufia* and *khirbet dūbil* by *ed-dālie*. Aside from this, *wādi felāh* is the only Carmel valley which has a perennial water flow in places – namely, from *dustrē* until the ocean and further up the valley from *rās en-neba'* until below *esh-shellāle*.

When one follows *wādi felāh* from its outlet into the sea, where it is called *mōyet dustrē*, upwards, one arrives at the mountain after passing the plain where is first forms a narrow, fertile lowland. The same is bordered in the North by a high craggy rock face with large caves, the so-called *nawātif wādi felāh*. Then *wādi bistān* enters from the right; it will be discussed here with its branches at the conclusion. A mountain protrusion, *fersh musakkir bābu* (The Ridge that Concludes the Valley Portal), pushes forward here from the south towards the northeast through which the *wādi* is jammed into a narrow, rocky bed and is made impassable for riding animals. After a short distance, one finds *wādi 'l-mutemenna* (Valley of the Site of the Hindrance) on the right, then *a'rāq esh-shammās* (above *bayādat esh-shammās*, the Deacon Rock, respectively called Chalk of the Deacon). The cave *en-nātūf* is located opposite this; the *mughr esh-shiāh* (called *mughr ushāh* in *'usufia*) are situated slightly higher and to the east. At this point, the *wādi* takes a sharp turn, almost back-tracking, towards the northwest in order to orient itself directly eastwards again soon thereafter by running along the slope of *tell ez-za'rūr* situated in the North. Where the knoll *umm el-qarāmi* (Mother of the Root Stock) enters, strengthened by the ravine *el-munyasa* (Site of the Porcupine), from the latter, the valley turns southwards. It forms the ground *hāwi 'sh-shellāle* there with the garden *bistān* and the spring *'ain umm halāli*. A depression in the creek bed is called *ghadīr el-'abid* (Creek Hollow of the Slaves) at this point. Circumventing the hill with the village *esh-shellāle* in the south and running eastward, the valley acquires the *meshābik ruqtiyya*, or simply *el-meshābik*, (The Valley Net from *ruqtiyya*) from the south and, shortly thereafter, the ravine *en-naffākh* coming from *seyyālāt seq'ab* (Streamlets of the Mountain *seq'ab*). The small valley, *el-qannāshiyye*, then enters from the north; the slope lying opposite it to the south is called *ard el-'urqāni* (Rock Earth). The spring originates somewhat further eastwards on *rās en-neba'* (Spring Source). This spring is strong enough to irrigate the entire surroundings and previously propelled the mill from *esh-shellāle*. Now the valley turns southeastwards again whereby it takes on *shulūl āmina* with its side ravine, *khallet el-matāmīr*, from the north, i.e. from the ruin *ed-dawāmīn*. The riverbed receives the name *wādi 'l-balāt* (Creekbed of the Stone Slabs) near the ruin *khirbet es-sitt khadra* while at the same time the valley opening up to a well-formed plain assumes the term *merjet ez-zerā'a* (Garden Plain) on a longer stretch. The group of mountains in the northeast is called *'ishsh er-rikhame* (Eagle's Nest) and is bordered in the southeast by *wādi 'l-qasib* (Reed Valley) with multiple branches which has its origin at the *qambū'at ed-durziyye*. Opposite this, *ashlūl hajar rabāh* ascends to the *seq'ab* in the south. *Ashlūl el-huweishīri* and soon after it *khalāil ez-zbīb* (Small Raisin Valley) descend from the same height in a protrusion on the southern side. In the north, one sees the minor ravine *ashlūl ed-diyyiq* (The Narrow Ravine) and then the knoll *ashlūl el-murmāli* beyond *wādi 'l-qasab*. *Merjet ez-zerā'a* ends here by making another sharp turn further eastward. Thereupon the valley directs itself precisely to the east whereby forming a narrow ravine called *bāb el-hawā* (Gate of the Wind). *A'rāq el-wensā* rises on its southern side. It is closed in both the west and the east by a small valley on each side, both leading upwards to the south and both called *khallet el-wensā*. The northern slope is called *naqqār abu seif ed-dīn* (Stone Wilderness of the Father of *seif ed-dīn*). It is bordered in the west by *ashlūl eḏ-ḏīb* (Wolf's Ravine); we are already acquainted with its upper course under the name *wādi 'ain el-hāik*. The acclivity *ishkarāt* (شكاره) *barghōt* (Planting of the Bedouin *barghōt*, i.e. the flea) disembogues from the northwest into the lower course. The eastern border of this northern slope forms the small valley *'ishsh ghurāb* (Raven's Nest). The valley turns anew to the Southeast to bear the name *el-miqtali* (The Battle Ground) from now on in an extension. *Wādi* (or *jōret*) *abu 'abdallah*, descending from *rahārīh* on the Carmel Ridge, enters from the North at the bend. It is strengthened in its middle course by *khallet el-ghamīq* with the Leech Spring, *'ain el-'alaq*, and in its lower course by *khallet esh-shāsh*, or *khallet esh-shāsh el-qādi* (Valley of the Turban of the *qādi*), as it is named after the gleaming white chain of hills, *shāsh el-qādi*, abundant in reefs, in the south. *Khallet esh-shāsh* dispatches the small *khallet sa'd* at the eastern end of the village *'usufia* and ends as *merjet ez-zeitūn* south of the village which will be discussed in the eighth section. A striking round hill, *el-mudawwara*, rises from the plain at the southern end of the *miqtali*. The creek bed is named *wādi 'l-mudawwara* here. The adjacent slope to the North is called *rub'ān el-mādi*. *Khallet selāmi* borders it to the south; its upper course extends south of *rúus el-maqā'id* (Heads of the Seats) while the entire southern side of the *khalle* from *dahret en-namli* (Ant's Backs) is towered over by a ruin of the same name. *Wādi 'l-mudawwara* sends the small valley *el-'aqabi* (The Ascent) southwards and then assumes the name *wādi 'l-feshsh*, or *khūr el-feshsh* (Valley, respectively Plain, of the Camel Lice), in its southeastern course. The *'ishsh ghurāb* (Raven's Nest) branches off to the northeast. It immediately divides again: it continues in the same direction under the name *khallet a'bēd* in order to end as *khānūq ʾsmēt* at the *maqāzih* (Implantations) already known to us from the description of the routes to the *muhraqa*. It dispatches the slope *el-meshālih* eastwards which reaches up to *ma'sirat el-a'dām*. The floor of *rúus el-qabāla* (Chiefs in the South, namely from *'usufia*) rises to 520 meters above sea level south of *'ishsh ghurāb*. After *khūr el-feshsh* sent *khallet abu fāris* up to *rub'ān el-khurfēsh* (Terrace of Thistles) on the Carmel Ridge northeastwards, it acquires the name *khallet el-a'war* (Valley of the One-Eyed). It ends as *khallet hamze* on the Carmel Ridge opposite *khallet el-aswadiyye*.

The single larger side valley of *wādi felāh*, *wādi bistān*, mentioned in the beginning, extends from *fersh musakkir bābu* to the southeast when one follows the valley up the river where it acquires *wādi bedrān* coming from the East. The latter lies on the junction point in the north towered over by *sifār en-nāmūsi* (Block of Stone from the Sarcophagus); a short distance further, it sends *khallet ed-dukhān* (Smoke Valley) towards the southeast into which the ravine *jōret el-ma'ze* (The Goat's Pit) enters from the northeast. Traveling up *wādi bistān*, one arrives at the spring *'ain ez-zerqā* (Blue Spring) where the path coming from *ed-dālie* turns southwestwards towards the nearby village *'ain hōd*. After some time, one reaches the ruin of the former Druze village *bistān* (Garden) near which the spring *'ain en-nakhle* (Palm Spring) is located in the North. After leaving the southern cave *el-midān*, or *el-mayādīn*, on the right and passing the small valley, *wādi 'l-balāt*, coming from the massif *seq'ab* on the left, one finds oneself before the ruin of another Druze village, *umm esh-shuqaf* (Mother of the Shards). The valley here bears the name of the ruin, *wādi umm esh-shuqaf*. The small valley *bistān el-leimūn* (Lemon Garden) lies with a spring east of this, likewise issuing from the *seq'ab*. *Khallet el-'āsi*, originating by the ruin *dūbil*, then enters from the South, bordering the peak *rās el-'āli* in the North. The spring *'ain umm esh-shuqaf* lies on the point of outlet of *khallet el-'āsi*; *a'rāq el-'āsi* (The Wayward Rock) towers above it in the south. The valley divides itself until its end after an additional small depression, *khallet el-wāwiyye* (Valley of the Female Jackal) in the south in order to encircle the village *ed-dālie*. The southern branch includes *'ain el-qibliyye* in the south of the village; the northern branch, *khallet 'īsā*, contains *'ain esh-shimāliyye*. It drains *merjet enjas* (Pear Plain) in the North and the Northeast from *ed-dālie*.

Ed-dālie lies at the beginning of a plateau that climbs southeastwards towards the Carmel Ridge where it forms *fersh el-kerak* and finally ends in the peak of the *muhraqa*. It sends the previously mentioned side valleys of *wādi felāh* to the North and the also previously mentioned ravines of the eastern slope of the Carmel which descend to the Kishon to the East. The plateau is drained in the south by the ravines of *wādi a'rāq en-nātif* that end in *wādi 'l-milh* as well as by several small valleys. The ravines will be cited in Section 11. These small valleys flow partly into *wādi 'l-metābin* and partly through *wādi 'n-nahl* to *wādi 'l-maghāra*. The two last valley groups will be dealt with in the fourteenth section. In the southeast the massif of the plateau reaches until the lower peak of *umm el-benādik* (sing. *bendak*, food bale) which abuts the *b'ībish* in the north. *Rās el-muhellil* (467 meters above sea level) rises south of *ed-dālie*, separated from the slightly lower *rās el-'āli* only by a narrow ravine, *khallet en-nassār*. *Miqtalit umm esh-shuqaf* (Battle Grounds of *umm esh-shuqaf*) lies at the foot of *rās el-'āli* on the southwestern slope. The highest point of this portion of Mount Carmel associated with *wādi felāh* valley system, the *seq'ab*, lies between *esh-shellāle* and *ed-dālie*. It forms two peaks: the northern peak reaches 476 meters above sea level by *esh-shellāle* and the southeastern, located closer to *ed-dālie*, reaches 493 meters above sea level. The latter bears a ruin, *khirbet seq'ab*.

The lower course of *wādi felāh* on the shore and in the coastal plain will be described in Section 12 (on *'aṭlīṭ*). The valley runs along a brief stretch in a well-cultivated ground, often planted with olive trees, by the outlet from the mountain. However, a long, frequently winding, rocky and impassable party aligns itself here until *hāwi* from *esh-shellāle*. The villagers avoid entering this; the reason for this avoidance lies not only in the difficulty of the hike but rather more so in the fact that this portion of the valley is still inhabited by panthers which stalk the surroundings at night. The *mawārid* (sing. *mārid*), giant, diabolical ghosts, certainly bring about the greatest fear in the Fellāheen; according to general opinion, they reside here. If one wanted to develop a rational cultivation in the extremely fertile region in the middle and upper courses of *wādi felāh*, then one must lay out a path from *esh-shellāle* descending the valley which would nevertheless be associated with very large costs.

The settlement *esh-shellāle* lies on a hill surrounded by a creek bed in the middle of a well-irrigated and therefore very fertile plain which is suitable not only for planting haulm, legumes, and melons but also for gardening and more so for the cultivation of fruit trees. It receives its irrigation partially from the spring *'ain umm halāli* and partially in longer conduits from *rās en-neba'* which today still supplies the gardens whereas it once simultaneously lead to the former mill of *esh-shellāle*.[1]

The shortest and most comfortable connection between *haifā* and *esh-shellāle* leads across the Carmel Ridge from where one still has a three hour march before oneself. The path extends across the Carmel Ridge until the other side of *el-khrēbi*. Turning right at the climb to the *juneidiyye*, it reaches the rock portal of *wādi 'l-murrān* beneath *maghārat el-glīkh*. One arrives at the northern slope of *wādi felāh* by *ard el-mughrāqa* by ascending the elevation on the other side of *wāsit trābe* and bypassing the elevation of *esh-shēkh jebel* and its foothills, *a'rāq khālid*, in the west. One descends to the ravine of the *munyasa* (Site of the Porcupine), passes the beautiful, ancient quarry *ed-derejāt* and turns towards the rise with the settlement. While climbing, one observes countless building stones, among them two columns with small notches which are still more irregular than those of the column in *hawākir umm el-hīrān*. Slightly higher, one sees a *kharaze*, an opening stone from a cistern, through which a *sindyāne* has grown. Before entering the village, one passes a doubled, square rock extension with a level floor. A niche is found on one of the vertical sides of one of these. All of this presents the same image that the rock structure on *esh-shēkh jebel* does. While the ground there was, however, covered in humus and could not be studied, the level surface here is exposed.

---

1   The word *shellāle* refers to a small waterfall; however, such a waterfall does not exist in the region and according to the ground configuration may also have previously not existed. I, therefore, see no reason to doubt the statements of the villagers that *shellāle* means the torrent that once gushed from the lovely walled mill conduit onto the overshot mill wheel.

It exhibits a round, hollowed-out crevice in the ground in front of each of the two niches. The crevice is about twenty-five centimeters in diameter and thirteen centimeters deep. A round blood groove surrounds each of the crevices and empties into them. Undoubtedly, these are sites of ancient sacrificial altars. The transportable round altar would have been set up before a niche. The blood of the sacrificial animal ran down its outer side in order to be conducted by the blood grooves into the crevice below the altar. A completely corresponding arrangement, yet more primitive in its method of carving, is found in *esh-shēkh ibrāq* and will be described in Section 15 with the addition of an image.

An old age can be ascribed to the village of *esh-shellāle* as revealed by the remnants of an ancient culture. The hill is covered with ruins; the scultures among them date back to the Roman Imperial Era, the Byzantine Era, and the Crusades (Fig. 66). At the nearby *ard el-'urqāni*, I found a portion of a recently open, and unfortunately thereby destroyed, burial chamber. The carving here indicates Late Roman art (Fig. 67). The settlement may also have still existed during the Arab feudal period as the current state of the mill suggests. It would have then been abandoned during the general decline of the agriculture only to be populated again nearly 130 years ago by the Druses. The destruction of the Druze village, which falls in the time period shortly after Ibrahim Pasha's retreat from the region in 1840, is illuminated by a local tradition that was confirmed for me by the oldest men in *ed-dālie* and *'usufia*.

According to this tradition, a Muslim woman from *'ain hōd* by the name of *āmina bint abu 'l-hēja* proceeded to *ed-dawāmīn* via *esh-shellāle* to question a Christian *khūri* there about an ill person. Near *esh-shellāle*, she was, however, assaulted by Druses, killed, and burned in a *mashhara* (coal pile) in the nearby dell. Her relatives, disturbed by her absence, visited the clerics in *ed-dawāmīn* who must have told them they had not seen the woman. Thus, they searched the entire region until they found the half-charred *sma'di* (headdress)

Figure 66. Decorated stone from *esh-shellāle*.

Figure 67. Late Roman burial chamber ornament in *ard el-'urqāni*.

Figure 68. The mill at *esh-shellāle*.

Figure 69. Jewish burial portal from *khirbet ruqtiyya*.

from the woman in the coal pile. Enraged at this injury, unheard of in the Arab World where the custom is to provide women with special protection, the Muslims of *'ain hōd* banded together with their brethren from *ikzim* and *umm ez-zeināt* to avenge her death. The Druze village *esh-shellāle* was destroyed, and as the torch of war was kindled, the neighboring Druze villages, *bistān* and *umm esh-shuqaf*, as well as *ed-dawāmīn* must have likewise fell. The memory of these events lives on in the name of the dell where the coal pile stood, *shulūl āmina* (Amina's Ravine).

The *esh-shellāle* region was beaten down to create the village field of *'usufia*; the borders were already listed in its description. Recently, the dragoman at the Imperial German Vice-Consulate to *haifā*, Mr. Shukri Mansūr, had purchased the land. He has built a home and farm on the hill and gardens and basins in the plain.

The mill, which is of course no longer running, stands at the foot of the hill (Fig. 68). Based on its current appearance, the structure is of Arab design yet it is much older. The carvings on many of the stones used for its construction indicate the Era of the Crusades.

Figure 70. Sculpture from the mill at *esh-shellāle*.

One of them exhibits the sculpture which is depicted in the sketch given here (Fig. 70). It measures twenty-five square centimeters. It is exactly identical with the cross-shaped figure on a stone at a house in *ed-dālie*; it was brought there from the *dūbil* ruin.

The area surrounding *esh-shellāle* would allure both geologists and archaeologists for excursions. One finds lovely fossils of sand dollars (*Clypeaster*) and large see urchins (*Hemiaster*) nearby. The southern slope lying opposite the village, *en-naffākh*, consists of a brown, intensely weathered, volcanic basalt which, when chemically studied, revealed a composite of silicate, acidulated lime, magnesia, and especially, alumina, or clay, and iron. One reaches the large caves, *mughr esh-shiāh*, in the southwest after a brief half hour; today they are primarily inhabited by goat herds. *Nātūf esh-shiāh* is situated beneath the caves. The red rock face opposite these on the northern side of the valley, *a'rāq esh-shammās* (Deacon's Rock), likewise contains caves. Ascending from *mughr esh-shiāh*, one can turn westwards to arrive at *sayāfīr en-nāmūsi* passing over *hajar el-humr* (red stones) in *wādi 'l-mutemenna'*. A number of ancient garden walls extend across the ridge here; individual remnants of buildings stand between them. The visit to *khirbet ruqtiyya* (Ruin of the Turtledove) is more interesting. The path leads directly south of the hill from *esh-shellāle* across the *en-naffākh* slope and then through the valley of *meshābik ruqtiyya* (Valley Net of *ruqtiyya*) on the elevation which is identified from afar by a dominating hill bearing various trees. Of the ruin, only the foundation walls are still standing; they are made of medium-sized, well-carved ashlars. They give the impression of a medieval castle. Aside from this, columns, a large *kharaze* from a well, and door posts are still recognizable. A large column drum is still found next to these. It is like those which are present at so many sites on Mount Carmel. It implies that the settlement already existed in antiquity. This assumption is verified by the nearby burial chambers located in the East. One of these deserves our attention due to the shape of its foundation which is given in a sketch (Fig. 71).

As revealed in the symmetry of the structure, the burial chamber was first built as a family tomb in order to extend its almost square vestibule (a) to the loculi (b) on the side walls under the arched arcosolia. Later it was transformed to a Jewish grave with *kōkīm* (c). Whereas these *kōkīm* feature a rounded-off end, as is common here, a grave shaft (d) with a rectangular end is situated opposite the entrance.

Even the small dimensions of rooms designated for admission of the corpses at this burial site do not go unnoticed. The vertical height of the graves from the leveled floor to the horizontally smoothed ceiling measures roughly one meter. The portal is decorated with circles and stars outside, above and next to the entrance; this probably dates from the time of the extension of the chamber for the attachment of the *kōkīm* and implies Jewish origin (Fig. 69). This assumption is even more likely as, namely, the presence of multiple Jewish graves in the more southern portion of Mount Carmel demonstrates.

More carved columns, sometimes round and sometimes four-cornered, are found near the gravesite; a large boulder transformed into an oil mill is also found there. The stone slab

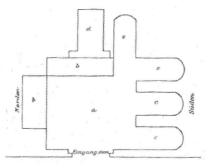

Figure 71. Burial chamber in rock at *khirbet ruqtiyya*.

is handsomely rounded on its sides and is treated above as *hajar farshe* (bed stone). It exhibits a raised edge and a not very large hollow in the middle as a socket for the vertical wooden dowel through which the lever was fixed which bore the *hajar bedd* (grindstone) on an arm rotating on the *hajar farshe*. A protrusion on the boulder contains a depression where the ground olives were deposited. Based on my knowledge, this is the only oil mill in the entire region standing outdoors and carved out of a boulder.

From *khirbet ruqtiyya*, one can either reach *'ain en-nakhle* southwards via *maqāmāt ruqtiyya* and *jōret el-ma'ze* and arrive at *bistān* where one meets with the path to *'ain hōd*, or ascend the mountain *seq'ab*. Turning eastwards on the latter option, one first ascends the elevation which rises above *esh-shellāle* (476 meters above sea level). Then one arrives at the higher peak (493 meters above sea level) in the southeast from where one enjoys a magnificent view of the southern portion of Mount Carmel and the entire region to the south and the west. This peak is crowned by *khirbet seq'ab* which is thoroughly destroyed yet suggests that it stems from a castle of the Middle Ages in its dominating position. In fact, it would be incomprehensible if the Crusaders had not secured this significant point. One descends from here to *ed-dālie* in a half hour.

The visit to *khirbet ed-dawāmīn* (or sing. *ed-dāmūn*), sitting enthroned on the northern slope of *wādi felāh*, is even more attractive. From the mill of *esh-shellāle*, one first climbs past a rock displaying many caves until one comes to the path which leads up to the hill of *esh-shellāle*. One stands before the lovely ancient quarry; it bears the name *ed-derejāt* (The Stairs) (compare Fig. 5) after the step-like rock carvings. Rather than climbing through the *munyasa*, one turns right and reaches the elevation with the ruin after a half-hour march. One enters the field of ruins near several small Fellāheen houses; the field lies between the two small valleys, *el-munyasa* and *shulūl āmina*, but still extends beyond these on either side with its tomb groups. It has an expanse of 600 meters from west to east and 300 meters from north to south. The remains of the Druze village are found in the middle. The village was founded in the second half of the eighteenth century and was destroyed after the year 1840. The number of the Christians settled here who could save themselves from the ravage in time sufficed to support a separate *khūri*. Innumerable remains from buildings, a large number of cisterns and grape presses, and various grind- and bed stones from oil presses lay nearby. A castle stood on the Eastern side; its enclosure walls can still be followed, and its

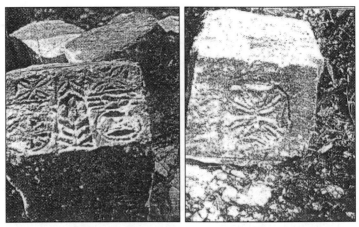

Figures 72 and 73. Cross sculptures at *khirbet ed-dawāmīn*.

outworks reach down towards the valley. Based on its construction style, it originated from the Crusader Era and possibly encircled a church. The stones carved with cross (Fig. 72 and 73) which I still saw there have since been used in the extension of the church in *'usufia*. A walled underground chamber that is now partly buried is located towards the northwest; however, it may date from antiquity based on its handsome structure. Still further to the northwest, one observes a deep, well-constructed rock cavern which is divided into two large rooms separated by a rock wall. A pillar rises in the center of each room; it probably once supported the ceiling which has now disappeared. Plaster is visible on the walls; the rooms may have served as water basins during the Middle Ages. However, three small niches exist on the western wall of one room which suggest the notion that the rooms date back to antiquity and were possibly used for sacral purposes. The carving of the pillars also implies the same. An almost uninterrupted row of rock burial chambers from the most varied epochs occupies the entire slope down to the valley. One finds ancient family tombs on *shulūl āmina*. The *maghāret et-tibn* (Straw Cave) presents a type of an incomplete Jewish grave with seven *kōkīm* above on the *munyasa*. A burial cave with a vault-like ceiling stands next to it. An additional rock burial chamber is also there; the head of an ox is depicted on its inner portal (Fig. 74). The sculpture is executed exceptionally crudely, and thus an archaeologist, an acquaintance of mine, leans to the view of ascribing a very old age to the grave. I have doubts about agreeing with him because this grave sculpture was made as a craft and was certainly often assigned to less talented masters of the craft. Furthermore, the handling of the graves located in the remaining sections differs in no way from the usual workmanship of antiquity in the local region. A stone slab (Fig. 75) which I found close by is somewhat more artistic; it may date from the Jewish Era. A number of Crusaders graves can be detected further in the west on the other side of the *munyasa*. They are much more spacious, and they exhibit several trough graves next to each other standing vertical to the vestibule under the arcosolia. The tomb covers which were adorned with the Crusaders'

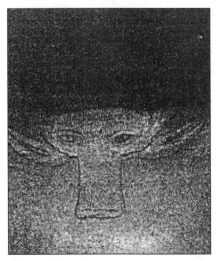

Figure 74. Ox head on a grave at *khirbet ed-dawāmīn*.

Figure 75. Sculpted stone slab from *khirbet ed-dawāmīn*.

coats of arms, have unfortunately been so destroyed that I could not even consider photographing them. The ruin is one of the largest and most intriguing in the entire region. Excavations of this site could possibly yield important findings. The village embodied in the remnants must have stood in significant prosperity for a long time. The return path to the Karmelheim can be taken through *khallet ed-dāmūn*, passing by *maghāret ed-dāmūn*, and through the eastern *wādi 'l-qil'* across *el-khrēbi*. A knoll attaches itself to the hills of *ed-dawāmīn* in the East; it is called *khirbet el-matāmīr* (Ruin of the Small Silo, i.e. granary). It is covered with a multitude of terrace walls amidst which several ruins of building can be recognized as with *khirbet sayāfīr en-nāmūsi*. They may have only been gardens with their corresponding garden houses. From there, one soon reaches the Ridge Path by *jibb 'usufia* via the *rahārīh*.

Following *wādi felāh* further upwards from *esh-shellāle*, passing the romantic creek bed covered with oleanders, one soon arrives at *rās en-neba'* (Spring Head) from which the various springs issue that irrigate the ground of *esh-shellāle*. Traveling southwards, one passes *khirbet es-sitt khadrā* (Ruin of the Lady *khadrā*). The cultivated eastern side presents little that is worth noting. The western side forms a steep rock slope towards *wādi 'l-balāt* yet is characterized by massive wall blocks which are certainly ancient. With this, the character of the high sanctity of the site corresponds with the views of the Fellāheen which also extend to the deciduous oaks (*mell*) already mentioned in the first section of this study. The four trees, long since dead, are not touched by any villager although its dry wood is sold for a high price in *haifā*. The plain beginning here, *merjet ez-zerā'a* (Cultivation Plain), is very fertile and well-cultivated. After the harvest, Bedouins settle in the stubble fields as is the case all over Mount Carmel; the Fellāheen owners of the fields are pleased with this because the nomads' herds fertilize the fields. The path restored by Mr. Oliphant from the Carmel Ridge to *ed-dālie* enters here from the north through *wādi 'l-qasab*. A few paces ahead of this, one can observe a carved *midbise* on a boulder under a large carob tree. A layer of porous volcanic tuff, *trāb el-murmāli* (or *trāb el-merāmīl*), stands on the northern slope where *merjet ez-zerā'a* ends. It is similar to the material already known to us at the spring, *'ain qatf ez-zuhūr*, by *et-tīre* which revealed basaltic components under the microscope. A *jurn* hewn into a rock slab is located in the approximate vicinity. One can leave *merjet ez-zerā'a* by way of the small southern valley, *khalāil ez-zbīb* (Raisin Valleys), in order to arrive at *ed-dālie* where one passes a small, unknown ruin high on the elevation. Hereto one, however, usually chooses the subsequent parallel valley, *khallet el-wensā*, that likewise passes a ruin, *khirbet el-wensā*. The latter is not very large; it consists only of a stone structure dating from antiquity and a *sīh*. East of this, near the eastern *khallet el-wensā*, a larger and better preserved ruin, also called *khirbet el-wensā*, is supposed to be situated. I did not search for it. The name *wensā* may have possibly been carried over from the ruin to the valley and *a'rāq el-wensā*. At this point, *wādi felāh* is constricted into a narrow ravine, *bāb el-hawā* that is oriented directly eastwards. On the other side of this, it expands to *el-miqtali* plain (The Battle Ground). It is crossed by the path leading from *'usufia* to *ed-dālie* which winds southwards on the elevation through the *'aqabe* in order to arrive at the village *ed-dālie* through *merj enjās*. A peculiar round hill, *el-mudawwara*, rises in the southern end of the *miqtali*. Opposite this, *dahret en-namli* (Ant's Ridge) bears a ruin that probably stems from a castle of the Middle Ages between *wādi salāmi* and *'ishsh ghurāb*. The ruin covers an area of roughly 150 square meters; the walls consist of medium-sized stones. A *sīh*, carved into the rock and furnished with an entry channel, can still be recognized. Its sides measure five and a half to three meters. Among the foothills of *wādi felāh* reaching to the Carmel Ridge between *'usufia* and the *muhraqa*, only *shāsh el-qādi* presents reason for closer consideration. It bears an ancient settlement on its ridge. This settlement has, however, been so intensely destroyed and weathered that it is difficult to determine its traces from the mature reefs. More often than not, one, at most, recognizes a pile of ruins. I observed the remains of a twenty-centimeter-wide, round conduit from a *midbise* and a circular hollow belonging to it there. A curious, larger grape press is, however, well-preserved; its form varies from every other type. An approximately sixty-centimeter-deep *birke* in the shape of an oval with axes roughly one and a half meters to ninety centimeters, respectively, is located next to a fifteen-centimeter-deep, four-cornered *mastabe* carved into the rock with sides roughly three by two meters. The conduit connecting the two hollows is not open but rather runs as a cavity through the edge of the rock of the *mastabe*. Due to the uniqueness of this type of press, I am not able to say from which time period the structure dates. Yet it holds the most similarity with the later reconfiguration of the primitive press structure on *esh-shēkh jebel*. The slopes of *shāsh el-qādi* are covered with a number of terrace walls. Another grape press is found on the side of *'usufia*, nearly at the foot of the hill, which assumes an association with the *midbise* in its proportions, the shallow carving of the *mastabe*, the open conduit, and the irregular handling of the corners of the *birke*. It lies above *a'rāq er-rāhib* in the valley of *et-tīre* and will be more thoroughly described. – The peaks, *rúus el-qabāla*, lying to the southeast, also host several grape presses.

The large Druze village, *ed-dālie* (The Vine), lies south of *a'rāq el-wensā*. Its full name is *dāliet el-kirmil* (The *dālie* in Mount Carmel) in contrast to *daliet er-rūhā*, officially called *daliet el-kirmil* and *umm esh-shuqaf* as a village community.

Paths. 1. From the Karmelheim on the Ridge until *jibb 'usufia*, then southwards through *wādi 'l-qasib* and *merjet ez-zerā'a* with an ascent through *khallet el-wensā* and a descent in *khallet 'īsā* totaling four hours.

    2. From *'usufia* through *khallet el-ghamīqa* and *wādi abu 'abdallah*, afterwards through the *miqtali*, the *'aqabi* and *merjet enjās*, totaling one and a half hours.

    3. One and a half hours from the *muhraqa*; see Section 9 above, path 3.

    4. From *haifā* through the coastal plain until *'ain hōd* and then through *wādi bistān* and *wādi umm esh-shuqaf* at the conclusion of this section, totaling five hours.

    5. Towards *umm ez-zeināt*, totaling one and a half hours.

The Kishon forms the border of the village field in the East; *ashlūl el-mansūra* and *ashlūl mansūr* form the border at the beginning of *wādi 'l-milh* where the region of *el-qeimūn* and *qīre* join, followed by *wādi 'l-milh* and the mouth of *wādi a'rāq en-nātif*. The border extends upwards on the slope south of the *muhraqa*; it runs through the region called *ez-zīghān* to the upper course of *wādi 's-sillame* and to *bayādat summāqa* until the *b'ībish*. Hereupon, it crosses *wādi 'n-nahl* and reaches *rās el-muhellil*, descends to the southwest where it also surrounds the *miqtalit umm esh-shuqaf* and extends northwards to *rās el-ahmar* in order to arrive at *wādi umm esh-shuqaf* across the *mīdān*. Outrunning this valley east of the *bistān*, the border cuts through *khallet ed-dukhān* and climbs the *seq'ab* by *khirbet seq'ab*. It arrives at *merjet ez-zerā'a* via *shulūl huweishīri* from where it from now on follows the course of *wādi felāh* until the ridge, adjoining the field from *'usufia*, and the course of *khallet el-aswadiyye* on the other side of *wādi felāh* until reaching the Kishon.

The large, lovely village *ed-dālie* (Fig. 76), surrounded on three sides by protecting elevations and accessible to the cool west winds only through the opening of *wādi umm*

Figure 76. The village *ed-dālie* from the Northwest.

esh-shuqaf in the west, has the reputation of having a healthy and mild climate. One sees *'usufia* from the eastern portions that are situated higher; one enjoys the view from the western slope of the charming valley of *umm esh-shuqaf.* The tower of *'aṭlīṭ* rises before the blue surface of the ocean on the other side of the valley. Three quality springs provide the village with water: *'ain esh-shimāliyye* in *khallet 'īsā* in the north, *'ain el-qibliyye* in the south, and the nearby *'ain umm esh-shuqaf* in the west. The settlement had already existed in ancient times as substantiated by the graves and other ruins and reached back to the most remote eras. It must have also thrived during the Middle Ages. Nearly 130 years ago, the Druze family *dār hassūn* from *mār ishāq* in *jebel el-'alā* by *hamā* settled here. Soon other fellow believers from *jindlāya* and *el-bīre* from the same region moved there. The dialect of these immigrants is purer than that of the Druses from Lebanon in *'usufia* who for this reason have to put up with a lot of mockery. The attack which wiped out the Druze villages from Mount Carmel after Ibrahim Pasha's retreat to Egypt seems to have ceased before *ed-dālie* probably because the population of this village was too many in number for the Muslims. Sixty-two years ago (1261 Hijrah) another terrible storm brewed across the village. A young Bedouin was found dead in the village field, and the Muslims believed that the Druses had killed him. This resulted in a very tense relationship between the Muslims and the Druses which soon led to hostility. The residents of *ed-dālie* who no longer felt secure in their Muslim surroundings decided to emigrate (*rahle*) and proceeded together, leaving behind their fields and houses, towards their co-religionists to *mejdel esh-shems* and *'ain fit* near *bāniās* where they next stopped. Meanwhile, the groundlessness of the accusation that they were charged with manifested. The authorities did not want to do without the industrious tillers and their tax revenue, and upon their departure, the shēkh of *et-tīre* at that time, Tāhir el-Yūsif, headed out with a hundred men on horseback to persuade the Druses to return to *ed-dālie*. After long negotiations, they decided to this since bonds were to be given to them in the future. Only individual families kept their decision and settled in *haurān*. Since this time, *haurān* is also the aim of the wishes of those who returned whereby it is influential to consider that the Druses there are not called on for Turkish military service. Mr. Oliphant settled in *ed-dālie* nearly thirty years ago; he built himself a spacious house there, planted vineyards, provided for the restoration of the path, and performed various good deeds to the Druses. His project to furnish the village community with a modern school failed due to difficulties caused by the government. He had to content himself with supporting the old reading school with money. His property went to his widow after his death; she appointed Jabbūr Effendi Qardāhi, a lawyer from *haifā*, as her administrator.

Ed-dālie counts 744 residents (*dīlāwi*, pl. *dayālni*) who have two *mukhtār* for secular affairs. The first of these, the actual village shēkh, is a member of the house of *hassūn*. At the same time, he is the representative of the Stella Maris Monastery and holds custody of the key to the chapel of the *muhraqa*. Spiritually, the Druses have a *shēkh ed-dīn* who also teaches at the school and is assisted by a second *shēkh*. He leads the religious service in the *khalwe* which I nevertheless visited during the day, that is, not at the time of the sermon. It is a handsome new building that one enters through a terrace adorned with a pomegranate tree. It is separated into two large, elongated rooms from the west to the east; the rooms are divided by posts and a curtain. In contrast to the mosques, the main room contains neither a pulpit nor a *mihrāb*. The cleric stands in the center of the room; the listeners gather around him while he removes the colorful covering from one of the holy books and begins the lecture facing south. The following inscription stands on the eastern wall:

نجيذنا مما نخاف ١٣٠٠   *nadjīnā mimmā nakhāf 1300*

يا خفى الالطاف   *yā khafiyya 'l-altāf*

It is to be read from the top to the bottom and means, roughly translated: "Oh, you whose favors are concealed deliver us from that which we fear. The year 1300 (1883 A.D.)." The expression *khafiyyu 'l-altāf* is also common among the Muslims but it has a special connection to the religion of the Druses. According to their highest dogma, God is, above all else, a God of that which is hidden. In addition, the room which is lighted by a window on the northern side contains a modern wall clock and various cupboards which hold the holy books as well as bedding. Namely, the *khalwe* is simultaneously a *menzūl*, i.e. lodgings for Druze shēkhs who come to visit from other villages. The southern room, separated by the curtain, accommodates the women during the service who in this way most likely hear the preacher but do not see him.

The preparation of a paper-thin flat bread called *'awīs* in a *tannūr* is unique to the Druses. The *tannūr* is a walled, plastered, cylindrical hollow placed vertically in the ground; a large fire is kindled on its floor. As soon as the flame no longer rises but the wall still glows, the formed dough is pressed on the wall by the women by means of a pillow (*kāra*) where it sticks until it is baked (approximately one and a half to two minutes). The *'awīs* tastes best fresh. Another trade unique to the Druses is the production of pottery which transpires in the most primitive method. For this one uses hard yellow clay found near the village. The clay contains silicates, some magnesia, and iron as well as calcium and is called *trāb qata'* (cut clay) by the Fellāheen. Softened by adding water, mixed with *tibn nā'im* (fine chaff) and ground *milh qāq* (calcite) and kneaded, the clay is shaped by hand into various simple vessels by the women without the use of a potter's wheel. Thereafter it is fired in the open flame. The vessels, which are very durable but not attractive, exhibit characteristic forms which one already finds in the oldest ceramic wares of the region.

The *maqām* of a saint, *abu ibrāhīm*, who the Druses claim is identical with *el-khidr*, stands in the middle of the village. Among ancient ruins, one observes a cave with an ancient oil press and two basins in the garden near Mr. Oliphant's residence. The closure stone from a Jewish burial chamber rests next to one of the basins. Mr. Oliphant transported this here from the *summāqa* ruin. It displays peculiar sculptures and has been published in his day. In building the school house on the northern side of the village, the arch of a Christian church was found. Incidentally, the houses of the entire village exhibit numerous walled-in sculptures from antiquity and the Middle Ages; some come from *ed-dālie* and some from the nearby *khirbet dūbil*. A rocky hill contains several burial chambers in the rock with *kōkīm* towards the northeastern end of the village, near the site where the *trāb qata'* is extracted. In the eastern portion of the village, on the other side of the threshing field, the path towards the *muhraqa* leads past an ancient ruin that has been destroyed beyond recognition. A maze of walls begins here which is reminiscent of the pre-historic settlement in the Monastery region. It continues eastwards until *tābūt jell fakhr ed-dīn* (Sarcophagus in the Terrace Gardens of Fakhr ed-Dīn) (Fig. 77). This has already been mentioned in the ninth section. This sarcophagus is one of the most unusual works of stone in the entire Carmel region. A stone colossus, ninety-one centimeters tall, has been transformed into a disk, 195 centimeters in diameter, through the rounding of the vertical walls. At first glance, the disk bears a certain resemblance to the oil press of *khirbet ruqtiyya*. The surface is, however, not that of a *hajar farshe* but rather it contains an orthogonal grave, oriented from the east to the west, that is 1.64 meters long, fifty centimeters wide, and thirty-seven centimeters deep. The eighteen-centimeter-tall border on the outer side of the surface apparently served in securing the grave cover. The ruins stand in direct proximity to a structure of massive, only crudely hewn blocks. One of these measures 1.5 meters tall, 1.8 meters long and eighty centimeters thick. A large stone slab is found next to it. It has been partially shattered though it displays a flat cupule at one point that is thirty-eight centimeters in diameter and thirteen centimeters deep. Similar piles of stones, partially leaning on walls, are still found here in several numbers. I discerned the remains of a sarcophagus under one of these; it corresponds with the above-mentioned *tābūt* in its carving.

The expansive *khirbet dūbil* lies a short distance away to the south. The path there leads past a pre-historic, orthostatic road, pointing north, as well as a paved Roman road next to it. The ruin, situated on a hill, extends over an area 400 meters by 250 meters in the lengths of their sides. The field of ruins has, however, long since been used as a quarry and partially supports agricultural fields so that one can no longer recognize the buildings. Among the items to name there are: a larger *sīh*, a small yellow marble column, several columns with notches, various *qubūr shemsiyye*, remnants of sarcophagi, graves with heavy

Figure 77. Sarcophagus by *ed-dālie*, called *tābūt jell fakhr ed-dīn*.

Figure 78. Small column with lion's head from *khirbet summāqa*.

sarcophagus covers, a *hajar farshe* from an oil mill, and several caves. Based on the findings of antiquities, the village flourished both in ancient times as well as in the Middle Ages. One would like to explain the word *dūbil* as *double*, as a double settlement next to *ed-dālie* from the Era of the Crusades. From *khirbet dūbil* one reaches the rise *rās el-muhellil* (Peak of the One who Praises God), 467 meters above sea level, in a solid half hour via the region called *ed-duweidār*. From here one has a magnificent wide view towards the entire south. Conversely, one easily recognizes this peak from the south, for example from the *khushm*, by the two trees, a *kharrūb* and a pine, that adorn it. One can reach *ikzim* southwestwards from *rās el-muhellil* through *khallet nassār* and *wādi ʿj-jāmūs*. The *miqtalit umm esh-shuqaf* lies west of the latter valley. It hosts an ancient castle ruin on a site called *murmāli* on a small hill. Only the substructure is still visible today; it is made of large orthostatic blocks. Ancient, roughly hewn caves are found nearby.

Although the well-known *khirbet summāqa* (Ruin of the *summāq* Tree, *Rhus coriaria*) is not situated in the region of *ed-dālie*, it is still easy to reach within one and a half hours. One proceeds east of the *dūbil* ruin through *khallet bīr dūbil* in *wādi 'n-nahl*. The latter takes its name from the fact that numerous swarms of the clever bee population have settled in unattainable holes in the southern rock faces of *rās el-muhellil*. After crossing the creek bed of the lovely *wādi* overgrown with several bushes, the climb to *fersh summāqa* begins on the other side. Whereas hewn caves and water containers are located deeper in the valley, one enters the plateau of the ruin by a *midbise* with a large *mastabe* along with a *birke* and *bīr*. One immediately sees a large cave and a cistern-like, open carved-out space which is hewn partly in circular and partly rectangular forms. Two columns lie on the ground deep below. One arrives at an ancient castellated settlement with well-built walls of large ashlars passing by large columns with notches and opening stones from cisterns. Mr. Kohl, Dr. Watzinger and Mr. Hiller conducted excavations on commission for the German Oriental Society in a cave inhabited by goat herders in 1905. This revealed the entrance to a temple-like building, perhaps a synagogue. The portal posts are carved in the manner of a relief. I noted a column-like figure, approximately fifty centimeters tall, nearby. Its head depicted a lion with, regrettably, a damaged face. At the center of the column, several rib-like curves are indicated. The flat column end still bears a lion's tail on the side (Fig. 78). A great number of columns with notches still rest near the ancient castle. Many of the columns are

Figure 79. Sculpted burial portal from *khirbet summāqa*.

comprised of remarkably crumbly lime chalk throughout the entire ruin. One frequently finds fossilized piddocks (*Nerinea cochleaeformis* Corn.) in them. Towards the south, a larger burial plot lies half-hidden, separated from the castle by a depression. The largest burial chamber has a sculpture over its entrance; a picture of this is included (Fig. 79). A bull on the left and a lion on the right are recognizable; the object in the middle portrays a vase. Whereas the image of the humped bull, characteristic for such monuments, is revealed in its identity with assurance, the lion, with his face turned towards the viewer, is poorly executed. One notices in his contours that the sculptor did not work in accordance with his own view. Similar observations can generally be made for the art of ancient times. Even the well-known, so-called Alexander sarcophagus at the Istanbul Museum which depicts human figures in realistic perfection and faithfully portrays horses as wells as hunting dogs distorts the wild animals. An egg and dart motif surrounds the portal of our burial chamber in rock beneath the main sculpture. This is also not executed artistically. Considering the latter item, one could transfer the sculpture to the Roman Era but must thereby assume that it originated from local sculptors. The portal leads into the rock to a vestibule with three-meter-long sides from which six arched *kōkīm* in irregular order and, to the right, a larger cave-like space extend. Several burial chambers in rock, partly with *kōkīm*, partly with loculi, are still found next to this. None of them display any sculptures; one must descend via a shaft for most of the chambers.

The small ruin *khirbet umm ed-derej* (Ruin of the Mother of the Stairs) is located three-quarters of an hour from *summāqa* above *wādi 'l-metābin* and west of *wādi sarār*. Its solid walls made of large ashlars in relation to beautiful columns indicate ancient origins. An additional ruin, which I, however, did not visit, is supposed to rest on the slope of *ed-damleh*.

The path from *ed-dālie* to *'ain hōd*, taking not quite two full hours, leads through the captivating and fertile *wādi umm esh-shuqaf* and *wādi bistān*. After the descent from the elevation of *ed-dālie*, one passes the spring *'ain umm esh-shuqaf* overtowered by *a'rāq el-'asi* (The Wayward Rock). Soon thereafter one arrives at the ruin *umm esh-shuqaf* to the right of the creek bed. As previously mentioned, this was once a Druze settlement which was founded at the end of the eighteenth century but was destroyed after 1840. An elderly Druze from *ed-dālie* who guided me here, showed me the remains of his father-in-law's home which are still overshadowed by a fig tree. Their field was joined with that of *ed-dālie* after the village's destruction. Only a few stone ruins remain from the Druze village. Between these, individual well-carved, large stones, several columns, and a *kharaze* of a well are found as witnesses of a larger, more solid, and older culture. Rock burial chambers lie further above on the slope; such is also the case in the west at *khallet el-balāt* which similarly still exhibits ancient quarries.

Crossing the creek bed, one arrives at *khirbet bistān* which is also a Druze settlement and shares the time of its founding and destruction with the previous settlement yet it was only half as large. A sacred stone, the *jurn el-'arūri*, is more interesting than the remnants located here; some of which also date from ancient times. The stone is located nearby under a fig tree draped with shreds of cloth. It lies flat on the ground where it has partially sunken in. It consists of meleki rock and has a diameter of 1.3 meters. It exhibits a round depression

Figure 80. Sculpture on the sacred stone *jurn el-'arūri*.

in the center as well as several carved grooves on the otherwise smoothed surface. This is depicted in Figure 80. The Muslims visit *jurn el-'arūri* when rabies (*marad es-sa'rān*) breaks out in a person or dog. One then proceeds there with the patient in the evening in order to spend the night there. Here, they pour water into the depression in the center of the stone. At daybreak, one ladles it out and gives it to the patient to drink who is supposedly immediately cured. Here we have a special case of a site dedicated to local superstition whereby the character of the sanctity is not a natural object, as with the sacred trees and springs, but rather is attached to an object of human manufacture. Here *el-'arūri* is regarded as the name of a "weli." The cloth shreds on the fig tree (*sharāit*, sing. *shirīta*) that one has either ripped from hems or specifically brought along represent the veils used at other *maqāme* which are hung as a symbol of a vow. Rather common in the entire Orient, these cloth tatters are rare in the Carmel region. Aside from here, I have only seen them on the tree of *shēkh mādi* by the *es-sawāmir* ruin.

The spring *'ain en-nakhle* (Palm Spring) lies north of the small courtyard separated from the *bistān* ruin by the creek bed. Today, the very old, recently newly walled well is, however, surrounded by eucalyptus trees instead of palms. From here on, moving downstream, the valley is no longer called *wādi umm esh-shuqaf* but rather *wādi bistān*. The residents of *'ain hōd* took possession of the estates of the former Druze settlement *bistān* after their destruction. The village of *'ain hōd* can be reached in a solid half hour from here.

11. Umm ez-Zeināt

Umm ez-zeināt is the village that lies furthest advanced to the southeast in our region. It is undoubtedly considered a part of Mount Carmel according to general opinion as it still lies on red soil although the white dirt of the *rūha* already begins directly at its feet.

Paths: 1. Through the plain; along the road from *jelamet el-mansūra* towards *jenīn* until *wādi 'l-milh* into which one turns in order to climb the elevation by the mouth of *wādi a'rāq en-nātif* or slightly later at the end of *wādi 'l-milh*. This takes one and three-quarters hours by foot from *jelamet el-mansūra*.

2. From the *muhraqa* via *bīr el-muhraqa* or directly by *khirbet el-mansūra*, crossing *khallet er-radjāde* in *wādi a'rāq en-nātif*. This takes one and a half hours.

3. From *ed-dālie*, crossing *khallet bīr dūbil* and likewise the valleys *khallet hajar el-bedd* and *khallet el-qudah*, going eastwards around *b'ībish* across the region of *umm el-benādik*, finally following the Ridge southwards in the southeast above *wādi a'rāq en-nātif*. This takes one- and three-quarter hours.

4. From *ikzim*, generally following the course of *wādi 'l-metābin*. Two hours.

Wādi 'l-milh comes from the south and enters the Jezreel Plain south of *jelamet el-mansūra*; it is bordered in the east by minor hills. The largest of which ascends towards the village *qīre* in the *rūha*. Following the valley upwards, one has *khallet el-manatt* (Valley of the Jumping Point) first in the west; it was previously mentioned in Section 9. It arrives at the bottom of the valley of *wādi 'l-milh* opposite *ard ishkāra* which already belongs to *qīre*. Thereafter, the valleys *ghurq et-ṭōr* (Subsidence of the Bull) and *khallet esh-shurbēta* come. The first issues forth in the North and the second southwest of *khirbet el-mansūra*. A smaller depression which divides above into three branches is called *khallet er-radjāde* (Valley of the Female Bearer of Sheaves of Grain). Hereupon, *wādi a'rāq en-nātif* turns into *wādi 'l-milh* from the northwest which runs in direct continuation into small valleys at the foot of *umm ez-zeināt*. The larger cave, *a'rāq en-nātif*, is located in a rock wall in this valley not far from the junction point. The slope above this to the North is called *rub'ān ez-zuwān* (*zuwān* means a germinating type of weed in a grain field[1]). Further northwestwards, two small valleys enter from the North; they approach each other below and are both called *khallet ez-zīghān* (Crows Valley). *Khallet en-nebhān* flows into the eastern *khallet ez-zīghān* from the Northeast. *Khirbet a'rāq en-nātif* is located by the junction point below in the valley bottom. *Bīr en-nātif* lies slightly further above this in the ground. The smaller cave, *a'rāq en-nātif*, is above this to the north on the slope. The next valley coming from the North is called *el-khōr* (The Lowland) by the residents of *umm ez-zeināt*; in contrast, the Druses from *ed-dālie* call it *ez-zurrādiyye*. It divides into two branches by a site called *jōret el-hajar* (The Stone Pit). The eastern branch, *khallet el-kerak*, extends up until *khirbet el-kerak* while the western branch, *khallet el-maqsabi*, does not arrive at the elevation. The last valley entering *wādi a'rāq en-nātif* from the North is called *es-sillame* (The Ladder). It acquires the ravine, *en-nezzāze*, from the Northeast

---

1   *Zuwān* is often identified with (undeciperable word) (Mathew 13:25) and is described as a type of weed present in grain fields with small black kernels in the shape of small acorns which has a strong numbing affect – i.e. the darnel, also common in Europe. These features, however, fit a type of grass which is called *taradān* in the Carmel region. The *zuwān* resembles the rice plant in its growth; its long, flat kernels display a groove on one side, and its white-yellow hue is lighter than the wheat. The *zuwān* numbs, or sedates, (*bizāwin*) when eaten but to a less intense degree than the *taradān*. The chickens eat *zuwān* but reject *taradān*.

not far from its source and extends to *b'ibish* (thus, according to the pronunciation of *ed-dālie* and the dialects of *'usufia* and *ikzim*, the hill is called *bheibish*) in the longest of its branches. In its upper course continuing northwestwards, *wādi a'rāq en-nātif* is called *el-meshābik* (The Valley Net) and falls into several branches of which one extends southeastwards towards *umm ez-zeināt* and the westernmost branch reaches to the low group of hills, *umm el-benādik* (Mother of the Feed Bundles). Others from this group of downwards-flowing streams belong to the *wādi 'l-metābin* valley system and will be seen in the fourteenth section.

When one bypasses the peak of the *muhraqa* in the plain when coming from *jelamet el-mansūra*, one leaves the road to *jenīn* in order to enter *wādi 'l-milh*. One stands before the large hill, *tell el-qeimūn*, with the ancient ruin which one would like to identify as the Yokneam, also Joqneam, on Mount Carmel mentioned in Joshua 12:22, 19:11. *Wādi 'l-milh*, well-known as forming the Carmel border, is a fertile valley with gently sloping hills and bears many beautiful deciduous oak trees (*mell*). The Bedouins prefer to stay in the valley after the harvest. After passing the point of junction of *wādi a'rāq en-nātif*, the path leads upwards towards *umm ez-zeināt* to a site which had already been used by the pre-historic orthostatic road. Still further westwards on the southern slope of *wādi a'rāq en-nātif*, one observes a striking grey-blue colored, jagged chalk reef. Attaining the elevation, one enters the fig and olive tree gardens of the village.

The name of the village, *umm ez-zeināt*[1], "Mother of the Adornments" is commonly interpreted as "Mother of the Beautiful Women." This view is generally shared among the population although the representatives of the finer sex living there could not seem to ascertain for me a special entitlement for the decorative nickname. At any rate, they must yield precedence to the female Druses from *ed-dālie*. Perhaps the village name stems from the ancient ruin, *khirbet zēni*, which is located near the village. *Umm ez-zeināt* is the

---

1   Whereas the *au* diphthong consistently flows into a *ō* on Carmel, the *ei* diphthong is sometimes preserved. One more frequently hears *ē* in place of this only in the northwest, near the city of *haifā*. The pronunciation *ei* predominates in eastern Carmel most likely due to the influence of a Bedouin environment where an older and more pure dialect is spoken. I am also transcribing strictly by ear, thus *umm ez-zeināt*, while the name of the ruin located immediately next to it is pronounced *khirbet zēni*.

only village within the actual Mount Carmel that is not directly built on top of an ancient field of ruins. According to tradition, however uncertain, Druses also lived here about one hundred years ago. Based on the appearance of the houses, the village is recent and may just barely be a few centuries old. The houses consist partially of clay and partially of stone with or without clay coating. Much larger ovens are built completely out of clay. The location of the village at the southeastern end makes it visible from many places in the south. The chapel of the *muhraqa* rises above it as seen from such a stand point. The residents are called *ahāli umm ez-zeināt* (the people of *umm ez-zeināt*). A *nisbe* (derivational word) such as in the names of the previously discussed Carmel villages is not formed. There are 630 residents. They are all Muslims and are considered to be fanatical. Despite this, they do not have a mosque but rather a *menzūl* where they also gather for religious services. They played a large role in the already mentioned destruction of the Druze villages *el-mansūra* and *esh-shellāle*. Concerning the women's dress, the color is noticed for the first time here and only infrequently which would have been standard on the *khushm*. While the *fistiān* in the northern Carmel villages are namely gaudy but of one solid color (often blue or red, seldom yellow), the dress here sometimes consists of long stripes, running from the top to the bottom, of red, yellow and green scarves of clothes. The language here is almost entirely Bedouin; one frequently sees the nomads' tents surrounding the village.

The village field touches *wādi a'rāq en-nātif* in the North on the already described border of *ed-dālie*. The region of *ikzim* previously extended until near the village *umm ez-zeināt* in the west. However, the residents of the latter gained possession of the region of *umm el-benādik* and *summāqa* several years ago. The largest portion of the community region lies in the *rūha*.

While the ancient walled village well, *bīr el-harāmis*, and *khirbet el-harāmis* immediately at the foot of *umm ez-zeināt* lie in the previously mentioned *rūha* and are therefore not discussed here, *khirbet zēni* (Ruin of the Village, "Adornment") still belongs to Mount Carmel. The ruin lies a few minutes away to the southwest on a remarkably steep slope slightly below the village. The slope only allowed for building houses on narrow terraces. For the most part, the stones from the ruin have been used for building living quarters in *umm ez-zeināt* though I still found several columns with notches, a cistern, a *jurn*, a *hajar bedd*, and several shattered sculptures. The not insignificant ruin dates from the era of classical antiquity as these and the large cubic wall stones indicate. West of the village, at a distance of a quarter of an hour, a small hill, *umm el-qudūr* (Mother of the Cooking Pots), bears additional ancient ruins. One repeatedly meets with a Roman paved or cobbled road on the path from *ed-dālie*. Still in the region of *ed-dālie*, while crossing the *khallet hajar el-bedd*, one observes one of the peculiar small towers that are called *rujūm baht* by the Druses. We are already acquainted with these from the path to the *muhraqa*.

Wādi a'rāq en-nātif contains traces of ancient cultures in a variety of places; only the most significant of these are mentioned here. *Khirbet a'rāq en-nātif* lies at the point where the two parallel valleys, both called *khallet ez-zīghān*, reach the valley bottom. The pre-historic road is first observed in the northwest; the remains of other orthostatic roads connect with it. The remaining material also consists of large roughly-hewn blocks as with *khirbet esh-shōmariyye*. Thick, column-like stones can be recognized among other items which were possibly used as stelae. Further remnants of the same style are embedded on the northern slope. A small natural hill rises from these ruins separated by the creek bed of *khallet ez-zīghān*. It gives the impression of being a castellated hill and is covered with similar walls. Among other things, a grape press is found here which is related in its construction to one found in the valley of *et-tīre* above *a'rāq er-rāhib*. It will be thoroughly described with the addition of a sketch. A *birke*, dug roughly thirty-five centimeters deep into the rock, lies next to a *mastabe*, carved shallow, which is connected to the press by a small open conduit. Its foundation is an elongated rectangle with crudely rounded corners. One sees chambers in the rock on the southern slope of the hill; at first glance, they seem to be burial caves. When one enters through the approximately sixty-centimeter-wide portal, one finds oneself in an almost cubic room with sides measuring nearly two meters. The back edges are however rounded and support a coarsely arched, carved rock ceiling; plaster is not visible anywhere. I, however, did not find traces of grave carvings in these rooms. – Several massive boulders rest opposite the hill on the slope on the other side of the valley bottom which is to be ascended southwards. The largest of the boulders bears a curious carving. Four vertical cuts, approximately one meter long and twenty centimeters wide, run parallel down the boulder two meters above the ground. An ancient stone quarry appears to stand above it. This ruin is evidently one of the oldest of the entire Carmel region. As suggested by the presence of the pre-historic road and the orthostatic structure, its period of origin joins with the epoch in which the monuments of *a'rāq ez-zīghān* and *rushmia* were built. Yet this, in contrast, seems to exhibit certain progress. Even the castle hill with its stonework seems closer to our perceptions of a proper fortification, and the rock chambers already reveal an incipient certainty and greater ease in the stone carvings. This is, however, namely also the case with the grape press. One has to assume that it was indeed constructed, although without an angle measure, with tools better than that which the Stone Age offered. Hammers and other tools may possibly not have been made of iron but rather bronze. The complete picture which the ruin presents is that of a culture which lay between the Stone Age and the Iron Age. The experts may confirm the assumption that we are dealing with an earlier Semantic or Canaanite settlement here. The ruins of *esh-shōmariyye*, *tell el-batta* south of *et-tīre*, and the *murmāli* in the *miqtalit umm esh-shuqaf* fall into the same category.

Bīr a'rāq en-nātif, a deep well walled with boulders, lies in the valley bottom several minutes to the northwest. The smaller elevation, *a'rāq en-nātif*, can be seen above it on the northern slope. Unfortunately, I was unable to visit this site as well as the larger because it is located further down the valley. Yet I would not rule out that both caves exhibit similar traces of late antiquity as the *maghārat umm ahmed* does. I also heard of a ruin on the slope of *wādi 's-sillame*.

12. Atlīt

Along the road following the shore from *haifā* by foot three hours, by wagon one- and three-quarter hours; from the Karmelheim via *et-tīre* and then southwestwards via *bīr el-bedawiyye* by foot three hours, on horseback two hours.

By *dustrē*, the path to which is already familiar to us from Section 5, *wādi felāh* breaks through the dunes with its southerly tributaries, forming an alley. This narrow course contains water throughout the year whereby the region, to a great degree, transforms into a swamp during the rain season and in spring. One notices an old Crusader well on its western side; a water conduit leads from here to *'atlīt*. South of this opening the dune[1], which had already been used in ancient times as a quarry, rises to a greater altitude. Here it bears *khirbet dustrē*, a former fort of the Knights of the Temple that was carved directly into the rock and serves as a lasting witness to the craft of building fortifications during the bellicose era of the Crusades (Fig. 81). Amidst deeply carved avenues, the castle was cemented in spots that were recessed in the rock. Its remnants with cisterns and water installations still amaze us today and help us realize that with *'aṭlīṭ* they withheld the advances of the Mamlukes long ago.

East of *dustrē*, the road extends southwards for a short stretch where it crosses *wādi felāh* by means of a stone bridge next to an old Crusader well which bears the name *el-hannāne*. The bridge was erected in 1898 for the Kaiser's journey with his wife and has recently been repaired. Two Israelite blockhouses stand on the other side of the bridge; the wagon often stops here. They are called *bēt el-khasheb* (wooden house) because of their wooden construction which is a rare occurrence in the region. From here, the road turns directly to the west as it follows a man-made cut through the dune. Its name, *bāb el-'ajal* (Wagon's Gate), indicates an epoch in which the use of the wagon was more common in the Arab period prior to our modern times. In fact, this cut, like many others with which we will immediately become acquainted, may date from the Roman Era which left behind so many mighty works of rock. Before the arranged expansion of the passage in 1898, ancient niches and carved-out rooms could still be seen on its side walls. Similarly, this is still seen today in *bāb et-tantūra* which is mentioned in Section 15. The passage located here was especially important as a strategic point wherefore the Knights of the Temple laid out the just cited

---

1   The dune deserves a more thorough study in its entire extension from the north to the south. There is no other point in the region on which one receives the impression of the successive centuries of culture that passed over the region. As my focus was directed to the mountain range of Carmel itself, I was only left with the time to more closely observe the points of the dune which seemed most important to me. Some will be discussed in this section and some in Section 15.

Figure 81. *Khirbet dustrē.*

Figure 82. *'Aṯlīṯ* from the North.

fortification for protection. The name *dustrē* (*Districtum, Détroit*) or *Petra incisa* (The Rock Incision) possibly also stemmed from this; the latter term, nevertheless, was also sometimes extended to *'aṯlīṯ* during the Middle Ages.

One observes many ancient niches, individual graves and *midbise* in the dune rocks on either side of the passage. Immediately to the right, next to the entrance, two massive carved symbols are located on the incline, roughly eight meters above the ground. Dr.

Schuhmacher published these in his time (PEF[1]. Quarterly, 1889, p. 191). While kindly pointing this out, he added that the reproduction of his drawing does not correspond with the original. That is why I have copied the latter again (Fig. 82a). The symbols were mounted

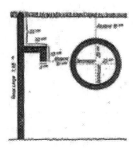

Figure 82a. Carvings in rock at the entrance to *bāb el-'ajal*.

on a once smoothed but now intensely weathered rock surface 1.05 meters tall. They are seven centimeters deep and five centimeters wide. Pending the experts' verdict, I would like to recognize the Phoenician letters *'Ajin* and *Tāw* within the images. These are perhaps the beginning consonants of the name *'aṭlīṭ* which possibly reaches back to a very early era as will be mentioned below. In this case, one could view the inscription as the boundary marker of this village's region. The site is still nearly one kilometer far from the village, and, based on the terrain, one can assume that a path already led through here before the construction of *bāb el-'ajal*. – After crossing the passage which also uses the new telegraph to *jāfā*, one arrives at *'aṭlīṭ* via an often marshy terrain (Fig. 82).

Aṭlīṭ was the *castellum peregrinorum* of the Crusaders and often served as a point of disembarkment for them. It was the strongest bulwark of the entire region and the headquarters for the Knights of Temple. We were more precisely instructed in the structure, the building of which began in 1218, by a lucky coincidence as the papal legate Olivarius from Cologne and the French Cardinal Jacques de Vitry, named Bishop of Akko in 1216, described it as witnesses[2].

---

1   Translator's note: This is possibly a reference to the Palestine Exploration Fund.

2   Compare with Rey, *Etude sur les Monuments de l'architecture militaire des croisés en Syrie et dans l'Ile de Chypre*, Paris 1871, pp. 93. I was able to view this work at the library of Joseph University in Beirut. For this as wells as many other

Hereafter, near the structure of the fortification, one encounters multiple ancient walls, several fresh water springs and, furthermore, a treasure of ancient gold coins of unknown mint which offered a welcome contribution to the building costs. The structure is to have been one of the most magnificent and beautiful buildings which the Crusaders built and is still recognizable in the ruins today. The promontory upon which *'aṯlīṯ* is situated is surrounded on three sides by the ocean to which steep slopes descend and, in addition, were covered with massive walls. The solely accessible eastern side, aside from the dune with the fort *dustrē*, was protected by a triple row of fortification structures. The outer-most wall began in the North by the tower that is built out into the sea which is called *el-habis* (The Jail) today. It extended southwards until the hill, *el-muntara*, where a strong tower likewise stood. From there, it turned westwards until the ocean. A glacis rose before the fortification; its periphery could have been placed under water on both sides. The actual castle walls, built of massive blocks which were set in lime mixed with mussels, first began on the other side of the glacis ditches. The wall exhibited a portal in a protruding tower corner on the southern half. The wall ended with a large tower in both the north and the south. The towers each contained two-storied arched halls and rested on similarly arched store rooms. A round tower is located on the southern side of the promontory, in the vicinity of a hexagonal church in the southwestern corner which Pococke, like Wilson (1843) and Barth (1846), still saw in his journey to the Orient taken between the years 1737 and 1742. The western side contained a castle and the port facilities.

The *castellum peregrinorum* was appointed with municipal law and venue jurisdiction. The flourish of the fortification, incidentally, did not last long. Indeed, it was able to stave off the Sultan of Damascus, el-Melik el-Muazzam 'Īsa, in 1219, and the Knights of the Temple successfully defied Kaiser Friedrich II's order to surrender the castellum to him in 1228. Yet it sustained the advances of the Sultans of the Egyptian Mamlukes, who crushed the rule of the Crusaders in the same century, just as little as the remaining towns and castles. It fell in 1291[1], just barely one and a half months after the fall of

---

favors, I have the honor to express my obligingly gratitude to the professors of the university. Further compare with Ritter, Palestine III, pp. 615.

1   According to Abu 'l-Fidās' History (ed. Constantinople 1286 Hijri) Vol. IV pp. 26 at the beginning of the month of *sha'bān* 690 Hijri = July 30, 1291 A.D.

Akko, with the exception of Tortosa, the last Franconian possession, during the command of Qilaūn's son and successor el-Melik el-Ashraf Salāh ed-dīn Khalīl who broke its walls. Since then, it has only served as a quarry because it was never rebuilt. Its defeat is one of the few events that have left a permanent impression on the people. The local tradition reports that *aṯlīṯ* was the town of a *melik esh-shīḥ* by the name of *jemāl ed-dīn*. His residence was in the castle from which the tower, *el-qarnīfe*, still remains today; his government building was in the western side of the castle on the harbor while his mother, *shīḥa*, lived at the current *khirbet shīḥa* at the foot of Mount Carmel. A powerful king from the south advanced towards it and blew up the southeastern fort, *el-muntara*, and thereafter destroyed *aṯlīṯ*. The legend has thus distorted the facts and in addition embellished it with oriental names in which older memories can, however partially, still continue to live on. Only the two facts that the enemy was a king from the south and that the attack came from the southeast seem exceptional. In actuality, the existence of the Templar fort *dustrē* may have made an onslaught from the northeast very difficult. – The coin findings and the discovery of ancient walls near the castellum structure indicate an ancient settlement that one has identified as *Mutalio Certha* according to the *Itinerarium Burdigalense* from the year 333 A.D. Nonetheless, it must be noted that the Muslim authors use the name *aṯlīṯ* as one that has apparently long been well-known[1]. The same cannot be explained from the Arabic, and it is therefore possible that the old native term is revived here. *'Akkā* also presents a similar occurrence whereby the ancient Phoenician name *'akkō* admittedly must have yielded the word *Ptolemais* in the Greek-Roman period but appeared anew as the form *'akkā*, still common today, after the Arab conquest.

---

1   The name عثليت occurs in Abu 'l-Fidā (*l.c.*) and Yāqūt *mu'jam el-buldan* (ed. Cairo 1324/1906, Vol. IV, pp. 122) which also quotes the term *husn el-ahmar* and informs that the castle was taken by Saladin in 583 H. (i.e. after the battle from *hattīn* 1187). Since the structure of the *castellum pereginorum* from 1218 seems to have been a new building, the information probably refers to the fort *dustrē*.

Figure 83. Chambers in the rock at the Fort *el-muntara*.

The current remains of the fortification still look imposing and belong to the most beautiful monuments of the region. Traces of the outer-most wall are still preserved as well as the tower *el-haris* built out into the ocean on the northern border and the fort *el-muntara* in the southeast of the hill. The latter contains several caves on the western side that were possibly casemates. Peculiar rooms have been carved on the southern and eastern sides,

Figures 84 and 85. Ruins on the western port side of *'aṭlīṭ*.

Figure 86. Arch in the castle at the port of *'aṯlīṯ*.

Figure 87. The castle wall at *el-qarnīfe* from the south.

though already outside the fortification, which may have served as shops or even as stables (Fig. 83). The glacis and its ditches are covered with sand. The southern tower has disappeared from the main wall. Warehouses are still discernable on the southern side; other than that, a pier has been added there. The western side is abundant in ruins, massive columns, docks (Figs. 84 and 85), and the still-preserved remains of the first floor of a castle with lovely arches (Fig. 86) which were probably used as a watch point. The middle still houses several ruins, and the northern side was flanked by the walls which were partially immersed in the sea. The northeastern tower deserves the most attention. It bears the name *el-qarnīfe* (The Tower) and is visible from afar as the landmark of *'atlīt* (Fig. 87). Its northern wall towers high, and one can best recognize the construction of the Crusader buildings of the thirteenth century in it. Massive ashlars, or blocks, set in lime are piled up on either side; the middle was likewise filled in with rubble set in lime and smaller stones in order to give the walls the necessary thickness. Lovely pointed arches in the upper story are perceptible on its southern side. They rest on corbels that depict two human heads. The room to which the pointed arches belong was possibly a hall of knights. The wall of the *qarnīfe* which displays the lost splendor is certainly no longer undamaged; "this too, already shattered, can topple overnight." Beautiful arches are still located in direct proximity; today, goat herders use them as stables.

Eighty to one hundred Fellāheen (*'atlīti*, pl. *'atāliti*) reside in squalid huts amidst these ruins; a mukhtār stands in authority over them. As a result of the unhealthy, marshy surroundings they are almost constantly with fever to which the previously given expression refers. Linguistically, I noticed an Egyptian articulation of the letter *jīm*; the word *jezīre* (island), for example, is pronounced like *igzīre* by the Fellāheen here. Not long ago, the residents of *'atlīt* were forced to sell their village field to a man from *haifā*. As Baron E. v. Rothschild in Paris wanted to acquire the same for the purposes of colonization, the Turkish military treasury, however, declared that *'atlīt* was non-negotiable as a fortification. Accordingly, the promontory was separated from the village field with another incorporated area. Its northern border begins by *bīr el-bedawiyye* and follows the dune southwards until the point where it lies opposite *bīr et-tilāl* near the ocean. The border reaches the latter via *bīr el-khuneizire*. It has been made discernable by a new wall. As a fort, *'atlīt* has a post which consists of an *onbashi* (corporal) and two soldiers. The Rothschild Settlement, which has transferred administration to the Jewish Colonization Association, surrounds the remaining portion of the village field. Its border runs east of the dune north of *dustrē* until the entrance of *wādi felāh* in the plain; then it follows the path along the mountain's foot, touching the regions of *'ain hōd* and *el-mezār*. It enters here, pushed back by the protruding region of *ikzim*, again westwards towards the dune which accompanies it southwards until *wādi 'l-mālha*. Upon reaching the ocean, it turns northwards until the area of the fort. The previously-mentioned blockhouse, *bēt el-khasheb*, belongs to the Jewish region.

The near surroundings of *'aṯlīṯ* in the south deserve a more thorough observation. An elevation begins by the fort *el-muntara*; it stretches between the ocean and the dune and southwards, parallel to the latter. It portrays itself as a later dune formation. Not far from the fort, on the western foot of this hill, one observes an incision in the rock, called *rān* (Drinking Trough), and the *'ain ej-jummēzi* (Sycamore Spring) soon thereafter, which was once cast as a *hannāne* as exhibited by the large stones lying around on the ground. A few minutes later, one arrives at four additional springs in the south, the *'ayūn el-khuneizīre* at the foot of the *khirbet el-khuneizīre*. The latter is characterized by varied ruins among which orthostatic walls are most noticeable. In the most ancient times, when the location directly on the shore did not seem advisable for human settlement due to the then common piracy, a larger settlement may have stood here. A small depression, often covered with water, lies between this more recent dune formation, upon which *khirbet el-khuneizīre* is situated, and the sand hills (*tilāl*) which accompany the ocean's border. The depression bears the name *el-bassa*[1]. Its southern branches are now being built up although the marshy region is highly unsanitary, and man and beast are beset by numerous tiny black, blue-winged mosquitoes (*barghash*).

We bypass the *bassa* in the north by turning westwards from *'ain ej-jummēzi* and arrive via a small sand hill, *dabbet esh-shuweikāni*, at the round land projection which, bearing a small military guardhouse (*qolluq*), closes up the bay from *'aṯlīṯ* in the south. Deep incisions have been added in the rock between this and the first offshore island, *jezīret bēt el-milh*. The narrow inlet that runs through here is today still buried on both ends in the summer so that the sea water trapped this way evaporates. The salt that is left behind is lifted out by the soldiers on behalf of the government and taken to *haifā*. The site is called *bēt el-milh* (Salt House) from this extraction dating from previous eras. A small island still lies in the ocean, north of *jezīret bēt el-milh*; it exhibits traces of carvings just as its name, *jezīret el-maqtū'a*, conveys.

Following the sand hills by the ocean southwards, one arrives at a deep rivulet, *esh-shuqāq*, flowing into the sea; it has slightly brackish water. South of this, one finds long and wide, partially walled incisions

---

1   It is marked as *birket esh-shuweikāni* on the English map.

in the rock opposite *jezīret el-muqla'* (Quarry Island) on the seashore. The incisions extend through the sand hills until the *bassa* which was built for the purpose of their draining. I was shown an excellent fresh water spring (*bīr el-muqla'*), flowing around the salt tide, where the incisions meet the ocean. It can be deduced from the well-carved stones lying around that the spring was constructed during the Era of the Crusaders. One finds a water conduit (*qastal*) on the sand hills east of here. It turns towards the *bassa* after originating at a deep walled well, *bīr et-tilāl* (Sand Hill Well) where it disappears today. The conduit is formed by mutually corresponding upper and lower stones, concavely carved, on a stone substructure. The concave stones enclose clay pipes lying in solid mortar bonding. This is also the work of Crusaders and possibly once led to the *castellum peregrinorum*. A small cave with traces of highly primitive carvings lies slightly south of *jezīret el-muqla'*. Known as *maghārat es-sammāki* (Cave of the Fisherwoman), it probably dates from the time of the most ancient human settlement of the region. The small offshore island carries the name *igzīret el-mubaslata* according to the dialect of *'aṭlīṭ* which was explained to me as "storing island." Further south, the small islands, *jezīret en-naffākha* with one ruin and *jezīret wādi 'l-mālha*, are left to be mentioned.

Dabbet el-fukhkhār (The Clay Hill) forms the conclusion of the *bassa* in the south; rather than a ruin, one finds here a multitude of ceramic shards. Returning to *bassa* by way of this hill, one observes a wall on its border on the surrounding elevations; the wall bears a mound of boulders today on two rows of hewn foundation stones touching each other. It extends from *bīr et-tilāl* northwards until *bēt el-milh*, then turns westwards and arrives at the more recent dune by *'ain ej-jummēzi* from across *dabbet esh-shuweikāni*. From this point, it ascends to *khirbet el-khuneizīre*. This wall, which encircles the *bassa* in the north in a half-circle, is called *sansōl et-tilāl* (Wall of the Hills); I could not discover anything more precise about it. I found it reminiscent of the walls of the fortified camps of Arab armies such as I saw, for example, in *tlemsen* in Algeria. One may perhaps assume that an Arab army which proceeded to capture such a significant fortification as *'aṭlīṭ* must have planned for a longer period of besiegement and needed to protect against sudden raids. That the *castellum peregrinorum* could be attacked only from the south with hope for success is moreover illuminated by the already described fort grounds. The current state of the *bassa* with its climatic unfavorable conditions can probably not be made an objection to the choice of this camp location because, as we saw, arrangements were met for its drainage by the Crusaders. Only through such measures as well as the careful setting of all the region's quality springs by means of the *castellum peregrinorum*'s water supply can its existence on such a site be explained whereas the current military posts must be transferred for sanitary concerns in very short periods of time.

Such observations are convenient to allow the state of the region during the Era of the Crusades to appear enviable in comparison to the present. In addition, there is the magnificent former building activity which sowed the land with monumental fortifications, castles and monasteries whereas, with the exception of a few localities, the later history of the era of Arab feudalism and on barely witnessed the construction of a notable building in the entire region. We know that the administration of justice experienced a special consideration at the time because the *Assises du royaume de Jérusalem* was also held to be exemplary in the western world. Thus, the Holy Land experienced an epoch of great flourish like that which has never repeated itself since the time of the Roman emperors. An otherwise unusual order prevailed in the Levant on account of the strong rule of the Northern warriors under the auspices of whom fields, industry and trade could thrive. How much the Muslim subjects adjusted to such a government is illuminated in a report by the Spanish-Arab traveler Ibn Jubeir published in the year 578 Hijri (1182 A.D.)[1]. It describes the conditions of *bilād bshāra* (North Galilee), ruled by the Crusaders, which he passed through on his journey from Damascus to Akko in the following words:

"Our route continued uninterrupted through a chain of villages and well-arranged constructions. All of the residents are Muslims, and they got along well with the Franks – we seek refuge in God against (such) trials! ... And the trial has penetrated the hearts of the majority because they see with their own eyes the situation of their brothers, the residents of villages in the Muslim region, and their relation to their superiors because they find themselves, unlike them, living the opposite of a good livelihood and mutual benevolence. And this is among the afflictions which befall the Muslims in that the Muslim

---

1 رحلة ابن جبير, ed. Wil. Wright, Leiden 1852, pp. 305. I am grateful for the courtesy of Professor P. Lammens in Beirut for the knowledge of this passage.

complains of the tyranny of fellow believers who rule over him and praises the behavior of his opponent and enemy, the Franconian ruler. Surely, he leaves his rights behind. God help us in this situation!"

One cannot doubt the sincerity and impartiality of the commentator for whom this confession was certainly difficult since he does not use expressions such as *khanzīr* (pig) or "Allah curse them!" sparingly when mentioning the Franks.

The tall dune near the fortification, bearing the name *maqāti' 'atlīt* (The Quarries of *atlīt*), is just as interesting as the following area surrounding *atlīt* to the south. It was namely used as a quarry for many centuries in ancient times. Further south, one encounters sites where a large portion of the elevation has been gradually removed from east to west so that only a narrow ridge remained. The stones that have been garnered from the dune in its complete extension over time would have sufficed for the building of an entire metropolis. The road to Jāfā extends along the dune on its western border; it first leads to *bīr el-yazak* (Guardsman's Well), a Crusader *hannāne*. A few paces to the North from here, a similar rock incision, *bāb el-hawā* (Gate of Wind), as presented by *bāb el-'ajal*, leads up the dune. Due to its climb, I could never give it the same importance as with the first-mentioned gate which cuts through the dune until the niveau of the plain. For this, the carved-out wagon tracks are, however, still preserved; smaller indentations have been fixed between these for the hooves of the draft animals (Fig. 88). The wagon tracks resemble those in the paved tiling of ancient Italian cities such as were once present in Pompeii. On the eastern side of *bāb el-hawā* the stone is carved in handsome vertical walls. It is a charming spot for picnics where one can rest in the shade of large carob trees. There are two additional sites that bear the name *bāb* further to the south: *bāb es-saghīr* (The Small Gate) and *bāb es-sūr* (Gate of the Wall). Both are, however, not breaks in the dune like the previous, but rather points through which the path leads. *Bāb es-sūr* takes its name from an ancient fortification wall that runs along the dune that it crosses; the wall consists of large, unhewn blocks of stone. Shortly thereafter,

Figure 88. *Bāb el-hawā* with wagon tracks.

Figure 89. Ancient niches in the dune south of *'aṭlīṭ*.

one arrives at the southernmost intersection, *bāb el-maqāti'* (Gate of the Quarries), which exhibits small wagon tracks. After a few minutes, one observes peculiar niches (Fig. 89) which may have been intended for sacral purposes in ancient times. Crossing beautiful quarries, the *maqāti' ez-zeitūne* and *maqāti' el-butmi* (Olive Tree and, respectively, Terebinth Quarries), we reach the significant ruin of *shēkh ibrāq*.

Figure 90. *Maqām* of *shēkh ibrāq.*

Usually, one would prefer climbing the dune over using the road which incidentally offers nothing worth noting. Yet, *khirbet esh-shēkh ibrāq[1]* deserves a visit. It bears its name from the *maāam* of *shēkh ibrāq* which is a small stone house with a flat arched white dome which once bore a metal peak with a crescent moon (Fig. 90). Though the modern building presents itself as architectonically insignificant, the roll of the saint is, however, so great in the local tradition that he takes the first rank after Elijah-Khadr in this region. A pole erected near the shrine serves to run up a flag announcing the beginning of a festival to the surrounding residents. A now withered carob tree divides the meadow of the entire site. The great sanctity of the site suggests from the start that a sanctum previously stood here. The far-extending ruins lying around which stretch along the road and up the dune elevation prove through the ancient stonework, namely through the many orthostatic lime blocks, the significance the settlement already held in ancient antiquity.

An entire necropolis with many graves from antiquity (Fig. 91) and possibly from the Crusades lies in the beautiful stone quarry to the south. Among the graves, there are some with Jewish *kōkīm*; some are family tombs, and others are individual tombs. Here and there,

---

1   This name is substituted for the previous *khirbet mālha.* "*Mālha*" simply means the creek bed of *wādi 'l-maghāra* and its tributaries which connects with the ocean here through the dune.

one finds *qubūr shemsiyye* which are almost all oriented from north to south here and small *jurn* as well as a larger *sīh*. The remnants in the immediate vicinity of the current *maqām* offer the most interest. A large stone drum on the stone slab is first noticed; a round *jurn* is buried next to it. A large *sīh* of great length and width carved into the rock is located east of it. The plaster is still discernable on the *sīh*, and a low raised wall protrudes from its four corners. Next to it, one enters a Roman burial chamber by means of a descending staircase. An ancient sacrificial site (Fig. 92) deserves particular attention. A round *jurn*-like hollow nearly seventy centimeters in diameter and twenty-five centimeters deep is situated in the ground in front of a niche displaying a half-oval in which a smaller niche sits at chest-height. A wide groove encircles the hollow and disappears into the hollow. A larger, circular depression, roughly seventy centimeters away from this, should be considered as belonging to the arrangement. An idol to which the sacrifice was made probably stood in the smaller niche. The transportable altar would have been placed on the edge of the *jurn*-like hollow. The blood of the sacrificial animal ran down the side of the altar in order to be collected in

Figure 91. Ancient burial chamber from the necropolis of *shēkh ibrāq*.

Figure 92. Ancient sacrificial site by *shēkh ibrāq*.

the blood grooves on the ground and thereby directed to the hollow below the altar. The circular depression added next to it is the pit into which the remains of the sacrifice and the ashes were thrown. The highly primitive execution of the stone carving indicates a very old age for this sacrifice site. We have already encountered this same type in a more ideal version by *esh-shēkh jebel* in the *wādi* of *et-tīre* as well as on the hill of *esh-shellāle*. A second sacrifice site differs from this kind; it is found at *shēkh ibrāq* in direct proximity to that which was just discussed. It consists of the same *jurn* with blood grooves but does not include a niche but, in contrast, has three steps which lead up to the *jurn*. A cistern with plaster lies east of here; next to it, a similar cistern is located but with a still existing *kharaze* (entrance stone); further on, there are a *midbise* with plaster and two large *midbise* of the usual type. Many of these basins are used as *jōret milh* (salt extraction sites) today. Further northwards, one observes a large circle recessed in the rock surface next to an ancient sacrificial slab. It encompasses an area of a circle greater than two meters in diameter. The circle itself rises roughly fifteen centimeters above the ground with a width of twenty-five centimeters and has an incision on the side in the following shape:

I could not determine the purpose of this circle. The entire hill is covered with stone works from which only three tomb groups with loculi and a large *midbise* will be mentioned. The latter was not for wine but rather for *dibs* preparation as evidenced in the *bīr* present at the site. The ruin of *shēkh ibrāq* is indeed worthy of a thorough study by experts.

13. The Southern Portion of the Western Slope of Mount Carmel until Wādi 'l-Fureidīs; 'Ain Hōd, el-Mezār, Jeba', 'Ain Ghazāl and el-Fureidīs.

The less notable elevations of the western slope of Mount Carmel have been listed among the villages in the regions in which they lie. The descriptions of the valleys flowing from the mountain into the plain are the following from north to south: 1) *khallet abu sba'*[1]; 2) *wādi hajali* named after *khirbet hajali*, called *wādi 'l-meshāhir* (Valley of the Coal Pile) in the upper course; it sends the ravine *el-qfāf* (The Baskets) northwards towards *'ain hōd* and *wādi bistān* to *khirbet bistān*; 3) *khallet ez-zeitūne* (Valley of the Olive Trees); 4) *khallet es-serj* (Saddle Valley). These four valleys merge with *wādi felāh*. – 5) *khallet el-mezār* after the village *el-mezār*; 6) *khallet es-serrīsi* (Valley of the Mastic Bush, *Pistacia lentiscus*); 7) *wādi 'l-maghāra* (Valley of the Cave) which, along with its tributaries, will be discussed in the following section; 8) *en-nakhrūr*; 9) *el-bayāda*; 10) *ed-dakhnūn*; 11) *khallet jeba'*, north of the village *jeba'*; 12) *es-sullāji*, a small ravine directly south of *jeba'*. The valleys numbered 5 through 12 unite under the name *wādi 'l-mālha* in order to break through the dune south of *shēkh ibrāq*. – 13) *Ard el-menāra* is only an extension of the plain towards the mountain side; it takes its name from the hill lying to the North with the ruin *el-menāra* (the Lighthouse); 14) *wādi henu* which will also be described in the following section; it spills into the ocean north of *kufr lām* during flooding. – 15) *wādi esh-shāmi*; 16) *khallet el-'aēn* which leads towards *'ain ghazal*; 17) *wādi 'l-madībi'* (Valley of the Hyena Sites); 18) *wādi umm 'asīdi* (*'asīdi* is a sweet pastry dish described in the first section). The small valleys numbered 15 through 18 disappear into the plain

---

1 *Asba'* is a man who is missing a finger on one hand. Such deformations lead to nicknames which sometimes replace the actual names. Thus, I was told by a Bedouin, the *sittāwi* is named so because he had six fingers on each hand.

without their waters reaching the ocean. – 19) *wādi 'l-fureidīs* named after the village *el-fureidīs*. Augmented by the small valleys coming from the *khushm, khallet en-nazle* and *en-neffākha*, as well as by *khallet el-kebbāra*, it forms the perennial *nahr ed-difle* (Oleander River) in its lower course after the dune break. Above the effluence from the mountain by *el-fureidīs*, it takes on several side valleys from the left and right among which only the following on the Northern side are worth mentioning: the *meleff* (the Wrapping) by *shefeia, wādi mādi* which bears the name *wādi 'l-khalīl* in parts, *wādi hanāne*, and *wādi 'z-zibriyye*; and on the southern side: *wādi tātā* (after the *khirbet en-nebi tātā*) and *wādi mīna*, called *umm ed-derej* (Mother of the Steps) in the lower course. At the beginning of *bilād er-rūha*, it receives the name *wādi 'l-fawwār* (Valley of the Sparkling Mineral Water) and sends two larger branches, *wādi 'sh-shuqāq* (Valley of the Chasms) and *wādi 's-sanājiq* (Valley of the Flags), to the Northeast.

One arrives at the foot of the hill of *'ain hōd* (Basin Spring) either by wagon over the Jāfā road in two and one quarter hours, turning directly eastwards at *bēt el-khasheb*, or by foot from the Karmelheim via *et-tīre* in three hours. The path leads through the ravine, *el-qfāf*, and afterwards passes the ancient basin spring to which one descends a stairway. The beautifully situated village looks down on the western coastal plain. Its residents (*hōdāwi*, pl. *hayādni*), counting 283, are administered by a *mukhtār* from the house of *abu 'l-hēja* and maintain a school. Although they do not have a mosque, they are considered to be good Muslims who perform the prayer more regularly than the common Fellāheen. Their participation in the destruction of the Druze villages was mentioned with *esh-shellāle*. Since this time, they have been in possession of the terrain of *bistān*. *Shēkh muhammed, el-ghureyyib*, and *muslih* are revered here as holy persons.

The village field which meets with the regions of *et-tīre* and *esh-shellāle* in the North extends from *wādi felāh* and *wādi bistān* across *khallet ed-dukhān* and *jōret el-ma'ze*. It then turns, bounded by the region of *ed-dālie*, southwards to *mīdān* and *rās el-ahmar*, acquires *es-suwēdir* (The Gentle Slopes) towards the west, south of *khirbet hajali*, whereby it encounters the field of *ikzim*, and reaches the plain by way of *rbā' stambūl* and *khallet es-serj*. Here it encounters the Rothschild terrain described in the previous section not far from the path on the fringe of the mountain. The border is formed by a line that goes through *kharrubet en-nejame*.

As the *bistān* ruin and *'ain en-nakhle*, lying north of the ruin, were already described in Section 10, only the visit to *khirbet bellūh* and *khirbet hajali* still remain for us. *Khirbet belluh* lies barely a quarter of an hour southwards from *'ain hōd* on the other side of *wādi hajali*. Passing by several ancient graves, one arrives at the intensely damaged ruin covered with bushes. One observes burial caves, *midbise* of the usual type, and cisterns beautifully carved into the rock to the west of the slope. Various *hajar farshe* and other equipment, some with plaster, intended for the preparation of oil lie between them. I was shown a rock there from the inside of which a strong flow of good drinking water issues forth every two to three years after persistent rainfall but suddenly dried out. This phenomenon, which seems to actively occupy the imagination of the villagers, led them to give the spring the name *'ain el-meshūra* (The Enchanted Spring). A quadratic four-walled structure in the east with one-hundred-meter-long sides is better preserved than most portions of the ruin. Its southern side rises still higher and implies the Roman Era. The remnants of a tower stand on the eastern side. I also found an oil press with *hajar bedd* and a second larger oil press here; next to it is a well-executed construction block almost one and half meters long, a half meter thick and three-quarters of a meter wide. The *khirbe* seems to stem from a village which was very involved in the cultivation of olive oil in antiquity and possibly also during the Middle Ages. This corresponds with the fact that many of the ancient olive trees of the surroundings are referred to as *rūmi* (Byzantine) and that the small valley which borders the ruin in the south is called *khallet ez-zeitūne*.

On the path to *khirbet hajali* (Partridge Ruin) which requires roughly three-quarters of an hour from *bellūh*, one encounters heavily reddened lime with many piddocks. The ruin rises on a narrow, dominating elevation, oriented from the east to the west, which looks down on *sahil ikzim*. It measures more than 350 meters long yet only about sixty meters wide. One observes two altar slabs, the traces of the pre-historic road, a *bīr* carved into the rock, and diverse stonework reminiscent of the Crusades Era in the north. A large cave in the Northwest can be entered. *Kōkīm* have now been affixed but indicate a much more ancient origin in the presence of a *rōzane* (an upper light-hole). A half-circle wall is located in front of it. One observes portal posts nearby and a burial chamber in the rock south of this. A water conduit coming from a cistern with a double opening and an entrance stone that is still present leads into the actual structure which passes through a lower door bearing. A stone drinking trough stands in the immediate vicinity as well as an additional large cistern carved into the rock but walled on the top. One also finds several cisterns with *kharaze*, a *birke*, a large *mustabe* further on, various *midbise*, stone troughs, and a *sīh* (basin) in the west. To the southeast, one observes a portal and two large basins as well as a stone quarry. Castle terraces are discernable on the southern side whereas the extensive terrace on the western side stems from vineyards. The large number of cisterns is striking; the number of herds is about thirty. Nevertheless, it should be considered that the next minor spring, *'ain hajali*, lies nearly ten minutes away on the northern border of *wādi hajali*. According to its layout and type of construction, *khirbet hajali* was a castle from the Middle Ages. The many ceramic and glass shards found on site as well as several coins found in the caves also fit with this. Even the castle which dominated the entrance to *'aṭlīṭ* through *wādi 'l-maghāra*, could not have been without significance. The treatment of the altar slabs suggests the Roman Era, and the cave with the *rōzane* where Phoenician glass was also found indicate that the settlement already existed during an early historical period to which even the orthostatic road still reached.

El-mezār, a summer residence of the *mādi* family from *ikzim* (Fig. 93), lies on a low hill at the foot of the mountain only a short half hour south of *ain hōd*. Although it only consists of one large building surrounded by several smaller houses, *el-mezār* holds the rank of a *qarie* (village community) which counts seventy-nine residents. The small field is bordered by the Rothschild terrain not far from the path on the mountain fringe; it extends between *khallet es-serj* in the north and *khallet es-serrīsi* in the south eastwards up the elevation until *rbā' stambūl*. The southern portion of this is a point of controversy between *el-mezār* and *'ain hōd*. The minor and half-corroded *maqām* of *shēkh ahyā* is situated at the foot of the summer residence in *khallet el-mezār*. It has been identified with the site of a chapel of St. John of the Middle Ages. I was told the ruin of a *muntār* is supposed to lie on the elevation to the east.

One needs an additional solid half hour to reach *jeba'* from here. Halfway along the path, one crosses *wādi 'l-maghāra*; it gained its name from the multiple caves on the southern side. Among them, the largest of which is worth touring. The entrances, with the exception of one, have been sealed by massive lime blocks piled on each other which date from the most ancient time but were later bonded by lime mortar. One encounters well-carved foundation stones from an inner portal at the current entrance. The stones are not made of limestone but rather of *hajar ramle* from the dune. The cave initially presents itself as a large hall and contains several fireplaces, some of which are walled. The cave then extends some eighty meters deep into the mountain in a long corridor reminiscent of a gothic church on the side aisle where one encounters another fireplace at the end. Swarms of bats

Figure 93. *El-mezār.*

Figure 94. *Shēkh ʿamēr* by *jeba'.*

come flapping towards a visitor armed with a light. Sixty years ago the cave was a hideout for robbers who conducted their mischief at this significant entry point to Mount Carmel. A small unnamed ruin lies in front of the cave; it stretches southwards. Apart from piles of stones, I noticed a cistern along with several *jurn* and *midbise*.

The village *jeba'* counts 406 residents (*jeb'āwi*, pl. *jebā'ni*) who are considered to be hospitable according to the previously introduced expression and are under the authority of a village sheriff from the *el-hāmidi* family. Its not very considerable field is bordered in the west by the region of *es-surfend*, by *ikzim* in the north and the east, and by *'ain ghazāl* in the south. A steam mill is operated by a German in the west. The mill stands next to a *hannāne* from the Middle Ages that is still used; its type is like that of *bīr el-kneise*. The *maqām* of *shēkh 'amēr* (عمير) (Fig. 94) rises in the east on the mountain slope. Its modern building bears the following inscription:

أمر بعمارة   The erection ordered
هذا المكان أحمد   of this shrine by Ahmed
الحمدي سنة ٢٣٢   el-Hāmidi; Year 1232 (= 1817 A.D.)

Aside from multiple handsome oil presses, the village accommodates many *matāmīr* (silos, cistern-like storage bins for grain) and a large number of beautiful ancient columns. One of which is found in the steam mill. Recently, a lead sarcophagus of good quality was also found. Large arches are discernable at many points; several houses of the modern village have been built upon these. Considering the many traces of antiquity found here, it indicates a former village that was larger. The already previously suggested identification of *jeba'* with *Geba hippeon* mentioned by Plinius (*Naturalis Historia*, Vol. 17) where a cavalry brigade under Herod was stationed is indicative of this (see Buhl, Geographie des alten Palästina, 1896, pp. 210). The *hannāne* may prove that *jeba'* also flourished during the time of the Crusades.

The small ruin *el-menāra* lies southeast of *jeba'* on the elevation; I did not visit this ruin. The path leads southwards past it at its foot, crossing *wādi henu* towards the large village *'ain ghazāl* in a solid half hour; one arrives at the village via *khallet el-aēn*. The village's 883 residents (*ahāli 'ain ghazāl*, the form *ghazlāwi*, pl. *ghazalni*, seems to be seldom used) have a mosque and a school. They are considered to be hospitable as we know from the previously cited expression. An additional expression affirms this:

'ain ghazāl rās ej-jūdi (*'ain ghazāl* is the center of goodness, i.e. generosity). However, the lack of good drinking water makes itself tangible. *Shēkh ishhādi* is revered as a saint in a lovely domed structure. With regard to antiquities, I was told of a supposedly good sarcophagus which I did not visit. The village field, bordered by *kufr lām* in the west near the fringe of the mountain, extends northwards where it touches *jeba'*, runs through *wādi henu* until it nears *ikzim*, then turns southwards, and reaches the plain again north of *ard umm et-tōs* which belongs to *et-tantūra*. The ruin of a *muntār* lies on the path towards *ikzim* east of *'ain ghazāl*.

Wandering southwards further along the mountain fringe, one soon arrives at *es-sawāmir* which possibly takes its name from the Samaritans as is the case with *kufr es-sāmir* north of *et-tīre*. *Es-sawāmir* was a village even twenty-five years ago; now it has disappeared in a seemingly inexplicable way. One sees hardly a trace of any type of structure, and alone the cactus hedges, which are almost always present by settlements, indicate to the tourists that a settlement once stood here. I was told that the residents moved to *'ain ghazāl* and carried with them the better building stones for the construction of their new homes there. At any rate, this example of the obliteration of a Fellāheen village similar to that observed with the destroyed Druze villages yet not in such pronounced degrees is informatory. It illustrates the perception made in the excavations of ancient sites that often only a narrow line, several centimeters wide, remains of a settlement in the layers of ash lying upon each other. Today a single, very recently built house stands here though it is situated further above in *wādi 'l-madābi'*. In contrast, the handsomely walled ancient *hannāne* of the Crusaders on the creek bed has remained almost intact; it corresponds with the style of *bīr el-kneise*. The ruins of *khirbet es-sawāmir* lie south of the creek bed; the village probably flourished during antiquity and the Middle Ages. Its better material proved more resistant than that of the Fellāheen village. The simple tomb of *shēkh mādi* stands above this on the edge of the mountain, shaded by a carob tree hung with cloth tatters.

After an additional half hour, the path leads through *khirbet et-tōs*[1] where the beautiful old quarries on the mountain slope are first to attract the traveler's attention. A great number of graves have been

---

1   The earlier maps refer to this site with the name *khirbet esh-shīh* which is unknown to those in the area and transfer the name *khirbet et-tōs* eastwards to the elevation where a ruin is not to be found. – The word *tōs* means generous in the Fellāheen dialect; one speaks of *rizq tōs* as "of bountiful provisions."

built into the quarries as we are indeed acquainted with the relationship between quarries and burial chambers from the necropolis of *shēkh ibrāq*. The graves found here fall into two categories: Roman family tombs with loculi under arcosolia and handsome, larger chambers with throughs for Crusaders. Moreover, there is a peculiar double child grave in which two depressions are embedded in the ground in the style of the *qubūr shemsiyye* separated by a narrow middle room in the rock chamber. In this instance, an arcosolium has not been carved. In many chambers, one arrives at the inner room first after passing through the relatively small opening carved into the rock wall a few feet above the ground. Above these rock walls, a small depression extends eastwards on the elevation where one notices a plastered road leading steeply upwards. One can make out remnants from various eras in the actual ruins on the path. A castle possibly occupied the highest point; a temple may have stood somewhat further below where the pedestal of a column is located. Descending still further, one discovers a *jurn* and several T-like perforated columns, in other words, *lekid* stones from an oil press. A deep, well-walled well lies on the plain. A wide plastered road leads almost directly westwards past this through the plain; one can follow the road on the other side of the dune until *el-burj*. Finally, two cisterns as well as the remains of the pre-historic walled road are still to be mentioned to the southwest of our ruin. All these traces of various cultures prove that *khirbet et-tōs* existed as a settlement from the most ancient times through to the Roman Era and up until the time of the Crusades. The ruin and its surroundings extending up the eastern elevations, the so-called *ard umm et-tōs*, belong to the field of *et-tantūra*.

Figure 95. Perfected threshing board (*nōraj*) from *el-fureidīs*.

Nearly twenty minutes afterwards, *el-fureidīs* (The Little Paradise) is reached; it is a small village with 297 residents[1] who do not have the best reputation morally. Here I saw one of the perfected threshing boards mentioned in the first section of this study which is called *nōraj*. It seems to correspond with the *mōrāg* in Ezekiel 41:15 (Fig. 95). The village has nothing else of interest to offer. It has the site of reverence for *hāj hammād* in the form of a humble fenced-in grave and the domed building of *shēkh ighnēm* as *maqām*. The village field is bordered by *et-tantūra* in the west and the north, by *'ain ghazāl* in the northeast, and by the Israelite colonies in the east and the south. It extends in the plain until across *khirbet en-nazle* whereby it does not extend far into the mountain. One can reach *el-fureidīs* by wagon in four and a half hours from *haifā* as the road towards *jāfā* which leads from *et-tantūra* to *zummārīn* passes by it.

14. Ikzim[2]

From the Karmelheim via *et-tīre* and along the foot of the mountain until *wādi 'l-maghāra*, thereafter through the *sahil ikzim*

---

1   A *nisbe* (derivational word) does not seem to have been formed for the residents of *el-fureidīs*.

2   The place name is written as *ijzim* ((اجزم) and is also pronounced thus within the village. The *nisbe* there is *jizmāwi*, pl. *jizāmni*. However, in the rest of the Carmel region and in *haifā*, the word sounds like *ikzim* or sometimes *igzim*, and the *nisbe* is then *kazmāwi*, pl. *kazāmni*. In order to explain this discrepancy, one could think of the Egyptian pronunciation of the Arabic letter "*jim*" (ج) for the word *igzim* by which the "*jim*" is articulated as "*g*" rather than "*j*." Such a pronunciation is normal in *'atlīt*, as we have seen, and also occurs here and there in *haifā* where the refrain from a sailor song "*yā rigāli, sall 'an-nebi*" ("Oh, you men, pray to the Prophet"). However, the difficulty which the *nisbe* "*kazmāwi*" presents with its clear, even lightly aspirated "*k*" is not solved by this. I would like to assume that the occurrence can only be understood in the relation of the Ikzim dialect to the northern Carmel dialects which was referred to in the preliminary remark on linguistics in this study. In accordance with this, the residents of *ikzim* have also adopted the squashing of the "*k*" to "*tsh*" from the Bedouins which occurs when "*k*" stands before a light vowel or a consonant. The other residents of Carmel have naturally gotten used to interpreting this "*tsh*" as their "*k*" and to reproducing it accordingly as one can also make similar observations in other languages. Thus the Ottomans have noted that the

by foot takes four and three quarters of an hour. Following further along the foot of the mountain until *wādi henu* which one then follows upwards takes five hours, on horseback three and a half hours. For the purpose of wandering through the region of *ikzim*, as with the southern Carmel region, one would benefit in spending the night at Hotel Graff in *zummārīn*; one reaches *zummārīn* from *ikzim* across the mountain and *shefeia* or via *'ain ghazāl* and then along the foot of the mountain. This takes two and a quarter hours by foot and one and a half hours on horseback.

Ikzim, the most significant village in the southern Carmel region, lies on the southern border of the fertile plain *sahil ikzim* amidst a wide expansive region that stretches west-eastwards from the dune at the sea until the *rūha* and north-southwards from *rās el-muhellil* by *ed-dālie* until towards *shefeia*. It is primarily crossed by the valley systems of *wādi 'l-maghāra* and *wādi henu*.

The village field begins at *mālha* by the dune. It follows the dune northwards, then extends westwards along the Rothschild terrain towards the mountain's foot and turns again to the southwest of *el-mezār*. Attaining the elevations via *khallet es-serrīsi*, it is bordered by the field of *'ain hōd* below *khirbet hajali* and by the field of *ed-dālie* south of *miqtalit umm esh-shuqaf*. It climbs the southern slope of *rās el-muhellil* with *wādi 'j-jāmūs* and approaches the village *umm ez-zeināt*, enclosing *khirbet summāqa* and *umm el-benādik*. By way of the small valley *khallet ej-jamle* west of *bīr el-harāmis* as well as *ard abu shershūh* and *mōyet esh-shutub*, the field arrives at the abandoned German steam mill in *wādi 'sh-shuqāq*. *Khallet sa'īd* forms the border against *subbārīn*. Continuing from *drā'ismā'īn* crossing *khirbet umm qubbi*, the *zuēg*

Turkish "*tsh*" or "*dsh*" is replaced with "*z*" in Greek, and therefore they adopted the practice of rendering every foreign "*z*" with their "*tsh*". Thus, they call the well-known Prussian General Freiherr von der Goltz "Goltsh Pasha" albeit the sound association between "*t*" and "*s*" is not unfamiliar to them as is, for example, the verb form *etse* (if he had done) proves. A further peculiarity of the dialect of *ikzim* is the classic clear pronunciation of "*jīm*" with an audible preceding *d*-sound whereas the "*jīm*" elsewhere softens to a French "*j*." Thus, to the residents of the northern portions of Carmel, the "*jīm*" of the *ikzim* residents sounds almost like their "*tsh*". While they reduce the "*j*" of *ikzim* to their own "*j*" in other words which occur in their own idioms, the name *ijzim*, inexplicable in the Arabic language, presented them hereto no analogy. So they mistook the "*dsh*" for the "*tsh*" in this name and reproduced it with "*k*."

(*zuēq*) and *khirbet hanāne*, it meets with the terrain of the Israelite colony in the south. Then it turns to the North by the *suleimāniyyāt* where it encounters *ard umm et-tōs* whereat it is accompanied from the region of *'ain ghazāl* until *wādi henu*. The *fersh* separates it from the western *jeba'* until *wādi 'l-maghāra* which it follows to *mālha*, returning to the starting point. As already noted in Section 11, the residents of *umm ez-zeināt* have recently taken hold of the elevations *umm el-benādik* and *summāqa*. It is illuminated from the given points that the village field of *ikzim*, like that of *umm ez-zeināt*, encroaches across the Carmel boundary in the East out into the *rūha*.

Wādi 'l-maghāra, which reaches the union with the ocean south of *shēkh ibrāq* under the name *wādi 'l-mālha*, meets the large cave to which it owes its name by its exit from the mountain. This was described in the previous section. It acquires influxes from here on eastwards only from the North; still in the narrow passage, these are *wādi shilha* and *khallet umm nāsir*, which stretches towards the slope *es-suwēdir*. Following the water course towards the East, which from now on forms the Northern border of *sahil ikzim*, one thus sees *khirbet nāsūs* to the left. West of this, *wādi 'j-jāmūs* (Buffalo Valley) flows in; it first sends *wādi 'j-jimāl* (Camel Valley) to the northwest and then *khallet es-suwēdir*. The short *wādi abu khēl* (*tshhēl* in the dialect of *ikzim*) branches off to the north from the mouth of this. A rocky hill rises at the end of the latter. It is called *mellāt el-mustarāh* (The Deciduous Oaks of the Resting Point) after its former oak stand; it offers a lovely view. Thereafter, *wādi 'j-jāmūs* turns to the northeast and acquires *tezrībi* which issues forth from between *fersh hamad* and *rās el-ahmar*; then it bypasses the *miqtilat umm esh-shuqaf* known to us from Section 10 and continues again to the northeast after a sharp turn to the north. Here it is accompanied by a mountain ridge in the southwest which is first called *ed-duweidār* and thereafter *shaqīf el-ahmar* and merges with *rās el-muhellil*. *Wādi 'j-jāmūs* sends a small valley called *el-hallūfiyyāt* towards *shaqīf el-ahmar*. Here, it obtains the name *rbā' et-tawīl* (The Long Terrace) for a short stretch and ends as *khallet nassār* between *rās el-'āli* and *rās el-muhellil* not far from the ruin *dūbil*. A small valley, *qit'at el-mer'i*, extends northwards east of *khirbet nāsūs*, and, somewhat further eastwards, another valley called *khallet et-tūn* (Lime Oven Valley), as I was told, extends towards *duweidār*. A craggy knoll is visible east of *duweidār* in the middle of a small plateau called *rbā' el-ghuzlān* (Terrace of the Gazelles); I was told it was named *tell abu mudawwar*. At the eastern part of the northern end of *sahil ikzim*, the water course of *wādi 'l-maghāra* turns to the northeast towards a deep incision in the mountain taking on the name *wādi 'n-nahl* (Valley of the Bees). In a northeastern-bound sweeping curve, *wādi 'n-nahl* circumvents the *fersh* and *khirbet summāqa* as well as the well-cultivated hill, *b'ībish* (this is according to the dialect of *ed-dālie*, but according to that of *ikzim*: *bheibish*). It sends *khallet ej-jī'a* to *rās el-muhellil* where it joins *abu haddādi* east of the mountain slope which is bordered by two small parallel valleys, *khallet el-ghamīqa*, in the east. At the site called *bāb wādi 'n-nahl*, *khallet bīr dūbil* enters containing an influx called *khallet 'ali* in its upper course from the northeast from *birket ed-dālie*. The rocks northeast of *bāb wādi 'n-nahl* bear the name *balātat en-nadjārīn* (The Carpenter's Stone Slabs). The creek bed of *wādi 'n-nahl*, now called *khallet el-qudah*, ends by *bīr el-hūti* after it has also admitted *khallet hajar el-bedd* from *rujūm baht* here.

From the hills to both sides of *sahil ikzim*, the mountain range in the west was identified to me as *el-fersh* (The Ridge) and the elevation not far from the village in the east as *esh-shenna*. A small depression on the western side of the latter is called *shulūl sahil ikzim*.

During flooding, *wādi henu* flows through the dune depression, *muqtā' el-khiyār* (Cucumber Quarry), north of *kufr lām* to the ocean. From its exit from the mountain and on, it pursues a course directly eastwards for a considerable time. Before reaching *ikzim*, it acquires two smaller valleys, the *bayāda*, and the water course of *ard er-rumēli* which comes from *jebel 'īd*; the well of *ikzim* is located before its depression. An additional depression east of *ikzim* is called *bāb el-mutalli* (Door of the One Who Enters); the traveler's path from the *rūha* leads through this. Near *ikzim* itself, the creek bed of *wādi henu* takes on the name *wādi abu sa'īd* and, a short stretch further eastward, the name *mākūra* after *khirbet mākūra* which lies directly south of it on the elevation. The entire upper course, however, is called *wādi 'l-metābin* (Valley of the Small Rooms for Chaff). As I strode further eastwards from here, my guides proved less knowledgeable in the names of places. Thus, I give the following names here only with reserve. A region with a watercourse, called *ed-damleh* or *ed-damlehi*, lies southwest of *khirbet umm ed-derej*; it supposedly bears a ruin. I was told that another subsequent depression is termed *wādi a'rāq el-bissi* (Valley of the Cat's Rock). The slope *es-senāsil* merges with it here; its watercourse is called *el-feshshi*. An additional Northern inflow belonging to *wādi 'l-metābin*, known as *wādi 'l-khasheb*, bears the name *wādi sarār* in its middle course after it has acquired *khallet ez-zeitūne* from the Northeast. It sends a side valley to the Northeast which, I was told, is called *wādi 'j-juhfān*. *Khallet umm el-benādik* enters the latter from the North based on the notes I made. *Wādi sarār* is first called *karm enjās* (Pear Orchard) in its upper course, thereafter *el-madba'a* (Site of Hyenas) and then *khallet el-buim* (Terebinth Valley) where *a'rāq en-nahli* (Bee's Rock) rises to the east. Lastly, the same watercourse is called *wādi 'l-ghāra* east of the ruin *summāqa*; it has its origin at *b'ībish*. I cannot accurately name the other eastern branches of *wādi 'l-metābin*. One of the same to the west of *bīr el-harāmis* is called *khallet ej-jamle*. *Wādi 'l-metābin* itself originates in two springs next to *bīr el-harāmis* which were indicated to me as *'ayūn el-'ullōqa* (Blackberry Springs). I also could not determine the influxes of *wādi mādi* which drains the portion of the village field lying south of *ikzim* and enters *wādi 'l-fureidīs* east of *shefeia*. *Wādi mādi* itself bears the name *wādi 'l-khalīl* north of the ruin *umm qubbi*.

When the traveler coming from the coastal plain passes the ravine of *wādi 'l-maghāra* and enters into *sahil ikzim*, he or she can easily reach *khirbet nāsūs* to the left at the foot of the elevations south of *khirbet hajali*. Along with *khirbet 'alā ed-dīn*, *khirbet ed-dawāmīn*, *dūbil*, and *summāqa*, *khirbet nāsūs* belongs to largest ruins of Mount Carmel. It stretches nearly 400 meters from the north to the south and is 300 to 350 meters wide from the east to the west. A large cave called *ed-dīwān* lies in the south; a lime plaster mixed with ceramic shards and mussels is visible at this cave. While this fact is indicative of a later era, an air shaft built into the cave, a so-called *rōzane*, suggests that the site had already been used as a burial chamber during the earliest of antiquity. A grave-like hollow is, incidentally, located not far below the *rōzane*. The remains of the dungeon of a medieval castle are situated slightly above *ed-dīwān*. From here one has a lovely view of *sahil ikzim*. Next to this I found a *hajar bedd* and a perforated, T-like *lekīd* stone from an oil press. Going northwards across the settlement's field of ruins, which must have provided many stones for the houses of *ikzim*, one arrives at various cisterns and basins which may have belonged to a bath. Many glass shards, and, in part, very beautiful colored ceramic shards of medieval Arab fabrication lay around the field. Based on these signs, one may assume that a once considerable village which already existed in ancient times still thrived during the Middle Ages. From *khirbet nāsūs*, one reaches *ikzim* through a beautiful stand of olive trees.

This village presents itself as very charming when one enters it from the west via *wādi henu*. Two parallel ravines would be noticed by the tourists on the northern side of this fertile valley which is also planted with olive trees. The western ravine, the so-called *bayāda*, has a reddish-yellow hue while the eastern ravine, *ard er-rumēli*, has a grey-black hue. According to local tradition, copper was extracted from the first and iron ore from the second in earlier eras. The earth that I took from *bayāda* which I had melted did not yield any copper but that from *ard er-rumēli* had an iron content. The current appearance of the site (Fig. 96), nevertheless, suggests that this metal was once extracted though surface mining or open-cast mining. *Ard er-rumēli* which forms the slope of *jebel 'īd* is geologically characterized as volcanic eruption as Conder already detected. Its basalt masses have transformed into the black-grey dust through decomposition; this dust does not occur elsewhere on Mount Carmel. Very crumbly lime chalk, containing a vast number of fossilized mussels, is present directly contiguous and partially mixed with the basalt dust.

Figure 96. *Ard er-rumēli* near *ikzim*.

Figure 97. The village well of *ikzim*.

The well of *ikzim* (Fig. 97), an older construction, is located southeast of here; it contains quality drinking water which is accessible via a stairway descending into a deep shaft.

Seen from here, the village of *ikzim* almost gives the impression of an acropolis (Fig. 98) with its tall houses. The peak of the hill is occupied by the residences of the family of *dār el-mādi*. The houses (Fig. 99) even date from the Arab feudal era and differ markedly

Figure 98. *Ikzim* from the West.

from those of the Fellāheen in their castellated character. Likewise, favorable, the mosque, situated slightly below the peak, contrasts with the other liturgical rooms of the Carmel villages. It consists of a wide, clean courtyard (Fig. 100) with small chambers, in one of which a Quran school is held, as well as a rather large prayer room. An ancient Muslim sculpture can be seen over the entrance to the latter; it depicts a vase with flowers and fruits

Figure 99. Courtyard of a house from the *el-mādi* family.

Figure 100. Courtyard of the mosque in *ikzim*.

and is surmounted by the lettering *bismi 'llāhi 'r-rahmāni 'r-rahīm* (in the name of Allah, the Most Kind and Most Merciful). Below this, a later inset stone is located and framed on either side by similarly older, relatively crude sculptures. The sculptures each portray a pentagram within a circle and a chalice, and the stone bears the following Arabic inscription:

النوار ذكر الله فادخل و احتسب   جمع البها بجامع جمعت به

من راكع¹ يرج الثواب و يرتقب   وانظر لنضرة روضه كم قد حوت

ارخ صفاك بسر و اسجد و اقترب   مسعود شاد فاجزلن ثوابه

سنة ١٢٣٦

The beautiful radiance is unified in the mosque[2] where
The lights of the glory of Allah are united; so enter and make reserves for yourself (namely, of good deeds)!
And observe the fresh splendor of its enclosure, how much it encompasses
The one who bows down in prayer, anticipating and hoping for reward!
Mas'ūd built it; oh Allah, grant him great rewards!
(You, however,) note this date: your pure happiness on account of the power of "Pray and approach"[3]
In the year 1236.

The inscription is a so-called *ta'rīkh* (date poetry). The number count of the letters in the last half-line from the word ارخ (note this date) and on results in the figuring of the year 1236 (= 1821 A.D.). Mas'ūd was the great-grandfather of the region's current leader from the still influential and once powerful *el-mādi* family. He, however, may not have built the mosque from the ground up but had only rebuilt it as the presence of the older sculptures above and next to the inscription indicate.

---

1   Defective for يرجو

2   There is a play on words here; the word for mosque, *jāmi'*, means "unifying."

3   The expression, "pray and approach," forms the conclusion of the 96th Sūrah (chapter) of the Quran which, aside from the customary name Sūrah al-'Alaq, also carries the name Sūrah es-Sejde (Surah of Worship). The listeners prostrate upon the recitation of this expression according to general practice.

As previously mentioned, the following are revered as saints or holy persons: *shēkh qashqūsh* (almost pronounced as *kashkūsh* here), *shēkh isfār* and *shēkh ightāsh*, *shēkh yāqūt*, and *shēkh mahmūd* as well as a blissful beguiler (*el-mejdūbi*). The settlement dates from the most ancient times as evidenced in the present graves. The residents of *ikzim*, totaling 1519, are of a large, strong mold; their red-blond hair gave rise to the likewise already introduced *mu'nā* (proverbial expression). Due to their vastly expansive, fertile village field, they enjoy relative affluence. The produce from the field, namely wheat, barley and chaff, is transported by camels to *haifā* and bought there by the Germans preferably as the camel loads from *ikzim* are known for their full measure. Oil is sent by ship to Egypt via *et-tantūra*.

Several ruins in the surroundings are of interest. Since *khirbet summāqa* and *khirbet umm ed-derej* were already described in the tenth section as well as *khirbet nāsūs* in the beginning of this section, the visit of the remaining ruins is easily accomplished in a tour which at the same moment presents the opportunity to determine the southeastern Carmel border. From *ikzim*, one turns southeastwards through the depression called *bāb el-mutalli* (Door of the One Who Enters) to the plain of *wādi henu* which is called *mākūra* here. The fruit and vegetable gardens, resplendent with lush growth, are irrigated by various *hannāne*. The first of which may date back to the Crusaders though it was later rebuilt as suggested by the various still existent building medieval stones with their engraved crosses and other ornamentation. The fairly large but greatly damaged *khirbet mākūra* is located on an elevation lying to the south. Apart from walls, I found a cistern and several *jurn* here. The remains of a possibly antique building stand in the east (Fig. 101) while the southerly adjoining hill contains many graves also dating from antiquity. The path extending westwards from here towards *'ain ghazāl* passes by a *muntār* and crosses a number of terrace walls which also cover the plateau in the south until *khirbet es-suleimāniyye*.

Rather than follow this path, we stride eastwards in order to reach *khirbet qumbāze* (قنببازة, the well-known long dress) south of the valley course which is now called *wādi 'l-metābin*. It rises on a hill, and, based on its remnants, it possibly stems from a castle about which nothing more precise could be claimed. Another hill bears a similar ruin, *khirbet qotteine* (almost pronounced as *kotteine* here, Ruin of the Dried Fig), barely a half kilometer to the Southeast. The Carmel border coming from the east stretches between the two ruins at this point, following the small spring valley of *wādi mādi*. In general, the border runs southwards and is characterized by the ferrous red Carmel soil in the west and by the dull white-grey marl lime of the *rūha* in the east. To be certain while determining the border, I was accompanied by experienced persons from *umm ez-zeināt* and *ikzim* who declared which region was considered to be part of Mount Carmel and, respectively, to the *rāha* according to the appearance customary to each district.

South of a point in *wādi mādi*, which is called *wādi 'l-khalīl*, we ascend to *khirbet umm qubbi* which indeed lies close to the Carmel frontier but is actually situated in the *rūha*. In doing so, we pass by a large hewn burial cave, *maghārat et-tīni*, which takes it name from a large fig tree growing out of its entrance. Supposedly, many glass shards have been found in the cave. The entrance is a large square carved into the rock open to the northern side; it leads to chambers on the three remaining sides. To the left on the eastern side, one arrives at a well-hewn room downwards which is eight meters long, four meters wide and equally high; today it stands empty. Straight ahead, on the southern side, one enters a vestibule on almost level ground with three long *kōkīm* on each side. On the right, towards the west, one descends to a hollow of a kind I have otherwise not observed on Mount Carmel. A narrow, elongated room opens on the other side of the portal. The room is separated from a likewise narrow, long gallery running parallel to the vestibule by two pillars recessed in the carved rock and three pillars bearing arches. Still more burial caves lie on the slope somewhat

Figure 101. Ruin of *khirbet mākūra*.

Figure 102. Late Ionian column capital from *khirbet umm qubbi*.

above *maghārat et-tīni* which are called *mughr sayyūr* after a Bedouin. Among them, I found an ancient Roman family tomb; its loculi, though distanced from the arcosolia located above them, are still preserved. Next to an additional large cave, I also saw a tomb with three *kōkīm* three times to which one must descend through a shaft. I was told the actual *khirbet umm qubbi*, east of here, takes its name from a vaulted arch that recently disappeared. Along the way, many temple columns, column trunks, and a rather crudely executed late Ionian capital (Fig. 102) are embedded. A companion to the capital is found in the ruins of Caesarea. These antique ruins are now rapidly disappearing since they are used as good building stones in *ikzim*. *Umm qubbi*, only of little expanse, may have been an ancient shrine. *Khirbet hanna* lies as the remains of an ancient settlement on a hill sloping down northwards to *wādi 'l-khalīl* bordering directly in the Northeast. Its now cultivated site exhibits several column drums of which the largest has already been described in Section 4 on *wādi rushmia* with the inclusion of an image. Many shards of better quality clay as well as coins found here at *umm qubbi* indicate that both ruins flourished from the Roman Era on until the Byzantine Empire.

Khirbet hanāne (not *hannāne*) is located only a half hour away from here. It is on a hill which separates the eastern *wādi 'z-zibriyye* from the western *wādi hanāne* and is already considered part of Mount Carmel. Aside from more recent Bedouin graves, the site contains cisterns and deep burial chambers from the Roman Era as well as the remnants of two buildings with *lekīd* stones. The orthostatic walls of a square with sides measuring five and a half to six and a half meters still tower roughly one meter tall in the middle. Following the southern end of the Carmel border from here, one can reach the road of *wādi 'l-fureidīs* leading towards *zummārīn* on a path leading through *wādi 'z-zibriyye*. Only the visit to *khirbet es-suleimāniyye* lying just a brief half hour to the northwest remains for us. Its fortification walls stretch approximately seventy meters from the north to the south and approximately sixty meters from the east to the west. Various caves and burial chambers are seen at its feet. Door pillars, cisterns and *lekīd* stones are recognizable in the settlement itself. A large, round, flat stone which exhibits a convex indentation on its under side and two peculiar elongated stone slabs measuring six feet as well as a Frankish gravestone slab from the Middle Ages also lie here. The ceramic and glass shards merge with the architectonic remains in order to give us the impression of a smaller Crusader castle which was possibly still inhabited during the Arab feudal era.

15. The Western Coastal Plain South of ʿAṭlīṭ until the Crocodile River: es-Surfend, Kufr Lām and et-Tantūra.

One can travel from *ʿaṭlīṭ* to *et-tantūra* by way of three routes: 1. Along the shoreline where the following, mentioned in Section 12, lie: *jezīret wādi 'l-mālha, jezīret el-'ijāl* (Island of the Heifers, Young Cows), *jezīret en-naʿmi*, as well as a site called *maghsal el-banāt* (Washing Area for the Girls) located near *es-surfend*, and *jezīret el-makr*; I could not determine the position, as given to me, of the additional following places: *jezīret el-'ijāl, 'ain el-qantara, es-safra*, and *el-banāni*; - 2. On a path east of the dune until *es-surfend* which, with the exception of several quarries, seems to have as few sites worthy to note as the adjoining plain in the east; - 3. On the road west of the dune.

The road, on which one needs two hours by wagon from *ʿaṭlīṭ* until *et-tantūra* and which we already know until *wādi 'l-mālha* from Section 12, touches with the village *es-surfend* in the first point worth noting after *shēkh ibrāq*. The impoverished village on the dune lies on the site of an ancient settlement demonstrated by the quarries and graves found in the surroundings as well as its name. The name is ascribed to a Hebrew or Phoenician Zarpath but, however, is not to be confused with the town Zarpath (Sarepta) by Sidon mentioned in the Bible. Today, only a mosque, currently being renovated, towers over the Felläheen houses. The large manure piles which gave cause to the previously listed expression also stand out. The lovely, antique spring, *'ain es-surfend*, carved into the rock is still in use today. It stands on the road next to a large *dōm* tree (formerly scientifically termed *Rhamnus napeca*, now *Zizyphus spina Christi* Wild.). The indebted residents (*surfendi*, pl. *surfendiyyīn*), whose numbers amount to 220, were forced to sell more than half of their region to a notable resident of *haifā*, Rif'at Bey. The village field touches the Rothschild terrain from *'atlīt* and the frontier of *ikzim* in the north where it is bordered by *wādi 'l-mālha*. It touches the region of *jeba'* in the Wwst where it extends close to the mountain's fringe, the region of *kufr lām* in the south, and the ocean in the west.

Less than one and a half kilometers south of *es-surfend*, its sister village, *kufr lām* (Fig. 103), lies on the dune. The stone huts also built on the site of an ancient settlement[1] do not appear any less impoverished. However, a medieval castle occupies the northeast; it is better preserved than the similar remaining structures of the region which are often ascribed to the Crusaders. I would, nevertheless, like to leave it to the discretion of the experts as to whether this is an Arab building or not. It is well-known that it is often difficult to differentiate between the Crusaders' fortifications and those of their Arab contemporaries and successors when only ruins remain. The Frankish structures are sometimes simply characterized by more solid walls and better material, namely larger stone blocks[2]. Here the walls are now of such minimal strength that they do not reach two meters

---

1 The Arab geographer Yāqūt names a place referred to as (*balad*) *kafar lāb* in his *mu'jam el-buldān* (ed. Cairo 1324 Hijri = 1906 A.D., Vol. VII, p. 266), "near to Caesarea on the Syrian coast" which is possibly identical with our *kufr lām*. According to Yāqūt, *kafar lāb* was built by Hishām bin 'Abd el-malik, the Omayyad Khalif, who ruled from 724 to 743 A.D. This building can, however, relate to the initial founding of the village as the ruins present here primarily reach back to ancient times. It is to be considered that Yāqūt, who died in 626 Hijri (1229 A.D.), does not mention the existence of a castle whereas he usually lists the contemporary Crusader castles as *hisn*.

2 Nonetheless, the knights also built with smaller blocks during the twelfth century until the battles with Saladin. Even then the necessary strength was, however, achieved through the use of excellent mortar and the great thickness of the walls.

at the most stable of points. Besides, they consist of building blocks smaller than medium-size (Fig. 104). In addition, the Frankish castles suffered complete destruction at the hands of fanatical

Figure 103. *Kufr lām* from the North.

Figure 104. Section from the medieval castle at *kufr lām*.

Mamlukes during a conquest[1]. If many of the fortresses, such as *husn el-qrēn* (Montfort, also called Starkenburg, or strong mountain, is

---

1   The historian Abu 'l-Fida almost constantly accompanies his account of the capture of a Crusader castle with the expression *wa amara bihi fa hudima* (and he commanded over it that it would be destroyed). The few cases in

the oldest castle of the German Teutonic Knights east of 'akkā which fell to Sultan Bībar in 1271), still inspire our admiration in their ruins, then they have their massive construction to thank for this which partly defied the destruction. A relatively weak building, as such the castle from *kufr lām* represents, would have, however, possibly not escaped the demolition. In contrast, its better preservation helps to understand if its foundation first took place during the time when the great storm that devastated the land raged. - The castle looks northwards down on an opening in the dune surrounded by quarries and burial chambers in the rock. The opening is called *muqtā' el-khiyār* (Cucumber Quarry) and serves *wādi henu* as a drain towards the ocean at the time of flooding, or high tide. In addition to a great number of remains of a former culture, mosaic stones (*qālāt*), and oil presses, the village contains a spacious underground vault with two galleries which are separated by six arched columns recessed in the rock, walled upwards from chest height. One sells the tourists many antique glass items and *kharaze* (stone or glass beads for necklaces) as well as antique and medieval Arab coins. In the south, the dune displays *qubūr shemsiyye* and modern salt extraction sites; further on there are niches carved into the rock as well as basins and burial chambers in the west. The residents (*ahāli kufr lām*, without a *nisbe*) seem to lead a more miserable existence than those from *es-surfend*. Their small number which comes to only 136 persons makes the absence of a mosque understandable but does not make the inexplicable accumulation of debt from the relatively substantial scope of their village field comprehensible. The debt prompted them to sell a portion of their region to Rif'at Bey. Their straitened circumstances are probably induced by malaria which almost constantly afflicts the residents and has even become proverbially endemic there.[1]

The village field divides into two parts; the more northerly section is named after *kufr lām* whereas the more southerly bears the name of

---

which a more significant castle was spared for the purpose of further use, Abu 'l-Fida discusses more elaborately, for example, as with the *hisn el-marqab* (the Margat, or the Marqab, Castle of the Knights of St. John) between Tripoli and *lattaqiyye* which surrendered to Sultan Qilāūn on the nineteenth of Rebī' el-awwal 684 Hijri (May 25, 1285 A.D.) (History Abu 'l-Fida, Vol. IV, p. 22, ed. Stambul 1286 Hijri). – *El-qrēn* fell (ibid., p. 7) on the second of D̲ū'l-qa'da 669 Hijri = the twelfth of June, 1271.

1   See the correction of the translation of the expression referring to *kufr lām* in the amendments.

the ancient ruin, *haidara*. In the north, it convenes with the village field of *es-surfend* whereby the dividing line running directly west-east from the ocean passes a point lying in the middle of both villages, identified by quarries and a single Fellāheen house, called *et-tūti* (The Mulberry). In the east, it touches the frontier of *'ain ghazāl* on the other side of the coastal plain and the frontier of *et-tantūra* further in the south, receding somewhat westwards. In the south, the border forms a line against *et-tantūra* which likewise extends directly eastwards from *el-burj* by the ocean and crosses the dune north of *khirbet ed-drēhime* and then *kharrūbet abu shūshe*. The village field meets the ocean in the west.

Instead of using the road for continuing the hike towards *et-tantūra*, we prefer here to descend the eastern border of the dune and initially follow it southwards. After a few hundred meters, one sees *bīr qal'at el-melik*, a wide and very deep well shaft carved into the rock. A staircase of forty-five steps, reversing in the middle, attached on the eastern side, leads down to its water level. The residents extol the excellence of the water which stays fresh even in the hot summer because the sun rays do not penetrate the bottom of the shaft. A large necropolis extends upwards on the dune to the west of this well. It is in the middle of a quarry from where one initially sees eight *qubūr shemsiyye*[1] (Fig. 105) some of which are oriented from north to south and others from east to west. The countless other graves, likewise alternating in their orientation, can be, in part, characterized as antique family tombs with loculi and, in part, as burial chambers with six *kōkīm* which are especially frequent here, and, in part, as large graves with troughs for Crusaders. One of the plots combines a trough grave with two *kōkīm* on the right side of the vestibule and one *kōkā* on the left side. The trough grave lies opposite the entrance. Another contains an air shaft to the top. A boulder stands above the necropolis; it bears the foundation of an ancient tower on its surface. The walls are set in white mortar and enclose a circle that is no more than twelve meters in diameter. The tower is called *qal'at el-melik* (The King's Tower) and gave its name to the necropolis and the previously mentioned well.

---

1   These grave sites, embedded in the rock surface of the level ground, are not elevated from the ground if closed with a cover. If no humus lies on top, one can walk across them without noticing their existence. In his *Mission de Phénicie*, Renan shrewdly expounds from this the citation from Luke 11:44, "[Y]ou hypocrites, for you are like unmarked graves which the people walk over and know not."

When we reach the plain again, we notice the traces of the pre-historic orthostatic walled road which once accompanied the eastern border of the dune. Upon this, we climb the dune elevation afresh to view *khirbet haidara* (more seldomly pronounced *hēdara*). From the not very extensive site, I only saw two columns and a large handsome column capital with unfortunately mostly shattered embellishment further to the south aside from medium-sized and smaller building stones. The dune sends a small hill as an offshoot east of this site, the hill is crowned by *khirbet ej-jelālīm* (this according to the dialect of *kufr lām*; according to the dialect of *'aṯlīṯ, ej-jelame*). The foundation stemming from a castle constructed of larger than medium-sized, elongated ashlars forms a single square that measures sixty meters from the west to the east and thirty meters from the north to the south. The *'ayūn ej-jelālīm*, two shafts hewn into the rock, lie on the southern edge of the hill. One is reminiscent of *bīr qal'at el-melik* but no longer contains water; the stairs once leading to the water level are now overgrown. The other is of a very different character, and it seems doubtful to me whether it ever contained a spring as its current name would suggest. The ground, from which fig trees are growing, lies only about three meters deep, and the shaft is divided into two parts by a rock face. Several rows of small niches standing above each other are attached on the sides (Fig. 106). They appear similar to the *raff* of the Fellāheen houses which are used for storing household effects. This appearance led my

Figure 105. *Qabr shemsi* from *khirbet qal'at el-melik*.

Figure 106. Rock shaft, called *'ain ej-jelālīm*.

guides to the belief that the construction was once a *khammāra* (wine chamber). *Khirbet ej-jelālīm* lies in straight succession between *bir qal'at el-melik* and *zummārīn*. A straight row of stonework leads from here to *khirbet haidara* which stems either from a wall or a paved or plastered road.

A small protruding hill further to the East lies only one hundred meters south of *ej-jelālīm* and is called *kharrūbet abu shūshe*[1] after a carob tree distinguishing its peak. The ruin found here, possibly stemming from a small castle, is only minor and, apart from brickwork, exhibits a few rock carvings. Not far from here, one sees the traces of the paved or cobbled road which, running in a straight line through the plain, once connected the ruin of *umm et-tōs* with *el-burj* which will be immediately mentioned. Finally, we turn westwards

---

1   *Shūshe* is the name of a hairstyle among the Fellāheen that is now disappearing and is often only still seen on young boys. The heads are cropped short with the occasional exception of the forelock (*qudli*) and a tuft of hair rises upwards from the vertebrae. The analogy of this hairstyle with the peak adorned with trees that is otherwise bald has led to the naming of several locations of the region whereas the word *abu shūshe* (Father of the Tuft of Hair), which actually refers to the hill, is today often construed as the name of a saint, or revered person. Among these points, only the ruin site *abu shūshe* west of Megiddo and the location of *abu shūshe* by *ramle* are to be remembered here. The excavations of the *Palestine Exploration Fund* led by Mr. Macalister and still continuing today have brought the interesting ruins of Gezer, known from the Bible, to light.

again on the dune towards *khirbet ed-drēhime*. Its name was explained to me as the name of a plant with edible berries. The northern adjoining portion of the dune until the vicinity of *khirbet haidara* is an almost uninterrupted quarry which cuts completely through the elevation at various points. The material extracted here may have been used for the construction of the ancient Dora. One finds many ancient burial chambers in the rock and other stone carvings among the quarries. *Ed-drēhime* lies directly opposite between the current *et-tantūra* and *el-burj*, the ancient Dora. A great number of scattered building stones and ceramic shards reaching as far back as the Middle Ages lie at the site of the ruin which no longer exhibits high-rising remains. A deep well with a square-opening with one and a half meter long sides is worth noting. It bears no plaster, and, in place of stairs, it only has a vertical row of holes on one side which one must have used to climb down to the well floor. Aside from a midbise, a deep depression in the rock is also to be mentioned. It has a round, walled opening and was either used as a cistern or a silo. One finds a long canal that is open on the top on the western side towards *et-tantūra*. Before one descends to the road near *et-tantūra*, one passes a large burial chamber in the rock with two *kōkīm* each on the three sides built into the rock. The upper rock surface contains a large, flat *cupula* roughly forty centimeters in diameter.

If one follows the road from *kufr lām* until *et-tantūra*, one does not find much that is worthy of noting. After a bit, a spring, constructed in ancient times, with poor water lies on the right, and the quarries of the dune extend on the left. A large marsh lies north of *et-tantūra*; it compels one traveling by wagon to take an eastern detour. The buildings of the newly built Israelite Glass Distillery surrounded by eucalyptus trees and several palm trees presents a lovely image upon entering the village *et-tantūra* (Fig. 107). The houses have, however, been currently abandoned since this business did not bring a profit here. It is being considered using them for another purpose. Otherwise, the village, before which various rock islands appear in the southwest, makes a friendly impression with its many decorative, modern two-story houses and their red-tile roofs (Fig. 108). The village counts 737 residents (*tantūri*, pl. *tanātri*) and is incidentally flourishing. A branch of the *el-mādi* family from *ikzim* has settled here. To be precise, many sailing vessels anchor here at the end of the summer; they are loaded with the products of the interior. The harbor traffic of *et-tantūra* is the most significant along the entire coast south of *haifā*, and it surpasses that of Caesarea by far which is the reason for stationing a government customs officer in *et-tantūra*. Although the drinking water does not taste good, the climate is considered to be healthy as illuminated

Figure 107. The Israelite Glass Distillery in *et-tantūra*.

Figure 108. *Et-tantūra* from the South.

in the expression circulating about the village[1]. *Shēkh ʿabd er-rahmān el-mujērimi* is venerated here as weli.

The village field meets with the ocean in the west and *nahr ez-zerqā* (The Blue, or Crocodile, River) in the south. In the east, where

---

1 See the correction of the translation of this expression in the amendments.

it initially, more or less, follows the dune from the Crocodile River, it is separated from the mountain by the terrain of the Turkish demesne, *el-kabbāra*, then by the Israelite plantation *en-nazle* which lies within the jurisdiction of *zummārīn*, and subsequently by the frontier of *el-fureidīs*. Before the latter village, the field approaches close to the foot of Mount Carmel. It even reaches the elevations via *ard umm et-tōs* north of here. Then it turns westwards, merges with the region of *kufr lām*, and accompanies its border across *kharrūbet abu shūshe* until meeting the ocean.

With the name *et-tantūra*, the name of the ancient town[1] has been preserved which figured as Thora on the famous so-called Peutiger Map, an ancient road map from the Roman Empire. In this, its distance from Caesarea is given as eight Roman miles (approximately 1,480 kilometers). The report of the church father Hieronymus, who died in 420 A.D., agrees with this; according to him, "Dor is now an abandoned town which lies at the ninth milestone on the route from Caesarea to Ptolemais (*'akkā*)." The ruin, approximately twelve kilometers from Caesarea, today called *el-burj* (The Castle, The Tower), is located at some distance from the [word missing from text] modern village by the sea and occupies a considerable area. The tower, which lends the site its current name and was mentioned by many travelers of the previous century, has indeed almost completely disappeared today. Many caves and the ancient docks situated northwards (Fig. 109) are, however, still visible. The graves of the town stretch out over a long distance, extending across *'ayūn haidara* (Springs of *haidara*) until *rās et-tawīl*. They are eagerly plundered by the residents of *et-tantūra* and *kufr lām* whereby many antiquities perish because they are only hunting for treasures. Thus, I saw the broken pieces of the lion sculpture from a marble sarcophagus dating from better times next to a recently opened grave. An ancient cobbled road leads eastward from *el-burj*; next to this, one observes the large building blocks of a *hannāne* and several columns.

The history of this town reaches back into earlier periods. Even during the Pharaonic Era it was called Dor. In the reports from about 1200 B.C. attached to the victory of Ramses III over the "Ocean People", he boasts

---

1   Most of the following historical facts are extracted from Ritter, Palestine III, pp. 60, 192, 589, 608, and Eschmunazar's inscription from Schlottmann (Halle 1868).

that he had settled the Philistines in Shefela but moved the Zakkala "from Mount Carmel to Dor" from among the subjects (Vincent, Canaan, pg.

Figure 109. Docks in the ancient town Dor.

459 and Note 2). A Naphoth-Dor is mentioned in Joshua 12:23. Its ruler is listed among the kings conquered by Joshua. Even if the identity of this Naphoth-Dor is not fixed with our Dōr, it may certainly refer to the reports of Joshua 17:11-12 and Judges 1:27-28. According to this, Dor was engaged in the Tribe of Asher yet was assigned to the western half of Manasseh. "[A]nd Manasseh did not expel ... the residents to Dōr and its daughters..., and the Canaanites lived in the same region. Because Israel was powerful, the state imposed a tax on the Canaanites and did not expel them." All of Palestine actually came under the torture of the Israelites only at the beginning of the King's Era. According to the first Book of Kings 4:11, Solomon appointed his son-in-law, the son of Abi-Nadabs, as the magistrate over the entire dominion of Dōr. The Phoenician element was reinvigorated after the destruction of the Empire of the Ten Tribes by the Assyrians and the kingdom of Judah by Nebukadnezzar. The sea-worthy Sidon was an important ally to the Persians in the battle against the Greeks. Sidon, although tributary, could still retain a certain amount of independence. This half-autonomy seems to have been subsequently sustained as the Hellenistic influence overpowered, and Palestine and Phoenicia were conquered by Alexander the Great who ignored the Ptolemies. The Sidoean king Eshmunazar, about

whom it is disputed if he ruled during the time of the late Persian Empire or the first Ptolemaic dynasty, explains in his well-known gravestone inscription: "Furthermore, the Lord of the Kings gave us Dōr and Joppe[1], the mighty lands of Dagon in the plain of Sharon, as a reward for the tremendous deeds which I performed, adding them to the borders of the region that they will be united for eternity for the Sidonians." We have the Classical authors to thank for more reports. According to Claudius Julius, Dōr was a small village, populated by Phoenicians who settled there due to the craggy region abundant in Purpur mussels. They subsequently built walls and created a safe harbor. Hekatäus von Milet calls it a Phoenician town after the account from the late Stephanus von Byzanz; Skylax calls it a Sidonean town. During the wars between the Ptolemeans and the Seleucids, it served in brave opposition as a fortification. Polybius (Hist. V, 66:1) characterizes it as a very strong town. After the usurper Diodotos Tryphon had fled to Dōr from Sidetes, the Syrian King Antiochos VII (139-128 B.C), the latter destroyed the fortification. At that time, its significance sank so that Artemidorus, who wrote during the first pre-Christian century, only called it a small town. However, it was restored by Gabinius (Josephus, Antiqu. XIV 5:3), who was appointed the Roman proconsul to Syria in 57 B.C., whereupon it was raised to new glory in which it enjoyed a limited autonomy. Later, Dōra became a Christian seat of the Bishop within the main Palestinian province. Yet its splendor must have paled compared to that of the nearby provincial capital Caesarea. It had fallen into ruin by the end of the fourth century. According to the reports of the previously mentioned Hieronymus, the Roman matron Paula, who began her pilgrimage to the Holy Land in 383, was astounded by the ruins of the once very powerful town. Dōra seems to have been settled again during the Middle Ages; at least that is what early travelers who encountered considerable medieval buildings here report. They particularly speak of a castle built on older substructures on a rock protrusion, i.e. the *burj* introduced in the previous description of the ruins. An assumption about its character and origin can, however, no longer be expressed considering the lack of more extensive notes and the current condition of the ruins. Arab authors, of whom only Yāqūt and Abu 'l-Fida were at my disposal, or Occidental sources from the Middle Ages may

---

1   Translator's note: Joppe most likely refers to Jāffā.

possibly offer more pertinent information. The purpur[1] fishery has not been practiced in a long time. – With the exception of Sykaminum, in the proximity of which this region described by us begins, Dōr is the only town discussed here from which ancient coins are preserved. These fall into two categories according to de Saulcy, *Numismatique de la Terre Sainte* (*s. v. Dora*): autonomous coins of the town and coins of the Roman Empire. The first reach from 61 until 75 B.C., and the latter from Caligula to Heliogabal. Both often bear the legend *Dōreitōn* or *Dōritōn* (the residents of Dōr). The inscription is in Greek because in the completely Hellenized region the (second) official language was Greek also under the Romans. The current affairs offer an analogy for this in Syria where the Arabic language has likewise been maintained as the official language along with Turkish even though there has recently been an established push for Turkish.

The ancient road to *jāfā* extends south of *et-tantūra* via *qaisārie* (Caesarea). At one point, it crosses *nahr ed-difle* (Oleander River), the lower course of *wādi 'l-fureidīs*, on the dune that is becoming smaller here. The dune is called *hajar esh-shēkh* and will be described later. Additionally, it previously passed the Crocodile River, next to a mill, likewise on the dune and nearly one kilometer away from the ocean. However, a new bridge was built over

Figure 110. The Imperial Bridge over the
Crocodile River (*nahr ez-zerqā*).

---

1   Translator's note: This appears to refer to a type of sea snail, commonly called the spiny-dye murex, from which a pigment was extracted to be used in a purple-red dye.

the Crocodile River in 1898 for the Imperial couple's journey which is also still found in good condition (Fig. 110). It lies directly at the mouth of the river opposite a ruin called *melāt*; the road to it first leads southwestwards away from the dune. Wagons wanting to reach Caesarea, however, prefer the route on the shore due to the marshy terrain of the road. This route can be taken directly from *et-tantūra*. At the outlet of *nahr ed-difle*, the wagon must, nevertheless, turn onto a stretch far into the ocean. Before crossing the Imperial Bridge, one notices a small island from the shore. It lies in the sea surrounded by rock reefs, and is called *jezīret el-hamām* (Pigeon Island). In this manner, I traveled the route to Caesarea and back to the Karmelheim by wagon in one day whereby enough time still remained for me to view Caesarea. The path used today towards *jāfā* no longer leads through Caesarea but rather through *zummārīn*, the only location along the entire route that offers overnight accommodation. One arrives here by wagon after one and quarter hours from *et-tantūra*. This route attains the plain east of the dune through *bāb et-tantūra*, which will be described immediately. It traverses southwestwards until *el-fureidīs* whereupon it climbs as a southeastern curve to the elevation of *zummārīn* in the form of a good road.

In order to visit the points of interest on the still remaining portion of the coastal plain, we first turn on horseback towards *bāb et-tantūra* (Gate of *et-tantūra*) which lies directly east of the current village. Similar to *bāb el-'ajal* before *'atlīt*, it is an incision in the dune in which the rock has been removed down to the level of the plain, wide enough to easily admit wagons passage. On the western side, before the entrance, one observes several niches reminiscent of *maghārat es-sammāki* south of *'atlīt* in their crude carving. They may have served sacral purposes. The "gate" itself exhibits a multitude of round, cubic or right-angled, elongated chambers on both walls. Among these, some are equipped with smaller niches for erecting idols or images of saints. They may strengthen the previous assumption that these cuts through the dune stem from the Roman era. Ancient burial chambers in the rock can be seen on either side at the exit to the East. The new telegraph towards *jāfā* does not use the gate but rather moves a stretch further west of the dune in order to first surpass this and meet the route in the southeastern direction by *en-nazle* which follows the *khushm* on foot. After we pass through *bāb et-tantūra*, we accompany the dune southwards along its eastern border. Shortly, we encounter a modern, deep well shaft, *bīr et-tantūra*, with a pulley. It dates from 1904 and contains better water than found in the village after which it is called. Its water, like that of the many wells on the dune, flows underground from the mountain to the ocean. Soon after this, one sees a fig tree growing out of a cistern and then an antique well shaft with a square opening with sides measuring one meter. After we have crossed the telegraph line, we approach one of the dune's hills which projects eastwards with *khirbet el-mezra'a* (Ruin of the New Settlement). A well shaft lies on the path to the west; it is furnished with holes on the side for ascending similar to *khirbet ed-drēhime*. Its opening forms a rectangle with sides measuring two by one meter. A possibly recent modest burial chamber of a revered personage, the *maqām* of *shēkh muhammad el-mughrabi* is located at the foot of the hill. The enclosure walls of the ruin itself are still preserved. They represent a rectangle with thirty-meter-long sides from the north to the south and forty-meter sides from the east to the west. It was probably a small fortress that is supposed to have, until recently, only suffered little damage. An elderly shepherd, who I met there, insured me that the walls towered even higher than three meters according to his memory. Now only the southern and the northern sides are still in better condition. The former is approximately one and a half meters tall and one meter thick. The outer wall exhibits long, large ashlars set in mortar yet there are only smaller stones on the inner wall. A large stone disk, similar to a *jurn* rests on the southwestern corner. It has a large, four-cornered hole in the middle that does not penetrate completely to the bottom. The northern side of the fortress measures 1.75 meters tall but is thinner than the previous and built only out of smaller stones between which openings are sporadically located. The mortar used in building this seems to be very durable. It is mixed with small pebbles and ceramic shards.

Towards the south, the dune descends. After one has passed another well shaft with a square opening, one arrives at *nahr ed-difle*. A small and narrow Arab stone bridge leads over the river; it lies directly west of the northern end of *zummārīn*. The *nahr ed-difle* acquires not only *wādi 'l-fureidīs* which is often abundant in water but also *khallet en-nazle* which forms a marsh on the western border of the *khushm* as well as *khallet en-neffākha* and *khallet el-kabbāra*. It swells to a stream that floods the entire region during periods of flooding. In order to eliminate this danger, the dune was cut through in ancient times, possibly during the Roman Era. The careful carving of the slanting rock face that forms the sides of the creek bed still inspire awe today. The *wādi* here dries up in the summertime; the perennial water begins on the western side and reaches the ocean. A water mill stands next to the bridge, but it is only in operation during the rain season whereby it is supplied by a small open canal. Aside from a lowly stone hut (*khushshi*), a simple four-walled structure with a catafalque and a *mihrāb* rise in direct proximity. This site is called *hajar esh-shēkh* after the *maqām* of *shēkh el-qattānani*. From the creek bed by the bridge on, the dune extends southwards along an ancient open canal that is roughly a half meter wide. At the beginning, it is sixty centimeters deep but this changes later according to the terrain with a niveau gently sloping to the south. I followed this canal until *dabbet 'abdūn*; a guide from *kufr lām*, knowledgeable in the region, informed me that it reaches the Crocodile River and beyond until meeting Caesarea. This is likely because no larger settlements are found until Caesarea. From the situation, it appears that the shallow aqueduct running towards Caesarea drawn on the map does not have its origins at the Crocodile River, as previously supposed, but rather further to the North at *nahr ed-difle*.

Only ten minutes southeast of *hajar esh-shēkh*, a small hill, *dabbet 'abdūn*, rises. Ancient orthostatic masonry is stacked all around the foot of the hill. Bedouin graves are situated between these. The peak bears a likewise very old cistern-like hollow carved into the rock under the shade of a large carob tree. Its opening has an irregular, circular shape. One observes a simple four-sided structure built of boulders, the *maqām* of *shēkh 'abdūn*, next to the rock hollow. One also encounters orthostatic masonry of smaller dimensions. The settlement on *dabbet 'abdūn* incidentally belongs, based on the character of the ruins, to the oldest of the region and is reminiscent of the castle on *tell el-batta* south of *et-tīre* as well as the ruin in *wādi a'rāq en-nātif* by *umm ez-zeināt*. As other remains of buildings do not seem to exist there, the area may no longer have been settled during subsequent eras. The explanation of this occurrence can be found in its unhealthy surroundings as the swamp of *wādi 'l-kabbāra* stretches out in the East. It is a lowland that is sometimes settled by Bedouins but mostly by *ghawarni*. Perhaps the presence of the *maqām* indicates that a shrine once stood here because the current weli's indeed are frequently traced back to such and because the name *'abdūn*, which I have otherwise never come across, seems to have preserved an old word form. Accordingly, one could look for the Levite town *'abdōn* here mentioned in Joshua 21:30 which was drawn from the region of the Tribe of Asher. The distance of *dabbet 'abdūn* from the town of Dōr, which was similarly situated in the same region based on the previously mentioned writings, measures less than five kilometers. I did not invegtigate the dune group that lies further southwards because, according to my guide, there are no ruins there. Also, on this day, I wanted to view the foot of the *khushm*.

For this latter purpose, I must return to *hajar esh-shēkh* in order to bypass the swamp of *wādi 'l-kabbāra*. It is from this point that I arrived at *khirbet en-nazle*. The English map records *bīr abu bāze* as not being far from my route but I did not pass it. *Khirbet en-nazle*, belonging to the field of *el-fureidīs*, lies on the northwestern side of the *khushm* below *zummārīn*. A wide, passable road leads past this; the road leads around the western foot of the *khushm* in order to turn eastwards by the former *tāhūnet abu nūr* and meet with the new road to *jāfā* near *miamās*. The recently laid telegraph line accompanies it. *Khirbet en-nazle* is especially notable in its long row of antique burial chambers in the rock bordering the foot of the mountain. Along the way, I also noticed a grave site surrounded by boulders similar to the type of Bedouin graves but is oriented from the north to the south. Its dimensions measure more than twice that of the usual Bedouin graves. It bears a specific name, *el-hāshime*. A path climbs through *khallet en-nazle* towards *zummārīn*. Next to this, the *qastal* (aqueduct) carved into the rock from an ancient water conduit is recognizable at points. The new plantation lying to the south, within the jurisdiction of *zummārīn*, also bears the name *en-nazle*. The plantation primarily consists of a large orange tree garden and a eucalyptus forest adjoining in the southwest. The orange trees, in part, look wan as a result of the spraying of ingredients to eliminate a kermes[1] illness, until now unknown, that has afflicted the trees. It exhibits itself in the form of black spots on the peel of the fruit. In planting the eucalyptus forest, a surprising occurance in the region, *zummārīn* has rendered a great service in reoganizing the area that is susceptible to fever. We find a steam motor for agricultural use on the plantation as well as a water station somewhat further southwards which provides *zummarin* with the necessary amount of water by means of a large pumping station.

---

1   Translator's note: Kermes refers to an insect, the coccus ilicis, which infests oak trees.

On the other side of *khallet en-naffākha*, which similarly ascends a path to *zummārin*, one finds a simple, large, modern building on the left. It is known as *tshiftlik el-kabbāra* and is the private property of the civil list of the Ottoman Empire. It comprises the greater portion of the coastal plain between the *khushm* and the dune until the Crocodile River. At the same time, the *mudīr* (superintendent) exercises authoritative functions over the Arabs, Negros, and *ghawarni* settled in the area. Further to the south, one arrives at *khirbet el-kabbāra* (or *khirbet kabbāra*) from which primarily only a large grave site situated under a lovely walled arch with six *kōkīm* is to be mentioned. Several Fellāheen huts and the *maqām* of *nebi el-kabbāri* which is in poor condition stand next to this. From this Point, the view eastwards to the valley of *khallet el-kabbāra* is beautiful. The valley is divided into two parts by an imposing hollowed-out rock. After one has passed *khallet al-'asal* (Honey Valley) further on, one observes a Negro village on the left side of the path. It likewise bears the name *kabbāra*. These black people (*sūd*, or *'abīd*, i.e. slaves, often referred to with the customary word *takárni*, sing. *takrūri*, throughout the entire Islamic world, and sometimes with the word *dakrūri* here) admit to have already come to the land in previous generations where they were hired out at such sites for field work where the unhealthy climate did not permit the Fellāheen to cultivate. They seemed to exclusively use the Arab language; religiously, they are considered Sunni Muslims. It is curious that they did not adapt to local custom in respect to their residences but rather erected a kraal-like settlement here. The huts consist of a crude substructure of boulders with an often circular or elongated-round outline upon which an almost dome-shaped yet peaked straw roof rises (Fig. 111).

Finally, we reach the southern peak of the mountain, the *khushm en-nadīr* (sometimes pronounced here as *khushm en-nazīr*, i.e. the visible nose), which lent its name, *el-khushm*, to the entire chain of hills south of *wādi 'l-fureidīs* (Fig. 112). It is an imposing rock protrusion which is split into two halves by the small *khallet esh-shūni* (after *esh-shūni*, the second name of *miamās*), ascending abruptly from the plain, and, as its name implies, recognizable in the region from a distance. The mill that was once named after its previous owner, *tāhūnet abu nūr*, is located next to a bridge at the foot of the *khushm*. It is now in the possession of Jemāl Bey, the son of Sādiq Pasha, of Haifā. It was once named after him, and then the same owner of *bayyārat ez-zurghāniyye* located not far to the south. This is a lovely new stone

Mahmoud El Salman

building and is in operation throughout the year because the Crocodile River provides it with ample perennial water.

The Crocodile River, flowing into several small valleys of the *khushm*, lies only on the border of the region discussed here; it, however, receives the greater amount of its water from the *rūha*, namely the western portion of the so-called *wa'r er-rūha* still bedecked with lovely oak stands today. Therefore, it can no longer be discussed here. It will only be mentioned that it still deserves its ancient name because, just three years ago, the skin of a small crocodile killed here was for sale in *haifā*. In contrast, a few words about the magnificent aqueduct leading towards Caesarea built during the Roman Era will still be

Figure 111. The Negro village *el-kabbāra*.

Figure 112. *El-khushm en-nadīr.*

286

permitted. Aside from the open canal which can be detected near *hajar esh-shēkh* in the North, Caesarea drew its water from two different conduits. One of these begins at *rās en-neba'* by *miamās*. It runs through the plain and is today, for the most part, destroyed. The second, portrayed on the maps as the high Roman aqueduct, enters near *miamās* from the mountain where a larger, wider, and deeper course has been carved out for it. It can be followed eastwards until the region of *es-sindiāne*, and it is supposed to even reach beyond *subbārīn*. West of *miamās*, it stops for a short stretch at the foot of the mountain until it disappears again into the rock in order to finally run along the ground's surface. Near the mill, one observes that it contains three handsome parallel clay pipes, each thirteen centimeters in diameter, on a solid stone substructure. This second conduit is borne by lovely arches at the point where the bed of the Crocodile River sinks (Fig. 113). Here, the aqueduct divides itself into two branches whereby a portion turns southwards from the straight path in order to reunite with the other portion after a course in the form of a half-circle. I can only explain this arrangement in that at this point of the *zōr*, the structure was in the greatest danger due to flooding and that one had hoped the necessary supply of water for the town would be preserved in one section in the case of destruction of the other. On the other side of the *zōr*, the water conduit forces through the dune in order to disappear again inside. This point is called *maqātī' esh-shōmariyye*. The aqueduct appears again west of the dune, and, from here on, it accompanies the shore southwards until Caesarea. Today it is covered by sand piles here and there. This high aqueduct may have brought drinking water to the town while the two other water conduits may have served for irrigating the gardens and possibly also the needs of the baths. A small, apparently artificial knoll rises close to the mill and north of the aqueduct. I was told its name is *tell el-fellāh*.

Still another interesting occurrence is observed by the mill: the huts of the *ghawarni* (sing. *ghūrāni*), i.e. the residents of the *ghōr* (The River Plain). These huts consist primarily of *halfa* (Fig. 114). They are sometimes also hung with roofs of goat hair or completely composed of goat hair similar to the Bedouin tents. The half-nomadic *ghawarni* populate

Figure 113. Arch of the high Roman aqueduct
in the *zōr* of the Crocodile River.

Figure 114. *Ghawarni* in front of their hut.

several plains in Palestine such as *hāwi ʿakkā*, *jitru* (جدرو) east of *ʿakkā*,
but namely the Jordan Valley, aside from the *zōr* of the Crocodile
River. Their skin color is darker than that of the Fellāheen, and one
often sees swollen lips and kinky Negro hair which suggests a strong
addition of Negro blood among them. Their often weak constitution
may be explained through their long stay in the marshy area. However,
they seem to have assimilated to these climatic conditions in certain

aspects. With respect to medicine, they are interesting in that the malaria fever, which is so damaging to the Bedouins and Felläheen, occurs less frequently and to a weaker extent among them. The procedure they use for fever attacks is curious. Namely, they spread a plaster (*lezqa*) of mud (*samaqa*) over the stomach and lower abdomen; after which they lay down in their huts. Once the plaster has dried, it is removed, and they admit to feeling rejuvenated. Their language, which does not seem to be any distinctive idiom, comes closer to the Felläheen or the Bedouin dialect, depending on their surroundings. Even their clothing conforms to that of their neighbors. Often, they live in squalid conditions; some better-off members of the community keep buffalo. They live in small family groups without a division into larger clans. They are under the jurisdiction of the *mudīr* of the demesne *el-kabbāra* in the *zōr* of the Crocodile River. Despite their similar lifestyle, they are not considered to be equals by the Bedouins but are rather viewed with suspicion. They are also deemed to be inferior by the Felläheen although they are Sunnis in their belief and also bury their dead in the Muslim cemetery today. These outcasts are probably an ancient race, forced into their unhealthy place of residence by the Felläheen and the Bedouins. While the Felläheen view themselves autochthons and the Bedouins also still regard the West Jordan Land in the desert as their actual home, the *ghawarni* seem to know nothing of their ancestry.

One can best reach *zummārīn* from the mill via *miamās* and *umm el-ʾalaq*.

16. The Khushm and the Israelite Colonies

Whether and to what extent the *khushm*, the meaning of which has already been explained towards the end of the previous section, belongs to Mount Carmel is even disputed among the native population. Some consider *wādi ʾl-fureidīs* to be the conclusion of the Carmel region, and thus the *khushm*, lying south of this valley, is judged to be a separate region. Opposite this, most count the village *zummārīn* and its surroundings as still part of the Carmel. In fact, the hills projecting towards the coastal plain have characteristic features of the Carmel region in their wild rock precipices. Therefore, we believe to include the western portion in the framework of this description of the Carmel region based on the prevailing language use common to the area. An additional question concerns the issue of where the border of the *khushm* should be located to the East. The *ruha* and its forested southwestern end, *wa'r er-ruha*, begin east of the elevations *el-hēteri*, respectively east and southeast of the village *es-sindiāne*, according to the general opinion of the Fellāheen. I was, however, separately informed of the opinion that the region east of *zummārīn* and west of the *ruha*, *wa'r es-sindiāne*, is to be understood as a center which can neither be counted as part of the *khushm* nor the *ruha*. Others who seem to be better informed, explained to me that *es-sindiāne* cannot be geographically separated from *zummārīn*. This version may also be therefore advisable because the elevations of *zummārīn*, covered in red earth, stretch uninterrupted until *el-hēteri* in the East and until *es-sindiāne* in the southeast whereas the upper course of the northernmost branch of the Crocodile River has carved out a deep incision by this village. This forms a sharp border against the *ruha*, extending southwards as *wādi 's-sindiāne* and eastwards in the form of *wādi abu tahā* which flows in from the North. In concordance with the most knowledgeable men among the local people, we would thus like to include the entire *khushm* which reaches near *tāhūnet abu nūr* and *miamās* as far as the Crocodile River in the south and as far as *es-sindiāne* in the southeast and even surrounds the wooded *hēteri* in the Northeast.

I could only partially determine the topographical nomenclature here because I often lacked guides who were as well-versed in the region's particulars as those who were available to me in the Northern Carmel region. The western border of the *khushm* is intersected by five valleys. The first three of which (*khallet en-nazle*, *khallet en-naffākha*, and *khallet el-kabbāra* which has its source in two branches), united by *hajar esh-shēkh*, flow into the lower course of *wādi 'l-fureidīs* in order to form *nahr ed-difle* from that point on. *Khallet el-'asal* and *khallet esh-shūni* at *khushm en-nadīr* follow these further southwards; both already belong to the valley system of the Crocodile River. *Khirbet mansūr el-'aqāb* lies north of the origin of *khallet esh-shūni*. Several small valleys enter from the *khushm* into the Crocodile River, i.e. into its northernmost branch called *wādi 's-sindiāne*. Among these small valleys, three originate near *umm el-'alaq* and depart the foot of the mountain east of *miamās*. One valley separates into three branches and reaches the plain by *khirbet er-russeisa*. Two additional valleys encircle the village *breki*; of these two valleys, the western valley is called *khallet esh-shēkh* and the eastern *khallet el-hummus*. *'Ain ismā'īn* lies with the ruins *khirbet el-kharashi*, and *khirbet 'ain ismā'īn* is located where *wādi 's-sindiāne* enters from the hills. The perennial spring *'ain el-miyy̆ ti* issues somewhat further up the valley south of the village *es-sindiāne*. As a conclusion to the *khushm*, *wādi abu tahā* enters east of the village *es-sindiāne*. In the North, the *khushm* sends various small valleys to *wādi 'l-fureidīs*. The first larger valley is called *wādi tātā* after *khirbet en-nebi tātā*. The valley following eastwards after this is called *umm ed-derej* at the entrance but *wādi mīnā* further above; it extends southwest of the elevation *el-hēteri* with which the *khushm* arrives at its end there. A route towards *el-merāh* leads from *khirbet en-nebi tātā*. The knoll adjoining in the west is called *el-mukhalla'āt*. The narrow point *el-meshedd* merges with this in the south as well as *il-bastawiyye* further southwards. One arrives at *brēki* south of here whereas *khirbet es-suwēdi* lies to the northeast. Because I am not well acquainted with the eastern portion of the *khushm*, I have adhered more to the earlier map in the draft of the map sketch as I previously did with the southern and eastern sections of the region of *ikzim*.

In earlier eras, the *khushm* had attained great significance through the settlement of the Israeli colonists. For this purpose, Baron E. v. Rothschild purchased a terrain of nearly 19,000 donum (app. 13,946 square kilometers) which is now administered by the *Jewish Colonization Association*. The opportunity is offered to individual settlers to acquire ownership of the prosperities they have cultivated. However, they prefer to avoid the formalities of the land registry so as to not let any material rights demise. The core of the colonies is *zummārīn* (Zichron-Jakob, Jacob's Memorial). *Esh-shefeia* (Mayer-Shefeya) and the now abandoned Arab village *umm et-tūt* as well as *umm ej-jimāl* (Bath Shelomo, Daughter of Solomon) lie on *wādi 'l-fureidīs*. These villages form a contiguous complex that is bordered in the west by the demesne *el-kabbāra* and by the region of *et-tantūra* on the other side of the plantation, *en-nazle*. Further northwards, it is bordered by that of *el-fureidīs*. It meets with *ikzim* in the North and with *subbārīn* in the East. The villages fields of *es-sindiāne*, *brēki*, *umm el-'alaq*, and *miamās* form the frontier in the south. The Fellāheen village *el-burj* and *el-merāh* with handsome commerce buildings also belong to the Rothschild Terrain south of the Crocodile River. It should be noted that extensive stands of eucalyptus trees further south of Caesarea surround the additional Israelite colony, *khudēra*, which is part of a different organization. The Israelite villages are connected with each other and the plain by new roads which are fenced in by eucalyptus alleys near *zummārin*, otherwise often by fences of the thorny *'ambar* (*Acacia Farnesiana* Wild). Their aromatic yellow blossoms are exported and used in manufacturing perfume. In part, the colonies must battle difficult conditions. The large vineyards were completely devastated by phylloxera, a deadly grapevine pest. Since the colonists also do not shy away from great costs, the replanting with American vines in substantial quantities has already begun. The juice of the grape exported as "Carmel Wine," for the production of which expansive cellars, presses and distilleries have been built, plays a role in trade without attaining the quality of the wine of Northern Carmel. An entire literature about the Israelite colonies exists; it can namely be seen in the administrative reports and in the Zionist periodicals. I have heard a new map of the terrain is in preparation. The significance of the colonies for the region should not be underestimated. The arrangement of the roads, the orange gardens and vineyards as well as the preparation and the export of wine have brought a new life in the once desolate landscape. The importance of *zummārin* for the traffic, specifically also for the tourists, has already been indicated in the previous section. Since the founding of the village, the route from *haifā* to *jāfā* and *nābulus* runs through here where one can, with the exception of another hostel, find good accommodation at Hotel Graff. Generally, the wagons therefore stop here in order to arrive at their destination the next day. From *haifā*, one needs five to five and a half hours by wagon via *et-tantūra*; roughly the same amount of time is needed by horse along the foot of the mountain from the Karmelheim.

The new road turns from the plain into *wādi 'l-fureidīs* at *el-fureidīs* in order to pass over the creek bed on a stone bridge soon afterwards. Two caves are located above the bridge on the southwestern slope. Both were possibly once lived in. The first initially opens up to a larger room, behind which a natural shaft lies which receives the light from above. A lush elm-like tree with tasteless fruits similar to cherries thrives in the shaft; two species of the same plant stand near the entrance to the cave. It is, as Mr. Aaronsohn in *zummārin* informed me, the European nettle tree (*Celtis australis* L.) which otherwise does not occur in the Carmel region. According to him, the cave is called *maghārat* (or *a'rāq*) *el-meise*. The second cave, separated from the previous by a small ravine, is attainable only by climbing the low rock face. It is divided into two parts; one of which contains water from the beginning of the rain season until the beginning of summer which is the reason this cave is called *a'rāq en-nātif.* From the rock wall, one observes the remains of an almost right-angled, ancient structure with Cyclopean walls. The cave, which was similarly fortified like the large *maghāra* of *wādi 'l-maghāra* known to us from Section 13, offered a safer habitation because one did not lack water during a portion of the year.

From the bridge onwards, the road extends southeastwards until the ascent to *zummārīn.* Rather than use this right away, we first follow the road up the valley eastwards where it leads to the remaining colonies. Shortly thereafter, a road branches off to the Mayer-Shefeya colony lying on a hill which occupies the place of a former Arab village, *esh-shefeia.* The settlement contains decorative, modern houses in which thirty residents live according to the official count which is obviously too low. When one follows the valley upstream, the road bypasses the hill of the previous Arab village, *umm et-tūt,* which belongs to the colony. Its houses were abandoned as a result of illness and are now dilapidated. A massive alcohol celler has been set up in the hill by the colonists. Finally, the road arrives at the lovely colony, *umm ej-jimāl* (Bath Shelomo) which already lies in the *rūha,* likewise on the site of an ancient village.

The recently restored road to *zummārīn* makes a sweeping curve first to the south and then to the west at the previously mentioned ascent whereby one initially passes a small fertile valley, partially planted with bananas, and then the large wine cellars. The village *zummārīn* (Zichron-Jakob), already visible from the Karmelheim through its position on the elevation and the long eucalyptus trunks, has been built with considerable effort in a regular arrangement. To the time of its foundation, it was even furnished with street lamps. Aside from the settlers' houses and the previously listed hotel, the village contains a water tower, a hospital with a pharmacy that is directed by a permanently stationed doctor, a synagogue, a school, and a large administration building in front of a community garden. In the spacious hall of this building I attended a theater production in Hebrew. Hebrew is namely now taught in school as a living language so one often hears the children speaking Hebrew with each other. The state assessment of the number of the colonists at 536 persons was probably already too low in 1905. Because a substantial influx of immigrants from Russia has since ceased, the number may possibly be at 750 now. In addition to this, there are also a great number of Fellāheen who find work as well as accommodation here. They are, however, not listed in the official summery by the authorities because they are not entitled to civil rights here. Thus, the total number of residents approaches 1000. Similarly, *zummārīn* lies on the site of an ancient ruin which was already mentioned in the previous section by way of the ancient water conduit running through *khallet en-nazle*.

The remaining attractions of the *khushm* can be seen in a single tour. We first turn towards the southwest to *khirbet mansūr el-'uqāb* (The Ruin of Mansūr, the Eagle) situated close to the sharply descending rock face north of the origin of *khallet esh-shūni*. The site offers one of the most beautiful views of the entire region; the view wanders freely westwards across the coastal plain to the blue ocean tide, southwards across the yellow sand hills encircling Caesarea behind which the eucalyptus forests of *khudēra* appear, southeastwards to the vast *mell* and *sindiāne* stands of *wa'r er-rūha*. In the foreground, one observes the hill *ez-zurghāniyye*, the Israelite property *el-burj*, then the ruin *ihdidūn* (حديدون), the former Circassian settlement *safsāfī*, and further *ghābet es-serkes* (غابة الجركس, the Circassian Forest), similarly having fallen victim to devastation to the south. Further eastwards, *el-burēj* and *el-merāh* become apparent. *Mansūr el-'uqāb* is the name of a holy figure who is highly revered. For important disputes, people come from all parts of the entire region to make an oath here that is considered to be indissoluble. The *maqām* is, of course, very simple and unornamented; it is pictorially covered by an old carob tree which has been forced into an almost pine-like growth by the constant west wind. The ruin adjoining the shrine is not very extensive. Its walls, built partially from large and partially from medium-sized blocks, stretch roughly ninety meters from the north to the south and forty meters wide from the west to the east. They enclose the foundations of a tower in the middle. An orthostatic half-circle is visible in the east. In walking the grounds, I noticed a slab-like *jurn*-stone with a quadratic hollow in the center, the plastered *birke* of a *midbise* equipped with stairs, and a deep shaft with an opening shaped like a half-circle, one meter in diameter, which was plastered and partially carved into the rock and partially walled. It may have served as a cistern, silo, or also as a grave. The settlement may have flourished during the classical era but reaches further back than this time period. Today the stillness of the romantic site is only interrupted by the beating of the wings of the mighty vulture (*nisr*).

Directly east of here, *umm el-'alaq* (Mother of the Leech) lies; it is now in the possession of the *el-khūri* family of *haifā* known to us as the proprietor of *el-yājār*. It offers the typical view of the majority of villages of the region which are purchased by urban financers. The individual huts have made space for a large one-story building. It surrounds a spacious quadratic courtyard with living quarters and stalls on three sides while the gate and an adjoining wall on the right and left sides occupies the fourth side. Apart from this, a modest building projecting from the gate side figures as a mosque. The fate of the Fellāheen who gradually fell into debt is sad. They took monetary advances during the planting season until they were forced to relinquish not only their village fields but also their residences to the believers. Frequently, they are evicted from their native soil by the new property owner, and if they are permitted to stay there, they are under the complete authority of the *wekīl* (representative). Villages such as *ikzim*, which still have their hereditary large families, find themselves in a much more advantageous position because the families, who the Fellāheen have known for generations, take care of them and protect them against poverty. *Umm el-'alaq* with forty-five residents offers nothing further of interest. I did not come upon a Greek inscription indicated by Dr. Schumacher on page 192 of the PEF, Qu. St. 1889.

Now we proceed southwards on the road to *miamās* (ميماس, not *māmās*) lying at the foot of the mountain. Today it is most often called *esh-shūni* (The Grain Pile). This former village is the property of the *el-khūri* family; its location is occupied by a new large two-story building with two courtyards. In the terrain bordering the Crocodile River, such as by *el-yājūr*, mulberry gardens have been planted which are used in breeding silk worms. The cocoons acquired here under the guidance of foremen from Lebanon are sent to *beirūt* for the purpose of treatment. In the process of building the new structure, which houses fifteen Fellāheen and a *wekīl*, the previously described ruins, a castle, and a small Roman theater have disappeared. An eighty-centimeter-tall granite column with an inscription is still, however, preserved in one of the upper courtyards of the building. The inscription was indicated by Dr. Schumacher and published by Professor Zangemeister in Volume XIII of the ZDPV in 1890 and thereafter printed in the Corp.

Inser. Lat. (II, Suppl. Nr. 12082). Since a photograph of the latter has not yet been published, as far as I know, two images are depicted

Figures 115 and 116. Roman inscription on a column from *miamās*.

here (Figs. 115 and 116) in which the greater portion of the legend is visible. While I refer to the mentioned publications for all the details, I am content with taking an excerpt from the same for the reading of the inscription and the most important conclusions.

M•(arcum) FL•(avium) AGRIPPAM PONTIF•(icem)
Π VIRAL•(em)
COL•(oniae) Ī(primae) FL•(aviae) AVG(ustae) CAESAREAE•ORA
TOREM•EX•DEC•(urionum) DEC•(reto) PEC (unia) PVBL•(ica)

Marcus Flavius Agrippa, the Priest,
the old-duumvir (former mayor),
the Speaker for Colonia Prima Flavia Augusta
Caesarea (Messenger by the Emperor)
according to the decision of the Decurion (the city
senate), with fees from the Community (has set up [or
inherited] the community; the column, namely, bore the
statue of a man who is blessed with this honor).

According to the assumption of Zangemeister, approved by Mommsen, this M. Flavius Agrippa was the son of the well-known Jewish historian Josephus. The erection of his statue would belong to the reign of Trajan or Hadrain. The Latin is not unusual as Caesarea had become a colony founded by Vespasian for his Roman veterans. *Miamās*, which possessed a theater, must have been a suburb of Caesarea; the remnants of the wall and columns by the road which are still noticeable agree with this. It was already noted in the previous section that the high Roman aqueduct towards Caesarea exits the mountain here and that an additional water conduit, beginning directly southwards by *rās en-neba'* extends through the plain towards Caesarea. Unfortunately, nothing can be predicted today about the nature of the medieval castle.

Khirbet er-russeisa lies northeast of *miamās*, likewise at the foot of the mountain. Today one only recognizes the foundation walls of a quadratic tower on a small rise. Its sides measure roughly five meters, and it is near several ancient burial chambers in the rock on the slope. Almost directly westward at a distance of three-quarters of an hour, *'ain ismā'īn* issues into *wādi 's-sindiāne*. Before one reaches it, one sees *khirbet el-kharashi*, a ruin of average expanse, on the knoll on the left. Its site is now cultivated so that most of the traces of antiquity have disappeared. Aside from large building stones, several columns, and a very well-carved, though now split, *hajar bedd*, I only noticed three caves that had long since been cleared out. The middle cave contains a large antechamber from which three parallel galleries run out which are separated by two thick posts recessed in the rock. The internal

Figure 117. Cross-like drawing on a rock slab
above the cave at *khirbet el-kharashi*.

cave ceiling has been carefully smoothed. The rock surface of the final cave, situated somewhat more to the North, bears an incision which is depicted in the included picture (Fig. 117). If the carving is supposed to represent a cross built on a frame or a hill, then one can trace it back to the early Christian era with respect to the primitive execution. The remaining ruins could stem from the Classical period. Not far from here, in the vicinity of *'ain ismā'īn*, *khirbet 'ain ismā'īn* is to be mentioned. Similarly, its cultivated area exhibits only a cistern which still contains water today. I left the border of the *khushm* here in order to visit the nearby *khirbet es-sitt lēla el-mejdūbi* (Ruin of the Blessed Entrancer Lēla), already located in *wa'r er-rūha*. It is a small ruin built out of medium-sized blocks; its position would have suited a temple or a small castle. The *maqām* of the revered person which is still highly visited today is located not far from a collapsed cistern under the shade of a fig tree. The maqām is a small square of large, ancient stones that surrounds a handsome, yet undescribed marble slab. Only a few minutes eastwards, one arrives at a hill with *khirbet el-'ajami* which bears no *maqām*. From this ruin, only the medium-sized blocks of the low walls of a small tower remain.

Returning northwards back to the border of the *khusm*, one encounters the valley floor of *wādi 's-sindiāne* by the perennial spring *'ain el-mitťti* (Dead Woman's Spring) in order to ascend to the village *es-sindiāne* shortly thereafter. This village is one of the few that was not founded on the site of an ancient ruin. It is even considered to have been recently established. According to local tradition, it received its name because it was positioned in a *sindiāne* forest that was then stubbed out. The *en-nezzāli* family, to which the *mukhtār* belongs, belongs to the oldest of the settlers. They first migrated nearly 165 years ago. There are 543 residents. Apart from a modest mosque and the unornamented *maqām* of *shēkh 'abdallah* built in the village cemetery, the huts offer nothing in their architectural style that set them apart from the others of the Carmel region, respectively the *khushm*. Yet there was a rare surprise for me here. Upon asking the usual question, if there was an inscription located here, the village chief lead me to the house of a Fellāh. High on the wall, above his door, a stone with a Samaritan inscription was positioned. According to the information of the residents of the house, the stone stems from *khirbet el-'ajami* whereas the most likely better-educated *mukhtār* refers to *ihdeidūn* as the place of origin. The stone, which has a rectangular-shaped surface that is forty-two centimeters wide and twenty-six centimeters high, is walled in, though inversely, according to the width from the bottom-most to the top-most. Both side edges as well as the lower edge is less damaged but the upper edge (i.e. below by the inscription) is intensely damaged. The inscription, which occupies a somewhat smaller space, consists of twelve lines of carved writing whereby each word is separated from the following by a dot. It is framed in by straight lines which likewise separate line seven from line eight. From line seven on, the enclosed side lines move inwards less on the right but more on the left. Though I was not successful in photographing the stone alone due to the considerable elevation from the ground despite procuring a primitive ladder, I had to be content with making a cast of it which was the basis for the photograph prepared in *beirūt* (Fig. 119).

The learned Professor P. Sebastien Ronzevalle in Beirut, to whom I showed my copy and who in all graciousness made the necessary material for studying available to me, recognized the reproduction of the text of Deuteronomy 6:4-9 in the first ten lines at the first glance which begins with *shema' yisrāēl* (Hear Israel). This takes a prominent rank in the Israeli liturgy which is also considered to be the most distinguished commandment in the New Testament (Mark 12:29-30). The conclusion of the inscription ("and you should write them over the posts of your house and on your door") perhaps indicates that the stone, like that in *es-sindiāne* today, was fixed on the door of its previous location whether it was a private or a religious house. *Ihdeidūn* lies east of Caeserea where a Samaritan colony was situated based on the information from Professor Ronzeville. The critical treatment of the inscription was most kindly undertaken by the Imperial General Consul in Beirut, Mr. Schröder, the experienced expert of the region and its Semitic monuments. It will be given in an appendix to this section of the study.

We now turn northeastwards and arrive at *khirbet en-nebi tātā* on a hill, leaving the handsomely forested elevation, *el-hēteri*, on the right; the hill embraces the two branches of *wādi tātā*. *Bīr en-nebi tātā*, a spring carved into the rock in a deep shaft walled with large ashlars at the top, originates at the junction point of the two small valleys, at the foot of the hill. The ruin itself forms a circle about 400 meters in diameter; it consists of large, handsomely carved wall stones among which I found various *hajar bedd*, a large *jurn*, the *lekīd* stone of an oil press, a cistern, two altar slabs, several burial caves, and shards of quality Roman ceramics. If one is already inclined to assume the ruin is an ancient shrine on account of these remnants, one is encouraged in this assumption by the *maqām* of the revered person positioned in the center. The elongated rectangle of the *maqām*, draped with scarves, was first built from the ancient stones of a ruin during the Arab period. One, however, enters the interior in an underground, now naturally empty chamber. Its walls have been meticulously smoothed; the room measures two meters long, one and a half meters wide and eighty centimeters high. The walls possibly represent a megaron mounted under the temples. The shrine is held in the highest respect by all the residents. The title *nebi* (prophet) may suggest its age which is only allowed to be attributed to *weli*'s who have been venerated since primitive times. The site appeared to me like that of the type of "heights" which already play such a significant role in the Old Testament. Indeed, the hill is towered over by both the ridge of the *hēteri* stretching northeastwards and *khirbet es-suwēdi* in the south, but, incidentally, it, however, offers a lovely view northward towards the plateau of *ikzim* and the higher Mount Carmel. With its four shady deciduous oaks growing out of the debris, the ruin grants a delightful idyllic view which remains undisturbed by a small modern guard house standing slightly off to the side. The Cult of the High Places never fully died out in the region, and today a Muslim calls out the *tehlīl* "*la ilāha illa 'llāh*" when he has climbed the peak of a mountain which explains why so many points in the region are named *rās el-muhellil* (Peak of the One who Praises God). A happy coincidence occured here in that I witnessed a *ziāra* held to honor *nebi tātā*. From afar one heard a cadenced song approaching. A procession of women and children, of both genders, came through from *es-sindiāne* with multiple *sandshaq* (flags) at the head. After they testified their reverence to the saint, several of the older women began to prostrate themselves in prayer while others prepared the lauded meal for the poor (*tabkha*) from the foodstuff they had brought with them. Then a joyful festive atmosphere develops (Fig. 118). One sang, played, and danced, and, namely, during this I noticed an occurrence that I had not yet experienced in the Carmel region; a group of

Figure 118. *Ziāra* at *nebi tātā*.

pretty young ladies, stretching hands out to each other, circled a large oak in roundel in full of frolicsome gaiety, just like in Europe.

Khirbet es-suwēdi, an intensely damaged ruin, rises almost directly south of this; today one finds only a few medium-sized blocks on its cultivated grounds. These, however, still form the corner of a tower, and castellated terrace arrangements extend around the peak. Considering its dominating position offering a wide view one may assume a former medieval castle. One arrives at the hamlet *brēki* after a short half hour. It has 168 residents who saw it necessary to sell a portion of their field to the *el-khūri* family in *haifā*. The current village where much beekeeping is carried out holds nothing worthy of note except for two *maqām*, that of *shēkh abu 's-suwān* (Father of Flint) and *shēkh abu 'sh-sha'r* (Father of Hair). The first lies in the center of the village, adorned with many veils, small lamps, and small plates. It is built from old stones over a now buried cave. It is considered to be a great shrine where one trustingly places valuable items and before which oaths are pledged. The appearance of the *maqām* of *shēkh abu 'sh-sha'r* located on the eastern side of the village is evidently smaller. Even its rampart, in which a fig tree thrives, is built out of ancient ashlars. As is already to be indicated by the description of these graves, *brēki* lies on the site of an ancient ruin. This is supported by the presence of several broken marble columns and various burial caves. Among which, one with its entrance from the south exhibits several *kōkīm* and another exhibits a *rōzane* (air shaft) apart from the *kōkīm*. The copper and silver coins found here extend from the Diadochi Era until the Byzantine Period. An Armenian silver coin of Leon Takavor may have been transported here by a Crusader.

One returns to *zummārīn* by way of *bayyāret jādir*, an ancient manor with stone carvings that are still present. It has been activated again by Israeli colonists.

APPENDIX
TO THE SECOND SECTION

The Samaritan Inscription from es-Sindiāne
By General Consul Dr. Schröder

The inscription is forty centimeters long and twenty-five centimeters high and contains twelve lines. The first ten lines of this are excerpts from the Biblical text, Deuteronomy 6:4-9. We come across this text again, though only in abbreviations, on two Samaritan inscription stones from Damascus published by Dr. M. Sobernheim (MuNdDPV 1902, pp. 70), namely the stones referred to as "Samaritana VI" and "Samaritana V" (ibid, pp. 76 and 77) by Sobernheim[1]. Unfortunately, only the beginning of the last two lines (11 and 12) have been preserved. This is quite regrettable as it possibly contained the date of the dedication of the stone and the name of the benefactor (Ismael?). According to the copy as well as the photograph of the inscription it seems that some (5 or 6) weathered letters stand in the middle above the first line. From these, the two last letters look like יל or רל. – One or two letters are consistently missing at the beginning and the end of the first seven lines.

The inscription (compare Figs. 119 and 120) follows:

---

[1]   The beginning of the text שמע ישראל is found at the conclusion of the inscription on "Samaritana II" (Sobernheim ibid, pp. 74) so that the tablets "Samaritana II, VI, V" are thus lined up together. "Samaritana VI" contains Deuteronomy 6:4-6 and the first word from verse 7; "Samaritana V" bears verses 7-9. At the same time with Sobernheim and independently of these, Dr. Alios Musil also published and discussed the Samaritan inscriptions from Damascus in a publicized paper (Seven Samaritan Inscriptions from Damascus) in one of the protocols of the Akademie der Wissenschaften in Vienna (Philosophy-hist. class, Vol. CXLVII, 1903). Yet he is missing the inscription referred to by Sobernheim as "Samaritana VI." The inscriptions were once walled in as decorations in a house in Damascus. In the spring of 1906, I purchased them for the Berlin Museum where they are currently located.

Deuteronomy 6:4	[שמ]ע·י·ישראל·יהוה·אלהיכו·יה·אח]ד·[	1.
Deut. 6:5	[וא]הבח·אח·יהוה·אלהיך·בכל·לב]בך·[	2.
Deut. 6:5-6	[וב]כל·נפשך·ובכל·מאודך·והי]ו·[	3.
Deut. 6:6	[ה]דברים·האלה·אשר·אנכי·מצו]ך·[	4.
Deut. 6:6-7	[הי]ום··על·לבבך·ושננתם·לבני]ך·[	5.
Deut. 6:7	[וד]ברח·בם·בשבחך·בביח·בלכחך·בדר]ך·[	6.
Deut. 6:7-8	[בש]כבך·ובקומך·וקשרחם·לאו]ך·[	7.
Deut. 6:8	על·ידיך·והיו·לטטפוח·	8.
Deut. 6:8-9	בין·עיניך·וכחבם·על·	9.
Deut. 6:9	מזזוח·בחי]ך·[.....	10.
	שנח·בול·ה.....	11.
	ישמעאל	12.

Hear, Israel: Jahwe is our God, Jahwe is the One; and you should love Jahwe, your God, with your whole heart and with you whole soul and with all your strength; and these words with which I command you today should be kept in mind; and you should impress them upon your children and recite them when you are at home, when you are traveling, when you lay down to sleep and when you rise. You should tie them as a symbol on your hands, and bind them to your foreheads, and you should write it on the doorframes of your houses....

The inscription does not follow the Masoretic text but rather the Samaritan: line 6 בבית ללכתך (Masora: וּבלכתך), line 8 על ידיך at your hands (Masora: ידך, LXX τῆς χειρός σου), line 9 לטטפות complete with ו (Masora: לטטפת with defective spelling), line 3 מאודך (Masora: מאדך), line 9 על מזזות בתיך "on the doorframes of your houses" (LXX τῶν οἰχχίων ὑμῶν) instead of the Masoretic ביתך (of your house); in contrast, our inscription follows the Masoretic spelling (מזזות), not the Samaritan (מזוזת) in the preceding word. – In the first line, the divine name יהוה is abbreviated as יה for the second time. In line nine, the carver inadvertently omitted a ת before the third to last letter מ (כתבם instead of כתבתם). – Whether the concluding word from Deuteronomy 6:9 ובשעדיך "and on your doors" stands behind בתיך in line 10, remains doubtful. The available space would have been sufficient, but the poorly legible letters at the end of the line (left of the gap) could not be read as עדיך based on both the squeeze and the photograph.

The character of the script indicates a relatively old age for the inscription which may possibly date from the time before the twelfth century of the pre-Christian era. At individual portions it is no longer completely legible due to the weathering of the stone, particularly in

Figure 119. Squeeze of the Samaritan inscription in *es-sindiāne*.

Figure 120. Copy of the Samaritan inscription in *es-sindiāne* produced by Dr. P Schröder based on a squeeze and a photograph.

the first and second lines. The form of ה at the end of the first line is no longer fully distinct. The following forms are singular: ה as ... and א as ... .

* * *

Corrections and Additions to the First Section

Page 4, first paragraph, Introduction: The number of previously unknown ruins which I visited more than tripled in the course of a second, longer stay on Mount Carmel.

Page 4, third paragraph, Introduction: I became later convinced that one does not pronounce *'arāq* but rather *a'r āq* in the Carmel region. In order to be certain, I had the names of several sites written down by persons skilled in writing from various villages. All referred to as such were reproduced as اعراق. *A'rāq* is however not a plural form; on the contrary, the latter is *'urqān*. The form *a'rāq* can possibly be explained from عراق through the omission of the vowel of the first syllable and the subsequent shifting of an auxiliary vowel such as occurs with *ashlūl* next to *shulūl*.

Page 7, second paragraph, Section B: The ruin *umm qubbi* lies close to the Carmel border yet it lies outside of it. – As to the question of the southeastern boundary of Mount Carmel next to the *rūha*, the agronomist Mr. Aaronsohn of *zummārīn* kindly informed me that a geological boundary crosses through *wādi 'l-milh* based on his research undertaken in association with Professor Blanckenhorn. Cenomanian rock forms the main component of Mount Carmel in the northeast; the *rūha* in the southwest consists of Senonian rock. In the north, the line of separation between the two types of rock hereupon circumvents *umm ez-zeināt* and then turns towards *wādi mādi* which it follows until just before the ruin *hanāne* in order to arrive from there and on at *wādi el-fureidis* directly south. Likewise, Cenomanian rock forms the *khushm* until the village *es-sindiāne*. As evident from this, the purely geological line at the beginning and at the end corresponds with the Carmel boundary given in the text. There is, however, a conflict regarding the areas lying inbetween. The importance and noteworthiness of this enrichment to the geological knowledge of the region is unquestionable yet I believe that one can hardly divide Mount Carmel solely on a scientifically geological basis or a solely orographical basis. For geologists, a rock layer first comes into consideration when it reaches a certain thickness and forms more than a thin surface covering. On the other hand, the Fellāh, who deserves to be the principle regional expert with regards to assigning a locality to a specific area, forms his opinion mainly through consideration of the surface of the ground. For example, the site of the village *umm ez-zeināt* that lies on Senonian rock according to Aaronsohn and would therefore be considered part of the *rūha* is undoubtedly thought to be a part of Mount Carmel in the entire region. Only the difference of the weathered uppermost topsoil could thus be observed for the Carmel border incorporated in the text based on the statement of experienced residents of the region. The topsoil on the Carmel side displays a red hue as a result of the iron content; it has a white-gray coloring on the side of the *rūha* due to the prevailing marl. – Furthermore, Mr. Aaronsohn, the agronomist, had the kindness to provide me with numerous notes on the geological and botanical nature which have been partially utilized in the following corrections here and partially already incorporated in the second section of this work.

Page 8, third paragraph, Section B: rather than (قاموعة الدرزيه, Peak of the Female Druze) read (قَبّوعة الدرزيه, Bonnet of the Female Druze); after revised calculation, its height measures 551 meters above sea level.

Page 8, sixth paragraph, Section B: in place of *wādi fellāh* read *wādi felāh* (so is common).

Page 9, second to last paragraph, Section B: rather than *khānuq*, read *khānūq*.

Page 10, first paragraph, Section C: According to Aaronsohn, *nāri* is a product of weathering that is composed of both Senonian and Cenomanian rock. Based on the same source, *sultāni* and *meleki* are types of Senonian. *Yābis* is often called *mizzi* in Jerusalem.

Page 10, first paragraph, Section C: rather than *suwān*, read *suwān* (with dot under the "s").

Page 10, third paragraph, Section C: A volcanic eruption has already been determined by Conder near *ikzim* as explained in Section 14 of the second section.

Page 10, fourth paragraph, Section C: Rather than *zukūr*, read *zuhūr*.

Page 10, seventh paragraph, Section C: Rather than *natūf* read *nātūf*.

Page 12, third paragraph, Section E: The white crocus is *Crocus ochroleucus Boiss. Et Gaill.*; the bluish crocus is probably *Crocus hiemalis Boiss. Et Bl.*

Page 12, third paragraph, Section E: Urbanly, the cyclamen is called *zqōqia*.

Page 12, third paragraph, Section E: The lily-like *khusalān* is *Asphodelus microcarpus Viv.*

Page 12, third paragraph, Section E: The onion-like *basūl* is *Urginea maritime L.*

Page 12, third paragraph, Section E: The *lūf* is a type of Aaron's rod, *Arum Dioscoridis S. et Sm.*

Page 12, third paragraph, Section E: The grape hyacinth *basal ferk* is *Muscari comosum Mill.*

Page 12, third paragraph, Section E: The Fellāheen understand both several types of ranunculus and a multi-colored tulip with the name *berqōq el-khamīs.*

Page 13, first paragraph, Section E: Recently, the *sindyān* has been called *Quercus coccifera.* Incidentally, the botanical research has been made very difficult and in part confusing through the introduction of new terms in this as well as other cases.

Page 13, second paragraph, Section E: The blackberry *'ullēq mōy* is *Rubus discolor.*

Page 13, second paragraph, Section E: Rather than *Euphorbium antiquorum*, read *Euphoria dendroides.*

Page 13, second paragraph, Section E: The *murrān* is our laurustinus, or laurustine, *Viburnum tinus L.*

Page 13, fourth paragraph, Section E: The black-thorn *suwēd* is a type of Rhamnus.

Page 13, fourth paragraph, Section E: replace "berries" with not yet opened blossom buds (Correction from H. L. Bauer in Jerusalem).

Page 13, fourth paragraph, Section E: The *Verbascum Tripolitanum* is not counted among spiny plants.

Page 13, fourth paragraph, Section E: Rather than *aculentus*, read *aculeatus*.

Page 13, fourth paragraph, Section E: The *khilli* is not identical with *Ammi Visnago*.

Page 13, fourth paragraph, Section E (leading into page 14): *Eryngium* has thorns but is not considered to be among the thistles.

Page 14, top, Section E: Rather than *Botarium*, read *Poterium*.

Page 14, first paragraph, Section E: The *'unnāb* (*Zizyphus vulgaris Lam.*) is only seldom found in gardens. The likewise rare *Zizyphus spina Christi Wild* reaches the size of a walnut tree; its former scientific name is *Rhamnus nebeca*. Its fruit, often called *nebk* in the east, is called *dōm* in the Carmel region. This term has been transferred to the tree so that one seldom hears its actual name, *sidra*, among the Fellāheen. The bush-like *Zizyphus lotus* is present on the *khushm* and is called *rubbēd* by the Fellāheen.

Page 14, third paragraph, Section E: Rather than *na'ni*, read *na'na'*.

Page 15, second paragraph of Section F: The statement about the presence of a small type of deer is based on false information.

Page 16, second paragraph, Section F: The *rikhame*, possibly a vulture, only passes through the region. The *nisr* is native to here and is similarly a type of vulture. The *abu masas* is a falcon.

Page 16, fourth paragraph, Section F: The *qatā tatabōz* of Mount Carmel is the peewit.

Page 16, fourth paragraph, Section F: The *abu humār* is a type of shrike.

Page 16, fourth paragraph, Section F: The *warwar* is the European bee-eater (*Merops apiaster*).

Page 16, fifth paragraph, Section F: The *'arūs et-turkmān* is the European goldfinch (urbanly called *hassūn*).

Page 16, fifth paragraph, Section F: The *qumhiyye* is the common chaffinch.

Page 16, sixth paragraph, Section F: In addition, the stock also carries the name *abu sa'd* (Father of Good Fortune).

Page 16, seventh paragraph, Section F: Rather than *zilhiffe* elsewhere, read *zíhilfi* in *'usufia*.

Page 17, fourth paragraph, Section F: The *sultān ibrāhīm* is a species of the mullet (*Mullus surmuletus L.*).

Page 20, second paragraph of Section Gb: Rather than *'aql*, read *el-'aql* (likewise later on in the same paragraph).

Page 20, second paragraph of Section Gb: *El-khrēbi* is an ancient ruin (*khirbi kufriyyi*). The previous Druze villages, *el-mansūra*, *ed-dawāmīn*, *esh-shellāle*, *umm esh-shuqaf*, and *bistān* were not destroyed by the Egyptian Ibrāhīm Pasha but rather initially by the Muslim Fellāheen from the surrounding villages after Pasha's return to Egypt. The Druses migrated here only during the course of the eighteenth century. Some came from *jebel el-'ala* by *hamā*, and others from Lebanon.

Page 21, second paragraph of Section Gb: The *khalwe* is a small building with one window (not windowless) in Lebanon. The villages of Carmel, *'usufia* and *ed-dālie*, have larger and nicer *khalwe*'s. That of the last-mentioned village is described in Section 10 of the second portion of this work.

Page 21, second paragraph, Section Gb: Rather than the tomb of *behā allāh*, read a building that is destined for the tomb of *behā ullāh*.

Page 21, third paragraph, Section Gb: The Catholics first settled in the Carmel region during the course of the eighteenth century. Aside from *'usufia*, they had also previously lived in the Druze villages, *el-mansūra* and *ed-dawāmīn*.

Page 23, first paragraph, Section Gc1: Read in parenthesis: *jelamet il-'asāfni* for *'usufia* and *jelamet el-mansūra* for *ed-dālie*.

Page 24, fifth paragraph, Section Gc2: *'Ishsh* is not the cover but rather indeed a shaft in the wall in which the baskets were stacked up. The compression of the latter occurs by inserting a forked tree trunk with its thick end up into the shaft. Its branches jut out into the open. A massive piece of wood is horizontally attached to the branch. It bears a screw thread. A vertical spindle loops through this through which a lever can be moved. The spindle reaches into the stone of a column (*lekīd*), which deserves a more precise description, with its lower, horizontal pierced end. Often one and a half to two feet thick and three to four feet high, the stone has a vertical depression above which is approximately one foot long. It has an opening passing through the side which is connected to the vertical depression so that the intersection of these carvings represents an inverse Latin "T." A wooden nail has been pushed through the side opening. It passes through the pierced end of the spindle thus firmly joining the spindle with the *lekīd*. Now when the lever starts moving the spindle, it winds itself through the nut in the elevation with the attached *lekīd* as a weight, and the end of the tree trunk applies the intended pressure on the basket located below.

Page 26, second paragraph, Section Gc3: The exclamation *shimālak* (in *ed-dālie*: *shimāletak*) is not used by the passers-by but rather by the reapers. *Shimāl* (in *ed-dālie*: *shimāli*) means the left hand and the sheaf it holds. With the words "your sheaf," the reaper offers the latter in hopes of a *bakhshīsh* in a half-joking manner. However, if the passer-by had not greeted the laborer first, this offer is not permitted to take place.

Page 26, fifth paragraph, Section Gc3: Rather than cut the chaff, bring home the chaff.

Page 26, fifth paragraph, Section Gc3: Rather than female chaff cutters, read female chaff bearers.

Page 26, seventh paragraph, Section Gc3: Rather than *mūkhil* (with a dot under the "h"), read *mūkhil* (without a dot).

Page 27, seventh paragraph, Section Gc3: Rather than *fukhāra*, read *shughl il-fukhkhār*.

Page 28, third paragraph, Section Gc4: Rather than as well as, read such as.

Page 29, second paragraph, Section Gc4: Rather than *ftiri bijibni*, read *ftīri* (with a dot under the "t") *bijibni*.

Page 30, fourth paragraph of Section Gc6: The phonetic specification of the rhyme was very difficult to count out (*thadrija*) since children frequently speak unclearly and have no conception of the meaning of the words. Adults pay no attention to such things. I had the verses recited to me repeatedly and believe now to have come closer to the actual rhyme with the following version. Whoever knows from experience just how uncertain the notation of dialectic folklore songs, namely from the mouths of children, is, will pardon the imperfectness of the provided text.

> *Hudruj budruj, tammet tudruj;*
> *Min telāte, qurqu', hummus, fish.*

Repeat the counting rhyme, it moves in turn, it moved on in turn;
Of three, release, chick peas, nothing!

> *Hadāye, badāye, menājil tayye,*
> *Tili't azūr ma'a zarzūr*

Drive (to a march), beginning, sharp scythes,
I went out to pay a visit with a Staar (cataract?).

The counting rhymes often begin with one word that starts with an "*h*" sound and which is followed by a word beginning with "*b*." One can also observe similar occurrences in the counting rhymes among European children.

Page 40, third paragraph of Section Gc8: Rather than *hujājkū*, read *hudjājkū*.

Page 45, first paragraph of Section Gc9: And later repeatedly in the text, rather than *sahji*, read *saḥji* (with a dot under the *h*).

Page 45 and the following, Section Gc9: I also had the following songs here repeated, and this time by a literate person, whereby it resulted in some corrections and some better versions.

Page 45, line 5 of *Matlū'* 1, Section Gc9: Better:

Yā rēt mā jītū walā tallētu
Oh, if you had not really come, not entered!

Page 46, line 7 of translated *Matlū'* 1, Section Gc9: in the opening of the jar (as a flowerpot).

Page 46, line 7 of *Matlū'* 2, Section Gc9: *tallabuk*.

Page 46, translation of *Matlū'* 2, Section Gc9: It should be noted to line 3 of this that the masculine form is preferred in the Arab love songs even if the beloved is a female such as, for example, in the verses at hand.

Page 46, line 4 of translated *Matlū'* 2, Section Gc9: Read: will be gathered together in the flowerbed rows (for binding a bouquet).

Page 46, line 7 of translated *Matlū'* 2, Section Gc9: on which your hand was asked for.

Page 47, preamble of the *ḥāshi*, Section Gc9: *Ḥābis yā māl il-qōm*.

Page 47, translation of the preamble of the *ḥāshi*, Section Gc9: Stop! You will be the property of the enemy, i.e. Stop! Or you will be the property of the enemy.

Page 47, translation of the preamble of the *ḥāshi*, Section Gc9: For the dōm-tree, compare with the correction for page 14, first paragraph, Section E.

Page 47, line 1 of *Haddāwiyye* 1, Section Gc9: Rather than *sarrabha*, read *sarabha*.

Page 47, line 5 of *Haddāwiyye* 2, Section Gc9: Rather than *abāyi*, read *'abayyi*; likewise, rather than *el-'ūja*, read *el-'auda*; *'abayyi* is the name of a noble horse breed, such as *khēli* and *siglāwi*.

Page 48, line 1 of translated *Haddāwiyye* 1, Section Gc9: Read: Hear the new song, from the tip of my tongue it flows down; *sarabha* is here rather than *sarabat* for the sake of the rhyme. Such a change in the pronominal verbal ending with the verbal suffix occurs more frequently in the vernacular. Thus a youth calls out to another provocatively: *ta'a lahōn in kannak shātir*, come here if you are brave where *kunnak* stands for *kunt*.

Page 48, line 5 of translated *Haddāwiyye* 1, Section Gc9: Rather than the noble, read the *'abayyi*; similarly, rather than the lame, read the old.

Page 48, line 8 of translated *Haddāwiyye* 1, Section Gc9: Rather than the people, read the enemy.

Page 48, line 2 of *Haddāwiyye* 2, Section Gc9: Rather than *Tobannā yā tobannā*, read *yā hāshīnā tiwanna*.

Page 48, line 2 of translated *Haddāwiyye* 2, Section Gc9: Read: Our *hāshi*, act carefully!

Page 48, line 6 of translated *Haddāwiyye* 2, Section Gc9: Read: you have not taken a horse of prey (*qli'a* only refers to horses).

Page 50, expression referring to *kufr lām*, Section Gc10: Read: (regarded as feverish), unfold your beds and lay down.

Page 50, expression referring to *et-tantūra*, Section Gc10: Read: *et-tantūra umm el-'atūra*: *et-tantūra* is the mother of strength (health).

Page 52, first footnote, Section Gd: Rather than the previous section, read Section 14.

Page 52, Section Gd and repeatedly within the text. The names of the villages *es-surfend* and *et-tantūra* bear the article in Arabic, likewise *es-sindiāne* mentioned in the last paragraph of the page.

Page 52, last paragraph, Section Gd: The exact population counts of *brēki* and *es-sindiāne* are, respectively, 168 and 543.

I thank the kindness of Dr. Kampffmeyer for several of the linguistic corrections; Director Kandler most kindly provided me with corrections in the botanical field.

Printed in the United States
By Bookmasters